BEER PLACES

FOOD AND
FOODWAYS

SERIES EDITORS:
JENNIFER JENSEN WALLACH
AND MICHAEL WISE

Beer Places

THE MICROGEOGRAPHIES OF CRAFT BEER

EDITED BY DAINA CHEYENNE HARVEY,
ELLIS JONES, AND NATHANIEL G. CHAPMAN

The University of Arkansas Press
Fayetteville
2023

ISBN: 978-1-68226-223-8
eISBN: 978-1-61075-788-1

27 26 25 24 23 5 4 3 2 1

Manufactured in the United States of America

∞ The paper used in this publication meets the minimum requirements of the
American National Standard for Permanence of Paper for Printed Library Materials
Z39.48-1984.

Library of Congress Cataloging-in-Publication Data

Names: Harvey, Daina Cheyenne, editor. | Jones, Ellis, 1970– editor. |
    Chapman, Nathaniel G., editor.
Title: Beer places: the microgeographies of craft beer / edited by Daina
    Cheyenne Harvey, Ellis Jones, and Nathaniel G. Chapman.
Description: Fayetteville: The University of Arkansas Press, 2023. |
    Series: Food and foodways | Includes bibliographical references and
    index. | Summary: "Beer Places is both a road map for craft beer and an
    academic analysis of craft beer's ties to place. Collected into sections
    that address authenticity and revitalization, politics and economics,
    and collectivity and collaboration, this volume blends new research with
    a series of 'postcards': informal conversations and first-person
    dispatches from the field that transport readers to the spots where
    pints are shared and networks forged"—Provided by publisher.
Identifiers: LCCN 2022040205 (print) | LCCN 2022040206 (ebook) |
    ISBN 9781682262238 (paperback; alk. paper) | ISBN 9781610757881 (ebook)
Subjects: LCSH: Beer—Social aspects—United States. |
    Microbreweries—Social aspects—United States. | Cultural geography—
    United States.
Classification: LCC GT2890 .B444 2023 (print) | LCC GT2890 (ebook) |
    DDC 394.1/3—dc23/eng/20221103
LC record available at https://lccn.loc.gov/2022040205
LC ebook record available at https://lccn.loc.gov/2022040206

CONTENTS

SERIES EDITORS' PREFACE

The University of Arkansas Press Series on Food and Foodways explores historical and contemporary issues in global food studies. We are committed to representing a diverse set of voices that tell lesser-known food stories and to provoking new avenues of interdisciplinary research. Our strengths are works in the humanities and social sciences that use food as a critical lens to examine broader cultural, environmental, and ethical issues.

Feeding ourselves has long entangled human beings within complicated moral puzzles of social injustice and environmental destruction. When we eat, we consume not only food on the plate, but also the lives and labors of innumerable plants, animals, and people. This process distributes its costs unevenly across race, class, gender, and other social categories. The production and distribution of food often obscures these material and cultural connections, impeding honest assessments of our impacts on the world around us. By taking these relationships seriously, Food and Foodways provides a new series of critical studies that analyze the cultural and environmental relationships that have sustained human societies.

Relationships between food and place have garnered much scholarly attention over the 2010s, as the so-called spatial turn in the humanities and social sciences has more fully encouraged the critical sensibilities of cultural geography to spread across the field of food studies. This volume comprises the interdisciplinary work of twenty-eight contributors and three editors who bring to bear the latest geographical approaches in a book that not only provides a global consideration of the specific socio-spatial contexts of craft brewing, but also presents a state-of-the-field showcase of how food studies writers and scholars can generate crucial cultural insights using precise and imaginative spatial analysis.

One of the most striking aspects of *Beer Places* is the expertise and familiarity with practices of craft brewing that each of the editors and contributors brings to this study. Their fluency with the technical details—and their ability to communicate those specificities with readers—allows their arguments to emerge with clarity and convincing honesty. Informed as well with references to a wide range of work in social and cultural theory, the volume also connects the seemingly esoteric world of craft brewing to much larger conversations about urban and rural development, social justice, and the political economy of food and memory in the twenty-first century.

Beer Places wears these weighty scholarly contributions lightly, however, returning page after page to its central concern: parsing the spatial meanings of beer, taking seriously the role of place in affecting "taste" in a multitude of ways. More than just borrowing from the spatial concerns of food studies, this volume—perhaps the first true edited collection in "beer studies"—contributes its own new perspectives to the literature and should appeal to both academic and nonacademic food writers.

JENNIFER JENSEN WALLACH and MICHAEL WISE

BEER PLACES

The Place of Beer

DAINA CHEYENNE HARVEY AND JULIAN BAKKER

Stoneman Brewery is a nano-brewery on a multi-acre farm nestled in the rolling hills of northwestern Massachusetts. The area looks and feels more like Vermont, and if you happen to get lost on your way to the brewery, it is easy to wander across the border. I (Harvey) was told that cell phone reception would be spotty, that the brewery was near Vincent Brook, and that if I passed Sanders Brook it would mean I had gone too far. Stoneman Brewery was my first destination for a three-year research project on New England brewers. At the time, it was the sole brewery in New England that used only local ingredients. According to Justin Korby, owner and brewer, the beers were supposed to taste like New England.

When my colleague Ellis Jones and I arrived at the farm, Korby gave us a quick tour of the brewery. The brewery was in a shed. I guess I should say it was a shed; maybe 320 square feet. Korby had three or four fifteen-gallon fermenters, a couple of kettles, and that was it. It was a slightly scaled-up version of what I was doing every other month in my dilapidated, two-hundred-year-old barn.

Korby looked the part, though: tall, with a beard past his waist, wearing Carhartt overalls and scuffed-up work boots. He looked like he was getting ready to make something. He kept squinting as he talked, pushing his glasses back up his nose; somehow looking part farmer, part scientist. We talked with Korby for about ninety minutes. He went through the process of turning grain into wort and wort into beer. He walked us through the equipment and showed us the closet where he was using temperature-controlled fermentation. He showed us the sustainably planned community across the way and an open field next to the brewery where his pigpen was going to go—basically so he would have something to feed spent grain to. Then Korby gave us some glassware and apologized for not having any beer for us—he had just delivered it all to Pine Hill Orchards. Ellis and I stopped at Pine Hill and bought a few bombers on our way out of Western Mass. When I arrived home, I rushed inside and opened a bottle of King Korby Imperial Stout. Yeah, it tasted like New England.

Our conversation with Korby was mainly about beer—but beer as community, as a specific place. Korby explained to us that he wouldn't make beer unless he could make it with all local ingredients. He described his relationship with Valley Malt, the first micro-maltster west of the Mississippi in recent history; how he sourced hops from Four Star Farms; his relationships with other farmers; how he would only sell at certain local stores; and his collaborations with other brewers. Indeed, when we left Stoneman, we went to the People's Pint in Greenfield, Massachusetts. Chris Sellers, the head brewer, and Alden Booth, the owner, laughed when we told them where we were coming from and explained how they brewed with Korby often. In fact, Booth mentioned that they were tapping some kegs and hosting a bottle release at River Valley Market that afternoon. Sellers explained that it was a collaboration among Stoneman, the People's Pint, and the market. They got together, designed the beer, brewed it, and now were going to share it with friends and family. We were invited to stay.

Making beer is pretty simple. You add water, at about 140°F to 160°F (60°C–71.1°C), to grain and steep it (what brewers call mashing) for about an hour. You collect what is now called the wort and boil it in a kettle. During the hourlong boil you add various amounts of hops. After the boil you get the wort down to around 70°F (21.1°C) and stir in yeast, then put it in a carboy or a bucket with an airlock for carbon dioxide to escape. This ferments for about two weeks. You can keg this or add some sugar and bottle it. It's beer. It's simple. It's been made for about seven thousand years. But frequently, the brewers we spoke with, as with Korby, were increasingly interested in talking about beer less as a process and more of as a place. A place of ingredients, but also a place of interactions.

Increasingly, beer was being discussed in the same way you would expect people to talk about wine or cheese. As someone who spent most of their life around New Orleans and South Texas, I immediately recognized it as a type of boosterism, similar to what food scholars have written about as locavorism, as a way to carve out an identity—as a way to belong. In New Orleans, you regularly hear newcomers and tourists argue about food being Cajun or Creole. In South Texas, fierce arguments can be had over whether a particular sauce for an enchilada is Tex-Mex or something else; don't even bring up BBQ there unless you are ready for a lecture. When I was in New Orleans, I drank Abita because it was more or less from there. Same with Shiner in Texas. But I had never heard anyone talk about those beers *in that way*—as part of a culture, as a movement, as a practice, as authentic, as community, and as belonging. For me, beer used to be just beer, but now it seems like something else.

Beer Places is, at its most basic level, a roadmap of craft beer.[1] We make a number of stops, from North Carolina to Helsinki, from New Jersey to Zimbabwe. We stop in different types of places: taprooms, breweries, and bottle shops. And we focus on different-sized spaces: streetscapes and scenes, states and regions. Although we can't stop everywhere, it is our hope that readers will get a good idea of what craft beer looks like in different places. We leave it to them or to other authors to fill in the rest of the map.

At another level, *Beer Places* is an academic analysis of craft beer and place. Here our various contributors, representing several different fields, analyze the relationship among beer, culture, and geography. Readers will get a sense of how economics and politics limit craft beer production and consumption in various towns and cities; how craft beer creates community and identity; whether craft beer spaces are inclusive; and how beer is revitalizing place. We see this book as both a broad overview of work in what we call beer studies, and what we understand to be an emerging, and important, component of food studies.

We conceived *Beer Places* as simultaneously an academic analysis of craft beer and as a foray into the popular culture of craft beer. To accomplish this we combine academic chapters with shorter "postcards." The collected chapters build on theories, methods, and substantive fields—and yes, they feature a lot of beer, too. All of these chapters inevitably lead to the conclusion that beer is increasingly inseparable from place and vice versa. The postcards range from brief forays into a particular place—say, San Francisco or New Orleans—to more detailed descriptions of, for example, brewing beer in Suomenlinna, Finland, or what it's like to work at the Brewers Association in Boulder, Colorado.

Some read like shorter academic chapters (because academics wrote them), whereas others are from professional beer bloggers and thus read like short stories. It is our hope that by connecting beer to place in these various ways, everyone gets something enjoyable from the trip.

Beer in Food Studies

The field of beer studies does not exist. The Association for American Geographers has a specialty group, "Wine, Beer, and Spirits," and the Popular Culture Association has "Beer Culture" as a subject area, but that is about it. Beer studies is an orphan among academic disciplines.

If, however, you look at the industry trends and how both pop-culture writers and academics talk about it, craft beer looks a lot like food. This, of course, should not be surprising. Both involve highly intimate acts (putting something into your body), but both also are highly democratic—everybody eats and close to 80 percent of Americans drink alcohol at some point in their life. Both are activities that function in a socially centripetal way—bringing people toward one another—and both have similar production ecologies (Paxson 2013) and have been reconfigured and reimagined in "posttraditional" ways.

Whereas the postmodern is teleological—as a hyperconnected and hypermobile inevitability (Giddens 1991; Urry 2000) that expands upon the modern and separates us from traditional patterns of life—the posttraditional returns to traditional ways of doing things. The post-traditional cannot escape problems associated with nostalgia and must be critical of the actors and interactions that traditional ways of life engendered (and the reproductions of those systems and interactions that exist today),[2] but much of food studies can be understood as an embrace of the traditional.

In her book *The Life of Cheese*, Paxson (2013) shows the reader how cheese went from agrarian to industrial to artisanal. Of course, most cheese today is still produced in an industrial way (one might even say we have arrived at the postmodern production of cheese—think how nondairy cheese rivals artisanal cheese), but the way we think about and value cheese has significantly changed over the 2010s. Artisanal cheese has become a *crafted* product, the production of which includes a specific narration of place—the "local, organic, artisanal, farmstead, terroir" (Paxson 2013, 12)—and an interrogation of the traditional.

For many of us, though, most of the food we consume is a placeless

(Feagan 2007; McMichael 2009) globalized commodity (Bloom 2019). Since the 1980s, we have witnessed a number of food movements that have attempted to help us reconnect to our food. As Hess (2009) and others (e.g., Hinrichs 2019) have pointed out, reestablishing the local is often spurred by a fear of a homogenizing force that is transnational and de-territorialized. This is why the slow food movement in Italy emerged in the 1980s (Starr 2010) and the locavore movement (Gray 2014) arose thereafter. Other movements (e.g., sustainability, sovereignty, etc.) have likewise reinscribed links between food and place (Hedegarrd 2018) but have been less successful. These movements, which have guided much recent work in food studies, also help explain the rise of the craft beer movement.

As Levkoe (2011) notes, alternative food initiatives focus on social justice, ecological sustainability, community health, and enhancing democracy. Although craft beer has suffered from serious issues of diversity and inclusion, attempts to move the production and consumption of craft beer toward more ethical consumption (Jones and Harvey 2017) or reflexive consumerism (Goodman and DuPuis 2002) are underway. The need to be critical of the ways that the food and agriculture system structures what we eat and, by association, what we drink has become a small but burgeoning movement in craft beer (Chapman and Brunsma 2020).

Relatedly, craft brewing, traditionally seen as a white space (Anderson 2015; Withers 2017), has slowly begun to engage with social justice issues. J. Nikol Jackson-Becham (Dr. J), for example, was hired by the Brewers Association as their first diversity ambassador in 2018. Dr. J has worked with a number of organizations and breweries to help them become more inclusive spaces. We have also seen the emergence of Fresh Fest in Hilltop, Pennsylvania, the first Black beer festival in the United States, and Black Brew Culture, which is dedicated to curating black beer spaces and diversity. Breweries like Denizens Brewing Company in Maryland have become pro-LGBTQ spaces, whereas 5 Rabbit Cerveza in Chicago touts itself as the first Latin American brewery in the United States. Likewise, we increasingly see women as head brewers or in other leadership positions at many breweries (Chapman et al. 2018; Dunn 2017).

In their work on New England craft breweries, Jones and Harvey (2017) found that immediately after their priority of producing good beer, brewers are concerned with sustainability and community.

Breweries like Maine Beer Company (whose slogan is "Do What's Right") and Allagash have prioritized making their breweries as green as possible—through installing solar panels, sourcing local grain, and using motion-sensor lights to mitigate energy waste.

Likewise, community health and the link to craft beer can be seen in the re-creation of community through craft beer. In 2017, the town of Marlboro, Massachusetts, put a call out in the local newspaper (which was subsequently picked up on social media and by industry publications) in an attempt to lure a brewer to Main Street with tax incentives and other benefits. As Barajas, Boeing, and Wartell (2017) write, many cities are changing municipal codes and states are altering laws to make it easier for craft breweries to find success therein. Reid and Gatrell (2017) also show how the revitalizing of place is happening throughout the United States (but also elsewhere; see Cabras [2017] for places in the United Kingdom). These studies show that rather than creating gentrification—a common trope with brewers[3]—breweries are becoming embedded in communities as local institutions. In this light, breweries offer an avenue for making places known and embodied—for making spaces tangible (Fletchall 2016) and countering the homogenization of communities by corporations like McDonald's and Walmart over the last forty years (Schnell and Reese 2003).

For many who have appreciated the transformative aspects of alternative food movements, craft beer is a natural segue. Beer is a signifier of cultural norms and folkways (Tyna 2017). And as our relationship to food transforms, so does our relationship to beer. As the following chapters demonstrate, beer is best thought of as a foodway, and thus one must use place and all of its constituents to fully understand craft beer.

Place and Space

Beer tastes, naturally, like the end product of a variety of social, technical, and organic processes, and perhaps there is no real reason why any specific beer could not be competently made in various locations, given the same knowledge, capabilities, and ingredients. Nevertheless, many local and regional beer styles have developed across the globe, and contemporary craft beer has become known as much for individuality and idiosyncrasy as it has been about the recovery of earlier traditions. Over time, the culture of craft beer has grown and been reproduced through the evolution of new recipes, the emergence of new spaces for production and consumption, and shifting social practices related to craft beer. Alongside these changes, beer tasting and criticism has matured from a discussion of various flavor components such as malts, hops, yeasts, and waters to a broader understanding of the techniques and processes involved in beer making. Writing about and describing craft beer continues on this trajectory, and now must include an understanding of where and when the beer was made, the background of the brewer, and whether a beer adequately expresses these characteristics.

Increasingly, the idea of place as a component of the craft beer experience has been foregrounded by brewers and consumers alike. We can read about how tourists perceive the sense of a place in a brewery, or the particular taste of place that consumers feel a highly localized beer embodies, as well as the spaces of production—often referred to as *the brewery space* as opposed to *a place for brewing*. This distinction is interesting and important, demonstrating an experiential difference in the understanding of both terms, and challenges us to consider the concept of space in its own right, as opposed to a blank, abstract canvas upon which a brewery's sense of place emerges. By borrowing from the geographer Doreen Massey the idea that space is the dimension in which we encounter other beings and the world, one can show how definitions of space reveal assumptions about space. For example, relegating space to the calculative or abstract demonstrates a primary concern with apprehending space as political technology in order to exert control over resources and politics.

In what kind of space can a brewery take place? Certainly there are calculative, economic spaces, spaces for socializing, spaces for production and consumption, and border places where the brewery's identity must engage with the broader landscape, both influencing and being influenced. If one so desired, each of these attributes could be mapped, revealing distinct, nonidentical spaces, some measured perhaps in distance, others in influence, and still others in temporal extent—drawing on past influence or creating them with an eye to the future. In these multiple layers, space does indeed provide a background (though place is not a derivative of space) to the places where craft beer is made and experienced. Like the layers of this imagined map, great writing about craft beer thoughtfully approaches the multiple spaces, or dimensions, in which beer is encountered, such as identity, social situations, ingredients, architecture, and many more.

Place, considered in this framework, is much simpler to define than space, but more complicated than is typically understood. It might be argued that the previous discussion of place could be seen as a blueprint for describing places. In keeping with the desire to include various types of space, place can be considered a particular, local configuration of various meanings and materialities. Places do not have to have a strict, single, and unchanging identity (although a place might), but because of the multiple opportunities for encounters, places can contain and support a variety of identities. It is the nature of places to be, as Pred (1984) and others have described, in an incessant state of becoming.

This complicates the task of describing a sense of place and how a taste of place is transmitted. Without a placemaking checklist, of which there are many, how does a researcher evaluate the ways in which places are successful at being places? If certain places are missing attributes, or are just downright terrible, do we deny that they are places, perhaps to the faces of those living there? The discussion of place and placelessness within the social sciences provides a useful way to think through these difficult questions. Rather than fall back on distinctions between space and place—or between place and not-place—as if such things were discrete entities, we can discuss types of places, qualities of places, and the degree to which a place exhibits traits most associated with successful placemaking. These are not morphological, architectural, or design features. Borrowing from geographers such as Tuan and Relph, one characteristic of place is that place experience results in meaning making for the place and people in it. Another characteristic, drawing on the work of Edward Casey, describes places as being "thick" or "thin," referring to the experience of bodily engagement in a place, either with other people or the material world around us.

A taste of place will be rich in opportunity to perceive and be involved in the world. It might connect an individual identity to a group, a locale, or an influential person. A great sense of place implies multiple dimensions in which to explore and be confronted by the world, creating individual and social meanings through abundant embodied experiences. When we consider the sense of place of a beer or brewery, it will undoubtedly be rich in bodily sensation. The taste of place then refers to the unique flavors and experience of each beer, and how these embody the webs of ingredients, social networks, and layers of place that converge in the production and consumption of craft beer.

INTRODUCTION

A Place for Beer

Craft breweries and their tasting rooms are recognized for having a strong sense of place, or a unique, local taste of place, and so a variety of groups from real estate developers, to urban planners, to academics have taken an interest in how these breweries *take place*. The reasons for this interest vary. Perhaps some groups are interested in the role that breweries can play in placemaking—revitalizing old places and adding value to new ones. Others might wish to explore the processes by which craft beer places emerge, as well as possible similarities and differences between these places. The tastes and places explored in this volume are a deep dive through our many-layered map, exploring the relationships among people, spaces, histories, objects, identities, and the biosphere as each author describes their unique experiences of beer places.

Two tendencies should be avoided while engaging with these works. The first is reverting to a default understanding of place that views space and place as distinct categories, rather than highlighting that space is the background material of experiencing beer. Beer helps create an emotional attachment to layers of spaces, and hence to a place. The second is thinking in terms of a place–nonplace binary, particularly when reflecting on how new places emerge. A more useful approach is to think about the various processes and practices that contribute to the experience of place, and those that detract from it. The shorthand for this would be place and placelessness—movements, not categories. Placemaking at its best pushes back against the worst manifestations of modernism, the tendency toward sameness and efficiency, the dominance of mass production, by recentering places on lived experience. Places of craft production and consumption clearly manifest these ideals ideologically and as a means of differentiating their products via a taste of place. Placemaking in craft production is achieved through stories, narrative, and place names (Baso 1996).

In sum, craft beer contributes strongly to a sense of place, one that embodies a certain ideal sense of society and space. These places are co-constitutive with their locales, drawing deeply from regional spatial resources and creating new place identities in a process called *neolocalism*. Drawing on local histories and landscapes, neolocalism includes the recovery of industrial spaces, older manufacturing techniques, and traditional craftsperson identities. Recovery is part of an antimodern search for authenticity, and craft beers in general promote the idea that their tastes of place are an authentic way of experiencing the town, city, or bioregion in which they are located. Histories and other stories have many threads and authors. By drawing on existing experiences of place, neolocalism creates new narratives of place.

As in all processes of place, craft breweries practicing neolocalism preserve some local imagery and stories while minimizing or erasing others. These histories can be the stories of local residents, the brewery's interaction with the surrounding landscape, the area's legislative history with regard to alcohol production and consumption, and even records pertaining to old brewery sites and local recipes. Repurposing historical buildings, including older breweries, and relying on light-industrial architectural features are common strategies breweries use to locate a sense of authenticity on the physical landscape. Patterns of prohibition, explosion, and consolidation are typical in the beer industry, with the craft beer explosion capitalizing on the value of place against a landscape of placelessness and the weak experience of mass-produced beers.

The concept of terroir is often used to describe the taste of place associated with craft beer. A beer's terroir may be stronger or weaker depending on the ability of a brewery to successfully narrow the spatial extent defined as local for the purposes of acquiring the base ingredients and adjuncts for brewing beer. *Terroir* is a loanword coming from the world of wine via the broader discussions of the concept in food sciences and marketing. In these contexts, it refers specifically to the way that a food or wine conveys a specific, spatially defined taste of its home soil. As such, it is not a perfect analog for the taste of place associated with craft beer. Some craft breweries are able to grow their own ingredients on a site related to their brewery, and claim their beer reflects this in its taste sensation. Others may source their ingredients from a wider region, basing their taste of place on a network of inputs while claiming that this experience of place can be conveyed via the taste sensation. These inputs include the ingredient suppliers, the social milieu that informs the culture of consumers at the brewery, and the stories, images, and architectural influences that inform the look and feel of the brewery itself.

On one hand, any given beer can be recreated given the right conditions and set of ingredients, regardless of place. On the other hand, beer and place and intrinsically linked. I'd argue that a key factor for the rapid growth of craft beer is the desire for opportunities to be in a given place, and to knit oneself and one's identity in a more deeply meaningful way to place. Following placemaking theory, the opportunity to identify with specific places creates an more satisfying overall sense of engagement with a town, city, or region. The rich sense of place associated with craft beer ought to be tempered by an awareness that placemaking may not also result in great places. A new place identity will attract certain people that wish to be associated with it, whereas other people—potentially even those living in close proximity to new places—may not be brought into the new identity. Who do the places of craft beer serve? Should they be a template for placemaking in areas struggling to create vibrant spaces? The sense of place associated with craft beer goes beyond terroir, and the reproduction of these tastes and experiences is challenged by a new wave of conglomeration that threatens the viability of new craft producers. Will there be a line of succession, both for the businesses that brew craft beer, and the places they create? Do the people continue, or do the beer styles continue? Does the particular sense of place continue?

This is the same concern that preservation and heritage have: How can we preserve while not mummifying or Disneyfying the cities and spaces in which craft brewing takes place? Describing these special places, and understanding the processes and people that are involved in creating them, provides a valuable well of knowledge for anyone wishing to engage more deeply with their local producers, along with insights that can be used by new scholars, new craft breweries, and new developments as they strive toward experientially deep tastes of place, and cities that offer meaningful, positive ways to engage with a variety of spaces and opportunities.

Indeed, we are increasingly seeing beer discussed *as* place and place *as* beer. In *The United States of Beer*, Huckelbridge (2016) writes, "Local beers actually helped to shape the distinctive regional cultures that would cohere and combine to build a nation. Beer, like America, has prevailed not because of uniformity, but because of diversity" (8). It's telling that Huckelbridge divides the book into six chapters, each representing a different region of the United States. He goes on to note that beer, culture, and identity are irrevocably merged; they define how we see ourselves as northerners or southerners, New Englanders or Milwaukeeans.

In his book on Egyptian beer, Foda (2019) uses Stella (no, not that one) to show how the production of beer in Egypt mirrored Egyptian modernity from the late 1800s to now. Beer here is used to establish a new class, the *effendiyya*—the modern, secular Egyptian who associated beer with Western social values. Beer thus becomes a tool with the power to communicate a cosmopolitan identity (2019, 7). Under Nasser and a period of nationalization, beer—Stella in particular—is used to promote Egyptian identity and progress to other nations. Nasser, despite the growing influence of Muslims on national policy, wants Stella on shelves in other Arab countries. With the rise of the Sunni fundamentalist *al-Gama'a al-Islamiyya* movement, beer in Egypt became increasingly problematic. The company that made Stella was sold back to foreigners and increasingly produced nonalcoholic beer. For Foda, however, Stella charts the social, technological, economic, political, and religious change in Egypt. Stella's story, as Foda writes, is the story of Egypt (2019, 196).

Likewise, in *Brewed in Japan* (2014), Alexander follows beer production there from the 1800s to modern times. As in Foda's Egypt, beer in Japan was used to communicate imperial expansion, postwar recovery, and (much like today in America) the success of consumer culture. Initially brewed as a "German" product, war rationing and the imposition of American rule created an atmosphere where sourced ingredients could only produce a lighter, lager-style beer. Alexander argues that beer in Japan, much like Japan itself, has had an uneven and difficult history. This includes periods of imperialism where beer was used as an agricultural product to subjugate populations into being wage workers. The story of beer in Japan, as in Egypt, begins as one of foreigners, but ultimately becomes one of Japanese identity, as heavily managed by the government. Although rooted in business studies, Alexander nonetheless portrays how the social, economic, and political actors fixated on the authenticity of place and a desire to demarcate Japan from the West to produce beers that would be associated with Japan.

Borer, a contributor to this volume, likewise focuses on the relationship between beer and a specific place—Las Vegas. In his 2019 book, *Vegas Brews*, Borer shows us how, through myriad local (and translocal) interactions, a craft beer scene was produced in Vegas. The scene in Vegas has to deal with the fact that, symbolically, Las Vegas is the Strip—the place that tourists understand as Las Vegas. As Borer notes (2019, 8), craft beer drinkers embrace an identity predicated on authenticity, community, creativity, and the locavore—all of which stands in stark contrast to the cultural homogenization of the Strip. For locals, though, craft beer represented a way to reclaim the city—to find and reestablish community. The Vegas beer scene, however, is always battling against the city's "reputational constraint," and thus comes to look like no other craft beer place. Like Hucklebridge, Foda, and Alexander, Borer is telling us beer can tell us a lot about place.

Chapter Summaries

We divided the book into three parts. The first part deals with common themes in food studies, and readers will not be surprised that some of these have also become central points of contention in work on craft beer. The four chapters in this section focus on authenticity as a guiding determinant of the legitimacy of craft beer, or how craft beer is distinguished from big beer.

In the opening chapter, Koontz and Chapman look at what makes a brewery "authentic." Analyzing BeerAdvocate, one of the primary social media websites for beer, they examine whether the success of microbreweries can be explained through an authenticating process centered on breweries situating themselves around the hyperlocal. They use the term *localized authentication* to conceptualize this process. This is an interactive, collaborative process between consumers, the product, and producers that ends in a vibe judged by the consumer to be authentic or inauthentic to the place where the interaction occurs.

Using 4,500 unique reviews of breweries, they focus on three topics consumers discuss: the quality of the beer, comments on the localness of the beer/brewery, and the space. They note that these reviews help reveal how consumers contribute to or question the identity of the brewery. Importantly, however, they discover that there are "tipping points" in reviews. In other words, a brewery might excel enough in one of the three areas to tip the review to positive; conversely, in one area the space might be so bad that, despite good beer or being hyperlocal, it tips the review to negative. They find that reviews tend to tip toward the negative for only two reasons. First, the beer is so bad the other two areas cannot compensate no matter how local or enjoyable the space may be. Second, the aesthetics of the space fail to meet expectations to such a degree that they render the overall experience negative. Confirming what others (Grazian 2003; Milligan 1998; Urry 1995) have found, consumers need to have spatial fantasies confirmed by the actual space. Hence beer places need more than just good beer to be a good place.

In their chapter, "From Mill District to Brewery District: Craft Beer and the Revitalization of Charlotte's NoDa Neighborhood," Reid and Nilsson explore how craft brewing is changing one particular neighborhood—the NoDa (North Davidson) neighborhood in Charlotte, North Carolina. In doing so they focus on one of the key debates within craft beer: Are breweries gentrifying or revitalizing downtown areas? In other words, what kind of spaces attract breweries and what do breweries do to spaces once they are there?

Their chapter mirrors much of the discussion on Florida's work on the creative class (2002) and creative cities (2008) and the fallout from the gentrification that has occurred in many of the creative cities (see Moretti 2013 but also Florida 2017). Although Florida would probably champion breweries as hallmarks of the creative city (see Ocejo 2017), others point to the gentrification of places by breweries; still others note that the relationship is mixed, with breweries causing gentrification in some instances, and following and perhaps solidifying it in others (Walker and Miller 2019).

NoDa has ten breweries in a two-square-mile area, so it shows significant clustering. Although evidence for clustering of breweries is mixed, it seems to occur in smaller spatial units (e.g., on neighborhood levels; Carr, Fontanella, and Tribby 2019); however, we know very little about what clustering does for revitalizing or gentrification. Like Barajas, Boeing, and Wartell (2017), Reid and Nilsson find that breweries seem to be followers rather than leaders of change. As they write, "In the case of NoDa, it appears that the breweries have been drawn to the former mill district and are following signals of other investments, both private and public, as well as the influx of new residents and residential developments." As they conclude, the future of beer places, due to clustering, is probably going to be at the level of the hyperlocal rather than the regional or even at a smaller level—shelf space. This bodes well for cities or neighborhoods that are already beer places (think the Portlands, Asheville, or Denver), but might prevent other beer places from forming.

Roberts and DeSoucey's chapter also explores beer places in North Carolina. As they note, North Carolina has the most craft breweries in the South, and the state guild boasts that it is "the State of Southern Beer." With the recent arrival of craft (or once-craft) behemoths and a thriving scene with stalwarts like Burial, Fonta Flora, and Resident Culture, North Carolina is quickly becoming one of the most significant beer places in the United States. The question Roberts and DeSoucey explore is how North Carolina's identity has become wrapped around craft beer when brewing has not historically been important to the state.

Examining the process of what Berger and Luckmann (1966) termed *retrojection*, they find that social actors in North Carolina reinvent beer history to make their beer authentic. To do so, brewers pursue three different strategies. First, they use mnemonic bridging (Zerubavel 2003). Here they select mnemonic markers such as people or events to create historical continuity with the past. Second, they reinvent tradition through local ingredients—recreating the *Reinheitsgebot* (a six-hundred-year-old Bavarian brewing code) with place-specific foodways (think Fonta Flora's Bloody Butcher, an Appalachian grisette with red heritage corn). Last, they simply rewrite history to create an uninterrupted temporality. Here the past, present, and future are all the same. These strategies create a continuous biography (Zerubavel 2003) of craft beer in North Carolina. A spatial permanence is established, linking the centuries-old geography of moonshine to today's latest saisons. As they conclude, the cultural process of retrojection is less about the past than it is about the future. And the future of North Carolina cannot be imagined without its beer places.

The final chapter in this section takes the focus off of larger spatial constructions of authenticity, such as states and regions, and looks at taprooms. As Rice notes, and as previous chapters have alluded to, authenticity, much like place, is socially constructed. Here Rice focuses on gestures and space, which as Reynolds (2004) notes are mutually constitutive. Similar to Koontz and Chapman's chapter, Rice's discusses how taprooms use the rhetoric of space to communicate certain places, ideas, or images rather than others. As Mountford (2001, 41–42) states, "*Rhetorical space* is the geography of a communicative event, and, like all landscapes, may include both the cultural and material arrangement."

Rhetorical spaces differ from one another. For Rice, the space of the bar is one of inebriation, the space of Bukowski or Thomas. The space of the taproom, however, offers an "imaginary [that] is experiential." It is here in the taproom that we become initiated into the world of craft beer, finding like-minded others, seeking recommendations, and making connections. Unlike the bar—"where everybody knows your name" and perhaps everyone is like everyone else—the taproom is a space where anything can happen. By contrast, the bar is where everything that could happen probably already has occurred. Finding the connection between the rhetorical and the spatial allows us to understand culture and the relationship between place and identity.

Using the work of Augé (1995) and Barnett (2012), Rice situates the taproom in the spatial turn; it is somewhere between non-place and place. It is space with the potential to become place. But that placeness is destined to occur. For Rice, the authentic taproom offers banal authenticity. Its authenticity is ubiquitous even if historically questionable, as Roberts and DeSoucey show in their chapter. That is, any repurposed industrial building can be a taproom. But this banal authenticity can give rise to an authentic self, even, as Rice notes, if that self is itself banal. It is a space that is implicated in the "material realities of a particular time and place" (Barnett 2012). As Rice writes:

> Like a typical Starbucks, a taproom projects an authentic identity via rhetorical construction built out of the myth of banality: material things. This might include its ability to reclaim abandoned factories and garages as authentic locales; offer unique variety to differentiate its products from the conglomerate, mass-produced beer made by InBev, Heineken, and Molson Coors; promote local events and build an ethos of community; and create a unique signature among a given city's other leisure options.

Rice's chapter thus situates the oldest, and yet the most modern of beer places, as geographically everywhere and somewhere. They are, like any other place, what we make them.

In part 2 the chapters focus on the intersection of craft beer, identity, politics, and economics. Beer spaces are increasingly becoming third spaces, where the self and the other merge (Saunders and Holland 2018). Here the production and consumption of beer spills over geographic and symbolic borders. Here beer is not just beer; beer becomes a useful entity. Beer can be used to signify social and political relations; it is a performance that can be understood dramaturgically and can give us insight into broader structural issues in social life.

This section begins with Jones's work on life in Zimbabwe during a period of massive economic displacement—where currency devaluations often occurred daily. One of the earliest victims of the historic hyperinflation was Delta Corporation, which at the time had monopolistic control over the Zimbabwean beer market. Zimbabweans resorted to the dearth of alcohol by smuggling in cheap spirit and lagers. Mandoza, a pseudonymous man with whom Jones regularly interacted as part of his ethnographic work on young men and the absence of formal work (begun before the economic collapse), resorted to building a *shebeen* ("speakeasy") in his front yard in Chitungwiza. Following Mandoza, we get to see how every few days he made a five-hundred-mile overnight journey to Botswana to buy supplies, smuggle them back over the border, and then brew beer. The reasons Mandoza brews, however, is what makes for such a compelling story. As Jones details, beer and drinking play an important role in Zimbabwean culture, as of course they do in others. In Zimbabwe, one drinks to be "straight," where straightness can be understood as "living correctly." Living straight involves a particular circuit of home–work–bar. The monetary collapse rendered straight life impossible not only economically (i.e., work), but also socially (the local bar). Hence Mandoza's brewing beer attempted to fix a crisis of meaning.

As Jones notes, his chapter is interesting within the volume because the country, the beer, and for certain the economic situation is different from those of other places surveyed in this section. Still, the story ends up being similar to the others; they all stress the importance of having a beer place, but also note that beer places are formed and re-formed through politics, economics, and identity.

Drain's chapter, "Landscapes of Beer Consumption in Helsinki," analyzes two streets in different Helsinki neighborhoods. Surveying five years of change, Drain compares the working-class street of Vaasankatu in the Kallio neighborhood and the upper-class street of Iso Roobertinkatu in the Punavuori neighborhood to see how food and drink consumption helped drive neighborhood change. Elsewhere in Western cities, local governments have developed policies aimed at renewing working-class spaces. Quoting Hubbard (2017), Drain notes that "'successful' High Streets are depicted as those that have cast off any taint of working-class consumption, while failing ones are depicted as 'toxic,' harbouring 'unhealthy' stores potentially off-putting to more affluent consumers and tourists" (18). Urban policy as such doesn't want to rid the neighborhood of beer places, they just seek to sanitize them for middle- and upper-class consumers.

While the city experienced its own version of gentrification, a craft beer boom hit Helsinki. Drain finds that the boom fit right in on Iso

Roobertinkatu. Here one finds little variation in beer styles or prices. Beer places are differentiated on aesthetics alone. On Vassankatu, however, there is a good deal of diversity, with a mix of middle- and working-class culture and beer places. Beer on Vassankatu has the ability to mediate diverse social groups. Thus, by mixing neighborhood dive bars with more modern craft beer spaces, the neighborhood of Kallio creates a space where everyone is welcomed. As Drain observes, the street there is a mix of immigrants, students, and long-time patrons. It is a shared space. Hence, while having a gentrifying effect, craft beer spaces can also foment interactions between dissimilar groups.

In their chapter, situated in New Jersey, Saunders and Fogarty look at how state policies can affect beer places. Most notably they are interested in how breweries negotiate the law in New Jersey that visitors to taprooms must take a tour before they can sample the beer. They collect qualitative and quantitative data on five breweries in New Jersey and the policing of brewery spaces, with a special focus on the restrictions placed on bodies within the taproom. As they note, these laws and other unfriendly policies place New Jersey near the bottom of rankings on breweries per capita in the US.

In their examination, they contrast different ways that breweries engage in "placemaking" (Fletchall 2016) and how breweries construct their space so that it is legible within the context of the community. Saunders and Fogarty also find that an unintended consequence of the New Jersey law is that communities that are receptive to beer places experience clustering, whereas other parts of the state remain craft beer deserts. Another consequence is that brewers and brewery owners have to be strategic in how they work with or around the law. Some breweries have videos that act as tours of the brewery, others do a quick demonstration of how beer is made, and yet others take the tour objective seriously. A few years ago, Harvey stumbled upon Troon Brewing in Hopewell. Troon has since become one of the most well-known breweries in New Jersey, if not the United States. They are also famous for not having beer. They have a weekly limit release of about two or three cans per person, and usually run out of beer within one or two hours. Almost all of their beer goes to the Brick Farm Tavern, a farm-to-table restaurant on the property. Peeking in, Alex the head brewer, and at the time sole employee, exclaimed while sitting on a couch, "No beer . . . no tour," thus finding a new way to perhaps skirt the law.

The final chapter in this section deals with how the most important people in beer end up in beer places. Elliott's study of North Carolina breweries looks at how people become breweries; that is, how do they identify themselves as brewers? Elliott describes how "the personal inspiration evident in craft beer's growth represents a broader development in late capitalist markets." Brewing is a unique industry, where a postmodern guild system is still largely responsible for establishing careers. Elliott examination finds three common routes to becoming a brewer: the ideal pathway, never macros, and not-fans-prior.

The ideal pathway involves what Elliott calls the "enchanted consumer." Here the pathway to becoming a brewer blurs the boundary between work and consumption. This route, by far the most common, involves people who become enamored with craft beer, which turns into a lifestyle, which then becomes a career. Elliott notes that although the trajectories of work experienced by the brewers resembles the social critique of capitalism, whereby people embody market logic and come to identify as their job, craft brewers are different. They are passionate about their work, but they see their primary job as not to be a successful businessperson, but rather to educate people about the nuances of craft beer—and of course, to spread the joy of drinking good beer.

The chapters in part 3 deal with aspects of the craft beer industry that make it unique. In our research—as in these chapters—almost all brewers went to great lengths to communicate to us how collaborative and supportive the industry is. Unlike other industries or small businesses where competitive capitalism structures operations, craft breweries simultaneously embrace and eschew the traditional tenets of capitalism.

Borer focuses on a little-known aspect of the craft beer scene— bottle shares. A bottle share is, as it sounds, a gathering of people who each typically bring rare or locally hard-to-find beers. Most bottle shares are done in homes and thus are private, but Borer's bottle share takes place in public, at a bottle shop, which makes things more interesting in terms of the constitution of a craft beer community. Borer also brings attention to one of the major arguments in favor of consuming craft beer: it's local. As just noted, however, most bottle shares feature beers that are not locally available. As such, bottle shares promote beer from nonlocal places. Yet Borer argues that because they take place in particular places, they are situated in place, and thus are localized public rituals. As he emphasizes, we need to think of the idea of local as the point of consumption rather than just production.

Working from a symbolic interactionist perspective, Borer looks at the collective performance of the bottle share. He shows how bottle shares have an integrative function—bringing together individuals with different levels of beer capital, so that novices can learn what constitutes a good beer, and also marking particular places (in this case a bottle shop) as nodes in the craft beer scene. As such, the beer scene requires many beer places for it to succeed, but paradoxically beer places become ephemeral. They are any space where beer is shared, and as such they are shared spaces.

In the next chapter, Bianchi takes us to the United Kingdom to see the resurgence of community-owned pubs. Here residents are engaging in collective efforts to create and sustain local businesses by owning and managing pubs. Part of this has been made possible through the Campaign for Real Ale and also the Progressive Beer Duty, which reserves a lower taxation level for small breweries, but for the most part this collective ownership has resulted from the realization of the importance of beer places. As Bianchi notes, this is partly due to the rediscovery of craft beers, but also the desire for community.

For residents in many UK villages, the pub remains the last place to gather and socialize. In Somersham, East England, after years of pub closures, residents campaigned to "Save the Duke." This resulted in yet another Community-Owned Pub (COP) revitalizing the community. Bianchi also describes how a Toppesfield COP, the Green Man, has led the community to co-own other stores besides pubs and also provide services for schoolchildren and seniors. This has been supported by legislation, as noted, but also by the Pub Loan Fund, which allows pubs to borrow money for helping with myriad social problems. The government is literally banking on the historic role of the pub to provide social cohesion.

In "Craft Beer Ecosystem or Ecosystems?" Keller and Ghatak describe what they see as beer ecosystems. By looking at well-known beer places, such as Portland, Oregon; Portland, Maine; Cincinnati, Ohio; Kalamazoo, Michigan; Asheville, North Carolina; and Kansas City, Missouri, they argue that the industry functions more as a collective than as independent operators. Using the framework of entrepreneurial ecosystems from business studies, they find that breweries both contribute and depend on ties to other businesses. This process replicates itself across regions.

Similar to Elliot, they find that most brewers rely on other brewers rather than formal educations to help start their breweries. Also, as other authors in this volume observe, there is a benefit to clustering. As Keller and Ghatak note, clustering provides a cooperative culture where the ecosystem can draw from many different levels of businesses (local, regional, or national) and have crossover effects on other ecosystems. Understanding beer places as entrenched in ecosystems helps explain sharing and networking within the industry. As a number of breweries have indicated to Harvey and Jones during interviews, "A rising tide lifts all ships." Although these ecosystems can have both strong and weak ties (Granovetter 1973) to other industries and ecosystems, they are nonetheless rooted in particular places. Thus ecosystems will look different in different places as they draw from local businesses and trends.

As others in this book have noted, beer places can easily be thought of as scenes. In their chapter, McInerney, Adkins, Peña, and Behrends look at how scenes occur through the emergence of collective organizational identities. They focus on collaborative/competitive dynamics and show how these relationships tie organizations together to produce a scene. Using literature related to scenes, such as "fields" (Fligstein and McAdam 2013), they look at how breweries work together and as a result legitimize both the field and the rules that help govern it. Here brewers engage in "coopetition": while competing with other another, they also cooperate, to ensure success at the field level.

Using social network analysis (see also Skaggs and Gibbons's chapter), McInerney and coauthors study 150 breweries around Chicago, then argue that coopetition has shaped the scene through four aspects: (1) geographic subdivisions, (2) size and market footprint, (3) style and product portfolio, and (4) collaboration. Essentially they find that the geography of beer places matters. Breweries within Chicago city limits are much more likely to collaborate, and hence contribute to the scene, than are breweries in the suburbs of Chicago.

Fittingly, our last chapter is geographically set in Asheville, North Carolina, and focuses on brewery collaborations. Many of the collaborations that Skaggs and Gibbons examine are with food producers— which, as McInerney and colleagues would note, are part of the scene, and Keller and Ghatak would remind us, are part of the ecosystem. As Skaggs and Gibbons note, these collaborations help build not only the Asheville beerscape but also the local food scene.

Skaggs and Gibbons use Instagram posts to reconstruct social relationships among brewers and other local businesses. In doing so, they analyze both the social connectedness of members of the ecosystem and the number and "thickness" of those connections. As they argue, although digital relationships do not reveal all collaborative activity, they do reveal the relationships that breweries want to make visible to the public, ultimately creative a collaborative digital identity. Through social media, breweries are active in "creative placemaking." Skaggs and Gibbons find, much as McInerney and coauthors do, that geography matters for collaboration, but also that collaboration is the key to survival. Breweries that are socially isolated ultimately tend to get pushed out of the craft beer ecosystem. This example of collaboration between craft breweries in Asheville clearly demonstrates the relationship between social geography and spatial geography.

Notes

1. The definition of craft beer is somewhat controversial. Officially, the Brewers Association defines it as beer produced by a brewery that produces fewer than six million barrels of beer a year. In recent years, the industry has moved to using the term *independent* over *craft*. For a brewery to be independent, it cannot have 25 percent or greater ownership by a brewery that is itself not a craft brewery or brewer. Other terms such as *microbrewery* or *nano-brewery*, although generally used by individuals in the industry, likewise have little agreed-upon meaning, but are usually related to how much beer a brewer can brew in a single batch (i.e., three barrels, seven barrels, fourteen barrels, etc.).
2. I'm thinking here of authors who have looked at the omission of race and gender from foodways and foodstuffs to recenter our understanding of those products and productions in inclusive ways, such as Deetz (2017), Tipton-Martin (2013), and Zafar (2019).
3. This is not to say that gentrification does not happen in places where breweries are established or where a number of breweries conglomerate, but that gentrification is more complex than the simple equation of "brewery = gentrification."

References

Alexander, Jeffrey W. 2014. *Brewed in Japan: The Evolution of the Japanese Beer Industry*. Honolulu: University of Hawai'i Press.

Anderson, Elijah. 2015. "The White Space." *Sociology of Race and Ethnicity* 1(1):10–21.

Augé, Marc. 1995. *Non-places: Introduction to an Anthropology of Supermodernity*. New York: Verso Books.

Baso, Keith. 1996. *Wisdom Sits in Places: Landscape and Language among the Western Apache*. Albuquerque: University of New Mexico Press.

Barajas, Jesus M., Geoff Boeing, and Julie Wartell. 2017. "Neighborhood Change, One Pint at a Time." Pp. 155–76. In *Untapped: Exploring the Cultural Dimensions of Craft Beer*, edited by Nathaniel G. Chapman, Slade Lellock, and Cameron D. Lippard. Morgantown: University of West Virginia Press.

Barnett, Scot. 2012. "Psychogeographies of Writing: Ma(r)king Space at the Limits of Representation." *Kairos: A Journal of Rhetoric, Technology, and Pedagogy* 16(3).

Berger, Peter L. and Andrew Luckmann. 1966. *The Social Construction of Reality: A Treatise in the Sociology of Knowledge*. New York: Anchor Books.

Bloom, J. Dara. 2019. "Globalization of Food: The World as a Supermarket." Pp. 133–45. In *Twenty Lessons in the Sociology of Food and Agriculture*, edited by Jason Konefal and Maki Hatanaka. New York: Oxford University Press.

Borer, Michael Ian. 2019. *Vegas Brews: Craft Beer and the Birth of a Local Scene.* New York: New York University Press.

Cabras, Ignazio. 2017. "A Pint of Success: How Beer Is Revitalizing Cities and Local Economies in the United Kingdom." Pp. 39–58. In *Untapped: Exploring the Cultural Dimensions of Craft Beer*, edited by Nathaniel G. Chapman, Slade Lellock, and Cameron D. Lippard. Morgantown: University of West Virginia Press.

Carr, Jake K., Shaun A. Fontanella, and Calvin P. Tribby. 2019. "Identifying American Beer Geographies: A Multiscale Core-Cluster Analysis of U.S. Breweries." *The Professional Geographer* 71(2):185–96.

Casey, Edward S. 1996. "How to Get from Space to Place in a Fairly Short Stretch of Time: Phenomenological Prolegomena." Pp. 14–51. In *Senses of Place*, edited by Steven Feld and Keith H. Basso. Santa Fe, NM: School of American Research.

Chapman, Nathaniel G. and David L. Brunsma. 2020. *Beer and Racism: How Beer Became White, Why It Matters, and the Movements to Change it*. Bristol, UK: Bristol University Press.

Chapman, Nathaniel G., Megan Nanney, J. Slade Lellock, and Julie Mikles-Schluterman. 2018. "Bottling Gender: 'Accomplishing Gender through Craft Beer Consumption.'" *Food, Culture, and Society.* 21(3):296–313.

Deetz, Kelley Fanto. 2017. *Bound to the Fire: How Virginia's Enslaved Cooks Helped Invent American Cuisine*. Lexington: University Press of Kentucky.

Dunn, Jennifer C. 2017. "Does Craft Beer Culture Have a Place for Women?: A Co-cultural Autoethnography." Pp. 15–34. In *Beer Culture in Theory and Practice: Understanding Craft Beer Culture in the United States*, edited by Adam W. Tyma. New York: Lexington Books.

Fletchall, Ann M. 2016. "Place-Making through Beer-Drinking: A Case Study of Montana's Craft Breweries." *Geographical Review* 106(4):539–66.

Foda, Omar. 2019. *Egypt's Beer: Stella, Identity, and the Modern State*. Austin: University of Texas Press.

Feagan, Robert. 2007. "The Place of Food: Mapping Out the 'Local' in Local Food Systems." *Progress in Human Geography* 31(1):23–42.

Fligstein, Neil and Doug McAdam. 2013. "Toward a General Theory of Strategic Action Fields." *Sociological Theory* 29(1):1–26.

Florida, Richard. 2002. *The Rise of the Creative Class*. New York: Basic Books.

———. 2008. *Who's Your City: How the Creative Economy Is Making Where to Live the Most Important Decision of Your Life*. New York: Basic Books.

———. 2017. *The New Urban Crisis: How Our Cities Are Increasing Inequality, Deepening Segregation, and Failing the Middle Class—and What We Can Do About It*. New York: Basic Books.

Giddens, Anthony. 1991. *Modernity and Self-Identity: Self and Society*. Stanford, CA: Stanford University Press.

Goodman, David and Melanie DuPuis. 2002. "Knowing Food and Growing Food: Beyond the Production-Consumption Debate in the Sociology of Agriculture." *Sociologia Ruralis* 42(1):5–22.

Granovetter, Mark. 1973. "The Strength of Weak Ties." *American Journal of Sociology* 78(6):1360–80.

Gray, Margaret. 2014. *Labor and the Locavore: The Making of a Comprehensive Food Ethic*. Berkeley: University of California Press.

Grazian, David. 2003. *Blue Chicago: The Search for Authenticity in Urban Blues Clubs*. Chicago: University of Chicago Press.

Hedegaard, Liselotte. 2018. "(Re)tasting Places." *Gastronomica: The Journal of Critical Food Studies* 18(1):66–75.

Hess, David. 2009. *Localist Movements in a Global Economy: Sustainability, Justice and Urban Development in the United States*. Cambridge, MA: MIT Press.

Hinrichs, Claire. 2019. "Food and Localism." Pp. 295–311 in *Twenty Lessons in the Sociology of Food and Agriculture*, edited by Jason Konefal and Maki Hatanaka. New York: Oxford University Press.

Hubbard, Phil. 2017. *The Battle for the High Street: Retail Gentrification, Class and Disgust*. London: Palgrave Macmillian.

Huckelbridge, Dane. 2016. *The United States of Beer: A Freewheeling History of the All-American Drink*. New York, NY: William Morrow.

Jones, Ellis, and Daina Cheyenne Harvey. 2017. "Ethical Brews: New England, Networked Ecologies, and a New Craft Beer Movement." Pp. 124–36. In *Untapped: Exploring the Cultural Dimensions of Craft Beer*, edited by Nathaniel G. Chapman, Slade Lellock, and Cameron D. Lippard. Morgantown: University of West Virginia Press.

Levkoe, Charles Zalman. 2011. "Towards a Transformative Food Politics." *Local Environment* 16(7):687–705.

McMichael, Phillip. 2009. "A Food Regime Genealogy." *Journal of Peasant Studies* 36:139–69.

Milligan, Melinda. 1998. "Interactional Past and Potential: The Social Construction of Place Attachment." *Symbolic Interaction* 21(1):1–33.

Moretti, Enrico. 2013. *The New Geography of Jobs*. New York: First Mariner Books.

Mountford, Roxanne. 2001. "On Gender and Rhetorical Space." *Rhetoric Society Quarterly* 31(1):41–71.

Ocejo, Richard E. 2017. *Masters of Craft: Old Jobs in the New Urban Economy*. Princeton, NJ: Princeton University Press.

Paxson, Heather. 2013. *The Life of Cheese: Creating Food and Value in America*. Berkeley: University of California Press.

Pred, Allan. 1984. "Place as Historically Contingent Process: Structuration and the Time-Geography of Becoming Places." *Annals of the Association of American Geographers* 74(2):279–97.

Reid, Neil and Jay D. Gatrell. 2017. "Craft Breweries and Economic Development: Local Geographies of Beer. *Polymath: An Interdisciplinary Arts and Sciences Journal* 7(2):90–110.

Reynolds, Nedra. 2004. *Geographies of Writing: Inhabiting Places and Encountering Difference*. Carbondale: Southern Illinois University Press.

Saunders, Robert A. and Jack Holland. 2018. "The Ritual of Beer Consumption as Discursive Intervention: Effigy, Sensory, Politics, and Resistance in Everyday IR." *Millennium: Journal of International Studies* 46(2):119–41.

Schnell, Steven M. and Joseph F. Reese. 2003. "Microbreweries as Tools of Local Identity." *Journal of Cultural Geography* 21(1):45–69.

Starr, Amory. 2010. "Local Food: A Social Movement?" *Cultural Studies Critical Methodologies* 10:479–90.

Tipton-Martin, Toni. 2013. *The Jemima Code: Two Centuries of African American Cookbooks*. Austin: University of Texas Press

Tyna, Adam W. 2017. *Beer Culture in Theory and Practice: Understanding Craft Beer Culture in the United States*. New York: Lexington Books.

Urry, John. 1995. *Consuming Places*. New York: Routledge Press.

———. 2000. *Sociology beyond Societies: Mobilities for the Twenty-First Century*. New York: Routledge Press.

Walker, Samuel and Chloe Fox Miller. 2019. "Have Craft Breweries Followed or Led Gentrification in Portland, Oregon? An Investigation of Retail and Neighbourhood Change." *Geografiska Annaler: Series B, Human Geography* 101(2):102–17.

Withers, Eric. 2017. "Brewing Boundaries of White Middle-Class Maleness: Reflections from within the Craft Beer Industry." Pp. 236–60. In *Untapped: Exploring the Cultural Dimensions of Craft Beer*, edited by Nathaniel G. Chapman, Slade Lellock, and Cameron D. Lippard. Morgantown: University of West Virginia Press.

Zafar, Rafia. *Recipes for Respect: African American Meals and Meaning*. Athens: University of Georgia Press.

Zerubavel, Eviatar. 2003. *Time Maps: Collective Memory and the Social Shape of the Past*. Chicago: University of Chicago Press.

PART I

Authenticity and Revitalization

CHAPTER 1

Crafting Community and Drinking "Local"

Constructing Authenticity and Identity in the Craft Beer Culture

AMANDA KOONTZ AND
NATHANIEL G. CHAPMAN

Over the 2010s, the craft beer movement grew tremendously. According to the Brewers Association (2018), the number of breweries in the United States eclipsed seven thousand in 2018. Although this rapid growth continues, brewery closures have sharply risen, too. In 2017, 165 breweries closed their doors—a 70 percent increase from 2016 (Fumari 2018). Brewer's Association data show that "microbreweries and brewpubs delivered 76% of the craft brewer growth in 2017 as consumers' preferences shift to beer made more locally (than regional brewers) and available onsite neighborhood taprooms and brewpubs" (Schoup 2018). The difference between local microbreweries and regional breweries is the number and reach of their distribution networks. Regional breweries can have out-of-state distribution and typically cover a larger geographical region; local microbreweries may only sell onsite or to a select few retailers. Bart Watson, chief economist for the Brewers Association, contends that "beer lovers are trending toward supporting their local small and independent community craft breweries. At the same time, as distribution channels experience increased competition and challenges, craft brewer performance was more mixed than in recent years, with those relying on the broadest distribution facing the most pressure" (Fumari 2018).

As the craft beer market expands, the particular qualities that contribute to a microbrewery's success can become clearer as each faces greater internal competition, versus being the only alternative to macro-brewers (e.g., Anheuser-Busch). This expanded differentiation helps to further problematize the dichotomy between "inauthentic large" and "authentic small" breweries. Demonstrating the extent to which the consumption of cultural products entails consuming ideologies, Watson further notes that "beer lovers want to support businesses that align with their values and are having a positive impact on their local communities and our larger society. That's what small and independent craft brewers are all about. The ability to seek beers from small and independent producers matters" (Fumari 2018).

To explore what craft beer consumers consider authentic in a microbrewery and its product, we performed a textual analysis of BeerAdvocate.com, a popular social media review website, to determine if the success of microbreweries is based in authenticating processes, with a particular focus on whether consumers draw from and foster a sense of being a part of the "local" (i.e., the authentically local) in their evaluations of microbreweries. Sensitized by the local, we seek to answer the broad question: What are the traits, as perceived and expressed by consumers, that differentiate a microbrewery for better or worse? More specifically, we explore the ways in which consumer reviews integrate geographical and cultural constructs of space and place, and in turn, if a sense of localism is integral to consumers' expressed experiences of a microbrewery. In doing so, we focus on craft breweries as a site through which we can examine how geographical and cultural constructs of space and place foster a sense of localism and, relatedly, how a brewery's commercial success or expansion plays a part in consumers' reviews.

We find that what we term *localized authentication* is critical in differentiating successful or popular microbreweries. We define localized authentication as a contextualized and collaborative process, during which interactions among the products, producers (and/or representatives), and consumers result in the situated experiences of a "vibe." Individuals' judgments of the vibe of a physical space and place are the basis of their craft brewery reviews, which range with the felt authenticity and inauthenticity the vibe generates. We find the extent to which a reviewer deems their experience as authentic is based on three traits: quality, the "local," and space. Each trait has a tipping point; whereas each can help balance the imperfection of another, our findings suggest a recipe of "just enough" of each trait creates the best possible vibe and resulting review. Building from previous research (Koontz and Chapman 2019), this chapter also helps to understand what intangible components of a "vibe" contribute to the commercial success of cultural venues, particularly in a time when increasing competition can both expand and contract the boundaries of localism, or what is considered to be "local."

Our findings additionally expand research on sense of place, as we argue that consumer reviews help reveal how consumers collectively create, reinforce, or question the identity of a brewery and place. Consumers compare the image of their own local hometown with their expectations for the city/region and brewery they are visiting, which reinforces their expectations and reputations of the place and the brewery. This, in turn, influences how the "local" is and will be perceived by future consumers. As such, authenticating microbrewery narratives re-envision a sense of localized tradition, which can craft community and allow audiences to literally partake in the local, offering sought-after experiences of embodied connectedness and uniqueness that can otherwise feel lost in a consistently globalizing economy.

Literature Review

Although there are various terms and approaches to the current economic trends, such as *postindustrial economy, experience economy*, and *globalization*, each relates to the importance of experience and "consuming culture." Here we review key concepts that help us understand consumers' reviews of craft breweries and the meanings of vibe, and build up to the concept of localized authenticity.

AUTHENTICITY

As authenticity is a socially constructed concept of what is genuine or original, it seems logical that there is an ongoing debate over what creates a sense of place and, beyond that, a localized sense of an authentic consumption-based place. For instance, MacCannell (1976) introduced a continuum of authenticity from front-stage experiences, or staged performances for tourists (least authentic), to backstage experiences, in which tourists could get a glimpse of the local (most authentic). Cohen and Cohen (2012) build on Selwyn's (1996) terms of "hot" and "cool" authenticity (both of which worked to build from MacCannell's [1976] distinctions). They define "cool" authenticity as related to scientific and personal knowledge, so that it can be understood more as definitional and in terms of statements. Alternatively, "hot" authenticity is related to the more social desire to construct an authentic self and authentic other, typically through experiences. Cohen and Cohen (2012) argue that "hot" and "cool" authenticity, rather than expressing a dichotomy, should be approached as potentially integrated, as authenticity can have both a tangible origin and arise through an individual's perception.

To help further situate these discussions, one can also consider the importance of Baudrillard's work on aura and simulacra to places or objects being considered "real." Whereas authentication started out closer to "cool" authenticity, based in art history and determinations of objects' origins, these distinctions became muddled with the increase in mass reproduction and popular culture (e.g., cultural industries) as we know them today. As it became increasingly easy to reproduce products more swiftly and precisely, as duplicants became increasingly common (including photography), and as mass culture increased (i.e., chain businesses), using the same lines of reasoning for what is authentic became more difficult. As demonstrated through Baudrillard's work, the ideas of essence or aura, deriving from the original place or artist's hand, became more important to demarcating an object or place as authentic. Continuing in this line, Baudrillard also helped to capture issues of authenticity and consumption through concepts such as floating signifiers and simulacra, in which there never was an original. A commonly repeated example is Disneyland, featuring Main Street (the main street of a small town that never actually existed as such) and Fantasyland (which creates a fantasy of something that was never real except in that "falsely" created space).

With these questions and concerns established, theorists and researchers have increasingly adopted social constructionist perspectives of authenticity. Rather than being grounded in one reality, social constructionist perspectives hold that authenticity must be understood as an ongoing negotiation of perceived realities. For instance, Leigh and colleagues (2006) describe how members of a car subculture (MG owners) compare their vehicles to a showroom ideal, authenticating preserved cars through an interplay of collective memory and heritage, while romanticizing a constructed past British time and place (the company closed in 1980). Further, they explain how the physical experience of driving and fixing cars, along with gaining knowledge from individuals who can pass along sought-after expert knowledge, helps foster authentic experiences and identities. For example, Wang (1999) offered the concept of existential authenticity, arising from consumers' search for an experience that makes them feel they are in touch with a real world and their real selves. In an approach arguably reflective of the Thomas theorem and the social construction of reality, if the individual feels the subjective experience to be real, then the results are accordingly real in their authenticated outcomes. This is particularly the case for tourists, who may enter a liminal space where they feel allowed to drop the pretenses of everyday life. As such, research in authenticity increasingly emphasizes the importance of perception and experience to the judgments of authenticity; although authenticity can be integrated with more objective standards, these findings also relate to shifts in the broader socioeconomic context.

EXPERIENCE ECONOMY AND PLACE-BASED IDENTITIES

As trends in authenticity suggest, "experiences" are increasingly the focus of consumption and social sciences research, particularly in relation to debates surrounding the influences, forces, and consequences of globalization as it affects consumption and sense of place. The term *glocalization* has emerged to account for the transnational forces of globalization—the integration of the local into particular geographic areas (Ritzer 2003). Globalization and cultural homogenization both stoke concerns, as national and corporate interests take over and cross boundaries to create a sense of sameness through chain businesses and the spread of Western cultural traditions and norms. Alternatively, glocalization suggests that unique combinations of global and local forces influence particular geographical locations. Others have argued that with shifts accompanying globalization, we have shifted into an "experience economy," which Pine and Gilmore (1999) state reproduces itself through the practices of consumption and experience of culture. More specifically, Pine and Gilmore (1999) argue that we have entered a new economic age, where not just goods but services—and thus the total staged experience—have been commodified. One may see how the staging of experiences—in which being in a particular place matters—can relate to these unique integrations of global trends and a particular locale.

Further, Miles (2010, 66) suggests that culture has been appropriated within the "broader reinvention of the post-industrial economy" through "cultural quarters." *Cultural quarters* are places of concentrated cultural activity, such as museums, performing arts institutions, metropolitan cultural districts, and creative design centers (Miles 2010). According to Montgomery (2007), these centers do not exist in isolation; rather, their popularity and success depend on the extent and ways in which consumers engage with the aura or buzz of an area or scene. Silver and Clark (2016, 31) define *scene* as a "powerful conceptual tool for discerning the range and configurations of aesthetic meanings expressed within and across various places, for seeing the clumpiness of cultural life." What must be highlighted, though, is how authenticity research can again offer insight into how expectations can influence the consumption, perception, and success of cultural quarters or scenes.

Debate also continues on whether cultural scenes are essentially depersonalized to appeal to the largest crowd, or whether place *does* still matter and that identities are place based. According to Miles (2010), although culture and art are integral to cultivating the economy, cultural scenes are essentially homogenized to appeal to the largest crowd. The ideas behind the cultural products become more important than the products themselves, which ironically can diminish those underlying ideas (e.g., purchasing a mass-produced product with a regional slogan). Brown-Saracino (2018, 4–5) adopts a different approach, making the key point that people, beyond being social, are fundamentally "local creatures." She thus defines identity culture as "geographically specific, composed of those who share a defining demographic trait, and spans multiple friendship or institutional groups." Whereas Brown-Saracino focuses more on identities at the individual and group levels, Silver and Clark (2016, 140) name local authenticity as one of fifteen key dimensions of scenes, explaining that the "primary appeal of the local is the expectation that one can find something here that you can get only here, something distinctive, not (yet?) homogenized by the standardizing forces of global capitalism." Similarly, Gotham (2007, 10) describes "localization" in relation to urban branding as a "process by which local actors and organizations appropriate 'global' imagery and symbols to reinforce 'local' sentiments and inscribe 'local' meanings into products and cultural creations." However, Gotham further specifies that this relates to commodification, because localization is driven by corporations branding urban culture as an object for consumption.

Anthropologist Appadurai (1996, 179) argues, however, that even though concern for the loss of the local is due to globalization and cultural homogeneity, the construction of the local should be understood as a fundamentally "fragile social achievement." Appadurai claims that even rites of passage, including scarification, are related to creating "local subjects"; although he maintains that the spatial component has been understudied, arguably these rituals are performed to integrate a sense of the local. This supports Brown-Saracino's (2018, 5) argument that place identities help answer fundamental questions of self-identities and how we should relate to others around us. For instance, Gotham (2007, 150) states that residents of New Orleans's French Quarter created a "repertoire of authenticity," creating boundaries between those who are *of* a space (residents/locals) versus those who are *in* a space (tourists/visitors). This prizes "the local," as residents are defined as being more real and the authentic voice of a place. In the realm of Chicago blues and adopting a more liminal tourist role, even as a resident, Grazian (2003, 63–64) offers the term *nocturnal self* to describe the "personalities that pleasure-seekers craft as they negotiate their way through the nightlife of a city." This draws attention to the diversion from everyday life that can be experienced in a particular space and place, where people can temporarily create a world that is closer to "their dreams." Grazian emphasizes the more active role that audiences sometimes take, which again highlights the interactivity within creating the space: a place of consumption needs to meet enough consumer expectations to be able to create the world they want to temporarily inhabit.

EXPECTATIONS

The component of expectations overlaps judgments of authenticity and experiences, as demonstrated by Grayson and Martinec's (2004) extensive marketing research differentiating two primary types of authentication: indexical and iconic. Indexical authenticity can be associated (at risk of oversimplification) with "cool" authenticity, because it is more factual and related to being an original. Consumers evaluate a given object depending on whether it is "real" or "original," versus a copy, then judge its authenticity on whether they can physically connect it with the sociohistorical context (time, place, materials, etc.). The object at hand is judged according to whether it is the "real" or "original" object, versus a copy. Consumers' evaluations are then based on judgments where they determine if an object physically can be connected with the socio-historical context (time, place, materials, etc.). Alternatively, iconic authenticity, by contrast, is based in individuals' expectations for how something should be. In Newman and Smith's (2016, 611) summary, "Iconic authenticity is not concerned with a specific spatiotemporal fact, but rather with the degree to which the item satisfies one's prior expectations about how something ought to be, which can be reflected in terms such as 'authentic reproduction' (Bruner 1994; Crang 1996; Peterson 1997)."

Further, past research reveals how consumers of cuisine—particularly ethnic cuisine—bring expectations with them into the restaurant and their dining experience. For instance, Lu and Fine (1995, 540) explain that "ethnic food can only be accepted by adapting it into a cultural matrix and by creating a set of culinary expectations." Writing about Mexican restaurants, Gaytán (2008, 315) further explains that in a "world where soft drinks are marketed as 'the real thing' (Handler 1986, 6) and restaurants are named 'The Authentic Café' (Halter 2000, 19), consumption serves as a means through which authenticity becomes a measure of the quality, efficacy, and legitimacy of one's experience in a particular setting." Lu and Fine (1995, 545) find that consumers of "connoisseur-oriented restaurants" tend to have more time to invest, along with greater economic and cultural resources, with resulting concerns for how the "characteristics of the food meets their expectations." Consumers generally emphasize the character of the food (and connections with its origins), importance of service in creating an occasion of dining, quality of ingredients, and experimental ingredient combinations.

Gaytán (2008, 317) also describes how, with the consumptive emphasis on authenticity, stereotypes created a desire for "pre-determined images as opposed to spontaneous proceedings." Particularly related to this chapter's focus, Lu and Fine's (1995, 547) study highlights an interesting combination of experiences and expectations: they find that restaurants must work toward a good *reputation* more than good *food*, so that their styles must continue shifting—even if away from tradition—because consumers place the most emphasis on the "primary sensory satisfaction" (547). As related to expectations, Gaytán (2008, 321) offers that "a restaurant's atmosphere is vital to an assessment of authenticity," yet reviewers and consumers go beyond the menu, recipes, or even ingredients in their judgment—typically describing the ambiance more in terms of the other people in the space than decor. Although also focused on ethnicity, Gaytán's (2008, 322) findings uphold that there is "more than one way to achieve authenticity," because it relates to how these characteristics are expressed. For our purposes, Gaytán's conclusion raises questions as to what components are considered part of the authentic experience, and in what ways this includes or trumps product quality.

VIBE

Although research is limited, terms that help address such ideas surrounding experience relate to what is often referred to as the "vibe" or "atmosphere" of a place. Stemming from a more philosophical perspective, the conceptualization of affective atmospheres describes interactions between people and space, and how spaces are emotionally charged (Anderson 2009). Affective atmosphere goes beyond what Goffman noted regarding how the setting of interactions holds preestablished norms and limitations for how one can and should act (see, e.g., Goffman 1997), in that theories of affective atmosphere describe how a place has "a vibration" that comes from its aesthetics and the emotions that are brought into and derive from interactions there (Michels 2015, 256).

Sociological research on vibe is also scarce, and when available, typically limited to music subcultures or scenes. However, the available research offers groundwork for examining what is otherwise a seeming intangible "feel": physically being at a place and becoming a part of that place is what is unique and valuable to the interactional experience. For example, Driver (2016, 194) discusses how participants at hardcore music events, as a form of subculture, deem certain fellow participants authentic based on their "perceived potential to contribute to the 'vibe'—or 'atmosphere'—of hardcore music events." Driver uses the terms *vibe* and *atmosphere* interchangeably; both describe how cultural and creative production can be experienced as collaborative. Thus there is transference between producers and consumers, both of which can be deemed authentic based on their ability to perpetuate and transfer the cultural meanings of the product in combination with their own personal histories and identities (Driver 2016; Ingold and Kurtilla 2000; Thornton 1995). In these ways, vibe may be an updated term for the ephemeral experience Durkheim (2008) described as "collective effervescence"—when a community of people gathers to experience something together, which helps to elevate and ignite the group and therefore unites them again. What can be noted throughout Durkheim's account is how this is an embodied experience; there is an importance to how people interact, negotiate, create meaning for, and take up a space.

Methods

This chapter builds on previous research and data (Koontz and Chapman, 2019) in which we identified the ways in which brewers constructed an authentic identity for themselves and their breweries through the narrative of a journey. We extend this inquiry by assessing the authenticity and identity of the brewery from the perspective of consumers. We collected and analyzed our data through an iterative two-phase procedure. First, we used BeerAdvocate.com's search function to compile a list of craft breweries that met the following criteria: (1) an overall rating of 4 out of 5 or higher, (2) at least one hundred user reviews, and (3) production of at least fifteen unique beers. We chose BeerAdvocate as it is a leading consumer review site whose brewery ratings are user generated. These ratings are then standardized by BeerAdvocate's rating system using five weighted criteria: vibe/atmosphere (10 percent), quality (30 percent), service (25 percent), food (10 percent), and selection (25 percent). This search yielded 135 craft breweries. Our goal was to analyze breweries that were viewed as both successful and popular to consumers in order to conceptualize a model of authenticity and legitimation for craft breweries.

Second, we randomly selected thirty breweries from our list using a random number generator. We then examined 150 user-generated BeerAdvocate reviews for each brewery to gauge customer reception. This generated 4,500 unique data points. We examined only the 150 most recent reviews for two reasons: they would be most likely to reflect the current "vibe" or "scene" of the brewery, and several breweries mentioned new facilities, locations, and expansions. Recent reviews would better reflect these changes and the current experience at each brewery.

Using grounded-theory techniques and coaxial coding (Hussein et al. 2014; Strauss and Corbin 1990), we identified several key themes across the reviews. Grounded-theory techniques allow the researcher to develop a more in-depth understanding of the data and the ability to conceptualize themes as they emerge from the data (Hussein et al. 2014, 1–15) These techniques involved constructing gestalts for each brewery from customer reviews to get a sense of their overall feel. Both reviewers then open-coded the gestalts to identify several themes that reflected the authenticity and experience of customers at each brewery. Using the constant-comparative method, we identified several themes: physical space, connection to locals and localness, vibe and atmosphere, and overall service and quality. Based on our previous research and our grounded process, we determined that these themes are connected to "tipping points": the idea that a brewery could be viewed as positive in some areas, but negative in others. In our analysis of these themes, we found that breweries may have been deficient in one theme, but mitigated this negative perception by excelling in another area. For example, several breweries were negatively reviewed based on their service. Reviewers would then mitigate this assessment by adding something to the effect of "at least the beer is good" or another form of positive review. Hereafter, we analyze these themes as tipping points and how reviewers perceive a brewery's sense of authenticity.

Analysis

We found that consumers, in the process of localized authentication, construct a place and its associated vibe from three traits: quality, the "local," and space. As mentioned, each trait can be understood as having a tipping point, in which there needs to be "enough" of the trait to meet consumer expectations. The intersection of these traits leads to a place having a "good vibe." To judge the three traits of quality, localism, and space, consumers based their reviews on a comparison of locales. By *locales*, we mean that consumers compared breweries to their hometown, to their own place and sense of authentic "localness"—closer to a collective memory that is actively being constructed, deconstructed, and reconstructed with the addition of breweries to the repertoire. Although this is most certainly a relative experience, the process was similar across reviews; we therefore support findings that the overall sensory experience is critical to positive reviews of microbreweries.

However, we build from this to show how consumers' judgment of their sensory experience is not contained in that one event, but instead is both contextualized and cumulative.

Visitors' localized authentication process is accordingly extremely comprehensive; to authenticate a brewery, they can draw from the entire surrounding locale. Our findings uphold Grazian's (2003) suggestions (if from a different realm) surrounding the nocturnal self, in that consumers appear to want their fantasies upheld in their visits. Reviews show how consumers authenticate breweries using a number of traits, so that even if the breweries do not encompass one trait, they can compensate with another. Our data reveal that consumers, when rating breweries, often negotiated or rationalized a rating if the brewery compensated for a particular deficiency by exceeding expectations in another area. For example, customers would complain about the size of a particular brewery, but then tout it as exemplifying the "local vibe." One reviewer described such an experience as follows: "Not fancy by any stretch of the word, but you get a slight hometown feel here." When a brewery is deficient in one or more traits (e.g., perceptions of quality, authentic identity and connection to the "local," or the brewery itself), it may receive negative consumer feedback—revealing in turn how it did not meet consumers' expectations or needs to craft the positive experience. Breweries can thus also be authenticated based on what they both can and cannot control. For instance, a brewery can benefit by having its physical location (e.g., the mountains) taken into account in reviewers' experience of the establishment, or can compensate for a less desirable location (e.g., strip mall) by having proper decorations and from the quality of beer. Reviews thus suggest that even if certain cultural scenes may arguably be depersonalized to attract the largest crowd, consumers will interpret the place in such ways that "relocalize" the brewery, constructing reviews that support definitions of authenticity as geographically based and distinctive due to a combination of traits that cannot be experienced elsewhere (e.g., Brown-Saracino 2018; Gotham 2007).

QUALITY

Quality includes both the quality of the product—in this case, the beer itself—and of the service. A brewery's the tipping point—or balancing act—for quality is that as long as consumers perceive the quality of its beer to be good enough, it can compensate for poor service. Alternatively, as long as the service makes the customer feel welcomed and is quick or attentive enough, the quality of the beer does not have to be as high. In the case of localized authenticity, the ideal breweries that receive the highest ranking therefore will have both high-quality beer and service.

A part of what makes up a good vibe relates to this sensory experience, in that positive feelings are associated with consumers' feeling like they are a part of an inclusive interactive experience with others, both within a unique space and while they are having an individualized moment with the taste of a good beer. When a place offers both these aspects, consumers report that it has a good vibe. A negative review, though, can be rather revealing of what it takes for consumers to define a good vibe. The following example comparatively describes all of the ways the brewery did *not* fulfill their expectations. (All review excerpts reflect spelling, punctuation, and capitalization used in the source.)

> I must be getting old but wow was this an obnoxious stop—I was ready to move on to the next as soon as I stepped in. And finding a parking spot wasn't easy either. Being in an industrial parkway that curves and loops, street parking seems to be the only option, and due to the nature of the zoning this can turn into an unnecessarily long walk when there seems to be large groups of people driving solo to meet each other at Hardywood. . . . The line for taps in that space ran directly through the crowd trying to watch the band, and it was almost impossible to get a single beer. It was a hassle for all involved, including the bartenders who acted like we should be there to watch the band and not drink the brewery's beer, which was bland when contrasted with the dumpster fire happening before us. It's a shame that their secondary spot right next door was closed to the public, because it appeared to have 10x the space, with a cleaner look and more tables and taps.

Here, we can see how the perceived accessibility, exorbitant crowds, service, usage of space, integration of community (i.e., the band), and quality of beer are collectively critiqued.

Alternatively, other reviews show how a vibe may only be "okay" if consumers find the quality in only the beer *or* the service. Reviewers still may consider the brewery for additional visits or further attention, but typically the reviews explain how it is worth it to go for one particular reason (e.g., one beer option, the experience if you are visiting the city for another reason, etc.). For example, one reviewer described a place having a "pretty good vibe, but the taproom is fairly small and was pretty packed. Service was still pretty quick though and I had the PB [peanut butter] porter, which was great. Would return for this alone." Two others reviewed a brewery they defined as okay or worth dropping into—"The beers here are pretty standard. They're well made, but not much to write home about. They get a lot of hype, but I think it's just good marketing. The food is pretty good, and it's definitely worth dropping by if you're going to a ball game"—while another reviewer explained that they "had an enjoyable time here. Service was great. Atmosphere was OK, a bit sterile for a brewery."

Still another reviewer made very similar comments about a different brewery:

> The vibe of the place wasn't all that special and there weren't a lot of people there either. Their selection wasn't super impressive, it was pretty standard stuff really which was a little disappointing. The service was good though, I can't complain about that at all. I have to say though, it seems like they're getting less business due to the rise of some of the smaller/newer places opening up in the Richmond area.

Ensuring that customers receive prompt service is one way to keep customers coming back and to compensate for other components of the atmosphere or vibe. Yet, we can also understand service in a way that connects with the local community, as explained by another reviewer about the same brewery: "Large, spacious indoor/outdoor facility that seems to work exceptionally well with the community, hosting local bands, authors, and charity activities." These reviews demonstrate that individual consumer experience is relative to what the consumer perceives as authentic. The first reviewer posits that the brewery is losing business to smaller and newer breweries and that the beer is "pretty standard stuff," whereas the second seems to prefer the large space and how it can accommodate local interests such as music and charity events. The second reviewer never mentions the quality of the beer, but refers to the space in very positive terms. With such seemingly malleable boundaries for what can compensate for quality, it is interesting to reconsider Appadurai's (1996) perspective on locality as a fragile social achievement. Using their reviews, consumers appear to be helping the brewery, and potentially themselves as brewery insiders, to save face. As a form of mobile community, the microbrewery scene maintains a collective sense of authenticity through making sense of their experiences by helping to scaffold microbrewery reputations when possible. Reviews such as these seem to defend the perceived shortcomings of a brewery by touting the impact it has in the community. Thus its value to the locals seems in some ways more about how it reflects the surrounding location or community than the actual beer or service.

With quality being related to taste, evaluations of the beer's taste help interpret when the vibe feels right, because in the case of microbreweries the experience of the taste is integrated into the experience of the place. As Trubek (2008, 7) explains, "Taste evaluations must occur through language, a shared dialogue with others." Consumers' social expectations are brought into what reviewers or experts have defined as tasting good in the microbrewery world, usually based on a connection with quality ingredients, baseline recipes, and then something creative or outstanding enough to make a consumer choose that particular beer over others. As Bernot (2015) notes, "Choosing a beer that is 'locally made' . . . has increased in importance" for consumers, and aspects such as "flavor, freshness, aroma, ingredients, bitterness level, whether it was independently brewed and appearance" were all ranked high in terms of factors influencing craft consumers. Even so, we find that this can be understood as a two-way street: the taste makes the place, just as the place makes the taste.

Although research shows that ingredient origins matter to discriminating taste (e.g., Lu and Fine 1996; Trubek 2008), the following reviews reveal the integration of critiquing the quality of where one consumes the beer with assessing the quality of the beer. A quality beer can overcome a low-quality space, or vice versa, yet the best "vibe" comes from a high-quality place within which to consume a high-quality beer; quoting one reviewer, "the vibe is casual and the staff is laid back (in a good way)." Although another reviewer used the term "atmosphere," the combination of traits also supports the importance of quality of place and taste when they state, "staff is friendly and fast. It does get packed and noisy on the weekends but I still love the atmosphere of the building." This combination of traits also leads to consumers describing breweries as "destinations" and "must-stop" locations. For instance,

> A must-stop in a town absolutely packed with must-stops. I prefer the OG spot downtown. It just has the vibe. It was so packed I had

to stand outside the bathroom door. It was worth it. They make so many of my favorite beers and the ones you've probably had are probably on tap.

This review also highlights the role of originality (*OG* stands for "original gangster," a term appropriated to mean "original location" in this instance) in the construction of a vibe. Craft consumers seem to prefer original (i.e., pre-expansion) locations as they offer a more authentic experience. The typical reason for expansion is a lack of space—apparently a major determinant in whether a brewery is reviewed positively—yet originality of location seems to offer more value in terms of quality and authenticity. This can be seen in the following review:

> Very nice building and taproom, albeit on the small side. If this was a nano brewery that would be appropriate, that's for one of the big boys in the state it seems out of whack a little. I guess they do also have the spot on 19th and Arapahoe, but I read they want this place to be a destination spot and I just don't see how the current set up would allow that, at least once the weather gets crappy and the outdoor seating is no longer an option.

Although brewers frame expansion as benefiting consumers (e.g., Koontz and Chapman 2019), this review demonstrates the tension between brewers and consumers when it comes to expansion. Reviewers displayed a preference for visiting the original location: "Stopped by the original location for a few beers. Fairly small space, they have a bar and some standing room in the front, and a few high top tables in the back in view of the brew house." To some, visiting the original location offers a more authentic vibe and adds to the mystique of the local: "I was so stoked to finally get to check this place out. hop devil is one of the beers that got me into craft in the first place way back when, and this felt like somewhat of a pilgrimage to go to the original victory brewery." Expansion can be a double-edged sword, as breweries wish to avoid negative reviews on quality of service and/ or overcrowding, but microbreweries in particular also must produce enough beer for consumers. However, expansion comes with monetary and nonmonetary costs (e.g., harming the authenticity of the brand). By expanding and opening additional locations, breweries must now manage two identities. They must maintain a sense of originality while demonstrating how the expansion was in the best interest of the customer, rather than simply being economically driven. As these reviews show, it is difficult to maintain a sense of originality and authenticity while expanding into larger spaces.

THE "LOCAL"

Brewery traits that reviewers consider local involve location (e.g., the neighborhood or scene), the representation of the local (through ingredients, themes, etc.), and the actual people defined as "locals." The tipping point for the local, then, relates to consumers' comparison of expectations of what a local brewery "should" be, based on their personal locale (e.g., hometown and social location) and the locale of the brewery (region, city, site), and is therefore relative by definition. Reviewers then gauge its aesthetics from their own interpretations and experiences to evaluate and provide a review of the brewery. Their notion of local is thus twofold: it arises from their own locality and their experiences of "local" culture, and from their interpretation of what a particular scene or location "should be" as a projection of their own experience. For example, one reviewer compared the brewery to their hometown bar saying, "The bartender was filled with stories and silly jokes. Had us cracking up the whole time. Plus the locals were very friendly and fun to chat up. It was like being back home in a bar we had been to a hundred times." Although the term *beer scene* may be used for a particular place, and scenes are related to styles of life versus ways of life (i.e., a scene does not necessarily represent a subculture), the process of authenticating beer scenes remains comparative.

We also found that consumers who identified as tourists (e.g., "This place is a must visit when in _____ area") were conflicted in their view of the "local feel" of breweries. Some found this experience positive, whereas others felt it discouraged nonlocals from visiting the brewery. Some reviewers indicated that breweries need to make customers feel they are in a brewery distinct to that location, with enough locals to contribute to that feeling, yet not so distinct that the visiting consumer feels like an outsider. Others described seeking recommendations from locals to ensure that their experience was authentic: "This place came highly recommended by all the locals we talked to, it seems it's a favorite on the scene here, and I can see why. they had a cool metropolitan feel, neat old building, coffee shop vibe, maybe ten or so beers pouring." Again, reviewers use their own experiences to determine to what degree they want to feel like a tourist or a local, and often report seeking the advice of a bona fide local.

For example, one reviewer relates experiencing the local with a perceived or universal understanding of what it means to be a craft brewery: "The atmosphere and ambiance of this brewery was a healthy mixture of downtown Healdsburg and craft beer attitude." Another reviewer expressed the deep connection of the brewery to the surrounding area, and how that brewery stands out as local: "Truly imparts the heart and feeling of modern Wisconsin brewing. Located in a field in Amherst Wisconsin, this brewery appears a small stone in the sparse landscape. Almost instantly I feel immersed in the atmosphere, the layout so casually implies the connection with the region and community." Other reviewers made similar comments and touted a brewery that was large and received national distribution, but still managed to maintain a small, local vibe: "For a place with nearly national distribution their brewpub had a laid back, small town feel to it. Even on a weekend night when places just down the road were packed and lively my party still managed to find a table without any wait and enjoy a few beers."

Reviewers also embraced the locals and how their presence added to a brewery's vibe. In this review, the reviewer weighed another review against their own experience, while noting that the local feel provided a sense of authenticity:

> Despite being one of the better/more reviewed breweries in Asheville, you can find negative reviews about this place. Both here and on food sites like Yelp and Urbanspoon. A common complaint I found online was that this is very much a "local" watering hole, and somehow that the "locals aren't friendly." This was not our experience at all. It's a cool little spot, off the beaten path, with a large outdoor area. . . . It did feel like it had a "local" atmosphere to it, but I felt like that gave it some authentic charm. Nobody was even remotely unfriendly or rude to us. Just a lot of happy, smiling people, having some family-friendly fun and enjoying the beers.

In addition to touting the "local" in terms of the place, reviewers also related the presence of "locals" to authentic experiences. Reviewers also differentiated between the sort of locals that help keep the atmosphere of a certain status level, and those that make the brewery feel too much like just a bar or a college scene and therefore disrupt their expectations surrounding what a local brewery should be. The tipping point is typically a balance of locals and a welcoming vibe that makes visitors "feel like a local." Such quotes support yet expand upon Driver's (2016) research; in a parallel to hardcore fans, reviewers discuss locals as holding the potential to represent both the cultural history of the location and knowledge of the brewery itself. This "transference" can occur when visitors interact with locals and describe this as offering "authentic charm." When reviewing Half Acre in Chicago, one reviewer noted how the space seemed to transform its vibe to accommodate different types of crowds while still maintaining a sense of authenticity:

> Half Acre's Tap Room, much like the neighborhood it inhabits, is pretty much a mix of everything geared for, well . . . everyone. During the day, Half Acre is a mecca for Midwest beer geeks in search of its fabled nectar (a.k.a. Daisy Cutter)—during the afternoon, it turns into a drinking hole for the locals and the college students getting out of class; at night, it turns into a classy lounge for the young and hip elite of Northern Chicago.

Here we see that a space accommodates three very different crowds, each combining to create a different vibe. Such distinctions help reveal how the time of day and social class of the drinker, along with where they come from, influence the localized authentication process. We can see how localized authentication occurs as differing groups embody the same space and, by interacting, make it into a new place. First, the reviewer describes the brewery as a destination, or "mecca" for beer geeks—a term used to describe the most elite and dedicated beer drinkers—and refers to one of Half Acre's flagship brews, Daisy Cutter, as "fabled," suggesting that this beer and brewery are well known and sought after among beer geeks. Second, the reviewer describes the brewery as a "drinking hole for [. . .] locals and [. . .] college students." On the surface, the term *drinking hole* connotes a lesser-quality experience, but also hints that locals prefer it this way. It seems to suggest that beer travelers and locals do not necessarily mingle; certain times of the day are for certain types of drinkers. They share the same space, but at different times, and this is understood by travelers and locals alike. Last, the reviewer suggests the space transforms yet again, into a "classy lounge for the young and hip elite of Northern Chicago," distinguishing between this group and the "locals" who occupy the "drinking hole." These descriptions support findings on affective atmosphere, in that a place has "a vibration" (Michels 2015, 256)—or vibe—that arises from its aesthetics, the emotions (and arguably styles) brought into the space, and the resulting atmosphere that derives from interacting and partaking in the place.

SPACE

We define the trait of space in relation to the physical environment, encompassing the physical area, location, and decor of the brewery. Therefore, space can include what influences its "feel," such as the saying of an "industrial feel." A critical component to reviews is the size of the space. For microbreweries, the tipping point for reviewers is whether the space feels intimate enough, while offering enough room to socialize, get served quickly, and comfortably interact with (and hear) others. This can lead to the perceptions of a smaller space feeling intimate and cozy, or cramped and crowded. Alternatively, an industrial space can feel large but still inviting, or too spacious and thus cold. Overall, a brewery's space can contribute to localized authentication by offering visitors the chance to feel they are a part of local history, at times in a form of backstage access to production processes or historical buildings they would otherwise not typically be able to access. The connection of a place to local history relates to localization in that there are certain significant symbols that people can use to reinforce local symbols and meanings (e.g., an industrial space is recognizable for the brick, wood, and exposed piping, yet has particular meaning based on the local industries). This relates to localization, in that there are certain significant symbols that people can then use to reinforce local symbols and meanings (e.g., an industrial space is recognizable for the brick, wood, and exposed piping, yet has particular meaning based on the local industries). This also further supports Silver and Clark's (2016, 140) definition of local authenticity, in that the "primary appeal of the local is the expectation that one can find something here that you can get only here, something distinctive, not (yet?) homogenized," although we find this can be the case in and beyond urban spaces.

Many craft breweries inhabit older spaces that once housed various industries. Old industrial spaces provide the needed room to house large brewing equipment and create an opportunity for customers to feel like they are part of the production process. For example, "The atmosphere is great for a beer fan, you're basically smack dab in the middle of the brewery, drinking next to the giant fermenters." Larger industrial spaces also have a certain flexibility in their layouts. One reviewer appreciated such a space as it allowed for adaptability to the weather: "I walk into a beautiful tap room and smaller retail area. Very roomy and Industrial and has a cool lift up [. . .] garage door for warm days." Even if the space is physically limited, its distinct history can compensate. For example, one reviewer writes, "They don't have a ton of beers on tap, and the space is fairly small. But the vibe is a lot of fun, and they have games to play. Apparently the space was an old bank before it was the taproom, so there is not a ton of places to sit either, but it gives it a cool vintage ambience." In this way, certain points of practicality that otherwise may appear unacceptable (e.g., seating) are forgiven amid the overall sensory experience; being a part of something that is believed to be a locally authentic venue compensates for other spatial issues.

When spaces seem small, they are often described as cozy, such as, "Cozy tap room with a bit of a retro vibe, but it totally works." Reviewers who hedge their comments about a space being small show how, although they almost always use *cozy* positively, it can also connote "small" negatively when service suffers and customers have to wait for a beer, or lack sufficient space to enjoy their beer. This hedging is demonstrated by the reviewer who stated, "A neat little space in Dunedin. They have a nice, but small area for seating outside and some inside the tasting room. Really good vibe, great service, will be back!" Another reviewer writes about how a brewery was small, but "in a good way," writing, "Really small and quaint, but in a good way. The inside was very close quartered, again, in a good way. After experiencing people soup to the highest degree at every previous brewery in Asheville, this was a super refreshing gem." Here we can see how the physical trait of size can help control the number of people that enter a space. In these instances, it appears service quality remained high enough that a smaller size was seen as "quaint" and thus made the spot a hidden "gem." The balancing act remains ensuring that the space feels distinctive, by maintaining comfort in small spaces and a personalized feel in large places to prevent the experience of "people soup."

Similarly, reviews help demonstrate how larger breweries can accommodate more customers and recreate the vibe of a beer hall, or offer a larger gathering space where customers can interact with each other, while still maintaining the "cozy" vibe. For example,

The place is huge inside, despite not being much of a looker from the outside, it's enormous. they have a big dining room right when you walk in with a very long bar and bar area in the back, made to feel cozy with dark wood and copper accents around the place, and it was absolutely packed. . . . I like a bustling beer hall vibe, a tall glass [of] quality brew, and feeling like I am part of something cool, and that's exactly what you get in here.

As the former bank demonstrates, reclaimed or repurposed spaces are in a unique position, but not only due to size. Such spaces offer insight into how vibe is not inherent in a space simply because it used to be something else, but rather in how the owners are able to translate that history thematically into decor. In remodeling the old space, their choices in selectively maintaining, highlighting, or recreating aspects of the former business/industry can be critical to constructing what reviewers will understand as a successfully localized, authentic place. For example, "Nestled in among the art galleries, in a three-story building originally used for livestock distribution, this place has some serious character. Outside, railings, tables, chairs are all made of welded 'found' metal tools and items. Just wandering around the place is a treat!" This brewery maintains a sense of authenticity by being connected to the former industry (livestock distribution) and the new surrounding vibe (nestled among the art galleries). Depending on the overall feel of an area, a more industrial space can add to the vibe of a place. Some reviewers viewed the repurposing of older businesses as a sign of revitalization and connection to an up-and-coming community, "A short ride on the W1 (or W2) bus from downtown drops you off in the River Arts District, an evolving neighborhood where old warehouses have been converted into galleries, restaurants, cafes and one excellent 1300-barrel brewpub called Wedge Brewing Company." Highlighting how the local (community or context) is related to space, breweries can benefit from a larger localized authentication effort, as demonstrated by a "district." As a form of cultural scene, the brewery both benefits from and contributes to the vibe of a historical, place-based, yet trending scene.

Alternatively, how a space was previously used can also taint consumers' perceptions of a space. One brewery included in our study occupies a space that had been a medieval-themed family restaurant. Reviewers seemed confused by the thematic decor, which in turn influenced the overall sensory experience and vibe the space embodied. As one reviewer commented, "Not the most appealing location or building to the eye, but it's definitely worth the stop. It looks like it used to be some old Italian Pizzeria or something . . . kind of a long, banquet style building, typical of what you would see in the Detroit 'burbs. A really hometown-y feel to it." Another review of the same brewery found the decor amusing but not a positive contribution to the overall feel: "hehe. It's kind of funny in Dragonmead. It has the whole medieval thing going on, but from my point of view, it's entirely too clean in there. I mean, it's almost pristine, kinda clean in there. It somewhat doesn't fit imo [in my opinion]. But it's a pretty chill vibe." When occupying a previously owned space, brewery owners must negotiate the aesthetic and experience of the previous business while carefully incorporating aspects in a way that complements their brewery identity and, most importantly, meets visitors' expectations.

Similar to this experience, some breweries can focus too much on a particular theme or decor in their space, creating a negative customer experience. A reviewer noted how a brewery relies on an outdoors theme, but that it does not translate well to the entire space: "The really odd thing about the entire place was the vibe/atmosphere. It has an outdoors theme throughout, which is done pretty well in the tasting room area. However, when you get seated to eat, the vibe goes from outdoors to outdoors theme in a very dark, almost strip club like room." Reviewers who have a negative experience also may judge the scene and/or the drinkers on one particular aspect. For example, one reviewer equated a poor space and experience with the generally poor taste of the locals: "Expansion just opened, which I haven't been able to hit yet, but the old spot was plagued by overcrowdedness and an awkward mixture of outdoorsy + modern decor. Definite strip mall turned brewery feel. Not really a place I enjoyed hanging out at, and the beer could be pretty hit or miss, but the crowds obviously indicate a lot of folks like it. Either that or the East Valley crowd is seriously deprived of halfway decent drinking spots." As the preceding reviews show, the "feel" of a place can evoke an emotional reaction that translates into negative reviews that incorporate the brewery's location. Confusion can arise when reality (medieval family restaurant, outdoors, strip mall) does not match expectations (cozy contemporary brewery), resulting in a brewery tipping past the point of rescuing their reputation.

Discussion

The rising number of microbreweries exemplifies their popularity, but so does the increasing competition microbreweries will face against other craft producers versus just the larger macrobrewers. Building on research that suggested places to be important to how breweries construct authentic identities (Koontz and Chapman 2019), this study sought to answer the broad question of what traits, as perceived and expressed by consumers, differentiate a microbrewery for better or worse. We explored the ways in which consumers drew from space, place, and geographical traits to construct positive or negative reviews for microbreweries; or more specifically, to determine from these reviews whether localism is integral to breweries' authentication process.

We did find forms of "the local" to be critical to consumers' reviews, both positive and negative. To help explain this phenomenon, we offered the term *localized authentication*, defined as a contextualized and collaborative process during which interactions among the products, producers (and/or representatives), and consumers result in the situated experiences of a "vibe." We highlighted which intangible components of a vibe contribute to the commercial success of cultural venues, because consumers' reviews tend to judge a space as more or less authentic due to the vibe of a space and place.

Whereas prior research has highlighted the importance of consumers' experiences and expectations, our findings reveal the extent to which their sensory, collective, contextualized, and embodied experience—compared with their expectations for that experience—matter in localized authenticity and felt vibe. Individuals' judgments of the vibe of a physical space and place are the basis of their craft brewery reviews, which vary with the felt authenticity and inauthenticity that vibe generates.

We found that reviewers judge the authenticity of their brewery experience against three traits: quality, the local, and the space. These traits are only analytically distinct, as each combines to shape the consumers' experience and attendant review. Although we found quality to be based on the product quality and quality of service, we also found that one can compensate for the other, even if the resulting rating is lower than if both were rated high. Even so, the space also can influence the perceived quality. For example, reviewers forgave breweries with uniquely designed spaces or those located in historical spaces (e.g., former bank) that were too small, because of the quality of their brews and the vibe gained from the history of the space, perceiving them as "where it all began" or "vintage-y." Our findings additionally expand research on sense of place, jumping off from Baudrillard's emphasis on aura to the reasoning behind the authentication of the original micro-brewery and visiting the place itself. For breweries that have expanded to additional spaces, the OG location has an "aura" that cannot be felt at newer outlets. This also relates to the authenticity research by Leigh and colleagues (2006), albeit in a very different setting than the ideal of a showroom MG car, in that we can see how the "truly authentic" microbreweries gain a sense of the sacred. Each trait is contextualized based on the local, whether it be the patrons ("locals") that gave rec-ommendations or welcomed the visitors in the space, the integration of local history, or the location of the brewery (e.g., in a brewery dis-trict). As such, localized authentication arises from the brewery having "enough" of each of these traits for the reviewer to have a felt positive experience and a part of a good vibe.

We therefore also agree that even with breweries' commercializa-tion and potential attempts at mass appeal (e.g., Miles 2010), consum-ers performing these reviews attempt to personalize the place and their experiences. Such testimonials described breweries as having a "home-town feel," reflecting the local area/region, or seemingly being a "locals hangout." We also believe this to be another reason for breweries' abil-ity to compensate for weaker traits with stronger ones, as these con-sumers possibly may look to microbreweries for this sense of the local. Breweries generally received more extensive negative reviews for two reasons: they lacked both service and product quality or the theme/decor did not meet expectations to the extent that it detracted from the overall sensory experience. In these cases, breweries failed to compen-sate for such global disconnects between expectations and experiences with other traits. This offers insight into certain intangibles of a vibe. As expectations often accumulate over time, through informal experiences and building a form of cultural knowledge, those in a microbrewery scene may not explicitly realize that they have specific expectations for their experiences. As such, disconnects or dissonance between expe-riences and expectations are then "felt" rather than explicitly real-ized. Although taste can be translated into language, the integration of the product into the space, place, and interactions can muddy the waters, leading reviewers to make a more holistic judgment of the sensory experience. This is also likely why each trait has a tipping point; although each can help balance out the imperfection of another, our findings suggest a recipe of "just enough" of each trait creates the best possible vibe and resulting review.

Authenticating microbrewery narratives reenvisions a sense of localized tradition, which can craft community and allow audiences to literally partake in the local, providing sought-after experiences of embodied connectedness and uniqueness that can otherwise feel lost in an increasingly globalizing economy. Romanticizing a collective memory of a space or place, which reviews can foster, may help "reappropriate" places from a perceived anonymous, generalized globalizing force. Although a beer scene can correlate to one city (e.g., Asheville, North Carolina), judgments that go into the localized authentication process are comparative, making the microbrewery scene collective. Critically speaking, microbrewery visitors will consist of a more privileged subset, those with the luxury of time and resources to invest in the construction of a "local" that meets their expectations and emotional needs. However, this arguably leads to the interesting finding that consumers appear to work toward giving microbreweries the benefit of the doubt. Although our research cannot grant insight into reviewers' intents, such work may occur for multiple reasons. In line with prior research on affective atmosphere and vibes, reviewers may recognize themselves to be a part of the "scene," and therefore feel their own reputations are at stake because they are cultural experts and thus part of creating the vibe. Additionally, as reviewers may still feel a sense of "us" (local craft scenes) versus "them" (larger macrobrewers), they may recognize the importance of microbreweries' overall reputation (as also suggested by Lu and Fine in relation to reputation over specific quality of food). Reviewers must then make a communal commitment to these objective ideals and role performance to remain authentically in the subculture. Again, microbreweries and consumers both benefit from this experience, because if they go to an "authentic" microbrewery, they reconfirm their authentic identity and have an opportunity to play that role. In this way, constructing the local also helps to bridge traditions with imagined identities, offering future constructs of the local that help create continuity in collective identities.

This form of localized authenticity may therefore be a phenomenon deriving from and helping to perpetuate the experience economy.

Authenticating a place based on a locale ironically requires a comparison to another locale. For reviews to fit within a scene, symbols and discourses must be shared enough to help build expectations and a shared (even if implicit) understanding. Localized authenticity, as envisioned in the brewery reviews we studied, offer a unique link between globalizing forces and the importance of physicality and being somewhere—the sort of vibe that can only derive from interactions between people in a space, sharing a particular taste experience, in a certain location.

References

Anderson, Ben. 2009. "Affective Atmospheres." *Emotion, Space and Society* 2(2):77–81.

Appadurai, Arjun. 1996. *Modernity at Large: Cultural Dimensions of Globalization* (Vol. 1). Minneapolis University of Minnesota Press.

Bernot, K. 2015. "Here's Why (and Where) We're Buying Craft Beer, According to Nielsen Data." Retrieved February 12, 2019 (https://draftmag.com/nielsen-data -craft-beer-trends/).

Brewers Association. 2018. "Brewers Association Celebrates the Year in Beer." Retrieved March 7, 2019 (https://www.globenewswire.com/news-release/2018 /12/11/1665393/0/en/Brewers-Association-Celebrates-the-Year-in-Beer.html).

Brown-Saracino, Japonica. 2018. *How Places Make Us: Novel LBQ Identities in Four Small Cities*. Chicago: University of Chicago Press.

Bruner, Edward M. 1994. "Abraham Lincoln as Authentic Reproduction: A Critique of Postmodernism." *American Anthropologist* 96:397–415.

Cohen, Erik and Scott A. Cohen. 2012. "Authentication: Hot and Cool." *Annals of Tourism Research* 39(3):1295–1314.

Crang, Mike. 1996. "Living History: Magic Kingdoms or a Quixotic Quest for Authenticity?" *Annals of Tourism Research* 23(2):415–31.

Driver, Christopher. 2016. "'Bringing the Vibe': Subcultural Capital and 'Hardcore' Masculinity." Pp. 193–204. In *Youth Cultures and Subcultures: Australian Perspectives,* edited by S. Baker, B. Robards, and B. Buttigieg. London: Ashgate.

Durkheim, Émile. 2008. *The Elementary Forms of the Religious Life*. Oxford: Oxford University Press.

Fumari, Chris. 2018. "A Record Number of Breweries Opened in 2017, but Closures Are on the Rise." Brewbound. Retrieved July 5, 2018 (https://www.brewbound .com/news/record-number-breweries-opened-2017-closures-rise).

Gaytán, Marie Sarita. 2008. "From Sombreros to Sincronizadas: Authenticity, Ethnicity, and the Mexican Restaurant Industry." *Journal of Contemporary Ethnography* 37(3):314–41.

Goffman, Erving. 1997. *The Goffman Reader*. Edited by C. Lemert and A. Branaman. Malden, MA: Blackwell.

Gotham, Kevin Fox. 2007. *Authentic New Orleans: Tourism, Culture, and Race in the Big Easy*. New York: New York University Press.

Grayson, Kent and Radan Martinec. 2004. "Consumer Perceptions of Iconicity and Indexicality and Their Influence on Assessments of Authentic Market Offerings." *Journal of Consumer Research* 31(2):296–312.

Grazian, David. 2003. *Blue Chicago: The Search for Authenticity in Urban Blues Clubs*. Chicago: University of Chicago.

Halter, Marilyn. 2000. *Shopping for Identity: The Marketing of Ethnicity*. New York: Schocken Books.

Handler, Richard. 1986. "Authenticity." *Anthropology Today* 2(1):2–4.

Hussein, Mohamed El, Sandra Hirst, Vince Salyers, and Joseph Osuji. 2014. "Using Grounded Theory as a Method of Inquiry: Advantages and Disadvantages." *The Qualitative Report* 9 (13):1–15

Ingold, Tim and Terhi Kurttila. 2000. "Perceiving the Environment in Finnish Lapland." *Body & Society* 6(3–4):183–96.

Koontz, Amanda and Nathaniel G. Chapman. 2019. "About Us: Authenticating Identity Claims in the Craft Beer Industry." *Journal of Popular Culture*. 52(2):351–72.

Landry, Charles. 2006. *The Art of City Making*. London: Earthscan.

Lash, Scott and John Urry. 1994. *Economies of Signs and Space*. London: SAGE.

Leigh, Thomas W., Cara Peters, and Jeremy Shelton. 2006. "The Consumer Quest for Authenticity: The Multiplicity of Meanings within the MG Subculture of Consumption." *Journal of the Academy of Marketing Science* 34(4):481–93.

Lu, Shun and Gary Alan Fine. 1995. "The Presentation of Ethnic Authenticity: Chinese Food as a Social Accomplishment." *The Sociological Quarterly* 36(3):535–53.

MacCannell, Dean. 1976. *The Tourist: A New Theory of the Leisure Class*. New York: Schocken Books.

Michels, Christoph. 2015. "Researching Affective Atmospheres." *Geographica Helvetica* 70(4) (2015):255–63.

Miles, Steven. 2010. *Spaces for Consumption: Pleasure and Placelessness in the Post-industrial City*. London: SAGE.

Montgomery, John. 2007. *The New Wealth of Cities: City Dynamics and the Fifth Way*. Aldershot: Ashland.

Newman, George, E. and Rosanna K. Smith. 2016. "Kinds of Authenticity." *Philosophy Compass* 11(10):609–18.

Peterson, Richard. A. 1997. *Creating Country Music: Fabricating Authenticity*. Chicago: University of Chicago Press.

Pine, B. Joseph II, and James H. Gilmore. 1999. *The Experience Economy*. Boston: Harvard Business School Press.

Ritzer, George. 2003. "Rethinking Globalization: Glocalization/Grobalization and Something/Nothing." *Sociological Theory* 21(3):193–209.

Schoup, Mary Ellen. 2018. "Brewers Association: Craft Brewery Closures Will Likely Increase as Market Gets More Competitive." BeverageDaily.com. Retrieved July 5, 2018 (https://www.beveragedaily.com/Article/2018/03/28 /Brewers-Association-Craft-brewery-closures-will-likely-increase-as-market -gets-more-competitive).

Selwyn, Tom. 1996. *The Tourist Image: Myths and Myth Making in Tourism*. New York: Wiley.

Silver, Daniel Aaron and Terry Nichols Clark. 2016. *Scenescapes: How Qualities of Place Shape Social Life*. Chicago: University of Chicago Press.

Strauss, Anselm and Juliet M. Corbin. 1990. *Basics of Qualitative Research: Grounded Theory Procedures and Techniques*. Newbury Park, CA: SAGE.

Thornton, Sarah. 1995. *Club Cultures: Music Media and Subcultural Capital*. Cambridge: Polity.

Trubek, Amy B. 2008. *The Taste of Place: A Cultural Journey into Terroir*. Oakland: University of California Press.

Wang, Ning. 1999. "Rethinking Authenticity in Tourism Experience." *Annals of Tourism Research* 26(2):349–70.

Postcard from Worcester

DAINA CHEYENNE HARVEY AND ELLIS JONES

Alec Lopez, along with Sherri Sadowski, founded the Armsby Abbey in Worcester, Massachusetts, in 2008. It has built a reputation as a hub for craft beer and slow food lovers alike throughout the region. It was, for many years, one of the only places one could get Hill Farmstead beers on tap outside of exclusive parts of Vermont. (Hill Farmstead has long been considered the brewery that established and perfected the New England IPA style and is regularly rated as the number one brewery in the world.) The Abbey has built a strong following for its selection of local, US, and international craft beers on tap that is unrivaled in New England.

ELLIS JONES: What I want to talk about is just your experience in this area: starting the Abbey and what you think this helps reveal about New England, about Worcester, about this area, about beer and the kind of culture that goes along with it. Like, what's our little part of the world look like in comparison to other places?

ALEC LOPEZ: Think of the early exponential growth of beer. If we look back to 2008, when Armsby opened—let's say there were probably about fourteen hundred breweries in the US at that point. I know I'm close. We're over seven thousand now. That's a big shift. So that's breweries. Now, places that have good beer for sale have grown exponentially as well. When I started selling beer to the Dive Bar, the network was really small. We felt like everyone knew each other. We knew all the brewers. Like, going to the craft brewers' conference, there were only like a few hundred people there. It was a very tiny world. Now you go and it's sixteen thousand people there. And I'm still asked to speak about every year, so I get these weird snapshots . . . like annual growth in the industry. Curating, there's something we really valued, and there were a few of us that would band together to get certain beers together we found that we loved in Spain or Belgium or Germany working with importers, and it was this fun atmosphere.

My point is today, one of the main differences I see is that the artist curating is, like—it's still as small as it was fifteen years ago. I think there's very few people that actually understand beer that are selling beer. And it's still a very tight network of the people that truly have their passions one hundred percent in it. The shift has been in the way distribution works, the way the whole industry works. You know, we're always at the mercy of distribution on our side of the equation. But you'd want to order your beer from a distributor. There weren't many that had good beer. And you would know that they carried this brewery, but you wouldn't know what they specifically had. Right? So you'd place a wishful order and then like nothing, or 1 percent of that, would show up. You'd be mad.

For me, that was a catalyst to do two things: really dig into my relationship building with breweries, with traveling all around Europe and the US. I think ultimately that's one of the reasons we are where we are today . . . accessibility for certain, that's one of the reasons. But another thing was changing the way distribution works here in Massachusetts. It took me a while to get this to happen. But the change I made was I made an actual on-hand keg inventory that I could order from. And they did not want to do that. That was a very hard thing for them to do. They didn't want to show their hands, you know?

So it's funny, in the beginning there was an email to me from the inventory manager from one distributor . . . the whole on-hand inventory. Now for me I couldn't manage week-to-week what they had, what they got in. So I'd manage quality and time that way sometimes, and then all [of] a sudden there would be one more name on the email chain. And then another name. And now it's this dizzying array of every place that sells beer in the state. But I feel kind of happy about being responsible for that, because it made it possible for people to sell beer more easily. You know, before, the system didn't work for people trying to sell beer. Can you imagine ordering twenty things and one shows up? It's really difficult to work that way.

JONES: So that makes me think about this relationship stuff. I mean, one of the things I've noticed right off the bat—the first time I came, in 2009—was it was the only place to get Hill Farmstead. And

I've always heard that's because of the relationship you have with Shaun Hill. So tell me about that . . . those kinds of relationships which are a little off the map, more unique in really building that in this area.

LOPEZ: Just two real angles in this for me. One is, why are certain beers here at the end of the day? Because of how I do what I do, that's really the biggest catalyst. We pay meticulous attention to every detail . . . time, temperature, cleanliness, so I can manipulate every single draft line however it needs to be. I have one singular M.O. and that is to provide people—to give you access to the best beer that I have access to in the exact condition the brewer intended it to be. So that requires manipulating textures sometimes over a time arc of something beyond draft for a few days.

[Two, it] requires knowing not only about beer styles and what they need, but the actual individual beer and what it specifically needs. So I know that you know Edward [by Hill Farmstead Brewery], under perfect conditions, has this window. You know it's like a three-week window where it is what it's supposed to . . . what it can be. Right? It doesn't mean it's terrible after that; it's changing. So with beers that are, right now, I suppose most in vogue, the very aromatic expressions of hops, it's one of the most fragile things in the world of beer. Most people don't even know that. But if you allow the aromatic to fade, you change the perception of the beer so incredibly, because now you're giving the backbone of the beer a bigger stage, so when the aroma fades, now your perception of malt changes and the beer's very different. I do this with my staff quite often just to keep them sharp with their palate, with intentionally having varying vintages of something hoppy, like two weeks, four weeks, six weeks, just so they can get the spread of the sort of diminishment and the evolution.

Edward is an American pale ale produced by Shaun Hill at Hill Farmstead Brewery. Hill Farmstead names their foundational beers after family members, and Edward was Sean's grandfather. As of 2020, Hill Farmstead has been ranked as the best brewery in the world for six years in a row and seven of the last eight years by RateBeer, the world's largest, most popular beer review and rating website. The Hills' presence in the Northeast Kingdom of Vermont dates back eight generations, including

the building of the area's first tavern in 1809. On any given summer after-
noon, hundreds of cars dot the side of the farm road, as craft beer enthu-
siasts line up to grab bottles and cans from the barn and perhaps sip a
glass of Edward outside on the lawn.

But managing those things—and the glassware and how clean it is—that is why I think we continue to have access to such elegant and wonderful things. If you know the thing with Farmstead, people are quick here to say that it's about the relationship between Shaun and I. But the fact is the relationship came second. The only reason his beer is here is because he feels that I'm the only person that can sell it the way it needs to be—sorry, *present* it the way it needs to be presented. Certainly no better reflection of that than this lager series, Poetica. I have the Czech-made lager faucets. We exhausted ourselves with the learning curve of those faucets. And to be able to pour lagers in this really wonderful way through these faucets, that's amazing. But I think that overall is kind of more the tone.

Poetica is a variant of Mary, which is named after Shaun Hill's great-
grandmother. Poetica is a pilsner that is lagered off of Mary in oak pun-
cheons for two months and then slowly conditioned and carbonated for
three to four months.

I build relationships in multiple ways. I think one of the big catalysts for this place came in 2012. We already established a name, but working with the Shelton brothers, we did the first iteration of the festival here at Mechanics Hall. And that happened without the city even really knowing that it happened. So here we, we had 110 hotel rooms, many of the world's greatest brewers in one room, my room. We hosted everybody, Sherri, my wife, and I. We made these awesome welcome baskets for every single brewer and put them in their room, like a survival kit. They had a hand-drawn map of Worcester, bottles of water, snacks, et cetera, so we started off with this really nice impression. I had met half of these brewers at least. The other half, I hadn't. We set up a VIP lounge in the building with just brewers; a couple really good beers on all time, just for them. It was a free place to hang out. And then at the Dive Bar, we hosted them every single night privately with food. So for that weekend, I did more for Armsby in terms of relationship building than I have in the entire span of my career prior. Because I would fly to a festival in Brussels or Madrid, and maybe I'd spend time with two brewers, or three brewers, and start to build a friendship. Here I had a hundred in a room, solidifying the ones [friendships] that I had, and then building new ones. All those brewers in this room watching the attention to detail with our beer service and seeing how educated the staff were, I think really shot us forward in a lot of directions. So all these little moments, all the while maintaining focus on really just the service of beer, and the relationships of the brewers that I love.

The Dive Bar was a Worcester institution for twenty-five years before closing in 2019. It was regularly ranked by popular magazines as one of the best dive bars in the United States. On most nights in the late '90s there were more door guys than bartenders. Alec is credited with transforming it from a college bar to more of a beer garden. It was the first place in central Massachusetts to get craft beer.

JONES: So we're in New England, which at the moment is at the very top in the US in terms of craft beer. How would you describe the kind of evolution of the cultural scene, and the strengths and weaknesses that Worcester and Massachusetts have to offer the craft beer community?

LOPEZ: I exist in an odd microcosm within Central Massachusetts. Like if you walk into this room on any given day, a really serious percentage of the people have either come from a great distance to be here specifically, or because we're in this kind of Bermuda Triangle—Trillium, Tree House, and Hill Farmstead and everything else that matters to people in between. So anyone making the trek from down south, west—they're in Boston or New York for a business trip and they're a beer fanatic—they come here. So it's not so much—I don't feel like maybe the [People's] Pint or the Boynton would feel in terms of an audience. It's a very different experience for me. So I don't know how to comment on that specifically because I don't really interact with a broader version of the beer scene. I don't go out really hardly at all, so I kind of feel like I'm on an island in a lot of respects. And the island is global. It's so strange that Armsby in the beer community is a global brand. And that to me is forever mind-blowing. Sherri and I were in Helsinki last year, making our way up [toward the] Arctic Circle. We stopped at a little beer joint in Helsinki. The first interesting thing was an obscure little Swedish brewery [that] had a beer called Vermont IPA, which I thought was really cool. And then four other obscure little breweries from that area all had New England in their name. More interesting to me was the bartender. I was wearing an Armsby shirt, and he said, "Oh my God, how much do you love that place?" And I was like, "A lot." He said, "Oh man, I've only been twice, but if I'm even in the US for anything, I go there." And I was like, holy shit. He said all the brewers here [Helsinki] talk about [the Armsby]; they are all try- ing to get their beer there. And he says, "Do you live near there?" And I was like, yeah, I'm like two miles from there. I go there every day. He's just like oh my God. But then I introduced myself. He was really cool, but it's just amazing to me, people send me pictures of themselves in Rome, wearing an Armsby shirt. It is an interesting universe for sure.

And I think a lot of it gets lost. What's important to me sometimes feels like white noise in the context of what beer has become. You can go to Applebee's and they have their craft lines. And you know, when I started selling good beer, when I stopped selling shitty beer at the Dive long ago, the entire bar scene in Worcester, the bar owners I knew, they said I was an idiot and that I was going to go out of business. In fact, I was pretty alien- ated. Most of the people stopped talking to me. And people thought I thought I was better than them. It was a really odd time. I actually started second-guessing myself at some point. But I was very committed to my path.

Not that long after, I started getting calls in the other direc- tion. "Hey, I know we haven't talked in a while, but I was won- dering if, like, you had a suggestion for a beer?" At the same time I was doing my thing, as dumb luck would have it, the world of beer was coming up anyway, so everything I did was being pushed by the beer world at large. In this area, there was the thing called "the Dive Bar Effect." For a long time everything the Dive did was being mimicked. At one point the president from the Craft Brewers Guild said something to me. He said—I can't quan- tify it, but the Dive Bar is responsible for an epic proportion of growth in the craft beer world. I thought that was kind of amazing. And at this point I think it's hard to even think about these things. Then I started thinking about all the beers that are drawn to Mass, and it's just like, fifty, sixty that I went out and found out in the world. And I killed myself to make them available here.

Massachusetts is blessed with beer. Both Tree House and Trillium regularly rank in the top five to seven of the best breweries. The determined craft drinker could visit Hill Farmstead, Tree House, and Trillium in the same day, making what some have called the Trifecta. It's not unusual to pull up a stool at the Abbey and eavesdrop on conversations about the day's releases at Tree House, or have someone ask you how long it takes to get to Trillium, only to have someone else list off what is on tap in Canton or Boston. It's likewise not uncommon to read on Tree House or Trillium Facebook groups about out-of-towners asking if there is a place to drink somewhere in between the two breweries. The reply is always the Abbey.

JONES: Do you find that most of what you do is work with distributors; is that where you get most of your stuff?

LOPEZ: I'm an anomaly in a lot of ways. One way specifically is that I do not work with any sales reps; the only person that I will communicate with in distribution is whoever is solely in charge of management of their inventory. I don't like having people in my way. But because of the way I work, most things land in distribution already tagged for me. So a distributor for me is a necessary evil. But I don't like to work with any distributors. So I try to communicate strictly with the brewery. So kegs show up with a distribution tagged Armsby. All they're doing is delivering for me. It's an incredible amount of work. That's why there are very few people that do what I actually do. I'm a huge fan of German lager, one of the really difficult beers to get here. In fact, the American public has barely a clue as to what the German lager experience actually is. It's growing now, thankfully, but to try to get a keg from Germany to here is really difficult. If it's not refrigerated, sometimes customs reroutes East Coast to West Coast. So I mean they're kicking a boat all the way to LA to a port. Fuck . . . you know? It's not refrigerated. So certain beers I don't order in the summertime. I keep track of the customs pile-ups, so I know when things are shifting around. I work with importers. I work with the brewers in—you know—in this case Europe, so I know when a keg ships, when it travels. These things to me are every-thing. Managing those details costs me a lot.

JONES: I know here at the Abbey there's definitely an overlap for beer with food. One of the things we've researched is the crossover between the craft beer movement, the food movement, and the local farmers' movement. All of these things seem to overlap in some small or large ways. What is your sense of how craft beer overlaps with these other significant cultural contributions?

LOPEZ: So, it's the pursuit of the best experience you can get. Right? So local is important I think because if you're talking about local produce, you're more apt to be able to get a better quality product in much better condition. You know in our case, it's things that are harvested the way we want them. A lot of what we use, like green beans that just came in for us that were picked for us this morning—I could order local green beans through a distributor, maybe they were picked last week or a week ago—and it's these little details. I think culturally as a whole we're exhausting our-selves. Everyone's in this pursuit of the best experience. The best community experience. The best beer experience. Instagram's making it so much worse for people. Like, this is visually stun-ning. Well yeah, I spent hours making that shot for the fuckin' Instagram. Well, we've created this feeding frenzy of food and drink. And it's prurient. I'm pushing back in a lot of ways against that entire thing. I don't know if you follow Armsby's Instagram, I haven't posted anything on food in a while. It's kind of just beer shots. And the point of all of this to me is this is a place where you come in and you know that what you're going to get has been thought about. Like on the plate, in the glass, those are things that matter. I don't want you to be nervous when you're reading the menu and you don't understand these words. I want it to feel comfortable and approachable. And I think the world keeps doing this razzle-dazzle, like really complicated, overly produced thing and they're losing sight of the point of it all. The point of it is just to be able to go out and forget about whatever it is your day was, and, you know, have a beer . . . have some food. I think that part of it's about, what I think brings people a lot of comfort is know-ing that you're working within the local economy.

For me, beer, historically it was really difficult to get from New England. There just weren't a lot of good breweries here. Now it's like, shit, most of my board is from the Northeast. I remember trying to do a Massachusetts Tap Out twelve years ago, and I was just like, ugh. But now there's a lot of new things that keep happening. More and more people are farming. More and more people are brewing in little corners, and producing spirits, and thinking about cocktails, and making better soda. I think we've just culturally woke up and realized it doesn't have to be Coca-Cola and Applebee's all the time.

JONES: What are your general worries about craft beer in New England?

LOPEZ: We've . . . we've . . . we've fucked it all up. We spent so much time in the beginning demanding that people take beer seriously, that they put it on the dinner table, that you acknowledge that this complex beverage deserves to be next to your complex meal as much as that glass of wine. In fact, I could argue nine times out of ten that it can get you into far more interesting pairing experiences than wine, because it doesn't have these rules of the wine world. I'm not taking anything away from wine. Just like, imagine throwing lemongrass in wine. It's not going to happen, right? So we fucking screamed from the mountaintops in the '90s, the early 2000s, take beer seriously, take beer seriously. Well, now shit, it's everywhere. Beer dinners have become the meaningless thing that people do that barely understand either thing, beer or food. Fuck, they're everywhere. I stopped doing them a few years ago, because I couldn't even stand the thought of hearing the two words together, or seeing the place down the street do something. And I'm just like, ugh, man, that's an art. It's not a marketing shtick, you know? So that shit is difficult for me. People serving beer that don't understand the importance of the quality of the product or what the product means. People selling beer that are not educated at all about beer. What I put our front of the house through is like miles past what most would even consider for themselves as a proprietor of selling beer, let alone their staff. I'm excited that the whole world is growing around us, but it's also very bittersweet. At the end of the day probably, it's because I've always taken it too seriously; trying to overemphasize, to legitimize the little world of beer that we wanted more people to be a part of. And now we got what we asked for. And now a lot of us want less people to be involved in it in a way. It's too late. I mean we opened the gates, the industry, the distributors. It's never going to go anywhere now. How can you go back once you have something good? You can never go back. You're never going to drink Harpoon IPA or something like that. You know? Why would you?

While not doing dinners anymore, Alec is good at bringing in brewers and tapping kegs from their respective breweries. It's rare to get, say, Fonta Flora (Morganton, North Carolina) on tap in New England, but even rarer to be able to sit down and talk with the brewer. Ellis Jones and Daina Cheyenne Harvey have both cornered folks from Kent Falls Brewing Company (Kent, Connecticut) at the Abbey while drinking beers with them. In some ways the Abbey is a spiritual home for us. Ellis celebrates most of his birthdays there and Daina celebrated getting tenure with his colleagues there.

CHAPTER 2

From Mill District to Brewery District

Craft Beer and the Revitalization of Charlotte's NoDa Neighborhood

NEIL REID AND ISABELLE NILSSON

Introduction

The number of craft breweries in the United States has increased dramatically in the past four decades. In 1980, there were eight craft breweries;[1] by 2018, there were 7,346.[2] Growth in the number of craft breweries has been particularly rapid since 2010. Seventy-six percent (5,592) of US craft breweries in 2018 opened since 2010. Craft beer accounts for 13.2 percent of the American beer market in volume and 24.1 percent of sales (Brewers Association 2019c).[3] The growth in craft beer reflects the increasing preference for beer brewed in small batches at independent, locally owned breweries. Craft beer's popularity is particularly strong among the millennial demographic (23–38 years old in 2019), who are attracted by the diversity of styles and flavors of craft beer (Brewers Association 2016b).

As awareness of craft breweries increased during the 2000s, a growing number of communities began recognizing their potential as a catalyst for neighborhood revitalization (Funcheon 2018; ICIC 2018; Lubin 2016). In seeking a location for their breweries, craft beer entrepreneurs are often attracted to distressed industrial neighborhoods, where old buildings (churches, warehouses, automobile dealerships, etc.) are available relatively inexpensively. Through the process of adaptive reuse, craft beer entrepreneurs have discovered a new use for previously abandoned buildings (Reid 2018; Reid, Gripshover, and Bell 2019). In most cases, the arrival of a craft brewery in a distressed neighborhood is one piece of a larger gentrification jigsaw (Barajas, Boeing, and Wartell 2017; Walker and Miller 2018). When combined with other investments, from both the private and public sectors, craft breweries have contributed to the revitalization of neighborhoods across the United States. Cities where craft breweries have helped rejuvenate previously distressed neighborhoods include Denver, Colorado (RiNo District), Portland, Oregon (Pearl District), and Cleveland, Ohio (Ohio City neighborhood) (Alexander 2013; Gorski 2015; Walker and Miller 2018). Prospective craft breweries can access numerous federal, state, and local incentive programs. For example, New York's START-UP NY program offers qualifying breweries multiple tax incentives for up to ten years if they locate in specific neighborhoods (Nickerson and Hall 2017). From a geographical perspective, a key characteristic of craft breweries is their tendency to cluster in space (Dennett and Page 2017; Nilsson, Reid, and Lehnert 2018), doing so to exploit what Dennett and Page (2017, 450) call the "economics of cooperation." For example, clustering in space allows craft breweries to more easily engage in collaborative brewing (a common industry practice), exchange knowledge, share customers, and promote the neighborhood to the growing number of "beer tourists" (Kraftchick et al. 2014).

The purpose of this chapter is to explore the growth of craft brewing in one revitalizing neighborhood—the NoDa neighborhood in Charlotte, NC, named after its main through-street, North Davidson Street. We focus on NoDa for two reasons. First, the neighborhood has experienced an economic resurgence after several decades of decline. Once a bustling early twentieth-century mill district, the textile industry abandoned NoDa, with the last mill closing in 1975. Abandoned mills, deteriorating housing, and vacant storefronts came to characterize the neighborhood. The mid-1980s witnessed the start of the neighborhood's rebirth, and today it is a vibrant arts and entertainment district. NoDa's resurgence includes investment by several craft beer entrepreneurs who have opened breweries in the neighborhood. Second, one of the authors is a Charlotte resident, making the neighborhood highly accessible for the purposes of fieldwork.

Craft Breweries and Neighborhood Revitalization

In 2019, the craft-brewing industry contributed more than $75 billion to the US economy, and it has generated more than 500,000 jobs (Brewers

Association 2019b).[4] At the state level, several commissioned studies have assessed the economic impact of the craft-brewing industry on specific states (California Craft Brewers Association 2013; Dangaran and Wruck 2016; Stonebridge 2015). In the case of North Carolina, the industry's estimated impact on the state economy is $2.18 billion, with the number of jobs generated estimated to be 12,409 (Brewers Association 2017). The growth of craft breweries, along with evidence that they are economically impactful, has resulted in many municipalities introducing and, where necessary, amending regulations to make their locales more craft brewery friendly. Many of the changes have focused on modifying zoning regulations to make particular parts of a city available to craft breweries as places to locate (Williams 2017).

As the number of craft breweries located within cities increased, some discernible behavior patterns emerged. Two are of importance here. First, craft brewers prefer old buildings in economically distressed neighborhoods. Such buildings are inexpensive and can be adapted to meet the brewery's needs (Reid 2018; Reid, Gripshover, and Bell 2019). Second, craft breweries geographically cluster near one another, creating what some have termed brewery districts (Reid 2018; Nilsson, Reid, and Lehnert 2018).[5] Clustering partly reflects the spatial distribution of appropriate real estate investment opportunities, as well as the fact that it allows craft brewers to avail themselves of the aforementioned "economics of cooperation" (Dennett and Page 2017).

The modification of zoning ordinances to accommodate craft breweries reflects the belief that these establishments can play an important role in neighborhood economic development, particularly in revitalizing economically distressed neighborhoods (Harne 2017). A key debate regarding craft breweries' role in this process is whether they are pioneers or followers. In other words, does a craft brewery entrepreneur's investment catalyze additional investment in the neighborhood and its subsequent revival? Alternatively, do craft breweries appear on the scene after other investors have kick-started the process of neighborhood revitalization? Support exists for both scenarios. In the case of Cleveland's Ohio City neighborhood, there is no question that the opening of the Great Lakes Brewing Company by brothers Pat and Dan Conway was catalytic in that neighborhood's revival (Alexander 2013; Gatrell, Reid, and Steiger 2018). Similarly, the vision of Jerry Williams and John Hickenlooper and the creation of the Wynkoop Brewery in the Lower Downtown (LoDo) neighborhood of Denver, Colorado, paved the way for subsequent investment and the neighborhood's revival (Weiler 2000). In both cases, entrepreneurs demonstrated a willingness to invest in what Barajas, Boeing, and Wartell (2017, 2) call "economically uncertain locations." Today, Ohio City and LoDo are home to numerous craft breweries and thus are considered vibrant brewery districts.

Whereas craft breweries clearly played a pioneering role in the development of LoDo and Ohio City, two other studies have uncovered evidence of another role. Walker and Miller (2018) analyze craft breweries' role, relative to other investments, in the gentrification of various neighborhoods in Portland, Oregon. They conclude that "most craft breweries have opened in a neighborhood following the onset of gentrification" (Walker and Miller 2018, 2). Using a national data set, Barajas, Boeing, and Wartell (2017, 156) arrived at a similar conclusion: "Newer and smaller brewers may not be *catalysts* of urban revitalization so much as *respondents* to changing neighborhood demographics" (italics added). Therefore, when it comes to neighborhood revitalization, evidence exists of craft breweries being both pioneers and followers; either way, they play an important role. A healthy, revitalized neighborhood is a kaleidoscope of different land uses, which together provide the vibrancy needed for success.

History of NoDa

Starting in the early nineteenth century, North Carolina became a leading center of US textile production. The state's first textile mill opened in 1813; by 1890, there were 91 (Glass 1992; Hanchett n.d.). In the case of North Charlotte (as NoDa was then known), textile production started in 1903 with the opening of Highland Park Mill No. 3. Two other mills subsequently opened in North Charlotte: Mecklenburg Mill in 1905 and Johnston Mill in 1916. Located three miles north of the city center, North Charlotte was geographically distinct from, but connected via rail to, Charlotte itself. Many mill owners employed the strategy of locating outside of cities, as it allowed them to avoid local property taxes and the jurisdiction of city government. A suburban location also gave mill owners more control over workers and their families (Glass 1992).

Adjacent to the Highland Park and Mecklenburg mills were mill villages, a common feature of the nineteenth-century North Carolina landscape. Constructed by the mill owners, these settlements provided homes for the mill workers. For greater self-containment, mill villages also had a school, a church, stores, and other community assets. At the nexus of the Mecklenburg and Highland Park mill villages was a commercial district. Among other services, this district included grocery stores, a barber's shop, a drug store, and a doctor's office (Livingplaces. com n.d.). Mill owners at this time adopted a paternalistic attitude toward their workers, organizing activities such as outdoor movies and band concerts for them and their families (Glass and Kress 2006). Mill villages had a strong communal culture and were places where neighbors looked out for neighbors. Glass (1992, 47) describes the "interdependent relationship of mill workers and their neighbors," with residents relying "upon each other for various kinds of assistance, including child care; maintaining gardens and livestock; help in emergencies such as sickness, fires or death; and entertainment." Eventually, as result of annexation, North Charlotte would become part of the city of Charlotte.[6]

The zenith of North Carolina's textile industry was the period around World War I. Demand for military uniforms, blankets, tents, bandages, and other items spurred an upsurge in production and the opening of new mills statewide (Glass and Kress 2006). Growth continued after the cessation of hostilities, but the Great Depression was just around the corner, which caused demand for textiles to fall and production to decline (Livingplaces.com n.d.). As a result, many mills were forced to close. Those that remained open operated only two or three days per week (Glass 1992).

By the 1970s, the American textile industry was facing a new challenge: low-cost labor in the developing economies of Asia and Latin America. Production shifted offshore and, by the mid-1980s, more than 40 percent of the clothing purchased by American consumers was imported (Glass and Kress 2006). As mills closed, workers were laid off, and the number of people employed in North Carolina's textile industry fell from 293,600 in 1973 to 211,300 in 1986 (Glass and Kress 2006). Both the Highland Park Mill No. 3 and the Mecklenburg mills closed in 1969 (Hanchett and Huffman 1986; United States Department of the Interior 1988), and the Johnston Mill closed in 1975 (Huffman 1993). The mill closures signaled the beginning of some challenging economic times for North Charlotte. People left the neighborhood. Homes were abandoned and fell into disrepair. North Charlotte "drifted into poverty and crime" (Markovich 2015) and became known for low-income hous-ing, drug houses, and prostitution (Infanzon 2019; Thomas 2018).

The revitalization of the neighborhood started in the 1980s, when two artists, Paul Sires and Ruth Ava Lyons, opened their Center of the Earth Gallery on North Davidson Street (Infanzon 2019). Other artists followed Sires and Lyons into the neighborhood, and North Charlotte quickly evolved into a small but thriving arts community. NoDa was still very much in transition, however; the art studios existed side by side with sex workers and drug dealers. As one local resident, Scott Lindsey, reflected:

> No one walked down 36th Street, because if you parked down there, your car got broken into . . . or you got robbed. Or some-one tried to sell you drugs. Or there were prostitutes on the street. People didn't go back in the neighborhood off the main strip, because that stuff happened all the time. (Thomas 2018).

The Great Recession irreparably damaged the neighborhood's artists' community; during difficult economic times, fewer people buy art. They still buy alcohol, however, so many of the art galleries became bars (Thomas 2018). The NoDa arts district also faced com-petition from studios located in the South End neighborhood (which also happens to be another hotbed for the city's craft brewery scene; Nilsson and Reid 2019), and many claim that South End is emerging as Charlotte's newest arts district (Newsom 2015). However, NoDa busi-ness owners have preserved NoDa as a market for art retail by pairing concepts, such as having art exhibits move into eating and entertain-ment establishments. Even the local YMCA contains an art studio (Oyler 2017b).

Today, NoDa is Charlotte's main arts district, although the neigh-borhood's economic base has diversified to include cafes, restaurants, bakeries, yoga studios, and breweries (The Littlejohn Group 2015). In terms of neighborhood culture, there are similarities between North Charlotte of yesteryear and NoDa today. According to resident Michael Fleming, "everyone knows each other and you're nice to each other" (Infanzon 2019). NoDa business owner Joe Kuhlman notes that "friendly conversations going on between neighbors and strangers, is one of the major things that sets NoDa apart from other neighbor-hoods in Charlotte" (Thomas 2018). Residents and businesses work together to organize neighborhood activities such as the NoDa Farmers Market, weekly softball games, and a Halloween party (Infanzon 2019). Just as there was a strong sense of community in the mill villages of North Charlotte, modern-day NoDa offers a similar feeling of togetherness.

The textile industry has long departed North Charlotte, but its visual and structural legacy remains. Although many have been demolished, NoDa still has a number of early twentieth-century mill homes. Beginning in the early 2000s, neighborhood residents began to preserve and protect these historic one-story homes by taking advantage of the availability of protective easements. These are legal documents, signed by both the homeowner and Preservation North Carolina,[7] that prevent current and future homeowners from making changes that will compromise the home's historical integrity (Oyler 2017a). In 2015, sale prices for refurbished NoDa mill homes ranged from the high $200,000s to the mid-$400,000s (The Littlejohn Group 2015). Highland Park Mill No. 3 has been converted into loft apartments (The Littlejohn Group 2015). Other statistics suggest that the neighborhood is rebounding. In 2015, NoDa had a population of 4,103, growing annually by approximately 1.3 percent (The Littlejohn Group 2015). More recent numbers from the Charlotte Quality of Life Study (https://mcmap.org/qol/) show a population of 4,289 in 2016 (compared to Mecklenburg County's total population of 1,044,726).

While NoDa is growing, so is the city itself. Mecklenburg County, for which Charlotte is the county seat, saw a 50 percent population rise between 2000 and 2016, during which NoDa saw a 29 percent increase. However, the neighborhood demographics have been changing, with an increasingly White population in what used to be a majority Black neighborhood. This is a common trend in many of Charlotte's trendy neighborhoods close to the urban core. Young (mainly white) professionals are moving into formerly low-income minority neighborhoods around the center city, including NoDa (Dunn 2017). This trend is not unique to Charlotte. Craft breweries often locate in postindustrial districts near urban cores. A few studies have explicitly examined the link between craft brewery openings and potential gentrification (Mathews and Picton 2014; Nilsson and Reid 2019; Reid 2018; Walker and Miller 2018; Weiler 2000). Their results generally point to signs of gentrification in areas where craft breweries are located, but as Nilsson and Reid

(2019) and Walker and Miller (2018) note, these areas already seemed on track to gentrify (or had already gentrified) before a brewery opened in the neighborhood.

As for the economy, job growth has been relatively strong in the NoDa neighborhood with a 55 percent increase in the number of jobs between 2010 and 2015, compared to the county rate of close to 31 percent for that period. The average NoDa home sales price also has been increasing at a higher rate compared to overall city trends (20 percent vs. 10 percent), comparing data from 2013 and 2015. Craft breweries are playing a key role in the neighborhood's revitalization (Markovich 2015).

The Evolution of NoDa's Craft Brewery Scene

Charlotte's first craft brewery, Dilworth Brewing, opened in 1989. This was the first beer brewed in the city since the closure of the Atlantic Ice and Coal Company brewery in 1956. During the 1990s, several other breweries (e.g., Mill Bakery, Eatery and Brewery, Johnson Beer Company, and Southend Brewery and Smokehouse) opened in the city. For various reasons, including distribution and debt-servicing issues, all closed. The first, still-operating brewery, Rock Bottom Brewery, opened in 1998 in the heart of downtown Charlotte, followed by Olde Mecklenburg Brewery in March 2009, located just southwest of downtown (Hartis 2013; Williams 2017). As of February 2019, there were thirty-one craft breweries inside Charlotte's city limits (Williams 2019).[8] Eight of these are in NoDa; as of this writing (May 2019), two new breweries were scheduled to join them in spring 2019. The city of Charlotte has 3.75 breweries per 100,000 population (based on 2017 population numbers).[9] This places it well below other cities with well-developed craft beer cultures. In 2016, for example, Portland, Denver, and Grand Rapids, Michigan, had 11, 8.7, and 7.2 craft breweries per 100,000 population, respectively (McCarthy 2016).

Craft breweries have played a vital role in the revitalization of NoDa. According to a 2015 consulting report, "The greatest contribution to the current commercial vitality of NoDa has been the influx and establishment of three award winning breweries all on North Davidson Street (NoDa, Heist and Birdsong). These facilities revitalized the entertainment scene as the loss of art galleries that were an integral part of the backbone art crawl tradition" (The Littlejohn Group 2015, 29).

NoDa Brewing Company was the first brewery to open in the neighborhood, in a building that used to host a fiber technology company on North Davidson Street. Owner Todd Ford had homebrewed for sixteen years before he and his wife Suzie opened a fifteen-barrel brewery in October 2011 (Childress 2012). Today, NoDa Brewing has two locations that together house a seventy-five-barrel system (Thomas 2015). In an interview with The Full Pint, Ford explains why they choose to locate in NoDa: "We saw this as being a fantastic place to found a brewery, the culture of arts and creativity kind of fit into the brewing scene. Also, because it was an old mill part of town, there were a lot of warehouses for rent or purchase that fit the requirements of a brewery, and most of them were vacant at the time" (The Full Pint 2013).

Chandra Torrence, co-owner of Birdsong Brewing, agrees with Ford. According to Torrence, one of the attractions of NoDa is its "great old mill buildings and the cool mix of people" (Daniel 2011).

As noted in the previous section, the choice of abandoned buildings in Charlotte's old industrial neighborhoods mirrors the locational preferences of craft breweries in other places. Across the country, clusters of craft breweries are found in postindustrial neighborhoods once home to manufacturing and warehouse activities. Part of the reason is to minimize start-up and initial operating costs, but in many cases zoning regulations also play a part. Charlotte, until June 2013, only allowed microbreweries to locate in districts zoned industrial, with limits regarding size and proximity to residential properties (Nilsson, Reid, and Lehnert 2018; Williams 2017). Ford's statement also seems to support research suggesting that breweries often respond to, rather than pioneer, urban revitalization (Barajas, Boeing, and Wartell 2017; Walker and Miller 2018). The NoDa neighborhood, at the time of NoDa Brewing Company's opening, had established itself as a well-known arts district, with other investments already going into the neighborhood. The attractiveness of an arts district to brewers may not come as a surprise given the artisan nature of craft brewing. Suzie Ford, the co-owner of NoDa Brewing, "often emphasizes the artistic side of brewing, likening the raw ingredients they work with [. . .] to an artist's paint" (Hartis 2015).

When the Fords decided to build their second location on North Tryon Street, only about a mile away from the original location, the scenery was rather different. The building, which as recently as spring 2014 housed a commercial, industrial, and institutional roofing and exterior maintenance company, is in an industrial area that is home to garages, auto body shops, and small strip malls along a busy road connecting Charlotte's northeast neighborhoods to its downtown. In an interview with CharlotteFive, the Fords say they think their brewery, as well as new businesses to come, can bring life to the neighborhood. "We've already seen that over here. [. . .] The city has a vision for this area, officially calling it North End now. They're really trying to develop it" (Hartis 2015). This remark suggests that although NoDa Brewing is perhaps considered first movers/pioneers in the revitalization of this area, commitment from the city about future investments and development was an important signal for the company.

The tendency of craft breweries to engage in adaptive reuse is also evident in NoDa. Birdsong opened in a vacant building on North Davidson Street, not far from the original NoDa Brewing Company, in a still relatively industrial area with a towing company and a tire shop as next-door neighbors. Heist Brewery is in the historic Highland Park Mill No. 3 building, once home to the largest textile mill in Charlotte; the parcel was rezoned from industrial to mixed use in 2001 (Acerni 2012). Kurt Hogan, Heist's founder, had decided that the artsy NoDa community was "a perfect fit" for his brewpub. However, the community was suffering after the Great Recession,[10] together with the economy as a whole. Art galleries and eateries that had helped define the eclectic community went out of business, but Hogan wasn't discouraged. He continued with his plans as apartment complexes in the neighborhood were fully leased, new businesses were opening, and the proposed LYNX light rail extension plans announced in 2011 showed promise of a revival in the arts district (Singe 2012).

When brothers Jeff and Jason Alexander, were looking for locations for their brewpub, Free Range Brewing, their first choice was in the Plaza Midwood neighborhood. They envisioned a space with an industrial feel that was a bit rough and rustic yet "soft enough around the corners" for families to feel comfortable spending time there (Hartis 2013). Instead, they ended up buying a former warehouse property in NoDa along North Davidson Street, across from the original location of Amélie's, the popular, French-inspired, made-from-scratch cafe.

Free Range Brewing's property was rezoned from general industrial to mixed use (retail and warehouse uses) in 2008. Since it was rezoned, the old warehouse building has hosted an antique mall and a youth center. Later in 2015, after the brewery's grand opening, the parcel was rezoned to transit-oriented mixed use to allow for residential developments there as well (City of Charlotte 2018b).

Salud Cerveceria is a nano-brewery with a small, one-barrel brewhouse inside Salud Beer Shop, a bar and bottle shop located in the heart of NoDa (Hartis 2016c).[11] The beer shop opened in March 2012 following the opening of NoDa Brewing Company and Birdsong. Prior to that, the building's downstairs had been home to various businesses, including a book and canvas shop and a comedy club. At the time of Salud's opening, the upstairs of the building hosted the Neighborhood Theatre. Two years later, one of Salud's owners and a few homebrewing friends started making sour beers experimentally. In 2016, after looking at a few locations in NoDa and adjacent neighborhoods, Salud's owners learned the space above the beer shop had become available and they reached a deal (Lee 2017). The small-scale brewery opened in June 2017.

Bold Missy is located just north of the heart of NoDa, in a building that formerly housed Quartersawn Woodworks, a cabinet manufacturing and restoration company. The building is surrounded by other brick buildings in a formerly industrial area that is undergoing revitalization with new stores, restaurants, and residential properties under development. "It's going to look completely different in three years. Which makes it a really exciting place to be," said Bold Missy's owner Carol Waggener when interviewed by CharlotteFive a week before the May 2017 grand opening (Hartis 2017). The area had already seen an influx of private capital prior to 2008, and this development has continued. Across the street from Bold Missy, Divine Barrel Brewing is in a building that used to house a distributor of engine parts, on a parcel that had been zoned general industrial (manufacturing/warehousing) as recently as February 2016. This parcel was approved for rezoning to mixed use in June 2016 (City of Charlotte 2018a). The former industrial space, branded as NoDa Market, also includes a comic book shop, a noodle bar, a paint store, and a coffee house and pub. (Hartis 2016b).

NoDa's breweries provide unique drinking and dining options for both neighborhood and Charlotte residents and, as such, improve neighborhood quality of life. They also provide an opportunity for the neighborhood to capitalize on the increasingly popular phenomena of beer tourism. Beer tourism is on the rise across the country and can generate millions of dollars for local economies. A study of beer tourism in Kent County, Michigan, found that the average beer tourist visited for 2.27 days and visited 3.7 breweries during that time. This suggests that beer tourists tend to engage in short trips (e.g., over a long weekend). The same study found the economic impact of beer tourism in Kent County to be just over $7 million (Giedeman, Isely, and Simons 2015).

In the case of Charlotte, "beer tourism is thriving . . . visitors are adding brewery visits and tours to Charlotte itineraries, and beer fanatics are planning sole trips to the Queen City as a top destination" (Rice 2017). Although many beer tourists find their own way to the city's breweries, many more participate in organized tours. Several tour companies in Charlotte specialize in brewery tours, giving visitors the opportunity to visit several breweries in the space of an afternoon. Charlotte Brews Cruise visits eight breweries on their tours, including three (Heist, Birdsong, and Bold Missy) in NoDa. The company that organizes and runs the Charlotte Brews Cruise was founded in Asheville, North Carolina, in 2006. In 2013, they expanded operations to offer brewery tours in Charlotte (Charlotte Brews Cruise n.d.).[12]

Summary and Discussion

As with many cities across the United States, Charlotte is home to a vibrant commercial craft-brewing scene. Many of the investment trends we have seen in other cities, we also see in Charlotte. These include the preference for adaptively reusing abandoned buildings in older industrial neighborhoods, and the tendency for craft breweries to cluster in such neighborhoods. Often, the neighborhoods in which craft breweries locate are undergoing an economic revival. This is the case with Charlotte's NoDa neighborhood. A key debate in the literature is the extent to which craft breweries are catalysts of neighborhood revival or simply contributors to a revival already underway. In NoDa's case, it appears that the breweries have been drawn to the former mill district and are following signals of other investments, both private and public, as well as the influx of new residents and residential developments.

Another debate that seems perennial in the world of craft beer is whether the sector's growth has reached its zenith. This question has been broached by the media in cities as diverse as Grand Rapids,

Michigan, and San Diego, California (Biolchini 2017; Glassman 2016). The question, "Will Charlotte's craft beer bubble burst in 2019?" has been asked here, too (Hartis 2019). As industry observers, our sense is that there is plenty of room for more craft breweries in the city of Charlotte. We feel that the same can be said of NoDa. Indeed, NoDa's recent growth shows no signs of slowing; according to one commentator, NoDa's going to see "dramatic growth over the next few years" (Thomas 2018), including more breweries (Hartis 2019). At the time of writing (May 2019), two brewpubs, Protagonist Clubhouse and Wooden Robot Brewery, are scheduled to open in NoDa (McKenzie 2018a).[13] Protagonist Clubhouse will continue the practice of adaptive reuse by locating in a building that once housed a grocery store (Peralta 2018b). In choosing NoDa, Protagonist's three owners, Ryan McKillen, Mike Salzarulo, and Ryan Owens, were attracted by the neighborhood's "established nightlife scene that is also in the midst of a growth explosion" (Thomas 2018). This suggests that NoDa has reached a tipping point in terms of being a desirable neighborhood for private investors. In contrast, Wooden Robot Brewery will open in a newly constructed 7,500-square-foot facility right by one of the new light rail stations on the recently opened LYNX Blue Line Extension going through NoDa (Peralta 2018c). This facility, to be called The Chamber by Wooden Robot, will be Wooden Robot's second brewery in Charlotte, the first having opened in the city's South End in 2015. "We pretty much knew we wanted to be in NoDa; it's a good representation of what we're trying to do with our brand. We love the area, hang out there a lot right now and are big fans of the arts and culture," said Wooden Robot CEO Josh Patton to *Charlotte Magazine* (McKenzie 2018b). It announced in a company statement that it "plans to engage with local [NoDa] artists to bring a unique aesthetic and atmosphere to the new space, as well as focus on community events." Wooden Robot's site is part of the new Novel NoDa apartment community that opened in 2017 (Peralta 2018a).

Charlotte is doing its part to encourage and facilitate additional brewery growth. The city's zoning regulations have finally caught up with the reality of the growth of the craft-brewing sector. Breweries used to be defined as alcoholic manufacturers for zoning purposes, with microbreweries only allowed to locate in light and heavy industrial districts with limitations regarding size and proximity to residential properties. Brewpubs, on the other hand, had looser zoning regulations, being allowed, for example, in mixed-use districts (Peters 2013;

Williams 2017). However, new rules were implemented in 2013 to ease zoning regulations surrounding craft breweries, allowing microbreweries to locate in mixed-use zones. In 2014, additional amendments to the zoning laws were introduced that reduced the required distance between residential areas and eating, drinking, and entertainment establishments (Williams 2017). This easing of the regulatory environment provides the next generation of craft breweries with greater flexibility and choice of where to locate; a good location being critical to the success of any retail business. Many of Charlotte's breweries have taken the opportunity to locate in these zones, especially around the newly implemented light rail running through NoDa, as these areas have attracted the demographic that matches the breweries' main target market (millennials and young professionals).

However, the growth of the NoDa neighborhood, together with other postindustrial districts in Charlotte, could make it harder for new breweries to open, because the prime spots they seek (e.g., older warehouses) are increasingly difficult to find as the city's real estate market is tightening (Portillo 2017). Although rents and property values have increased around Charlotte's breweries, these areas were associated with a premium even before the breweries opened (Nilsson and Reid 2019). Hence, although there are fears of gentrification and displacement in the city's two brewery districts, NoDa and South End, craft breweries are not the sole factor pushing up rents and property values. Both these areas have experienced major public and private investments since the early 2000s. Part of the reason why these areas have been attractive to investors and residents is their proximity to the city center, but the LYNX Blue Line (announced in 2000, opened in 2007) and its extension (announced 2011, opened in 2018), which runs through these areas, has also brought with it considerable investment, as the city has designated many of the underutilized industrial parcels around it transit-oriented and mixed-use development.

Although some breweries may desire to grow and serve increasingly larger geographic markets, the key to success for most craft breweries in the future is likely to be a strong focus on local markets. Indeed, these markets are even being characterized as "hyperlocal" (Morrel 2016). The most successful breweries are likely to "focus more on the surrounding neighborhoods and less on getting tap handles in neighboring states" (Grant 2019). Market focus, rather than market expansion, seems to be one key to future craft brewery success (Wesson and De Figueiredo 2001). This focus on local markets means that new breweries opening in NoDa are more likely to be brewpubs, rather than microbreweries. Both Protagonist Clubhouse and Wooden Robot are brewpubs. Microbreweries depend upon acquiring shelf space in retail outlets and tap handles at bars and restaurants to sell their beer. Competition for shelf space and tap handles is growing and is unlikely to recede in the foreseeable future. Profit margins are significantly lower for beer sold offsite, as both the distributor and the retailer must get their cut (Morrel 2016). Selling beer to customers onsite is much more profitable. Onsite sales also provide the brewer with more control over their product, allowing them to sell the freshest possible beer. Delegation of quality control to distributors is not without risks and can compromise the integrity of the beer (Brewers Association 2016a).

Last, the potential exists to increase the number of beer tourists visiting Charlotte in general and NoDa in particular. The Charlotte Visitor and Convention Bureau already highlights the city's craft beer scene on their website. Enhancing travel experiences and digital storytelling around craft beer would seem to be key to promoting Charlotte breweries to outsiders. Carefully crafted advertising campaigns can pay dividends (Skift 2016).

Charlotte breweries also face challenges. The city of Charlotte is perhaps best known as a hub for banking headquarters and other large corporations. Although it is a city in growth mode with heavy focus on economic development, the big-business focus may have left small businesses behind. In an interview with CharlotteFive, Birdsong Brewing Company's cofounder Chris Goulet noted that "it's challenging to start a business in Mecklenburg County. They're not small business oriented. When we sat down as a partnership group three years ago and said we were going to do a second brewery and add capacity, I was probably the one most adamantly opposed because I just didn't want to go through the whole process of building another business in Charlotte" (Hartis 2016a).

Notes

1. The eight craft breweries that were operational in the United States in 1980 were Anchor Brewing Co. (San Francisco, California), Boulder Beer Co. (Longmont, Colorado), California Steam Beer Brewing Co. (San Rafael, California), Cartwright

Brewing Co. (Portland, Oregon), DeBakker Brewing (Novato, California), New Albion Brewing (Sonoma, California), River City Brewing (Sacramento, California), and Sierra Nevada Brewing (Chico, California) (Eckhardt 2010).

2. In this chapter, we use the Brewers Association's definition of a craft brewery. To qualify as a craft, a brewery cannot produce more than six million barrels of beer annually. Additionally, no more than 25 percent of the brewery can be owned or controlled by an alcohol industry member that is not itself a craft brewer, and most of the alcohol it produces must be beer that derives from traditional or innovative brewing ingredients and their fermentation (Brewers Association 2019a).

3. Craft beer's market share is higher in dollar terms versus in volume because it sells at a higher price point than mass-produced beer.

4. The 500,000 jobs include 135,000 directly at breweries and 365,000 in industries supplying material inputs such as malted barley, hops, brewing equipment, bottles, cans, and so forth.

5. The geographic clustering of craft breweries has been observed not only in US cities but also in London (Dennett and Page 2017).

6. Annexation of North Charlotte was a gradual process, with annexations occurring in 1907, 1928, 1959, and 1960.

7. Preservation North Carolina was founded in 1939 to protect the state's landscapes and structures.

8. The craft beer landscape in any city can change rapidly. The 31 breweries referenced in this chapter comprise the thirty breweries listed in Williams (2019) plus the original NoDa Brewing Co location on North Davidson Street which, at the time of writing (May 2019), is temporarily closed.

9. American Community Survey 2017 five-year population estimates from the US Census Bureau for the city of Charlotte show a total population of 826,060.

10. We are referring to the Great Recession of 2007–9.

11. There is no official definition of what constitutes a nanobrewery although the generally accepted definition is a brewery that uses a three-barrel brewing system or smaller (Garrison 2012).

12. In addition to Charlotte and Denver, the Brews Cruise company offers brewery tours in Atlanta and Savannah, Georgia, Boise, Idaho, Chicago, Denver, Nashville, Tennessee, and Raleigh, North Carolina (Charlotte Brews Cruise n.d.).

13. Both opened on schedule and were still going strong as of August 2022.

References

Acerni, Aleigh. 2012. "Heist: The Rise of the Brewpub." *Charlotte Magazine*. October 25. Retrieved December 19, 2018 (http://www.charlottemagazine .com/Charlotte-Magazine/November-2012/The-Rise-of-the-Brewpub/).

Alexander, Dan. 2013. "Beer Entrepreneurs Fuel Comeback of Struggling Cleveland Neighborhood." *Forbes*. November 26 (http://www.forbes.com/sites /danalexander/2013/11/26/beer-entrepreneurs-fuel-comeback-of-struggling -cleveland-neighborhood/#14cc94c3574f).

Barajas, Jesus M., Geoff Boeing, and Julie Wartell. 2017. "Neighborhood Change, One Pint at a Time." Pp. 155–76. In *Untapped: Exploring the Cultural Dimensions of Craft Beer*, edited by Nathaniel G. Chapman, Slade Lellock, and Cameron D. Lippard. Morgantown: West Virginia University Press.

Biolchini, Amy. 2017. "Is the Craft Beer Market in Grand Rapids Saturated?" *Mlive.com*. March 22 (https://www.mlive.com/news/grand-rapids/index.ssf /2017/03/grand_rapids_beer_city.html).

Brewers Association. 2016a. "Role of Distributors in Managing Beer Quality." March 28 (https://www.brewersassociation.org/industry-updates/role -distributors-managing-beer-quality/).

Brewers Association. 2016b. "Today's Craft Beer Lovers: Millennials, Women and Hispanics." August 15 (https://www.brewersassociation.org/communicating -craft/understanding-todays-craft-beer-lovers-millennials-women-hispanics/).

Brewers Association. 2017. "Total Economic Impact 2017" (https://s3-us-west-2 .amazonaws.com/brewersassoc/wp-content/uploads/2018/08/State-by-State -Breakdown-2017.pdf).

Brewers Association. 2019a. "Craft Brewer Defined" (https://www.brewersassociation .org/statistics/craft-brewer-defined/).

Brewers Association. 2019b. "Economic Impact" (https://www.brewersassociation .org/statistics/economic-impact-data/).

Brewers Association. 2019c. "National Beer Sales & Production Data" (https://www .brewersassociation.org/statistics/national-beer-sales-production-data/).

California Craft Brewers Association. 2013. "California Craft Brewing Industry Economic Impact Report." Sacramento: California Craft Brewers Association (http://www.californiacraftbeer.com/files/Economic-Impact-Study-FINAL.pdf).

Charlotte Brews Cruise. n.d. "About" (https://web.archive.org/web/20170602182157 /https://www.brewscruisecharlotte.com/about/).

Childress, Tricia. 2012. "True Brew in Charlotte. Creative Loafing Charlotte." September 26 (https://clclt.com/charlotte/true-brew-in-charlotte/Content ?oid=2869720).

City of Charlotte. 2018a. "Rezoning Petition 2016–063." Retrieved December 19, 2018 (https://charlottenc.gov/planning/Rezoning/RezoningPetitions /2016Petitions/Pages/2016-063.aspx).

City of Charlotte. 2018b. "2015 Rezoning Petitions." Retrieved December 19, 2018 (https://charlottenc.gov/planning/Rezoning/RezoningPetitions/2015Petitions /Pages/2015-001.aspx).

Dangaran, Kirsten and Karen Wruck. 2016. "Economic Impact of Ohio's Craft Beer Industry 2015." Columbus: Ohio Craft Brewers Association (https://web .archive.org/web/20190120075152/http://www.ohiocraftbeer.org/wp-content /uploads/2016/01/EconomicImpactFinalreportwithAppendix2.pdf).

Daniel. 2011. "Meet Charlotte's Newest Brewery: Birdsong Brewing." Charlottebeer .com, February 17 (https://web.archive.org/web/20110301040212/http://www .charlottebeer.com/2011/02/17/birdsong-brewing-charlotte-nc/).

Dennett, Adam and Sam Page. 2017. "The Geography of London's Recent Beer Brewing Revolution." *Geographical Journal* 183(4):440–54.

Dunn, Andrew. 2017. "In Charlotte's Trendy Neighborhoods, a Culture Clash of Black and White, Rich and Poor." *Charlotte Agenda*. July 20. (https://www .charlotteagenda.com/97973/charlottes-trendy-neighborhoods-culture-clash -black-white-rich-poor/).

Eckhardt, Fred. 2010. "A Selected Chronology of Early Craft/Micro Brewers in the United States and Canada. *All About Beer Magazine* 31(2), May 1 (http://allaboutbeer.com/article/a-selected-chronology-of-early-craftmicro-brewers-in-the-united-states-and-canada/).

The Full Pint. 2013. Interview with Todd Ford of NoDa Brewing. February 28. (https://thefullpint.com/interviews/interview-with-todd-ford-of-noda-brwewing/).

Funcheon, Deirdra. 2018. "To Fight Blight, Cities Are Establishing Brewery Districts." *Bisnow.com*, May 9 (https://www.bisnow.com/south-florida/news/retail/breweries-economic-development-brewery-district-craft-beer-87854).

Gatrell, Jay, Neil Reid, and Thomas L, Steiger. 2018. "Branding Spaces: Place, Region, Sustainability and the American Craft Beer Industry. *Applied Geography* 90:360–70.

Garrison, Mark. 2012. "Pint Sized: How Nanobreweries—Fledgling Operations in Garages and Backyard Sheds—Are Revolutionizing the American Beer Industry." *Slate.com*, December 12 (http://www.slate.com/articles/business/drink/2012/12/nanobrewing_how_tiny_beer_making_operations_are_changing_the_industry.html).

Giedeman, Dan, Paul Isely, and Gerry Simons. 2015. "The Economic Impact of Beer Tourism in Kent County, Michigan." Allendale, MI: Grand Valley State University (https://web.archive.org/web/20160503215951/https://www.gvsu.edu/cms4/asset/7A028470-B5EB-E9D6-C17010124D94A01E/beer_tourism_report_october_2015.pdf).

Glass, Brent D. 1992. *The Textile Industry in North Carolina: A History*. Raleigh: North Carolina Department of Cultural Resources.

Glass, Brent D. and Kelly Kress. 2006. "Textiles." *NCPedia*. Last modified January 1, 2006 (https://www.ncpedia.org/textiles).

Glassman, Bruce. 2016. "Does San Diego Have Too Many Breweries? *San Diego Magazine*, March 24 (https://www.sandiegomagazine.com/Blogs/Behind-the-Brews/Spring-2016/Does-San-Diego-Have-Too-Many-Breweries/).

Gorski, Eric. 2015. "Denver's River North Neighborhood: The Brewing District." *The Denver Post*, February 16. https://www.denverpost.com/2015/02/16/denvers-river-north-neighborhood-the-brewing-district/.

Grant, Justin. 2019. "Going Hyperlocal, Craft Breweries Open in Riverview, Valrico and New Port Richey." *Tampa Bay Times*, January 3 (https://web.archive.org/web/20190103200056/https://www.tampabay.com/topics/specials/craft-beer/craft-beer-new-bay-area-breweries-get-hyperlocal-20190103/).

Hanchett, Thomas W. n.d. *The Growth of Charlotte: A History* (http://www.cmhpf.org/educhargrowth.htm).

Hanchett, Thomas W. and William H. Huffman. 1986. *Mecklenburg Mill Historic Overview*. Charlotte-Mecklenburg Historic Landmarks Commission (http://landmarkscommission.org/2016/12/15/mecklenburg-mill/).

Harne, Angela. 2017. "Breweries, Craft Beer Outlets OKd in Winterville." *The Times Leader*, January 14 (http://www.reflector.com/News/2017/01/14/Changes-allow-breweries-craft-beer-in-Winteville.html).

Hartis, Daniel A. 2013. *Charlotte Beer: A History of Brewing in the Queen City*. Charleston, SC: American Palate.

Hartis, Daniel. 2015. "NoDa Brewing Co.'s New Location Opens in Charlotte's North End Today." *CharlotteFive*, October 1 (https://web.archive.org/web /20151003203303/https://www.charlottefive.com/noda-brewing-co-s-new -location-opens-in-charlottes-north-end-today-look-inside/).

Hartis, Daniel. 2016a. "Birdsong Brewing Is Celebrating Five Years, So We Asked Co-Founder Chris Goulet Five Questions." *CharlotteFive*, December 8 (https:// www.charlottefive.com/5-questions-birdsong-brewing/; site discontinued).

Hartis, Daniel. 2016b. "Divine Barrel Brewing to Open in NoDa Next Summer." *CharlotteFive*, December 2 (https://web.archive.org/web/20161204182934 /https://www.charlottefive.com/divine-barrel-brewing/).

Hartis, Daniel. 2016c. "Salud Beer Shop to Release Two Waffle-Inspired Beers at Wafflemania Tonight." *CharlotteFive*, September 13 (https://web.archive .org/web/20161018080519/http://www.charlottefive.com/salud-beer-shop -wafflemania/).

Hartis, Daniel. 2017. "First Look: Bold Missy, NoDa's Newest Brewery, Is Set to Open Later This Month." *CharlotteFive*, May 5 (https://web.archive.org/web /20171012200900/http://www.charlottefive.com/bold-missy-brewery/).

Hartis, Daniel. 2019. "Will Charlotte's Craft-Beer Bubble Burst in 2019? Or Will It Simply Shift Shape?" *Charlotte Observer*, January 3 (https://www .charlotteobserver.com/entertainment/restaurants/article223872615 .html?fbclid=IwAR2jWZL3LYZMrqy-KVNhgLoFfY5Gjy23wRcd _HwPQTDOuPjOPSgDDIUgRCo).

Huffman, William H. 1993. *Johnston Mill Historical Overview*. Charlotte- Mecklenburg Historic Landmarks Commission (http://www.cmhpf.org/S&Rs %20Alphabetical%20Order/surveys&rjohnstonmill.htm; site discontinued).

ICIC. 2018. "Bottoms Up: Craft Breweries Help Spark Revitalization in Inner Cities" (http://icic.org/blog/bottoms-craft-breweries-help-spark-revitalization-inner -cities/).

Infanzon, Vanessa. 2019. "NoDa's Charm Is Like a 'Quirky Mayberry'— Neighborhood Stories." *Charlottestories.com*, January 24 (http://www .charlottestories.com/noda-neighborhood-stories/).

Kraftchick, Jennifer Francioni, Erick T. Byrd, Bonnie Canziani, and Nancy J. Gladwell. 2014. "Understanding Beer Tourist Motivation." *Tourism Management Perspectives* 12:41–47.

Krewson, Andria. 2012. "Why Is Restoring NoDa's Textile Mills So Hard?" *PlanCharlotte.org*, October 5 (http://plancharlotte.org/story/historic-noda -textile-mills-face-uncertain-future/).

Livingplaces.com. n.d. "North Charlotte Historic District" (http://www.livingplaces .com/NC/Mecklenburg_County/Charlotte_City/North_Charlotte_Historic _District.html).

The Littlejohn Group. 2015. "AC&W Railroad Relocation Analysis Market Study" August 10 (http://charlottenc.gov/Projects/Documents/1AC-W%20Railroad %20Relocation%20Analysis%20Market%20Study%20081015_NAL.pdf).

Lee, Cameron. 2017. "Salud Cerveceria Is a Classic Charlotte Small Business Story." *CLTURE*, June 15 (https://clture.org/salud-cerveceria/).

Lubin, Lisa. 2016. "Craft Breweries Help Lead the Charge in Buffalo's Rebirth." *Chicago Tribune*, March 29 (https://web.archive.org/web/20210619161222

/https://www.chicagotribune.com/travel/ct-buffalo-beer-fork-travel-0410
-20160328-story.html).

Markovich, Jeremy. 2015. "NoDa Is Charlotte's Island of Interesting." *Ourstate.com*,
February 17 (https://www.ourstate.com/noda/).

Mathews, V. and R. M. Picton. 2014. "Intoxifying Gentrification: Brew Pubs and the
Geography of Post-Industrial Heritage. *Urban Geography* 35:337–56.

McCarthy, Niall. 2016. "Which U.S. Cities Have the Most Microbreweries Per
Capita?" *Forbes.com*, November 1 (https://www.forbes.com/sites/niallmccarthy
/2016/11/01/which-u-s-cities-have-the-most-microbreweries-per-capita
-infographic/#4cb26c39e19b).

McKenzie, Matt. 2018a. "Protagonist Clubhouse Makes First Hire, With Much More
to Come." *Charlotte Magazine*, December 4 (http://www.charlottemagazine
.com/Charlotte-Magazine/December-2018/Protagonist-Clubhouse-makes
-first-hire-with-much-more-to-come/).

McKenzie, Matt. 2018b. "Wooden Robot Opening New Location in NoDa Next
Spring." *Charlotte Magazine*, April 10 (http://www.charlottemagazine.com
/Charlotte-Magazine/April-2018/Wooden-Robot-opening-new-location
-in-NoDa-next-spring/).

Morrel, Dan. 2016. "We've Seen the Future, and It Is Hyperlocal Craft Beer." *Boston
Globe Magazine*, May 25 (https://www.bostonglobe.com/magazine/2016/05
/25/seen-future-and-hyperlocal-craft-beer/2aytCha1eTtzG7KICTttiO/story
.html).

Newsom, Mary. 2015. "Charlotte Arts Districts Face Challenges, Study Finds."
UNC Charlotte Urban Institute, June 9 (https://ui.uncc.edu/story/artists
-neighborhood-gentrification-noda-and-south-end).

Nickerson, Mark A. and Linda Hall. 2017. "New York Pours Tax Incentives into the
Craft Brewing Industry." *CPA Journal*, October 17 (https://www.cpajournal.com
/2017/10/19/new-york-pours-tax-incentives-craft-brewing-industry/).

Nilsson, Isabelle and Neil Reid. 2019. "The Value of a Craft Brewery: On the
Relationship between Craft Breweries and Property Values." *Growth and Change*
50(2):689–704.

Nilsson, Isabelle, Neil Reid, and Matthew M. Lehnert. 2018. "Geographic Patterns
of Craft Breweries at the Intraurban Scale." *The Professional Geographer*
70(1):114–25.

Oyler, Melissa. 2017a. "How NoDa Residents Are Preserving Their Historic Homes
despite Charlotte Development." *Charlottefive.com*, February 23 (https://web
.archive.org/web/20181124141338/https://www.charlottefive.com/how-noda
-residents-are-preserving-their-historic-homes-despite-charlotte-development/).

Oyler, Melissa. 2017b. "NoDa Still Stands as the Arts District—You Just Have to
Know Where to Look." *Charlottefive.com*, July 13 (https://www.charlottefive
.com/noda-still-stands-arts-district-just-know-look/; site discontinued).

Peralta, Katherine. 2018a. "A Popular Brewery Is Expanding into NoDa." *Charlotte
Observer*, April 10 (https://web.archive.org/web/20180614171215/http://www
.charlotteobserver.com/news/business/biz-columns-blogs/whats-in-store
/article208478879.html).

Peralta, Katherine. 2018b. "Three Friends Think Charlotte Could Use More
Breweries." *Charlotte Observer,* October 18 (https://web.archive.org/web

/20201024032236/https://www.charlotteobserver.com/news/business/biz-columns
-blogs/whats-in-store/article220218625.html).

Peralta, Katherine. 2018c. "Wooden Robot Brewery Is Expanding to NoDa." *Charlottefive.com*, April 11 (https://web.archive.org/web/20200524165818/https://www.charlotteobserver.com/charlottefive/c5-worklife/article236139918.html).

Peters, Corbin. 2013. "Beer: Is It Zoned Out?" *PlanCharlotte.org*, February 6 (http://plancharlotte.org/story/beer-it-zoned-out).

Portillo, Ely. 2017. "Pricey Homes, Splashy Apartments, Uptown Shops: Our 2018 Charlotte Property Predictions. *Charlotte Observer*. December 28. https://www.charlotteobserver.com/charlottefive/c5-worklife/article236129883.html.

Reid, Neil. 2018. "Craft Breweries, Adaptive Reuse, and Neighborhood Revitalization." *Urban Development Issues* 57:5–14.

Reid, Neil, Margaret M. Gripshover, and Thomas L. Bell. 2019. "Craft Breweries and Adaptive Reuse in the USA: The Use and Reuse of Space and Language." Pp. 4083–4101. In *Handbook of the Changing World Language Map*, edited by S. D. Brunn. Cham, Switzerland: Springer.

Rice, Jenn. 2017. "Sip Jalapeño and Sweet Potato Beers in Charlotte, N.C." *USA Today*, September 20 (https://www.usatoday.com/story/travel/experience/food-and-wine/2017/09/20/charlotte-north-carolina-breweries/681423001/).

Singe, Kerry. 2012. "Betting on a NoDa Revival." *Charlotte Observer*, May 20 (http://kerrysinge.com/commercial-real-estate-features/heist-brewery-owner-betting-on-noda-revival/).

Skift, Greg. 2016. "Travel on Tap: The Rise of Craft Beer Tourism." *Skift.com*, July 28 (https://skift.com/2016/07/28/the-rise-of-craft-beer-tourism/).

Stonebridge. 2015. "The Economic Impact of Craft Beer on the New York Economy, 2013." St. Helena, CA: Stonebridge Research Group (https://www.governor.ny.gov/sites/governor.ny.gov/files/atoms/files/NYCraft_Beer_2013_Impact_Study_FINAL4.15.15.pdf).Thomas, Jennifer. 2015. "Inside NoDa Brewing's $7M Expansion Plans." *Charlotte Business Journal*, April 7 (https://www.bizjournals.com/charlotte/news/2015/04/07/inside-noda-brewings-7m-expansion-plans-photos.html).

Thomas, Alicia. 2018. "Is NoDa Going Through an Identity Crisis? Here's How We Keep NoDa, NoDa." *Charlottefive.com*, April 9 (https://web.archive.org/web/20180502223100/https://www.charlottefive.com/noda-identity-crisis/).

Thomas, Jason. 2018. "See Renderings of Protagonist Clubhouse, the New Nano-Brewery Coming to NoDa." *Charlotteagenda.com*, October 18 (https://www.charlotteagenda.com/145481/protagonist-clubhouse-brewery-taproom-noda/).

United States Department of Interior. 1988. National Register of Historic Places Registration Form for Highland Park Manufacturing Company Mill No. 3, Charlotte NC (https://web.archive.org/web/20121228101749/http://www.hpo.ncdcr.gov/nr/MK1164.pdf).

Walker, Samuel and Chloe Fox Miller. 2018. "Have Craft Breweries Followed or Led Gentrification in Portland, Oregon? An Investigation of Retail and Neighbourhood Change." *Geografiska Annaler: Series B, Human Geography* 101(2):102–17.

Weiler, Stephan. 2000. "Pioneers and Settlers in Lo-Do Denver: Private Risk and Public Benefits in Urban Redevelopment." *Urban Studies* 37(1):167–79.

Wesson, Tom and Joao Neiva De Figueiredo. 2001. "The Importance of Focus to Market Entrants: A Study of Microbrewery Performance." *Journal of Business Venturing* 16(4):377–403.

Williams, Alistair. 2017. "Exploring the Impact of Legislation on the Development of Craft Beer." *Beverages* 3(2):18.

Williams, Ted. 2019. "Complete List and Map of Charlotte's 30 Local Breweries, Plus the Most Popular Beer at Each." *Charlotteagenda.com*, February 20 (https://charlotte.axios.com/31429/breweries-in-charlotte/).

Postcard from New Orleans

DAINA CHEYENNE HARVEY

The Avenue Pub is in a ramshackle building that's easy to miss if you are riding down St. Charles Avenue on the bright red streetcars. You have to search for its pale blue bar with the second-story porch, but once you spot it, the conductor will let you off right in front. It's small and cozy and dark—a bit disorienting when you've stepped in from a bright summer day. Once inside, you notice lots of taps; beers you've heard of but never had a chance to try, beers you've never heard of, and some of your favorites. Once you take your beer to a small two-top table, you can watch the world go by through the window or read a book. Most months you can sit outside in the warm humidity, smelling the magnolias and listening in to the goings on of the Garden District—for some reason it makes the beer even better. People come and go. Some will engage you in conversations like you've been friends for decades. They'll invite you to a street or house party they're off to or tell you about some other place you should try later that evening: what's playing at the Prytania, where's the newest po'-boy shack, or who might be at the Apple Barrel. They'll give you a handshake or a hug and let you get back to your book. It's a special place. It is, as owner Polly Watts says, a neighborhood bar, but in such a way that it can be anyone's neighborhood. It is the quintessential beer place.

HARVEY: So how did the Avenue Pub get started?

WATTS: I helped my dad open it when I was a senior at Tulane. I went off and did my own thing. He got very sick before Katrina so I was down here a lot . . . he passed away after Katrina and I moved back.

HARVEY: Sorry to hear. How has it changed over time?

WATTS: My dad had really envisioned a sort of neighborhood bar. It was a pretty much a neighborhood bar. He did the late-night thing, the twenty-four-hours thing, about two to three years into him owning it. By the time I got a hold of it . . . Katrina had pretty much wiped out his customer base. We were more of a bad-decision bar than anything else [laughter]. So when I took over, obviously, [I] was just stabilizing, it took us about two years, all the equipment was broken, we didn't even have a functioning ice machine. The balcony was falling off the side of the building. Then about two to three years after he passed away we got NOLA Brewing. It just used to be Abita. And I got very interested in NOLA [Brewing]. So I'm one of those sort of typical beer people that comes in from a local interest and then the world expands from there. And this was pre-taproom. So probably for . . . the first five years, you know, a lot of those places didn't exist or if they did, they didn't have tap rooms, and the market has changed entirely. But at the time we were one of the places you could come . . . and I mean to some extent we still are . . . but you can go to NOLA and get NOLA or Urban South and get Urban South, but you can get a whole lot of local breweries at my bar versus just one.

Abita was the "local" beer for close to twenty-five years until NOLA Brewing opened in 2008 (Abita is about an hour away from NOLA if you go around Lake Pontchartrain and about forty-five minutes if you go over it.) Abita is still "from" New Orleans and has a large presence there, but for some reason they never built a taproom in the city. Because of that—and perhaps even more, because of other successful breweries around Louisiana—Abita is no longer the only "New Orleans" beer, and many now associate it with the "other" part of Louisiana (i.e., not New Orleans).

HARVEY: So, the Avenue is the place I always come when I'm in town. . . .

WATTS: That's cool, how did you find out about it?

HARVEY: I was born here, grew up outside the city in St. Charles Parish. But I moved back to the Upper Ninth in 2010 to help rebuild houses after Katrina and to work on my dissertation about Katrina. But since I've tried to maintain a connection with the city, I always stop by and I try and bring people here and I think they're pretty surprised, because while New Orleans is definitely a drinking place, it's not thought of as a beer place, at least before. . . . I mean in 2011 it was just NOLA Brewing and you didn't have Urban South or the Courtyard or Parleaux . . . so this [the Avenue] has always been a craft beer oasis.

So how do you see the Avenue compared to the rest of places in New Orleans?

WATTS: Well, in other cities you have beer bars with a capital "B." That's what they are. You know. That's all they do, and they do it well. I've been very true to what I consider my dad's goal—my goal—which is we're not a capital "B" beer, we are a neighborhood bar. There are still things you can get in a neighborhood bar that you can't get in taprooms or capital "B" beer bars. That's not to say we are the be-all and end-all for all people. We want the beer to be in a non-snobby setting, but served right and [with] a good rotating tap list, so if you are a regular there is always something different for you to drink.

This day was the first crawfish day at the Avenue. During crawfish season a lot of bars and restaurants will have a crawfish boil outside on their sidewalk. Locals and tourists alike notice the first few boils, whereas after a few weeks only tourists tend to be excited to see them. Despite temperatures already reaching summer digits, crawfish season signifies that we are officially in spring. The ingredients for a boil are minimal, but the cayenne wafting through the oak trees is enough to make your eyes water. Yet the smell encourages you to go and investigate. As is typical for the first crawfish day, dozens of locals and tourists walked past Watts and me to peer into the boil.

HARVEY: So, are most of your customers local?

WATTS: No—well oddly enough, yes, a lot of customers do live in the neighborhood and walk over to us, but despite that emphasis we have an awful lot of tourist regulars and you're a good example of one of those people, someone who lives out of town but visits fairly frequently, sometimes once a year but often multiple times a year. Maybe from Baton Rouge or Houston, but when they're in town we're their neighborhood bar. Most of them come in through the beer angle . . . they've heard of us from the beer angle. I always wanted to be at a bar where I can make the beer people really happy, but we weren't shunning people who didn't want beer, maybe a nice glass of French wine or a good whiskey or, I guess, even a Miller High Life—because we still sell that. We don't sell a lot of it . . . but we sell. . . .

HARVEY: So, you said things changed with NOLA Brewery. How have things changed since then? This area has exploded.

WATTS: There's been an explosion nationwide of course, but we see it emerge in a smaller way in Louisiana. We've already started to see, we're still building in terms of the beer community, but we are starting to see some drop-off, some that weren't successful . . . some have closed, several, but we have a couple opening in the next six months. Miel opened—he was actually a former employee, very briefly.

HARVEY: So that was surprising for me to see there are almost five in the Lower Garden/Irish Channel now.

WATTS [starts naming breweries] So there's seven in the city limits . . . there are several others just outside, maybe five or six, but you'd have to look up the numbers.

Pre-Katrina, the Irish Channel was for almost all of its existence a working-class neighborhood. In the 1800s, Irish immigrants flooded into this part of the city as they dug canals and built levees—the Irish were seen as expendable workers, less valuable than enslaved people. As with Irish neighborhoods in New York City and Boston, the Channel always had a reputation as a "rough" part of the city. Although it became more diverse in the 1960s, when it became majority Black, the neighborhood is still the center for the annual St. Patrick's Day Parade and is home to decidedly Irish bars like Parasol's and Tracey's. Since Katrina it has experienced rapid gentrification.

HARVEY: How do you make the decision of what to put on tap?

WATTS: So, I'm really lucky, because my customer base seems to like my palate. There are some basics that we try and have on tap most of the time, but nothing here gets a permanent handle. But 80 percent to . . . 90 percent of the time they're on, those tend to be the more session beers that people like to drink over and over again, like NOLA Blond. I took Parish Canebrake off and put on Bell's Oberon just to see, to give people a little change, but I'll probably have to put Canebreak back on. Great Raft Southern Drawl is one that we tap most of the time . . . but everything else is done, it's a mixture of special releases from local breweries, European imports, and then I try to basically balance the system. If I don't have a lot of stouts on, I add an imperial stout, and I'll look and see what's available. Sometimes I cellar stuff. Most of its personal taste. It's very accurate to say that it's curated. There's no formula.

HARVEY: How does being in New Orleans help the Avenue?

WATTS: I think there are a lot of things that got us attention in the early days that wouldn't have gotten us, you know if we were in Peoria. We're on St. Charles Avenue, which is a major tourist thorough-fare . . . with the streetcar. We're open twenty-four hours. But yeah, we're a tourist destination.

St. Charles Avenue was home to many of the area's most wealthy families from the 1850s to the mid-twentieth century. Many of the mansions are still there, though they've been converted to hotels, bed and breakfasts, apartments, and condos. The streetcar (and the street) runs from Canal Street in the Central Business District through the Garden District and ends up in Carrollton where Tulane, Loyola, and the Audubon Park converge. For $1.25 you can ride the car and hop off wherever you want to explore the different neighborhoods.

HARVEY: How would you like to see the Avenue in five to ten years?

WATTS: You know, it's hard to see where the beer world is going to go. Because the taproom pressure on beer bars is real and it's serious. We've been very lucky that we've kept our customer base and we're still growing. But if you look at beer bars across the country, they are suffering. The brewpub industry is cannibalizing beer bars. I think we're in a unique position here at our bar. We're a neighborhood club. I think we can ride out the storm. We carry a lot of things you're just not going to see in other places.

The microcosm of the path or trajectory that craft beer has gone in the United States is fascinating. We have an industry that, for lots of different reasons, expanded and flourished because of different laws, especially in regards to the three-tier system [customers, distributors, and retailers]. It's now reached the point where the breweries that expanded and benefited under that system now want to get rid of that system. So we've seen that, and it will be interesting to see as the three-tier system disappears in certain parts of the country—are we moving back?—and a lot of people in the industry think we are—are we moving into a set of laws that will allow the big conglomerates to decimate small, local craft? There's a part of me that says craft beer is too entrenched in the American psyche for that to happen, but when I see the growth slowed in the way it has and I see what people are getting excited about. . . . I see a lot people getting excited about sugar. Europeans were seeing this, sugar, sugar, sugar, and Americans have turned to that to capture part of that market. I wonder what that's doing. Are we attracting long-term customers, or are people just here for the sugar? We've seen market disruptions, the market has expanded and the conglomerates have had to accept craft beer, but now deconstructed, with the taprooms . . . and it's all happened in ten years . . . kind of the same way Uber destroyed taxis, what Airbnb has done to hotels, so I just wonder where we're going to be in ten years. If you had asked me ten years ago I could have told you . . . but now I don't know. But I know neighborhood bars will survive [laughter].

Pre-Katrina, New Orleans' neighborhoods (named, but rarely called, faubourgs) were like New York City's boroughs. It was easy enough to go from one to the other—to the untrained eye it was difficult to tell where one ended and another began—but people pretty much stayed in their own neighborhood. You had your neighborhood bar and your po'-boy spot and your grocery, so there was no reason to leave it. After schools were forcibly integrated, New Orleans went from one of the most integrated cities to one of the most segregated cities—and this in many ways reinforced reasons to stay in the neighborhood. When I was in the Lower Ninth I often spoke with people who hadn't been Uptown (north of Canal) for decades—despite it being just a couple of miles away. Things changed after Katrina, more so for whites than Blacks, because of the influx of people moving to the city from elsewhere who were not accustomed to staying put in one neighborhood. A bike culture emerged. All of a sudden you weren't sure if the person sitting next to you at the bar lived in the neighborhood or was just visiting. The new breweries, NOLA Brewing and Urban South among the first wave, followed more recently by Parleaux, the Courtyard, Miel, Port Orleans, Cajun Fire, and Second Line, to name a few, have added to the integration as brewery crawls have become a thing. Because of streetcars, bikes, and generally just ambling around, it's easy to visit five or six breweries by walking—drink in hand, of course; it's the rule in New Orleans. But as Watts notes, the taproom is beginning to compete with the experience of the neighborhood bar. Although the Avenue is still the only place in New Orleans to drink an Oud Bruin and then follow it up with something from Cloudwater, the locavore scene and the walkability of the Irish Channel/Garden District has made visiting multiple places more enticing. Neighborhood bars will survive, as Watts notes. Here's hoping that the Avenue is one of them.

The interview ends in true New Orleans fashion, with an invitation for another drink sometime later on down the road:

WATTS: You want some crawfish . . . I'm going to get me some. Do you know Brian Struke from Stillwater Brewing? He's coming by at five—you should come back then and hang out. He's going to pour some saisons and sours and eat some crawfish, so if you swing back by . . .

CHAPTER 3

Tapping History

Crafting Identity through Retrojection in the North Carolina Triangle Craft Beer Scene

NATHAN ROBERTS AND MICHAELA DeSOUCEY

Introduction

North Carolina has, relatively rapidly, become known as a "beer place." As of 2016, the state was ranked eighth in the nation for its number of breweries: more than 250 across cities, suburbs, and rural areas (Brewers Association 2016). Further accentuating this reputation, the North Carolina Craft Brewers Guild proudly proclaims the state to be "The State of Southern Beer" on its homepage Craft beer and especially brewing have become important components of what characterizes North Carolina's place-identity. Its breweries range in size from micro- and nano-breweries, to craft breweries that distribute through bottle shops and restaurants, to large craft breweries such as Sierra Nevada (founded and headquartered in Chico, California) and New Belgium (founded in Fort Collins, Colorado) that have expanded their national production and distribution by opening breweries in the western part of the state, in and near the city of Asheville (New Belgium n.d.; Sierra Nevada, n.d.). Despite some expectations that these scaled-up operations would be rebuffed in a city already known for its thirty-odd small, locally owned breweries, they have proven popular with locals and tourists alike (Bland 2014).

However, compared to other state-specific traditions of food and drink production, beer brewing has not always been important to North Carolina's cultural place-identity (or economy). Its history within the state is scattered and sparse, similar to many of the other places where European colonists and migrants from brewing cultures landed; they tended to use what was available to make something drinkable and intoxicating (Baron 1962; Kopp 2016; Myers and Ficke 2016). Even though the state's history does include some brewing (notably a brewery run by Moravians in the town of Salem between 1774 and 1813, a Stroh Brewery Company plant that opened in 1970, and a Miller Brewing Company plant that opened in 1978; Myers and Ficke 2016), production never reached a level or economy of scale even close to that of Midwestern states such as Wisconsin and Missouri (Baron 1962). Moreover, North Carolina's cities were early adopters of the "noble experiment" of Prohibition, with Asheville adopting legislation against alcohol production and consumption seven years before the nation as a whole, which outlawed its few existing breweries (Glenn 2012). After Prohibition's 1933 repeal, owners of mills and factories—ostensibly worried about employee no-shows—convinced state legislators to adopt a law imposing a cap on alcohol by volume (ABV) in beer produced, distributed, and consumed in the state (Hartis 2015).

Because of this limit, North Carolina's current beer scene has primarily been a twenty-first-century development. Although the first "craft" brewery opened in 1986 (Myers and Ficke 2016), the growth of the industry mainly followed the "Pop the Cap" movement and law, signed in 2005, that raised the legal ABV limit in beer produced and consumed in the state from 5.9 percent to 15 percent (Glenn 2012; Hartis 2013, 2015; Myers and Ficke 2016). In the years prior to Pop the Cap's enactment, an average of 1.5 new breweries were opening per year. Afterward, foundings averaged 14.1 per year from 2006 to 2014; openings since 2014 have continued to rise. If nothing else, the fact that North Carolina has the most craft breweries in the American South, both numerically and per capita, makes the state a newly veritable "beer place" in what has been called a modern national beer renaissance (Crouch 2010).

This lack of deep, embedded brewing history poses a curious paradox. Researchers have shown that in many other locales, breweries—especially craft breweries—use localized histories of beer production in marketing their businesses and their products as "authentic" (Aupers, O'Neill, and Houtman 2014; Hatch and Schultz 2017; Koontz 2010; Koontz and Chapman 2019), in differentiating themselves from other producers (Carroll and Swaminathan 2000), and in emphasizing the valued cultural particularities of place (Flack 1997; Mathews and Picton 2014; Schnell and Reese 2003). For example, the founder of Chicago's Goose Island Brewery—a nationally known craft brewery that opened in 1988 and was sold, to the dismay of many (Frake 2016; Noel 2018), first to another brewery in 2006 and then to Anheuser-Busch InBev in 2011—picked its specific location because Chicago was, according to its organizational materials, "a city classically set up for brewers."

But North Carolina—especially outside of the relatively isolated Appalachian Mountains, where some illicit distilleries may have survived through Prohibition (Stephenson and Mulder 2017)—lacks direct or strong historical connections to brewing beer. We ask, then, what happens when brewers have no clear-cut history or place-identity to draw upon? In this chapter, we explore how members of the craft-brewing industry in the Triangle area of North Carolina (Raleigh, Durham, Chapel Hill, and surrounding towns, comprising the state's most populated region) are distinguishing themselves and their offerings by using alternative, tenuous-at-best historical referents and narratives to root themselves in place.

Our analysis—combining insights from interviews with people involved in the craft-brewing industry, texts about the state's brewing history, and germane media and website data—reveals how craft brewers are *rewriting* local (non-beer) histories that connote place in order to situate and differentiate their organizations' identities in affective and meaningful ways. We find that, in effect, they are repackaging relatively disconnected past events and peoples for today's beer consumers and, as such, altering the historical narratives that characterize place. We argue that this altering of history and the dialectical reconstruction of place that comes from it clearly represents what Berger and Luckmann (1966) refer to as *retrojection*, or attempts by social actors to realign, rewrite, and shift understandings of the past by accentuating a few carefully selected historical actions to create threads of temporal continuity and legitimate the present reality. The result of retrojection, as Berger and Luckmann posit, is a shared sense of the practice's perceived inevitability. We argue here that retrojection has proven a culturally resonant strategy in allowing actors to "tap history" by creating and promoting narratives for others to integrate into their understandings of place and into the multifaceted ways place can shape identity.

Temporality and Retrojection

Central to sociological theories regarding the social construction of place—as "space" imbued with the meanings invested in a location (Gieryn 2000)—are ideas about shared history and custom for members of a particular community (Anderson 1983; DeSoucey 2016) and how we more generally relate to those around us (Brown-Saracino 2018). In other words, "place" is space that is somehow special. The act of writing history itself thus engenders narratives that influence feelings of affective belonging and group-level understandings of place. The narratives constructed around special places typically speak of the qualities that enrich them and set them apart from others. As revisionist historians have often noted, historical chronicles and arguments are never truly linear or fully objective, but rather are influenced by the authors' positionality and intentions (Zinn 2003).

This phenomenon aligns with social theorists' arguments that the past and future both exist principally as ideas situated within an ever-developing and dynamic present (Fabian 1983). Mead (1932) called this concept the *specious present* in his pragmatic theory of temporality (see also Flaherty and Fine 2001; Maines, Sugrue, and Katovich 1983); suggesting that social actors continually reorganize and realign understandings of the past (and, consequently, imaginings of the future) to marshal and maintain a sense of historical continuity with the present (Flaherty and Fine 2001; Katovich and Couch 1992; Mead 1932; Maines, Sugrue, and Katovich 1983). Berger and Luckmann (1966) further labeled this process *retrojection*.

The re-creation of history through retrojection—wherein actors reinterpret the past based upon needs and desires in the present— allows for a presumptive conception of social reality that can be used to hold groups together and give them purpose (Berger and Luckmann 1966; Fine 2013; Hobsbawm and Ranger 1983). As the retrojection process implies, histories may require revisions to be useful in the present. "Difficult" events or pasts, for example, undoubtedly require the renegotiation of meaning in order to avoid negative connotations or stigmatizing identities in the present and near future (Rivera 2008; Wagner-Pacifici and Schwartz 1991). By recasting the details and deeper meanings of historical events or places, groups externalize, objectify, and internalize their own framing strategies to make them comprehensible in particular ways (Berger and Luckmann 1966).

Prior research on craft beer and brewing has examined breweries' uses of history in their promotional work, though it does not enumerate Berger and Luckmann's theory as we do. This growing body of research has tended toward two main threads: authenticity and neolocality. First, drawing on Carroll and Swaminathan's (2000) population ecology analysis of authenticity and the early microbrewery movement, Koontz (2010) shows that brewers use "traditionalizing" narratives to describe their products and production practices in order to make them appear authentic. Similarly, Hatch and Schultz (2017) examined how the Carlsberg Group, one of the world's largest brewery groups, drew on the company's founding myths to brand a new craft beer product as authentic. Yet authenticity can be a fickle concept for beer consumers who profess to care about producer identity and product quality (Frake 2016). As Aupers, O'Neill, and Houtman (2014) argued in their analysis of historical narratives around brewing, an "aura of authenticity" can easily be challenged upon close scrutiny (see also Barlow, Verhaal, and Hoskins 2018).

Researchers also have identified craft brewers' strategic employment of historical resources and narratives to draw attention to place. This work of *neolocality* (Flack 1997) involves breweries using local historical reference points in identifying themselves and their products to opportunistically create attachment to place. These points include important historical events, such as Great Lakes Brewing's Burning River IPA (Schnell and Reese 2003), and making visible their reuse of derelict industrial buildings to house their brewpubs (Mathews and Picton 2014). Such use of historicized, place-specific referents helps to retroject symbols of place identity while drawing lines about who or what is included in the "local."

Data and Methods

We based our analysis of craft brewing in the Triangle region of North Carolina on qualitative data collected through mixed-methods research. Between July 2016 and January 2017, the first author conducted in-depth, semistructured interviews with thirteen people involved in the brewing industry in the region. We also analyzed three recent book-length texts written about the history of brewing in North Carolina, examining the discursive strategies used to emplace brewing within North Carolina's social history. To bolster these data, we collected and analyzed secondary data from brewery websites, newspaper articles about the state's craft beer movement and industry, blogs, and podcasts; and conducted a material-culture analysis of Triangle breweries' beer labels and advertising campaigns.

Our findings point to three strategies used by Triangle area brewers and breweries that require varying levels of retrojection to fit historical narratives into the present-day social context of North Carolinian craft brewing. First, brewers "tap" localized histories to authenticate their products and businesses using idiosyncratic historical events, figures, and geographical markers (Flack 1997). Second, they break from—and re-create—brewing traditions to make new beer styles that are unique and eclectic. This can include reinterpreting the meaning and stringency of long-standing brewing codes (e.g., the *Reinheitsgebot*) or introducing variations on a theme in standard beer styles by using local ingredients and creating place-specific styles and types. Third, they rewrite local histories, often reconfiguring linear notions of time and space, with the goal of orienting craft brewing toward placemaking and centrality in the state's place-identity.

Analysis

REWRITING LOCAL HISTORY

As mentioned, the history of brewing beer in North Carolina is relatively scant (Myers and Ficke 2016), generally equivalent to other locales where European migrants coming from brewing traditions established themselves (Baron 1962). Yet, the recent expansion of craft brewing in North Carolina, and the seeming need to have it appear as the continuation of a rich tradition, has involved a wholesale reconstruction of this state-level history.

Three recent books on North Carolina's craft-brewing history (Glenn 2012; Hartis 2013; Myers and Ficke 2016) use methodical archival and historical research—meaning they are not falsifying or mythicizing the past necessarily (see Maines et al. 1983)—to create and solidify readers' expectations about beer and place. In fact, we rely on these texts to inform our own understanding of North Carolina's brewing history and do not distrust their source material. The focus of our analysis, rather, is the narratives created in these sources that emphasize key elements in indexing practices and promoting North Carolina's beer scene as an "implied objective reality" (Maines et al. 1983).

The authors of each text proffer select events as hard evidence of the seemingly historical continuity and inevitability of brewing in the state. For example, Myers and Ficke's 2016 *North Carolina Craft Beer & Breweries*, which is based on archival research conducted at the University of North Carolina at Chapel Hill's libraries, confronts the general historical account of brewing in the state, and then offers a replacement narrative of an *obvious* progenitor of contemporary craft-brewing culture:

> Traditional histories of North Carolina say little or no brewing was done in the state's past. They cite the warm, humid climate and ignore the generation of British, Scottish, German, and Czech immigrants who settled North Carolina. Having arrived from beer-drinking cultures, those immigrants were unlikely to forgo their favorite beverage simply because of a little weather. . . . Christopher von Graffenried included in his Account of the Founding of New Bern . . . a letter from a colonist to a kinsman in Germany requesting that he send brewing equipment. (1)

The other two authors offer subtler approaches in situating their historiographies of brewing as a cultural practice in North Carolina. Glenn's (2012) history of brewing in the city of Asheville points toward the distilling of illegal whiskey, or moonshine, as a foundation for the popular craft-brewing scene there today:

> The first Asheville City Directory (1883–84) notes that when the first Buncombe County commissioners were appointed to select a location for the county seat in 1797, they originally chose a site roughly where Biltmore Village now sits. . . . The commissioners were swayed by a taste of the local "mountain dew" at a small tavern . . . unanimously changed their minds, and, acceding to the wishes of the tavern-keeper, decided the "*best place for a town to be* [our emphasis added] was where good whiskey was plenty." . . . And a town that was founded "where good whiskey was plenty" would be *destined* [our emphasis added] to become a city where good beer is plenty too (p. 22).

By claiming that moonshine production was *destined* to result in craft beer production, this excerpt portrays beer brewing as a foreseeable place-based and placemaking outcome. Alcohol production is alcohol production, in this narrative. This discursive construction of historical inevitability, as well as the centrality of the practices to bookending a city's history and identity, retrojectively helps to draw temporal continuity.

Through giving these histories a sense of direct linearity, authors of texts about craft brewing provide a purposive narrative of shared history around imagined communities (Anderson 1983). By emphasizing key events for readers, authors present common frameworks for making sense of such communities' past. The key event that was formative to craft beer and brewing in North Carolina is Pop the Cap, which has since become a key element of beer-making's "sticky culture" (Fine 2013) in the state. Each of the three texts we analyzed elucidates Pop the Cap as a turning point in the historical narrative before offering overviews of the recent craft beer scene.

Pop the Cap refers to a statewide movement organized in the early 2000s by local independent brewers, beer journalists, and craft beer connoisseurs to beseech legislators to raise the 5.9 percent ABV cap on beer sold to North Carolinians (Hartis 2015). The movement's successful outcome altered the social and legal landscape of North Carolina craft beer consumption, and then production. As one of the brewers interviewed in this study stated:

> It is important to understand Pop the Cap not as a "Oh, we finally have beers that are higher alcohol" and all that kinda stuff. What it did was it opened up the market to breweries and distributors that could talk to breweries that had portfolios that were halfway over 6 percent and halfway under 6 percent. . . . So, all of a sudden you have this rush of breweries on the market that were all over the country. It was really exciting to see that.

What had once been a barren desert of industrial beer and a tiny selection of craft beers became an oasis in the southeastern United States' craft beer market. Established craft breweries from elsewhere could now bring their larger beer portfolios into the state. This brewer's memory of Pop the Cap and the market changes it instigated was far from unique in our sample, highlighting how members of the brewing community position its historical legacy in the Triangle region and North Carolina more generally. Pop the Cap has even been commemorated in the culture of North Carolina craft beer production. Carolina Brewing Co. (located in the town of Holly Springs) paid homage to it with their 15 percent ABV "Old 392" Barleywine, named for the original law limiting beer ABV. Our interviewees' frequent references to this statewide event, and for a few their participation in it, has thus helped situate craft beer's role and importance in the production of state-level culture (Peterson 1997).

USING LOCAL HISTORY

North Carolina's (European-informed) history stretches to the foundings of the American colonies, with its earliest colony being located on Roanoke Island on the state's coast (Powell 1988). Breweries, in attempts to authenticate and neolocalize themselves and their products (Koontz 2010; Mathews and Picton 2014; Schnell and Reese 2003), have drawn widely upon this extensive state history. As Schnell and Reese (2003) argue, using local historical events signals that businesses are community insiders. Using such events also prompts retrojection into the specific referents to legitimize current brewing practices.

For example, Regulator Brewing Co. in the town of Hillsborough uses the story of the 1766 Regulator Movement as a localization strategy that emphasizes political motivation in their business identity. The Regulator Movement (which culminated in Hillsborough) was a farmer-led insurrection against the colonial elite in the eastern part of North Carolina over new taxes instituted to build the governor's mansion (see Powell 1988; Zinn 2003). Although concerns with agriculture indubitably played a role in the movement, the grievances mobilizing the farmers were primarily related to class inequality and distrust of political authority (Zinn 2003). Regulator Brewing has reconstructed an historical understanding of the movement to embed it in their brand identity. The "About Us" section on the company's website states, "The Regulators in pre-Revolutionary NC fought for the small farmers' right to participate fairly in the *local economy* [emphasis added]. Not only do we support this standard, we believe that products grown by local farms are better for us and our beer" (Regulator Brewing Co. n.d.).

A couple of elements are worth noting in this retrojection of the historical narrative. First, highlighting the role and importance of "small farmers" repeats a key marketing tool of many craft breweries by conceptually linking the craft beer and local food movements and thus valorizing local identities. Using local farmers and local agricultural sources—as suppliers as well as rhetorical devices—further gives these breweries' products an air of *terroir*, or a particularized taste of place (Bowen 2015; Paxson 2012; Trubek 2008), even in a place that lacks established or transgenerational breweries. Second, supporting fair prices for farmers within the local economy more than slightly alters the initial grievances of the Regulator Movement, which were also inextricable from evangelical Christianity (Kars 2002) and pre-Revolutionary North Carolinian social contexts. Through emphasizing consumer market participation as an analogous political action, Regulator has resituated what was initially a subversive and revolutionary fervor with its business identity and activities in today's market.

Triangle breweries also use locally resonant iconographies in developing their products and brand identities to emphasize their connection to place (even when the referents are not derivative of the Triangle itself). For example, the now defunct Mystery Brewing Company, also located in Hillsborough, created Queen Anne's Revenge, a black ale that they called a "Carolinian Dark Ale" (to play on the beer term Cascadian Dark Ale; Mystery Brewing Company n.d.). Named after the infamous pirate Blackbeard's ship, which he intentionally sunk off the North Carolina coast in 1718 (Powell 1989, Mystery's branding of this beer—whose label featured a pirate skeleton holding a pint of beer—not only taps into bygone events but also furthers their attempt to establish and popularize a new beer style particular to North Carolina.

BREAKING TRADITIONS

As we found across interviews, Triangle-area brewers treat existing brewing traditions as evolving cultures that may be altered, integrated, expanded upon, and in some cases even discarded. The sixteenth-century Bavarian brewing code, the *Reinheitsgebot*, represents the dominant tradition that brewers today more generally use as an interpretative culture. Created as part of a pre-industrial Bavarian tax code (Smale 2016), the *Reinheitsgebot* established the main ingredients local authorities allowed in beer: water, hops, barley, and (added later) yeast. Even though the *Reinheitsgebot* was only ever enforceable in Bavaria—and has since been integrated into conceptions of German cultural heritage (Smale 2016)—it has offered new American brewers a starting line for differentiating micro- and craft brews from industrially produced beer.

Nationally, a number of craft brewers have disavowed the *Reinheitsgebot* as outdated and stifling of creativity and craft (Smale 2016). Brewers within the Triangle region, however, hold contradictory perspectives on this centuries-old mandate. Red Oak Brewery, located in the town of Whitsett (on the region's edge), openly endorses adhering to the brewing code on its website, yet reframes its primary purpose: "Although the Law of Purity has undergone some amendments over the years, the bottom line is that we adhere to the Purity Law of 1516 by using only water, malted barley, yeast and hops. Red Oak Brewery is committed to *brewing the best beer possible using only the very best ingredients*" (Red Oak Brewery n.d., emphasis added). Instead of simply offering a list of ingredients to be used, Red Oak interprets the *Reinheitsgebot* as implying a broader goal: the use of quality ingredients to produce quality products. By recasting the law's purpose, Red Oak turns it into a living cultural artifact and tradition that can take on new meanings in different sociohistoric contexts.

Other (mainly veteran) brewers in the region also view the *Reinheitsgebot* as an important component of making quality products. When asked about his views on it, one longtime brewer stated:

> Almost all of our beers fall that way. . . . And that's going back to us being kinda old school. We don't make beers with strawberries, peaches, blueberries, coffee, chocolate—'cause all those things don't fall under the *Reinheitsgebot*, and you know, get you [disqualified] for that. So, 99 percent of the beers we make would fall under that anyway. . . . I think it's harder making a really good— not really good beer, but it's hard to make *eye-catching* beer or *newsworthy* beer or *flashy* beer [emphasis added] when you're only using the four.

This brewer views the limits set by the brewing code as necessitating higher levels of skill and craft. In his mind, working within the centuries-old framework creates a welcome challenge, forcing rather than stifling creativity. Yet this statement also reinterprets the *Reinheitsgebot*. Quality and skill, not ingredients, are at the forefront of how this brewer construes the code.

When asked directly about the *Reinheitsgebot*, brewers who are newer to the field tended to disavow and disregard it as outdated in the contemporary context of American craft beer. As one brewer explained, the *Reinheitsgebot* was once valuable but has outlived its usefulness:

> It was cool back in the day. I mean, like, in 1516 it was relevant . . . it was kind of important because people were adding additives that were toxic . . . But I mean the way beer is right now, people,

especially in the US where people expect all the hops, there's not much use for the *Reinheitsgebot*. Definitely, it came about as a necessity, obviously. After that it was cool for a couple hundred years, but it's not really applicable anymore.

Each of these interpretations of the *Reinheitsgebot* is based upon a present, though different, understanding of a given past. Each requires resituating the code and its accompanying benefits and drawbacks. Together they are prime illustrations of how retrojection influences brewers' activities and motivations.

Conclusion

Prior research on craft brewing has examined the importance of history to brewers' claims of authenticity and locality (Flack 1997; Koontz 2010; Kopp 2016; Mathews and Picton 2014; Schnell and Reese 2003). Other researchers have analyzed how growing consumer markets for craft brewing involve storytelling (Smith Maguire et al. 2017), rationalization (Elliott 2017), and the influences of larger political economic systems (Beckham 2017). We extend these lines of research to consider how the craft beer movement and industry in North Carolina's Triangle region situate history in its present and future activities, highlighting the selective representation and reinterpretation—what Berger and Luckmann (1966) called retrojection—of place-based referents, events, and objects. The dialectical effects of using these carefully chosen (but loosely interpreted) historical narratives—whether as savvy marketing or sincere attempts to embed brewing in the state's image and culture—indubitably create a sense of social order in this popular and growing craft beer scene.

Brewers' deployment of circumstantial narratives and place-based referents help locate themselves as members of a community with a common history (Fine 2010). However, brewers do not accept these circumstances wholesale, instead recasting events and entities—from pirate ships to Bavarian brewing codes—to legitimate their brewing processes, ingredients used, business size, and even who is allowed to participate in brewing. Retrojection is thus, we posit, a process of engagement. It allows actors to reinterpret and realign history with their current practices and desires, which potentially influences how others also speak to a sense of place and value. Part of the compelling charm of recognizable symbols like Blackbeard's ship and the Regulator

Movement is that they offer ways for entrepreneurial brewers to sub-stantiate who they are, as well as for their consumers to cognitively authenticate breweries' identities (Kroezen and Heugens 2012). And although this retrojection leads to neolocality (Flack 1997), it also pro-vokes subjectively informed transformations of place identity.

Craft brewers also use historical narratives to contextualize them-selves as headstrong newcomers in an old industry. Again, though, we see these narratives as reconfigured through processes of retrojection. Brewing practices, such as applying the "purity" of the *Reinheitsgebot*, offer a sense of legitimacy for products and businesses. Yet it is unreal-istic to assume that brewing rules established in sixteenth-century Bavaria have a direct influence on practices undertaken currently and thousands of miles away. Just as beer evolves within different organi-zational and political contexts, the historicity evoked through cultural rhetorics of quality, purity, heritage, and authenticity imbues breweries with a sense of significance. Symbols and representations of place often appear at moments where they can be put to use (Katovich and Couch 1992). As a result, new breweries present themselves as extensions of proud traditions of craft and independence in a global market domi-nated by a few multinational conglomerates.

Last, we note that actors with vested interests and nominally the same community can, through strategies of retrojection, create com-peting and contradictory understandings of the past. We suggest that conceiving of retrojection as a cultural process illuminates how actors connect the past with anticipated futures, which effectively shapes the present. As these histories are disseminated and accepted by commu-nities at large, they impact a place's identity anew. Within the Triangle region and North Carolina as a whole, retrojection by craft breweries and brewers has offered a new, unfolding storyline for the state in the twenty-first century. No longer bound to tobacco or textiles, North Carolina has indeed become a beer place.

References

Anderson, Benedict. 1983. *Imagined Communities*. London: Verso.

Aupers, Stef, Carly O'Neill, and Dick Houtman. 2014. "Advertising Real Beer: Authenticity Claims beyond Truth and Falsity." *European Journal of Cultural Studies* 17(5):585–601.

Barlow, Matthew A., J. Cameron Verhaal, and Jake D. Hoskins. 2018. "Guilty by Association: Product-Level Category Stigma and Audience Expectations in the U.S. Craft Beer Industry." *Journal of Management* 44(7):2934–60.

Baron, Stanley. 1962. *Brewed in America: A History of Beer and Ale in the United States.* Boston: Little, Brown.

Beckham, J. Nikol. 2017. "Entrepreneurial Leisure and the Microbrew Revolution: The Neoliberal Origins of the Craft Beer Movement." Pp. 80–101. In *Untapped: Exploring the Cultural Dimensions of Craft Beer,* edited by Nathaniel G. Chapman, Slade Lellock, and Cameron D. Lippard. Morgantown: University of West Virginia Press.

Berger, Peter and Thomas Luckmann. 1966. *The Social Construction of Reality: A Treatise in the Sociology of Knowledge.* New York: Anchor Books.

Bland, A. 2014. "Big Breweries Move into Small Beer Town—and Business Is Hopping." *The Salt,* May 28 (http://www.npr.org/blogs/thesalt/2014/05/28 /316317087/big-breweries-move-into-small-beer-town-and-business-is -hopping).

Bowen, Sarah. 2015. *Divided Spirits: Tequila, Mezcal, and the Politics of Production.* Oakland: University of California Press.

Brewers Association of America. 2016. "State Craft Beer Sales & Production Statistics, 2017." Retrieved November 22, 2018 (https://www.brewersassociation .org/statistics/by-state/?state=NC).

Brown-Saracino, Japonica. 2018. *How Places Make Us: Novel LBQ Identities in Four Small Cities.* Chicago: University of Chicago Press.

Carroll, Glenn and Anand Swaminathan. 2000. "Why the Microbrewery Movement? Organizational Dynamics of Resource Partitioning in the U.S. Brewing Industry." *American Journal of Sociology* 106(3):715–62.

Crouch, Andy. 2010. *Great American Craft Beer: A Guide to the Nation's Finest Beers and Breweries.* Philadelphia: Running Press Adult.

DeSoucey, Michaela. 2016. *Contested Tastes: Foie Gras and the Politics of Food.* Princeton, NJ: Princeton University Press.

Elliott, Michael. 2017. "The Rationalization of Craft Beer from Medieval Monks to Modern Microbrewers: A Weberian Analysis." Pp. 59–79. In *Untapped: Exploring the Cultural Dimensions of Craft Beer,* edited by Nathaniel G. Chapman, Slade Lellock, and Cameron D. Lippard. Morgantown: University of West Virginia Press.

Fabian, Johannes. 1983. *Time and the Other: How Anthropology Makes Its Object.* New York: Columbia University Press.

Fine, Gary Alan. 2010. "The Sociology of the Local: Action and Its Publics." *Sociological Theory* 28(4):355–76.

———. 2013. "Sticky Cultures: Memory Publics and Communal Pasts in Competitive Chess." *Cultural Sociology* 7(4):395–414.

Flack, Wes. 1997. "American Microbreweries and Neolocalism: 'Aleing' for a Sense of Place." *Journal of Cultural Geography* 16(2):37–53.

Flaherty, Michael and Gary Alan Fine. 2001. "Present, Past, and Future." *Time & Society* 10(2–3):147–61.

Frake, Justin. 2016. "Selling Out: The Inauthenticity Discount in the Craft Beer Industry." *Management Science* 63(11):3930–43.

Gieryn, Thomas. 2000. "A Space for Place in Sociology." *Annual Review of Sociology* 26:463–96.

Glenn, Anne. 2012. *Asheville Beer: An Intoxicating History of Mountain Brewing.* Charleston, SC: American Palate.

Hartis, Daniel. 2013. *Charlotte Beer: A History of Brewing in the Queen City*. Charleston, SC: American Palate.

——. 2015. "Pop the Cap Initiative Celebrates 10 years." *Our State Magazine*. Retrieved January 30, 2017 (https://www.ourstate.com/pop-the-cap-north -carolina/).

Hatch, Mary Jo and Majken Schultz. 2017. "Toward a Theory of Using History Authentically: Historicizing in the Carlsberg Group." *Administrative Science Quarterly* 62(4):657–97.

Hobsbawm, Eric and Terence Ranger. 1983. *The Invention of Tradition*. Cambridge, UK: Cambridge University Press.

Kars, Marjoleine. 2002. *Breaking Loose Together: The Regulator Rebellion in Pre-revolutionary North Carolina*. Chapel Hill: University of North Carolina Press.

Katovich, Michael and Carl Couch. 1992. "The Nature of Social Pasts and Their Use as Foundations for Situated Action." *Symbolic Interaction* 15(1):25–47.

Koontz, Amanda. 2010. "Constructing Authenticity: A Review of Trends and Influences in the Process of Authentication in Consumption." *Sociology Compass* 4(11):977–88.

Koontz, Amanda and Nathaniel G. Chapman. 2019. "About Us: Authenticating Identity Claims in the Craft Beer Industry." *Journal of Popular Culture* 52(2):351–72.

Kopp, Peter. 2016. *Hoptopia: A World of Agriculture and Beer in Oregon's Willamette Valley*. Oakland: University of California Press.

Kroezen, Jochem and Pursey Heugens. 2012. "Organizational Identity Formation: Processes of Identity Imprinting and Enactment in the Dutch Microbrewing Landscape." Pp. 89–128. In *Identity in and around Organizations*, edited by M. Schultz, S. Maguire, A. Langley, and H. Tsoukas. Oxford, UK: Oxford University Press.

Maines, David, Noreen Sugrue, and Michael Katovich. 1983. "The Sociological Import of G. H. Mead's Theory of the Past." *American Sociological Review* 48(6):161–73.

Mathews, Vanessa and Roger Picton. 2014. "Intoxifying Gentrification: Brew Pubs and the Geography of Post-industrial Heritage." *Urban Geography* 35(3):337–56.

Mead, George Herbert. 1932. *The Philosophy of the Present*. Amherst, NY: Prometheus Books.

Myers, Erik and Sarah Ficke. 2016. *North Carolina Craft Beer & Breweries*. 2nd ed. Winston-Salem, NC: John F. Blair.

Mystery Brewing. n.d. "Our Beer." Retrieved October 17, 2018 (http://www .mysterybrewing.com/our-beer.html).

New Belgium. n.d. "Brewery: Asheville." Retrieved October 17, 2018 (https://www .newbelgium.com/brewery/asheville/).

Noel, Josh. 2018. *Barrel-Aged Stout and Selling Out: Goose Island, Anheuser-Busch, and How Craft Beer Became Big Business*. Chicago: Chicago Review Press.

Paxson, Heather. 2012. *The Life of Cheese: Crafting Food and Value in America*. Berkeley: University of California Press.

Peterson, Richard. 1997. *Creating Country Music: Fabricating Authenticity*. Chicago: University of Chicago Press.

Powell, William. 1989. *North Carolina: Through Four Centuries*. Chapel Hill: The University of North Carolina Press.

Red Oak Brewery. n.d. "Law of Purity." Retrieved January 15, 2016 (http://www
.redoakbrewery.com/law-of-purity.html).

Regulator Brewing Co. n.d. "About Us." Retrieved January 15, 2016 (http://www
.regulatorbrewing.com/about/).

Rivera, Lauren. 2008. "Managing 'Spoiled' National Identity: War, Tourism, and
Memory in Croatia." *American Sociological Review* 73(4):613–34.

Schnell, Steven and Joseph Reese. 2003. "Microbreweries as Tools of Local Identity."
Journal of Cultural Geography 21(1):45–69.

Sierra Nevada. n.d. "North Carolina Brewery Tour." Retrieved October 17, 2018
(https://sierranevada.com/brewery/north-carolina/brewery-tour).

Smale, Alison. 2016. "Beer Purity Law, A German Tradition (and Marketing Tool),
Turns 500." *New York Times*, May 14 (https://www.nytimes.com/2016/05/15
/world/europe/beer-purity-law-a-german-tradition-and-marketing-tool-turns
-500.html).

Smith Maguire, Jennifer, Jessica Bain, Andrea Davies, and Maria Touri. 2017.
"Storytelling and Market Formation: An Exploration of Craft Brewers in the
United Kingdom." Pp. 19–38. In *Untapped: Exploring the Cultural Dimensions
of Craft Beer*, edited by Nathaniel G. Chapman, Slade Lellock, and Cameron D.
Lippard. Morgantown: University of West Virginia Press.

Stephenson, Frank and Barbara Nichols Mulder. 2017. *North Carolina Moonshine:
An Illicit History*. Charleston, SC: The History Press.

Trubek, Amy. 2008. *The Taste of Place: A Cultural Journey into Terroir*. Berkeley:
University of California Press.

Wagner-Pacifici, Robin and Barry Schwartz. 1991. "The Vietnam Veterans
Memorial: Commemorating a Difficult Past." *American Journal of Sociology*
97(2):376–420.

Zinn, Howard. 2003. *A People's History of the United States*. New York: HarperCollins.

Postcard from Boulder

ELLIS JONES

Avery Brewing, as of 2019, was the fifth-largest brewery in Colorado. In 2015, it moved from a humble space built inside a web of temporary storage facilities on the edge of Boulder proper to a state-of-the-art facility on a sizeable chunk of land just outside the city. Similar to Allagash Brewing in Maine, Avery invited smaller "satellite" breweries to pop up right next door where they could benefit from the proximity to and relationship with their larger neighbor. This has proven to be a fascinating part of the culture of craft brewing—the open exchange of tips, tricks, strategies, and guidance among brewers and breweries. But, as you'll read below, that culture is shifting.

Avery is also interesting because, to maintain its rapid growth, it ultimately sold much of itself to a larger, international beer company, Spain's Mahou San Miguel Group. What many craft beer purists call "selling out," swiftly growing craft brewers see as a necessary step to maintain growth and open new markets that aren't as saturated with options as the ones where they have been competing. This is quickly becoming the norm. Breweries are banding together (e.g., the CANarchy craft brewery collective), or larger breweries are buying smaller ones to try and improve their prospects in an industry bursting with consumer choices. And it doesn't stop there: to stay on the industry's cutting edge, craft breweries are now feeling pressure to expand beyond beer itself. This interview gives us one example (and perhaps insight into others) of how craft breweries are having to rework their own narrative of what it means to be making "craft beer" as they attempt to adapt to their own rapid success.

Joe Osborne is a very laid back, outdoorsy, marketing manager at Avery who has been with the brewery since the early days and has seen it (and the industry as a whole) grow and evolve.

JONES: So, tell me about how you've seen things around craft beer change since you got into it.

OSBORNE: It's no surprise that craft brewing [has changed] as a new industry in the mid-'90s to what it is now. And a big part of it was this transparency among everybody, [there] was really nothing proprietary ever. Everybody shared everything. And no more true than in Colorado, because this is obviously a hotbed of breweries, right? Like you think of California's population and Colorado's population and the amount of breweries that are open in Colorado rivals that of California [per capita]. Around the mid-'90s, [the] shelf space that we were able to jockey for and get is now at a premium, way more of a premium than it ever has been for us. There's a finite pie . . . the industry has become a mature industry. So numerically the sales are flat, just like mature market sales volume-wise. No surprise . . . you probably read about us—we accepted a partnership with Mahou out of Spain. They're a 130-year-old brewery out of Spain, and the way it works in Europe is totally different. You know they have, I think, about 30 to 35 percent of the market share in Spain. And then they're really strong in France, and really strong in a couple other western European countries. They're big. They also have international interests with large breweries made in South America and stuff like that. But either way, what they do is brew. And we lucked out. They're a privately owned company—like, six shareholders have Mahou in their last name, and it's still a 130-year-old European company. But the evolution of the industry in general, people like us want to grow, or want to do more, or kind of want to build our dreams. And to get there we have to change how we do business. The business of this changed. And these ownership arrangements have changed.

JONES: So, now Mahou owns Avery?

OSBORNE: Partially. So, they just moved to majority ownership—now it's 70 percent them and 30 percent Adam Avery and Larry Avery. They're privately held. And they're a long-term product-driven company. Right, that's the thing. So, all these ownership situations, there is a lot of VC [venture capital]. Fireman Capital or CANarchy, which is now the Oskar Blues Holding Company. What you're seeing right now is people want to move to ensure broad distribution. You have to gather up some brands. And so a lot of people are doing that. And on a local level, small guys are now doing it, but they're not small anymore. CANarchy is a big thing. It's a big investment company that holds multiple breweries. Like CBA [Craft Brew Alliance] did for a while back with Red Hook and Widmer and Kona. And then you're also seeing VC money come in to have those little five-year pushes in Hop Out. Like we just kind of saw a turn. Dogfish Head took on some investment back in the day, actually about five years ago. And we just saw the big news with them getting the partnership with Boston Beer Company. So that's evolution now.

So, where it was this really cool, homegrown, organic, US-made, Wild West story and industry—which felt really cool, too, because craft beer naturally has this self-identity tie-in with the consumers. It's like I'm in the NRA, or I'm a vegan, or I'm a CrossFitter, or whatever. With craft beer you're into what craft brewery you align with. It's a part of that identity, that core identity. So that's me—a marketing guy—talking. I guess my point there was just that, as we've evolved, the consumers have had to get a little bit more promiscuous. Whether it's Texas, or Nebraska, or Colorado especially, you're seeing there's too much new. So, then there's also a lot of new fighting over shelf space. And the other big thing right now is that breweries like us, we can't [rest on] our laurels. We're having to branch out into the BFY category, we're going to be doing a hard seltzer next year. We're having to diversify.

JONES: BFY?

OSBORNE: That's become the insider category acronym for "better for you," which is essentially low-calorie, gluten-free—I guess you could call it pure ingredients.

JONES: Like health beer.

OSBORNE: In a way.

JONES: Not even beer maybe.

OSBORNE: Yeah, yeah . . . FMB, fermented malt beverage. So, on the sales side, and distribution side in business, this journey into non-craft beer, FMB, is a diversification for your portfolio. It has become important, because we've also learned that people—just like they want more local craft beer to tie themselves into—as they venture away from beer and want a different alcohol beverage, they still kind of want that local thing.

JONES: That's interesting.

OSBORNE: So, it's like you're seeing Upslope release a seltzer. Denver Beer Co. just released—they actually created a whole off brand that's not even Denver Beer Co. [but once you dig a little deeper, it is]. And they're not a great big company, but they figured it was important enough to actually have this local, Colorado feel to hard seltzer. And then you have Wild Basin coming out of CANarchy, which is their hard seltzer. And that's because we're all looking at it like a business. You know? We all see the same report of quote-unquote craft brands with growth. Your top twenty-five in the last year or two, the majority has been BFY beers. I guess my answer is how we've changed is that we're all looking at business. We're still a craft company. We're still a local company—a local business—that has an offering for somebody: an alcoholic beverage.

JONES: Have you seen the laws change over time locally that have made things easier or harder in Colorado?

OSBORNE: Colorado specifically? I've thought about that a lot because that question comes up—why has Colorado been "the place," you know? Because you could argue that this is like Napa for craft beer. You've got New Belgium Beer. New Belgium is a twenty-five-year-old company that [annually produces] almost a million barrels of beer. And literally two people started it out of a garage. You know?

JONES: And look where it is now.

OSBORNE: It's insane, right? But they're in the same ebb and flow that we all are now. That being said, Colorado's been like this hotbed for those stories. New Belgium, O'Dell, CANarchy came out of here. CANarchy now owns what, Oskar Blues . . . it was just Oskar Blues and Dale. And I know the older guy who helped them sell it and it's like people I know, and have hung with, and drank with . . . *this* guy now is controlling an investment firm with brewery holdings! All around the country, Cigar City, and Terrapin, and—I think they've gone five breweries deep. Deep Ellum Brewing out of Dallas. And so, why Colorado, right? And so I've thought about that a lot, and my theory is that, the reason Colorado got to where it's at is because [of a] favorable regulatory climate for independent retail. And by that, I mean that Colorado, literally on January first, became just like the rest of the states in the country.

Before January first of 2019, there was a law here that made it so independent alcohol retail had a fighting chance. And because independent retail alcohol was around, like Union Jack in Louisville, Liquor Mart in Boulder—they're independent retailers because we're dealing with that—craft breweries who are small, independent companies did not have to fight through the business bureaucracy of getting into a chain. Talking to groceries and playing that game, which is not cheap. It is expensive. You have to hire people who know it and ask for big salaries. You have to play a sales and distribution game, specifically geared toward that retail model of chain and grocery. But in Colorado, all we had were independent dealers. And we all grew up with this access to literally be able to walk into one place, talk to one person at each place, who could make a decision. You can't do that in many other states.

And what you would have to rely on was the distributor relationship with that chain or that buyer. Like was it Kroger's—if you want to sell beer at a Kroger in Texas, you've got to go to Missouri to even get in front of that buyer and be taken seriously. And you have to have so much data behind you. So, Colorado craft breweries had all this success because the regulatory climate made it so all we had [were] independent retailers for a long time. Major volume does not flow through independent retailers in any other state. And now we're going to see that change with the Colorado law change.

JONES: Was that something you guys lobbied against or were you staying out of it?

OSBORNE: We're staying out of that because it was a sensitive spot for us as suppliers. It was very sensitive for suppliers because it was a rift between your distributor and your independent retailers. Your independent retailers didn't want it for the most part. And the distributors really wanted it because it's big business. And then you have to weigh both sides. So, we're talking about both our customers and the three-tier system. Our customers, the distributors, and our secondary customers through our distributors—the retailers. So, the suppliers stayed out of that.

JONES: Sure.

OSBORNE: That being said, you know, it's been good for us now that we're—

JONES: You're big enough.

OSBORNE: Yeah, yeah.

JONES: Do you guys find yourself involved in any kind of politics either via the laws or via other causes? Like some breweries are environmental, some have other things that they have going on.

OSBORNE: It's really just culture driven from our founder, you know. He has things that he cares about. But that's now what the brewery is about. That's been us. Upslope ties themselves to the Colorado outdoor identity. Oskar Blues ties themselves to that rebel country kind of thing. And O'Dell has a Colorado nature feel. New Belgium is about sustainability and the environment. Left Hand I would say is probably the most political or cause driven because they're employee owned, and they're staunchly behind the independent seal from the Brewers Association.

JONES: Oh, right.

OSBORNE: We don't fit into that technically anymore because of our ownership situation. So we all have these different identities. And we're seeing some things like Sufferfest. Sierra Nevada bought them, but Sufferfest was originally a BFY health brand. It's a better-for-you beer brand. All the beers they make are like that. And then they wanted to capture hardcore surfers, and hardcore bicyclists, and GoPro people. Whatever. So, I think what we're seeing is still more people adopting craft alcohol. And the demographic growing. More women are coming into the fold. More Latinos are coming into the fold. If you look at growth potential and categories, thirty-to-fifty-something males, with a college education and $50,000-plus income, are our core demo[graphic]. No surprise. But the growth ones are women. And getting more and more women interested in craft alcohol, and then more and more Latinos, that's a huge market coming.

JONES: Along those lines, has there ever been much of a focus on bring-ing people from that kind of macro-brew population to craft beer via crossover beers?

OSBORNE: That's a great question, and it's funny you ask that because I would say that a brewery that had specifically did that from early on—because the only way you can play with macros is price—you know, consumer habit is driven by two things. Price is number one, and accessibility's number two. Those are always the top two things that any customer's going to be looking for in any retail situation. Those are the primary decision-makers, especially in today's world.

JONES: Sure.

OSBORNE: No one wants to compete with domestic [macro-brewers]. Not only can we not do that with what we do . . . with our ingre-dients, and our process, and what our overheads are. But we don't want to. Right? It's just the story of cheap beer, and that's never what any of this has been about for any craft brewery. I think, though, there is a spot that's in between that and the $9.99 six-pack. There's a space in there that a lot of people are going after. We are. Everyone is. And some people just were early enough to the game, [Founders] All Day IPA is a great example. Man, even New Belgium has branched off with some brands that don't look like New Belgium at all. They tried out with Day Blazer, and they won their license agreement with CSU [Colorado State University] with Old Aggie. Just a price-sensitive lager, licensed for the local state college or university. And they're killing with that.

JONES: Interesting. One last thing. You know I've only ever seen this physically once before and that was in Maine with Allagash. And Allagash had, I think, Bissell Brothers and somebody else. They had their own brewery and then these little breweries started popping up next to them. And then they would share, and help, and collaborate. And they got them off the ground. And now some of them have moved away and are doing their own amaz-ing stuff. And I've noticed in this new Avery space—there are little breweries all dotted around us. And I was wondering about that collaboration. You mentioned it earlier in the evolution of the industry. And I was just wondering how Avery, and how Colorado, has fit into this practice where you help the little guy.

OSBORNE: It's funny—the podcast I was listening to with Dave and Scott, my buddies, Dave called it "co-opetition." That is a hallmark of the industry in general. And in Colorado, it's a huge part of the Colorado scene. And we have always been that. Here we were early adopters of a quality assurance program that involved a lab. Well, our original lab came because even we were drinking with people from Coors. And [the people from Coors] were like, "You want to come see a really cool lab?" And I was like, "Yeah." And they brought that back here. In the past we would actually have over any brewing upstart. We would let people come and shadow us for a while to see what our processes were. We'd share all sorts of stuff with them, like how we do our brewer's yeast. Like what we need to do on a small batch. So yeah, that's just built in. It's such a given.

JONES: How about customers? Have you seen the politics of craft beer consumers change?

OSBORNE: I see a lot of people from all over political spectrums and lifestyle spectrums drinking beer in the same place. You don't see that [in] many places. I'm proud of that. Personally, I do care who I vote for. Do I care who you vote for? I know what I'm into. If you're not into that, that's cool. The whole thing is that I see suits, sitting next to a family of friggin' sun dresses. So . . . it's great. That's what we want.

JONES: Yeah. Like back to the public houses maybe someday.

OSBORNE: Literally what we're going for is to put the *public* back in *pub*. Yeah.

JONES: I like it.

I wrap up the interview at this point, buy a couple of hard-to-find bottles of Avery's good stuff (they make an amazing raspberry sour), and jump on my bike to head back home.

CHAPTER 4

Taproom Authenticity

JEFF RICE

In the movie *Office Space*, the data-entry workers occasionally break away from the drudgery of white-collar cubicle work to have a beer at Chotchkie's, a TGI Fridays ripoff. In the TV show *The Office*, the characters escape the monotony of selling paper out of their office cubicles to drink at Bernie's Tavern. The show *Northern Exposure* took place largely in Holling's bar, the Brick, in remote Alaska, far from the city's daily workflow. In *The Wire*, off-duty police officers often got drunk at Kavanaugh's, whereas Avon Barksdale and Stringer Bell preferred the Red Star for plotting how to upend conventional sales. One of the most canonical TV bars might be Moe's Tavern, the rundown space of refuge in *The Simpsons*, where only one type of beer is served and a jar of pickled eggs sits uneaten.

I begin with this brief survey of popular representations of beer drinking in order to draw attention to the overall question of beer and authenticity, particularly regarding sites of beer consumption. The authentic place to drink beer, as posed in generic television representations, is in the generic idea of the bar. By contrast, craft beer—independent, not owned partially or wholly by a conglomerate such as InBev, Molson Coors, or Heineken, and made by a brewery producing fewer than six million barrels per year—defines its authenticity via the taproom. A taproom is not a bar. The taproom, the public space of a brewery where beer can be purchased and consumed on premises, serves as a focal point of a given community, not just as a site for drinking as my introductory examples attest. The taproom's authenticity is styled differently from that of the bar. Bars traditionally have been places of alcohol consumption; sometimes they are dimly lit, sometimes they offer Pabst Blue Ribbon,[1] sometimes they sell cheap whiskey and vodka, sometimes they offer pool and darts, sometimes they remain open into early morning. A taproom's authenticity is built into its design: it typically receives outside light, may have outdoor seating, is family friendly, may have couches and tables, sometimes sits behind a glass or open wall through which brewery operations can be observed, and doesn't serve hard alcohol.

In opposition to mass-produced, conglomerate-owned breweries, craft beer positions itself as authentic. The Brewers Association, the main craft beer trade organization, promotes craft beer authenticity via its "Independent" labels that brewers are encouraged to affix to bottles and cans. Being "independent," craft beer understands itself as outside of a bar-centric focus whose mass replication and genetic traits contrast with the craft beer ethos of individuality. My concern in this chapter is to switch representations of beer consumption away from the popular depiction of the bar to the taproom. Doing so, I contend, allows for an examination of the taproom as one type of authentic beer location. That authenticity, however, itself depends on a number of assumptions and rhetorical gestures. The first of these gestures is space.

Representational Space

Popular-culture representations of drinking beer depict the authentic beer locale as a bar, projecting its space as one of escape, of intoxication, of "having a drink" (the euphemism for numbing down the anxiety of daily life), of after-work crowds still in their suits—of, as the television show *Cheers* declared, a place where "everybody knows your name." Beer-drinking lore is no different. Anecdotes and fables so greatly romanticize beer drinking that authentic beer bars, such as the one William Least Heat-Moon searches for in "A Glass of Handmade"—one of the first popular publications on craft beer—seldom resemble the spaces one actually drinks in. When Least Heat-Moon stops by chance in a Seattle bar, he glances at the tap handles and notices "brands I'd never seen: Redhook, Pyramid Pale, Bridgeport, Hale's Pale American, Grant's Imperial Stout"—early craft beer. The perceived mystique of *craft beer* leads him to an epiphany upon trying one of these beers: "The beer rolled and jumped in my mouth, my head; it made me drink with palate, tongue, cheeks, nose, throat" (1987, 76). Authentic craft beer begins for many as a mystical experience.

Bars, on the other hand, do not offer mystique, but instead inebriation. In his poem "The Suicide Kid," Charles Bukowski (2006) avoids idealizing craft beer, opting instead for the romantic notion of complete drunkenness: "I went to the worst of bars hoping to get killed but all I could do was get drunk again." Dylan Thomas killed himself with drink at New York's White Horse Tavern and thus embodied the romanticized "drunken poet" narrative. New York's McSorley's Old Ale House earned fame for serving beers only "in twos" and glorified the "take it or leave it" narrative. "Buy one, get one free" offers attract bar customers who might otherwise not enter. And then there are bars with themes or specific clienteles. Dive bars. Motorcycle bars. Metal bars. Gay bars. Whatever the label, these drinking establishments fulfil an American imagination of beer consumption that typically focuses on limited commonplaces: Budweiser, fizzy lagers, and nightly specials. This imaginary bar provides a public space in American culture that stretches from literature to mass media.

The taproom imaginary is experiential. Taprooms differ from working-class, landlord-owned English pubs; instead, they are descendants of American taverns, colonial establishments with a dedicated space for relaxed drinking, dining, candlelight, and even a fireplace. According to Jack Erickson, early colonial taverns discouraged "bye drinking," which he translates as "quaffing a few mugs of beer and chatting with friends into the late hours" (1992, 8). Yet the contemporary taproom embodies the spirit of "a few mugs of beer" and conversation. The 1990s relaxation of laws prohibiting sale of beer directly to customers led breweries to open taprooms, where profit margins are far greater than on distributing kegs or packaged beer, and where, despite Erickson's one version of bye-drinking history, patrons can drink a few pints and relax with friends. Until state laws changed, for instance, the Three Taverns taproom in Decatur, Georgia, could only offer "samples" if one bought six wooden tokens, and the original Surly taproom in Minneapolis gave out free samples if a visitor took a tour. Neither had a taproom. Now, they both do. Authenticity has shifted to incorporate onsite experience. Mystique remains part of that experience.

Mythical Spaces

As Least Heat-Moon's initial craft beer experience was for him, the taproom is a mythical space for me. A myth communicates ideology by presenting a sign or signs as a natural occurrence and obfuscating them as being socially constructed. As Roland Barthes argued, myths are "types of speech" (Barthes 1972, 107). Although the inclination may be to prefer a taproom as representative of craft beer authenticity, a taproom also can be read as mythological; that is, its mystical experience can exceed direct representation of a lived experience (sitting at a bar, drinking beer). Taprooms are constructed from the interactions and relationships that form publicly, culturally, economically, and socially. With taprooms, we don't need—as Barthes wrote about Japan—to claim "to represent or to analyze reality itself"; instead, we can isolate "a certain number of features, and out of these features deliberately form a system" (1982, 3). Barthes identified in both physical and ideological spaces systems of communication shaped by specific norms and commonplace expectations. As one such system, the taproom offers what Barthes also called the "situation of writing" (Barthes 1982, 4). Barthes notes that such a situation is not a direct representation of a thing or place; rather, it is the composition of signifiers, objects, things, emotions, and spaces gathered into some medium as an expression. The taproom gathers beer into its space, but it gathers other objects and beliefs as well.

Taprooms are spaces that situate writing. As someone who writes in taprooms, I identify the space's authenticity similarly to how Barthes would. For some, taproom writing involves marketing. Taprooms, via visitor experience, promote brands. As Golden Road Brewing's Meg Gil states, "Bringing people in to have an amazing experience with your beers—and pairing them with great food in some cases—it's the best way to build long-term equity. It's marketing that you actually make money on" (quoted in Schumacher 2016). Taproom visits spread brand via what Malcolm Gladwell called "connectors," people who spread information and "give us access to opportunities and worlds to which we don't belong" (2002, 54). A taproom visitor tells others about a visit, either in person or online via Facebook posts, Instagram photographs, Untappd check-ins, or Twitter threads. They introduce beer to those who may not be aware of craft beer. In tis way, they resemble a social media friend or follower, circulating experiential information within a network of friends and associates, who in turn share with their friends and associates. This activity runs counter to marketing models historically run by beer conglomerates such as Anheuser-Busch and Molson Coors that depend on large-scale advertising, gimmick concepts, and a dominant retail presence in convenience stores, grocery stores, and sports stadiums. As Bernot (2017) argues, "Larger, nationally distributed breweries are realizing that it's crucial to foster regional and local connections to drinkers, who are presented with ever more competition for their beer bucks. A brewery, even if it's owned by a larger company, can become your neighborhood hangout, complete with a regular bartender who knows your name and remembers that you always order the chicken pizza." With this sense of the familiar, the taproom promotes experimentation and innovation, because it can scale production to consumer taste. The Brewers Association's Julia Herz argues that "tasting rooms often are the birthplace of many of today's craft brewers' greatest ideas. A tasting room is a place where brewers who pay attention can get instant feedback and a read on how beer lovers respond to their offerings" (Noel 2014). Invention supports taproom mythology: "ideas begin here." Many of my ideas come from sitting in taprooms. I'm not a brewer, but I invent in taprooms.

Emergent Spaces

When did taprooms emerge as sites of writing and communication? Very few beer ads, historic or contemporary, feature taprooms. The concept of sitting in a brewery and drinking its beer was foreign and imaginary. When New Albion Brewery, widely credited as the first modern craft brewery, began operations in 1976, it did not have a taproom. Nor did Anchor Brewing when Fritz Maytag bought it in 1965. Maytag discovered Anchor Steam beer by ordering it at a nearby San Francisco bar, the Oasis. Least Heat-Moon described his visit to Anchor in 1987, but he didn't sample any beer in the tasting room. Nineteenth-century American breweries, such as Gottfried Krueger Brewing Company in Newark, New Jersey, and Frank Jones Brewery in Boston, were massive industrial factories producing over 100,000 barrels of beer annually, but none had taprooms. Jack Erickson's early 1990s mapping of breweries across the country, what he called "the wild west," and "the big east," never mentions taprooms. If Erickson discovered a brewery where he could stop and sample the beers, he called it a brewpub, indicating food was served. Taprooms don't always sell food.

"Are taprooms the future of craft beer?" Zach Fowle asked in 2017. In the short, thirty-to-forty-year history of craft beer, the taproom is a fairly recent phenomenon. Despite the taproom's economic impact on craft beer—according to the Brewers Association, 9.4 percent of craft beer sales were on premises (Watson 2017)—few write about taprooms. Over seven thousand breweries operate across the United States; most cities, thus, host at least one craft beer taproom. Data analytics company Nielsen CGA reports "that 46 percent of legal-drinking-age consumers visited a taproom or brewpub" from 2017 to 2018. (Kendall 2018).

"On any given night," NPR's Aaron Schachter (2017) states, "I can walk out my front door and within a half hour be at one of *seven* different taprooms serving up amazing fresh beer, brewed on the spot." A good modern brewery taproom might have ten to twenty beers on tap. Among the offerings, there will be flagships (beers that sell well and are commonly ordered) and rare offerings (one-offs, small batches, barrel-aged offerings). On a typical taproom board—often a chalkboard or electronic display—you might find a gose, a porter, an imperial stout, a saison, a beer that tastes like cherry pie, a Märzen, a few New England IPAs, a kettle or blended sour, and any other number of styles. Taprooms typically serve flights, four to five four-ounce pours served in cutouts on a wooden or plastic board. Or they might offer a half pour, eight ounces of beer instead of sixteen—larger than a flight sample but small enough to allow for multiple tastings. The spatial experience of the taproom does not communicate inebriation; instead, taprooms offer sampling, tasting, experimenting, experiencing. Experience suggests authenticity.

Communal Spaces

The taproom competes for tourism's endless search for the authentic. This beer search is oppositional to the mass-produced Irish bars, or the drinking establishments styled after Bennigan's or Applebee's, scattered within any number of carbon-copy malls, hotels, and suburbs. Taprooms vary in size, historical connection to their locale, and offerings. The Three Floyds taproom is located in a Munster, Indiana, industrial park. Hill Farmstead's taproom is located off of a gravel road, on a farm forty miles from anything else. The Russian River taproom serves pizza in downtown Santa Rosa, California. The Rhinegeist taproom in Cincinnati occupies the second floor of a mammoth nineteenth-century Moerlein bottling plant. The Side Project Cellar sits on a nondescript street in the Maplewood suburb of St. Louis. Upright Brewing's taproom in Portland, Oregon, can be found in the basement of the Leftbank Building; there is no sign outside and no bar to sit at inside, just tap handles sticking out of the wall. The Tree House Brewing Company taproom in Charlton, Massachusetts, serves beer for onsite consumption only on Saturday morning, and patrons line up hours before the opening for the opportunity to purchase a maximum of two beers. The Lexington, Kentucky, West Sixth Brewing taproom is an old bread factory and shares the space with a fish restaurant, indoor farming, an artists' space, a women's roller derby practice ring, and a coffee roaster. *The Beer Geek Handbook* sarcastically advises, "When choosing a beer at a brewery taproom, it is imperative that a Beer Geek identify and order the rarest offering available" (Dawson 2016, 134). Geeks, though, constitute a small percentage of brewery taproom visitors. Geeks are the anomalies, the die-hard craft beer drinkers in search of whatever is new and different. Most communities support their taprooms via families and casual drinkers, not geeks. Taprooms are slowly becoming cultural community gathering spaces versus sites of intoxication. Their authenticity stems from gatherings.

On a given day where I live in Lexington, Kentucky, I can visit seven taprooms: West Sixth, Country Boy, Pivot, Rock House, Mirror Twin, Fusion, and Ethereal. When I moved to Lexington eight years ago, there were zero. Some of these taprooms open at eleven in the morning, others at four in the afternoon. Some offer food; others depend on the presence of a food truck. In order to compete or remain financially viable, a taproom must do more than serve beer; it must be the focal point of its community. Thus, taprooms host trivia nights, yoga, biking clubs, storytelling, magic shows, fundraisers for organizations like the Humane Society, holiday extravaganzas, retro-themed parties, cornhole tournaments, beer cheese contests, and other events designed not only to lure customers but also to reframe the typical commonplace of alcohol consumption—getting drunk—as a communal act. Taprooms offer their patrons the opportunity to sample leisure time along with beer. Seldom do I see someone drunk in a taproom, whether I am in Lexington or some other city. Instead, at two or three in the afternoon on a given workday, I see people huddled over laptops, slowly sipping an IPA, taking advantage of the free Wi-Fi to work or communicate with colleagues. The taproom is a coworking craft space.

Taprooms speak to aesthetics typically associated with craft culture: nostalgia, revitalization, and neighborhood ethos. Within this ethos, taprooms draw heavily on craft's material aesthetics as well. Exposed beams. Concrete floors. Exposed brick. Chalkboards. Reclaimed wood. Gerard Walen describes Jacksonville's Intuition Brewing's taproom as German beer-hall revival: "The brewery's taproom, in a part of the building originally built in the 1920s, evokes the feel of a German beer hall, with long community tables where customers can converse over a pint" (2014, 36). Rick Armon credits Cleveland's Great Lakes Brewing's taproom for its Prohibition connections: "The tiger mahogany bar serves as a major conversation piece, because it has bullet holes rumored to have come from the gun of Eliot Ness, the legendary crime fighter who led a group of law-enforcement agents known as 'The Untouchables' in Chicago" (2011, 39).

The West Sixth taproom features an indoor beer garden populated by communal tables. The Rock House taproom is located inside the 1923 Lexington Quarry office, a small stone building with a fireplace dividing the bar from a seating area. The Blue Stallion taproom's six-foot bar stands taller than most of its patrons; when I sit on a stool, my feet hang below me like a child in a high chair. In each of these carefully designed spaces, communities gather around chairs, tables, and bar counters, but also around craft culture itself—the belief in an authentic space of artisanal output distinct from what conglomerate culture provides.

Authentic Spaces

Which is the authentic space for community: the taproom or the coffee house? The coffee house traditionally has been described as the place of community gathering, or as popular writer Steven Johnson (2009) argues, the site of scientific invention or revolution. The seventeenth- and eighteenth-century coffee house, it has also been argued, served as the primary site of the Enlightenment. Coffee houses (or today, coffee shops) are the commonplaces of public intellectual work; they capture the public imagination as a space of work when one tires of the office or does not even have an office to work in. A coffee shop should stir the imagination, this narrative claims; it should reflect a public space of engagement worthy of its history as the focal point of communication and, hyperbolically declared, humanism. At its heyday, the coffee house signified intellectualism, conversation, debate, and the public sharing of ideas. Patrons read newspapers in coffee houses as political debates raged. The coffee house served as a centerpiece for information distribution; it thus circulated information from media to patrons and back into the community by word of mouth. Jürgen Habermas (1991) claimed that the coffee house played a principal role in the public shaping of opinion, whether in cultural norms or political engagement. The legacy of the coffee house is still seen today; coffee drinkers with their laptops open, headphones or earbuds snug, typing away at term papers, novels, and policy statements, or just writing code, in their Starbucks, Caribou Coffee, Peet's, Seattle's Best, or other local spot. Yet silence is the norm in today's coffee shop, and Wi-Fi, not spirited oratory, transmits ideas, circulating them through the keyboard and accompanying internet. (I, however, tend to drink my coffee at home.)

Rhetorician Greg Dickinson described a typical Starbucks as a rhetorical tapestry of meaning. The daily spaces we interact with, Dickinson argued, project the contradictions of material culture while remaining culturally persuasive in their ability to create ethos and mood. "One way of taking seriously the materiality of rhetoric," Dickinson writes, "is to turn to rhetorical 'texts' that resist purely symbolic 'readings'" (2002, 6). Rather than read a taproom or coffee house as indicative of late capitalism or resistance to conglomerate culture, one can read such sites as an example of material rhetoric. A Starbucks, for instance, promotes the rhetoric of individuality (one can customize a drink as one desires) while demonstrating conformity (all Starbucks look the same). The coffee-house feel of a Starbucks encourages connectivity among its patrons the way historic coffee houses did (the wooden, relaxed look; the soft background music; the properly displayed roasted beans; the comforting lighting), but often results in the opposite. Starbucks are located in hotels, Targets, grocery stores, highway rest stops, and airports, places not known for exchanges of ideas or social connections, but rather ones we pass through on the way to somewhere else. Can one tell one Starbucks from another? Does the original Seattle Starbucks differ dramatically from the one in one's hometown or nearby airport? Is there an aura or sense of authenticity to a reproduced Starbucks the way there may have been to an eighteenth-century English coffee house or a contemporary brewery taproom located in a nearby neighborhood? Or is aura simply something situated in memory (i.e., there once was a majestic tradition of intellectualism in public spaces) or romanticism (the glory of a space outfitted in wood or with bar stools)?

Authentic spaces demand connectivity. Anthropologist Marc Augé called public spaces where individuals pass through, neither staying nor making connections, *non-places*. Non-places, like an airport or a Target, discourage human interaction, Augé argued, and they lack origin or authenticity. Non-places are the signifiers of a cold, monotonous, impersonal consumer culture that has overtaken contemporary life. Fredric Jameson (1991), whose canonical takedown of the Westin Bonaventure Hotel in Los Angeles challenged postmodern spatial design, might agree with Augé. Jameson's critique rested largely on the notion that the Bonaventure, or postmodernism as a whole, borrows from the vernacular of non-places such as Las Vegas, where visitors pass through without any sense of meaning or desire to connect to one another or to the place itself. Jameson expressed concern with the "hyper crowd" who passes through such spaces; *hyper*, possibly, for their lack of real interest in a space, or a supposed authentic culture that reproduction endangers.

The mass reproduction of space, which has affected coffee houses as much as shopping, erases the authentic experience that idea exchange, invention, and human interaction supposedly once encouraged over a cup of coffee. This line of thought claims that innovative design or public discussion has been replaced by rote copying or even boredom. Authenticity, we are led to believe, involves communication, connection, and exchange. Reproduction, as Walter Benjamin (2008) famously argued, leads to distance and, we might add, boredom.

Taprooms exist somewhere between the coffee house image and the postmodern hotel. Patrons communicate beer-based experiences as they move in and out of these spaces. They also often rate these experiences on social media sites such as Untappd and RateBeer, telling friends, Facebook posts, Instagram images. As community members, patrons treat the taproom as a connective space, moving through it in ways reminiscent of Augé's critique, except they do so in order to establish contact. A taproom is a space one communicates, either in writing or by word of mouth. Who goes to a taproom and does not mention it to friends or on Facebook?

Banal Authenticity

I wrote most of my last book, *Craft Obsession: The Social Rhetorics of Beer*, in Lexington's taprooms. Despite their assumed craft and mystique, taprooms can be boring in the afternoon, typically occupied by a few scattered people working on their laptops. Sometimes I'm the only person present. I'm not bothered by the lack of intellectual exchange. The silence and boredom that penetrate my university office often leave me exhausted and burned out. As department chair, my workday may involve signing documents, promoting courses during registration, dealing with faculty or student complaints, and trying to recruit students to our major. The banality of the office space, not unlike what Homer Simpson or the characters in *Office Space* experience, overwhelms me even if it makes few physical demands on my body. The everyday sameness of any working situation, as popular culture often demonstrates, requires occasional escape or even mystique and myth. By contrast, a taproom—music playing in the background; the smell of sweet, dank wort drifting from the brewery into the common space; the friendly welcome from its staff or owners; the wooden tables or benches—offers me a brief getaway for an hour or until I have to pick my kids up at school.

Taprooms need day writers (the privilege of being able to sit and write in a common space at two in the afternoon) as well as families (the people who spend time on a weekend afternoon with a casual beer). Regarding families: a popular online debate asks, should kids be allowed in taprooms? Those who reject the presence of children cling to the mythological "authentic" commonplace of the bar: an adult venue for adult consumption where cursing, drunkenness, and inappropriate behavior accompany drinking cheap beer. Those who embrace the presence of children point to an alternative "authentic" commonplace: the European tradition of allowing kids in spaces where alcohol is consumed. After all, George Orwell's famous ode to the perfect pub in "The Moon under Water" included a space for kids. The Twin Leaf taproom in Asheville, North Carolina, features a kids' play kitchen in the corner. Southern Grist's taproom in Nashville has board games. Can the taproom remain authentic with the presence of children? I bring my kids to taprooms, but typically not when I am writing. For my children, passing the time (and avoiding boredom, or, at least, my boredom with daily life) is often done in taprooms. Taprooms are my children's authentic sites for afternoon malaise.

Like a typical Starbucks, a taproom projects an authentic identity via rhetorical construction built out of the myth of banality: material things. This might include its ability to reclaim abandoned factories and garages as authentic locales; offer unique variety to differentiate its products from the conglomerate, mass-produced beer made by InBev, Heineken, and Molson Coors; promote local events and build an ethos of community; and create a unique signature among a given city's other leisure options. The 4 Hands taproom in St. Louis offers free video games on its second floor. The War Pigs taproom in Copenhagen, Denmark, serves Texas-style barbecue. The Wicked Weed Funkatorium in Asheville surrounds patrons with barrels of aging sour beer. Each of these taprooms makes its own mythical claim for authenticity. Each welcomes kids. Each, with its specific spatial offerings, could easily serve as my writing space.

Within the public imaginary, authentic spaces for writing might include library cubicles, home offices, and work desks. The taproom, hardly authentic for an academic discourse focused on these common-places, offers me a ritualized space for writing when my office space bores. Writing spaces, like a public imaginary, can become anchored to personality. Great writers need solitude! Great writers work at standing desks! In the early afternoon, when I am walking down the hallway of our office floor toward the elevator, a colleague typically will say to me, "Going for a beer?" Other department chairs ask me for beer advice before our biweekly chairs meeting begins. I'm known at all the tap-rooms in town. I'm a regular taproom writer.

"What are you working on today?" I might be asked by the bar-tender, brewer, or owner. Brewery taprooms may be, like a Starbucks, a non-place as patrons come and go, but they also offer a contempo-rary alternative to the romantic ideal of the coffee house or the drudg-ery of the workspace. The taproom remains one of our last local spaces for individualized work and communal idea creation. If we can roman-ticize our other spaces of engagement or liquid consumption, we can romanticize the taproom as well.

Authenticity

Take Ethereal Brewing's taproom in Lexington, Kentucky, for instance. Located in the revitalized Pepper Distillery district on Manchester Street, the brewery occupies a small part of the former distillery, which closed in 1958. A high-end restaurant sits adjacent to Ethereal on one side; a pizza place is on the other. A biker bar can be found on the other end of the distillery compound, and a craft ice cream shop, ax-throwing site, and new small-batch distillery also operate in the district. Outside, on Ethereal's patio, one can sit on long wooden benches overlooking the Town Branch of South Elkhorn Creek. Inside the brewery, the Pepper Distillery's original brick interior is preserved, and a long wooden bar stretches out in front of the sixteen artisanally designed glass taps, each identified above the handles by removable chalk-written boards ordered along the facing wall. The brewery opens out to the patio via a large mechanical garage door that can be raised when the weather is nice.

Ethereal projects the industrial feel of Lexington's bourbon heritage along with the well-circulated commonplaces of craft and revitalization, which focus on material objects: exposure, wood, stone, chalk, garage doors, patios. In craft culture, abandoned spaces are transformed into functional spaces, and this gesture is often credited with the phoenix-like rehabilitation of neglected neighborhoods or disused buildings. There is much to romanticize in an old distillery (the pizza place next door maintains a grain silo and distilling equipment as part of its interior design). City residents and tourists want to revisit what has been forgotten—to be a part of a resurgence so that they can treat the everyday as unique. For consumers, such revival writes of a return to the authentic. *A distillery was once here. I am reliving Kentucky bourbon history.* In this case of reproduction, aura is reclaimed. I enjoy writing in Ethereal's space during the afternoon, the large garage door open to spring, the taproom largely devoid of people except for me, one or two others, and whoever is tending bar. It feels authentic, whether or not it really is.

What is the difference between writing in a coffee house or in a taproom? Coffee houses offer professional acceptability for academic writing in public spaces; they provide a scholarly imagination of the authentic. Taprooms suggest otherwise. None of my colleagues would question me if I were leaving work to write in a Starbucks. Writing spaces are ideological and thus mythical. Their cultural acceptance is based on the network of associations we bring to that space; coffee indicates intellectualism, beer suggests frivolity. In general, there exists a taxonomy of space that arises from romanticism, novelty, adventure, and appropriateness, among other traits. "Beer," as one taxonomic identification of place, signifies many things, but for academics it doesn't signify "writing" or "work" the way "coffee" does. If a colleague asks me, "Going for a beer?" I feel guilty. I don't feel guilty because I am "going for a beer," I feel guilty in the way that any public image of work, leisure, or pleasure can affect us. The public commonplace of the academic is that of leisure: teaching two courses a semester, having summers off, being able to sit in a brewery taproom in the middle of the afternoon, writing for a living. The internalized academic commonplace of work is being forever busy (the same items flipped from leisure to burden depending on perspective). Leisure, when associated with academic work, is a negative commonplace. Whether that commonplace is valid or not, does it matter if I maintain it by writing in a taproom and not the expected space of the coffee shop? How does one maintain an authentic scholarly position when the choice is craft beer over coffee?

All of us have been interpellated into believing in the coffee house as a public space for work and not the taproom. One is an acceptable public work space; one is not. Acceptability stems from the networking of norms, circulated imagery, ideology, habit, and influence. Barthes called this network "mythology." The mythology of acceptability relies on a binary judgment that an act or place is "okay" or it is not. Although Barthes never mentions beer, he summarizes wine's mythology as a similar contradiction: "For the worker, wine means enabling him to do his task with demiurgic ease ('heart for the work'). For the intellectual, wine has the reverse function: the local white wine or the Beaujolais of the writer is meant to cut him off from the all too expected environment of cocktails and expensive drinks" (1972, 58).

These contradictions abound. Is there a difference between public writing with a pint and public writing with a latte? If so, which is or is not authentic? The emergence of craft culture over the last thirty years has produced new types of cheeses, wines, breads, coffee, and beer for a public dependent on reproduction and sameness. Craft, of course, embodies other levels of acceptability—rejecting consumer culture, embracing the local, choosing organic sometimes, writing, individuality, the handmade, innovation, and remaining authentic. Although breweries are miniature factories reproducing their products in bottles, kegs, and cans, they are also spaces that embody the imaginary ethos of craft culture—the handmade, nonfactory, artisanal, authentic product resisting the supposed evils of conglomerate culture. Writing in a taproom is an exercise of crafting in a craft space, and therefore should be a public projection of the authentic. That I want to write in a taproom, however, still earns me distrusting looks from my colleagues when I am anywhere near the elevator on our office floor. If I write in a taproom, they seem to suggest, I am not an authentic academic writer. I should choose the local coffee shop instead—or our college library's Starbucks.

Despite our potential to romanticize all aspects of daily life, authenticity conveys limitations. Being authentic, we might believe, gestures toward something not reproducible, craft based, and original. Being authentic is to oppose the cultural movements of conformity that have taken over public spaces as much as they have conquered food, entertainment, shopping, and school. To attach any experience to being authentic, however, is to experience its limitations because authenticity is as mythological as acceptability. Authenticity also often dictates our situations of writing. Every taproom in my city features at least one IPA; often multiple IPAs are listed on the board. The IPA's authenticity depends on whether one believes its historical narrative (hopped beer preserved on the long voyage from England to colonial India) or that an IPA should be filtered (West Coast IPA) or unfiltered (New England IPA) or dry (brut IPA) or conventionally challenged (coffee IPA, sour IPA). The IPA writes the space as authentic (a brewery must make an IPA) or not (the market is oversaturated with IPA). Can IPA be the authentic taproom marker even though—with almost every single taproom featuring at least one—it completes a homogenous beer drinking experience across the country?

One can enjoy a coffee without changing the world or being an intellectual. One can order a Starbucks and still appreciate the aura of the coffee shop it is meant to evoke, authentic or not. One can discover authenticity in an IPA even though they are ubiquitous and banal. I write in a taproom. That is all. I embrace my situation of writing as authentic banality. Can a space remain authentic without the baggage of hermeneutics (i.e., what does this space mean?) or culture (i.e., the space represents the revitalization of the craft aesthetic and resistance to dominant consumer culture)? When I sit in a taproom, laptop open, I am not romanticizing the space as a modern coffee house. Rather, like the characters in *Office Space* or *The Office*, I am taking a break from white-collar banality. Barthes (1997) conflated writing with the banality of everyday life: shaving, getting a haircut, taking a nap, listening to the radio, pissing in his garden. I, too, understand my writing as a fairly banal process. Drinking a hazy IPA, sitting in a taproom, working on an article or book manuscript, checking Facebook, writing down ideas, being public and private simultaneously. I wrote a great deal of this chapter in the Mirror Twin taproom in Lexington during the work week, in the middle of the afternoon, a few miles from my campus office. As I wrote, the lunch crowd slowly faded away, returning to their own jobs and errands, until only I and one other patron remained. I looked over my shoulder, and there he sat on the wooden bench next to mine, wearing a baseball cap from another local brewery, sitting under a TV playing ESPN with the sound off, his attention fixed on an open notebook in front of him. He, too, it seemed, was writing.

Notes

1. Pabst was known as an everyman's beer for most of the twentieth century, but in the late 1990s, as many regional beers were facing diminishing sales and being pulled at bars (or had already become extinct), Pabst became adopted as a "hipster" beer that many craft beer drinkers sought out. Essentially, drinking Pabst became cool—one, if not the only, macro-lager that thrived for a brief period in the craft beer scene for a brief period.

References

Armon, Rick. 2011. *Ohio Breweries*. Mechanicsburg, PA: Stackpole Books.

Augé, Marc. 2009. *Non-places: An Introduction to Supermodernity*. Brooklyn: Verso.

Barthes, Roland. 1982. *Empire of Signs*. Trans. Richard Howard. New York: Hill and Wang.

———. 1977. *Roland Barthes by Roland Barthes*. Berkeley: University of California Press.

———. 1972. *Mythologies*. Trans. Annette Lavers. New York: Farrar, Strauss and Giroux.

Benjamin, Walter. 2008. *The Work of Art in the Age of Mechanical Reproduction*. Translated by J. A. Underwood. New York: Penguin Books.

Bernot, Kate. 2017. "Why Big Breweries Want to Go Local." *Draft*, October 2 (https://web.archive.org/web/20171004171336/https://draftmag.com/brewery-satellite-taprooms-brewpubs/).

Bukowski, Charles. 2006. *Slouching toward Nirvana: New Poems*. New York: Ecco.

Dawson, Patrick. 2016. *The Beer Geek Handbook: The Essential Guide to Living a Life Ruled by Beer*. North Adams, MA: Stoney.

Dickinson, Greg. 2002. "Joe's Rhetoric: Finding Authenticity at Starbucks." *Rhetoric Society Quarterly*. 32(4): 5–27.

Erickson, Jack. 1992. *Brewery Adventures in the Big East*. Reston, VA: Red Brick Press.

Fowle, Zach. 2017. "Are Taprooms the Future of Craft Beer?" *Draft*, May 2 (https://draftmag.com/are-taprooms-the-future-of-craft-beer/).

Gladwell, Malcolm. 2002. *The Tipping Point: How Little Things Can Make a Big Difference*. New York: Back Bay Books.

Jameson, Fredric. 1991. *Postmodernism, Or, the Cultural Logic of Late Capitalism*. Durham, NC: Duke University Press.

Johnson, Steven. 2009. *The Invention of Air: A Story of Science, Faith, Revolution, and the Birth of America*. New York: Riverhead.

Habermas, Jürgen. 1991. *The Structural Transformation of the Public Sphere: An Inquiry into a Category of Bourgeois Society*. Cambridge, MA: MIT Press.

Kendall, Justin. 2018. "As Brewery Taprooms Thrive, Industry Stakeholders Voice Concerns." *Brewbound*, March 30 (https://www.brewbound.com/news/brewery -taprooms-thrive-industry-stakeholders-voic-concerns).

Least Heat-Moon, William. 1987. "A Glass of Handmade." *Atlantic Monthly*, November, 75–86.

Noel, Josh. 2014 "Goose Island to Open Taproom, Begin Tours at Fulton Street Brewery." *Chicago Tribune*, October 2 (https://www.chicagotribune.com/dining /recipes/ct-food-1009-tap-rooms-20141009-story.html).

Schachter, Aaron. 2017. "The Next Big Thing in Beer Is Being a Small Taproom." *NPR*, September 27 (https://www.npr.org/sections/thesalt/2017/09/27/552351664 /the-next-big-thing-in-beer-s-being-a-small-taproom).

Schumacher, Harry. 2016. "The Rise of Taprooms." *All About Beer* 37(2). Retrieved May 1, 2016 (http://allaboutbeer.com/article/the-rise-of-taprooms/).

Walen, Gerard. 2014. *Florida Breweries*. Mechanicsburg, PA: Stackpole Books.

Watson, Bart. 2017. "Brewery Onsite Sales: Building Craft Brands." Brewers Association, April 5 (https://www.brewersassociation.org/insights/brewery -onsite-sales-building-craft-brands).

Postcard from Copenhagen

ROBERT A. SAUNDERS

With the summer fleeting all too fast, I found myself spending a surprisingly warm day touring the tap houses of Nørrebro, a neighborhood that can best be described as the Brooklyn of greater
Copenhagen, Denmark. My adventure began as I stepped off the
S-train at the Nørreport station in the heart of the city. Coming up
the stairs, I turned right onto Fredericksborggade, heading across the
Dronning Louises Bro, a scenic bridge that separates the Peblinge Sø
from its northern sister, the Sortedams Sø. Together with the Sankt
Jørgens Sø, these artificial lakes form the one of the most distinctive
elements of Copenhagen's topography, providing enticing promenades
for pedestrians as well as an easily navigable cycling route for those on
two wheels.

Crossing into Nørrebro, one notices a palpable change in atmosphere, if not necessarily architecture. One of ten official districts of
Copenhagen, the borough is known for its bohemian ethos, ethnic
diversity, and periodic bouts of social unrest, including a number of
violent riots in recent decades. However, on this particularly pleas-
ant Saturday afternoon, such worries were far from mind as I strolled
along Nørrebrogade, spying the kebab houses, electronic shops, and
Islamic garment boutiques. Distracted by the bright colors and weekend conviviality, I soon came to my senses as I approached the high
walls of Assistens Cemetery, the final resting place of such luminar-
ies as the writer Hans Christian Andersen and the philosopher Søren
Kierkegaard. After reviewing the wares of the locals who had gathered
along the promenade to sell family heirlooms and various baubles, I
ducked into the cemetery, which seemed a world away from the teeming streets of Nørrebro. I took a moment to gather my thoughts while
traversing this quiet green space, punctuated by the gravestones of
Denmark's most famous souls (one stone even sported Norse runes),
before pushing on to my first stop, Mikkeler & Friends (Stefansgade 35).

Situated on a corner abutting a park where neighborhood kids were playing soccer, this modest outpost of the growing empire of Mikkel Borg-Bjergsø did not disappoint. Having been to two of his other pubs, one in central Copenhagen and the other in San Francisco's Tenderloin district, I immediately felt at home—perhaps a bit too much so, with the flat echoes of American accents all around. I wasn't surprised to hear so many American beer-hounds, given that Mikkel is one-half of the great Danish beer twins, the other being Jeppe Jarnit-Bjergsø, whose Brooklyn watering hole Tørst serves, for many, as the NYC metro area's most important beer mecca. I bellied up to the bar and ordered one of Mikkeler's guest beers, the Twisted Verbena, a Berliner Weisse accented with that supernatural herb, which purportedly wards off evil. A collaboration between Barcelona-based Edge Brewing and the British brewery Magic Rock, this otherworldly beer proved to be just the right way to start my hop-centric journey, particularly when offset by a slab of Danish hard cheese and some smoked pistachios. Having just flown in from Newcastle, Northumberland, a city famous for its chocolatey ales, I chose to follow the verbena beer with one of Mikkeler's own, the Nørrebro Brown. As I downed this sweet and simple brew, I felt as if I was literally drinking in the environs. Rather than visiting Koelschip, Mikkeler's Belgian-style adjunct next door, I decided to push on to new pastures.

After a fairly short walk through an area clearly undergoing a robust wave of gentrification, I found myself at just-opened Tapperiet Brus (Guldbergsgade 29F), a well-appointed brewery with extensive outdoor seating just opposite an organic pizzeria and a bustling bakery. I considered ordering the Brettexit, a wild ale made with "non-European" hops, but instead settled on a curious hybrid entitled My Sour Pils from To Øl Brewing. Seated on a sunny park bench where I could watch the many passersby, I was able to properly appreciate the wonderful venue. Located in an old iron foundry and locomotive factory, Brus is a partnership with To Øl and the tony Copenhagen cocktail bar Mikropolis. Brus takes its name from the Danish word for the sparkling appearance of bubbling beverages, and with a baker's dozen fermentation tanks and seventy-odd oak barrels, it proclaims itself the heart of a burgeoning brewing culture. Interestingly, the Danes are the only Scandinavian nation that prefers ales to aquavit, shifting from a spirits-based culture to one of beer only in the last century.

Although I could have spent the rest of the day at Brus sunning myself and drinking tart pils, I pushed on to one of my favorite haunts in the Danish capital, Nørrebro Bryghus (Ryesgade 3). Heading down Guldbergsgade, I happened upon another, smaller cemetery, cordoned off by those now-familiar walls. After stopping to purchase a few old maps of Scandinavia (including one sketched before World War I), I overheard a local guide tell his charges to hop up on the bike racks and peer over the wall. I waited until they departed and discreetly followed his advice to discover the Jewish Northern Cemetery. Seeing the overgrown headstones inscribed in Hebrew, I thought back to the privations of the last war and how they afflicted this northern corner of Europe. However, I was quickly drawn back to the here and now by watching local youths in a skate park. One turn later and I was at the only brewhouse bold enough to take its name from the neighborhood.

Commanding a prime piece of real estate in a friendly corner of the borough, Nørrebro Brewery is a destination for any visiting beer lover. With the good weather, I was lucky to score a seat at one of the few park benches outside (sunny days draw Danes out into open air regardless of the temperature). Departing from form, I ordered a bottled beer known as "the Good." This refreshing Danish take on an American pale ale is in a new series from Nørrebro Brewing known as the Good Bad Evil. Its darker peers are a Belgian quadrupel (the "Bad") and a black imperial porter (the "Evil").

With the sky now totally blue, Nørrebro was teeming with Danes and international visitors alike seeking to drink in the waning days of summer, so I gave up my seat and headed south. I perused a pop-up market on the wonderfully eclectic pedestrian lane known as Blågårdsgade, before turning right onto Rantzausgade towards my next destination, Kølsters Tolv Haner at No. 56.

As I approached this organic-beer mecca, I noticed a heavy police presence on the streets despite the seemingly halcyon atmosphere of this brilliant Saturday. The experience immediately brought back memories of watching the Danish Swedish TV series *Broen/Bron* (known in America as *The Bridge*) and its foreboding depiction of the Nørrebro district in the episode on the "failure" of integration. But when I ordered a small glass of golden Højsommer, all thoughts of the oppressive grayness of *The Bridge* evaporated. I drank down that honey-flavored beer, which fittingly smacked of the midsummer days after which it was named, while in the front garden (the back was only for residents of the surrounding apartment complex) and staring at Brorson's Church as the sun dipped reverently behind its red brick.

Although the setting was perfect, the beer—brewed by the owners' father—proved to be the one disappointment of the day, lacking the effervescence (or *brus*) that had otherwise characterized the afternoon's menu. (Perhaps knowing that organic beers are less bubbly, the pub only serves its libations in "half" portions, or 20 centiliters).

Running short on time, I dashed back toward the inner city, intent on finding the newly opened pub that had come highly recommended by a publican across the Baltic Sea in Malmö, Sweden. After one wrong turn, I located Himmeriget (Åboulevard 27), co-owned by Mikkel's "evil twin" Jeppe. Small and serious, this little spot offered up ten craft drafts, of which almost half were American in origin, including one from my own hometown of Dunedin, Florida. Recognizing the value of this well-curated list, I settled on 25 milliliters of a low-alcohol, cherry-laced sour from the California-based Lost Abbey brewery and purchased a "to-go" can of Evil Twin Mission Gose, an ale brewed with salt and coriander with a bit of eucalyptus thrown in for good measure.

With my memorable jaunt winding down, I meandered back across Dronning Louises Bro, smiling at the growing crowds of twenty-somethings filling the benches on the span's northern edge to catch the late-afternoon rays of a setting sun. More than a dozen little parties were forming, each working up a good amount of *hygge* (that untranslatable Danish word for "making a cozy space") with their six-packs of canned Tuborg, one of Denmark's two mega-brewers. Although I was tempted to linger and let the late-summer vibe overtake me, I decided to hurry back to my hosts in northern Copenhagen, knowing full well that a home-cooked meal awaited me, with plenty of hygge on offer.

PART II

Identity, Politics, Economics

CHAPTER 5

Displaced Brews

*Unmaking the Geography of Beer
in Hyperinflationary Zimbabwe*

JEREMY L. JONES

In late 2008, while the global financial crisis was convulsing the economies of the north Atlantic countries, Zimbabwe descended into a
record-breaking (and largely unrelated) bout of hyperinflation. The
plunge followed a decade of grueling economic crisis and political tur-
moil (Chiumbu and Musemwa 2012). That November, the annual rate
reached an estimated 89 sextillion percent (Hanke and Kwok 2009).
Only once in history has that figure ever been bested, in post–World
War II Hungary. Formal-sector shops were largely empty, and when
supplies did arrive, they sold out in minutes (Jones 2010a). People
streamed across the border to neighboring countries, returning with
everything from building supplies to bread, toothpaste to toilet paper.
Armies of young men engaged in illegal foreign-currency deals and
elaborate forms of black-market arbitrage (Pilossof 2009). Civil ser-
vants dashed to spend their ridiculously meager salaries—often worth
no more than ten US dollars at the "real" (i.e., black market) rate
(Chagonda 2012).

It would seem surprising, then, that "Mandoza,"[1] a loquacious
wheeler-dealer in his late twenties, chose this very moment to start a
shebeen ("speakeasy") in his front yard in Chitungwiza, a city located
twenty minutes outside the capital, Harare. It made sense, though.
Shebeens have a long and storied history in the cities of southern
Africa (Chimhete 2018; Haggblade 1992), but his scheme was less a
matter of following precedent than profiting from the chaos. Starting
around August 2008, Delta Corporation, which held a near monopoly

on Zimbabwe's formal market for beer, drastically reduced its output. Aside from hyperinflation itself, the company was facing supply-chain deficits, a lack of foreign currency for imports, and punitive government price controls. And as it stepped back, informal traders moved in. Many smuggled cheap sugarcane spirits produced in Mozambique, adding fresh life to an illicit trade that is more than a century old (Duri 2012). Others imported lager that they purchased at retail price or sourced from expired stocks in South Africa, Botswana, and Zambia. Because the standard markup on these cross-border goods was around 100 percent, it could be an exceedingly lucrative trade.

Mandoza turned to another time-honored practice: homebrewing "traditional" opaque beer (Ambler and Crush 1992; La Hausse 1988). Normally, the low cost and widespread availability of Delta's mass-produced opaque beer, Chibuku, made homebrewing a profitless venture, but the factory taps were dry. Every couple of days, Mandoza made an 800-kilometer overnight journey to Francistown, Botswana, a border town packed with Zimbabwean traders. There he would buy a case of Mnanti, a commercial opaque beer mix made of a proprietary blend of maize meal, malt, yeast, and sugar.[2] He traveled on forged documents, and sometimes just jumped the border while coming back in order to avoid duties. Back in Chitungwiza, he added boiling water to the Mnanti mix. The fast-brewing concoction that resulted was similar to Chibuku: alternatively sweet and sour, it had a texture like thin gruel. In keeping with local nomenclature, he deemed it to be *chihwani* (i.e., "one," in reference to the one day required for brewing) or *chiko-kiyana* (a.k.a. *skokiaan,* of which more in a moment). Together with his wife, he sold it night and day to friends, neighbors, and anyone else who happened by, until the supply ran out and the cycle began again.

In this chapter, I want to contextualize Mandoza's brewing venture and consider what it might tell us about the relationship among beer, brewing, and "place." It is an interesting case for this volume partly because it is so unlike so many other accounts herein: the country is different, the people involved are different, the economic situation is different—even the beer is different. And yet there are also material and conceptual links to the brewing contexts described elsewhere in these pages. Zimbabwe's Delta Corporation is partly owned by South African Breweries, which in 2008 was itself the majority stakeholder in the global behemoth SABMiller. All of the lagers Zimbabweans drink come from the SAB stable, but the company has also had a finger in the industrial brewing of opaque beer for more than a century. Against the unique circumstances of Mandoza's shebeen, then, we find a recognizable global landscape of highly rationalized, capital-intensive lager production, as well as a hybrid African space of mass-produced "traditional" brews. I argue that this landscape of "external meaning" (Mintz 1986, 153) fractured amid the country's economic crisis (Jones 2014), and that the "place" of beer and brewing was fractured along with it, a process I term *unmaking* (cf. Weiss 1996). I start by exploring the position of beer and brewing in Mandoza's social world. Then I step back and set that configuration of social life and alcohol in historical context. After that, I return to some details of the shebeen, and address Mandoza's own response to the forces of economic displacement.

The Landscape of Everyday Ethics

Let me start by describing a discussion that first helped me crystallize the relationship between beer drinking and place. In 2006, I started ethnographic research on young men in Chitungwiza, Zimbabwe's third largest city by population, located about fifteen miles from the capital, Harare. Although I was interested in a host of matters related to youth and gender, I spent much of my time examining how young men eked out a living in the absence of formal employment and in the face of the country's growing economic emergency.

The first neighborhoods in Chitungwiza were developed in the early sixties to house workers employed in the white-run businesses of the capital, then called Salisbury. This represented the latest instantiation of a deeply colonial institution: the "native location." The first such locations emerged in the 1890s, soon after Cecil John Rhodes's British South Africa Company was granted a colonial charter.[3] They were prime evidence of the fundamental social principle of any colony: the color bar. All manner of business and employment opportunities were reserved for whites, and along with overcrowded "tribal trust lands" (cf. the US "reservation" system), native locations stood in painfully stark contrast to the verdant suburbs and commercial estates of whites. After the country attained majority rule in 1980, Chitungwiza experienced a decade of measured growth and stability. In the early nineties, though, amid a record-breaking drought, the government embarked on an International Monetary Fund structural adjustment program, with predictably devastating effects on the city's residents (Carmody

1998). Many were retrenched out of formal-sector jobs, including the local textile industry, which was largely shuttered. In the decades since, Chitungwiza has been subject to continuous urbanization without industrialization. By the turn of the millennium, before the worst of the economic crisis, most residents were scraping by on an uncertain mix of informal economic activities.

Young men like Mandoza bore the brunt of those developments. I knew him prior to my research, and he provided an entry point to a larger group of young men from his neighborhood. They had all grown up together, and often joined forces in both leisure and moneymaking ventures. One of my research methods with them was a bimonthly group discussion, carried out in the shade of one of their yards. I would set a basic topic for the day—usually just a key word or two drawn from my other research activities—but otherwise they did most of the talking. In keeping with their habits, as well as local standards of masculine sociability, I always brought along a half-dozen scuds of Chibuku (*scud* refers to the beverage's characteristic two-liter returnable brown plastic containers). Unlike lager, which is almost always consumed individually in Zimbabwe, scuds are customarily shared in a circle until the supply runs out. In this case, when the beer was finished, the conversation generally wrapped up, too.

During one such meeting in late 2007, we were discussing the vernacular concept of "straightness."[4] In keeping with local convention, Mandoza and company did not use "straight" to describe a sexual identity, as speakers of American English might, but rather to capture a diffuse sense of moral and ethical propriety, akin to "uprightness" or "respectability." To live a "straight" life or act in a "straight" manner was to do things properly, above board, and according to protocol or custom. Notably, though, most of the conversation that day concerned the *absence* of straightness in their lives, and how that absence owed to their economic plight. They insisted that in order to make ends meet amid the country's deepening crisis, they had to act surreptitiously, break laws, and set aside concerns about propriety. From earlier discussions with them and others, I knew that people often called this "crooked" logic of getting by *kukiya-kiya*, from the English word *key*. Strictly, to "key" something (*kukiya*) meant to lock it, and to be "keyed" (i.e., "locked") was also a synonym for being drunk (cf. "wasted," "plastered," etc.). The reduplicated form (*kiya-kiya*), however, suggested "grabbing" or "binding"—just the sort of actions required in an economy centered on opportunism, improvisation, trickery, and outright force. My goal for our discussion that day was to better establish how they understood the relation between kukiya-kiya and straightness.

I had started by playing them a clip from a recent episode of *The Mai Chisamba Show*, a TV show hosted and produced by Rebecca Chisamba, during which she facilitated audience discussion of cultural issues. The episode concerned kukiya-kiya and included an exchange between two men who embodied all the stereotypes of generational conflict: a free-wheeling, dreadlocked youth who spoke in urban slang, pitted against a (literally) straitlaced elder who spoke in "deep" Shona and channeled the rhetoric of the ruling party, ZANU PF, which was itself gerontocratic in both composition and ideology (Campbell 2003). The young man insisted that it was impossible to be "straight" in contemporary Zimbabwe: one had to do whatever was necessary to get by, even if it was unethical or dangerous. The older man addressed him in a patronizing tone, called him lazy, and insisted that the country was ripe with opportunity if only young people would work with government officials. If people wanted to engage in kukiya-kiya, he said, they should do so in a "straight" manner.

As soon as they heard this, Mandoza and the others erupted in angry laughter. Bennie, Mandoza's best friend and lifelong neighbor, mocked the idea that government officials would help with anything: "You'll go in and they'll be like, 'Beat it, kid.'"[5] The others quickly piled on:

LUCIANO: When we say kukiya-kiya, it doesn't mean that a person lacks the ability to do a certain job. You can work on something and get no money out of it, though. So you end up doing a little bit of everything [*zvese-zvese*]. Kukiya-kiya is doing anything and everything to get money [*kubudisa mari*] right then and there. . . . Of course you know there are risks, but there's no other move to make [*hapana yekutamba*].

BENNIE: Right, if you do things straight, you'll get nothing. You won't succeed [*haulume*].

SANCHEZ: Acting straight is a waste of time [*unopera bhutsu*].[6]

TINDO: These days nobody will come clean about what they're doing, and nobody does things straight. . . .

Perhaps, Bennie ventured, doing things "straight" meant making and handling money in visible ways, so that everybody could see.

Tindo agreed: straight economic activity had a paper trail, he said—pay stubs, receipts, and the like. It was not simply a matter of transparency, though, Bennie added after a moment of reflection; "straight," he said, "means living life with a pattern that everybody understands." He gave the example of his father, Sinyoro. For three decades, Sinyoro had enjoyed formal employment as an electrician in Chitungwiza's industrial complex, having migrated to town from a nearby rural area during the liberation war in the seventies. In the early eighties, he had acquired the family home through a housing scheme sponsored by the ambitious postindependence government. A steady, decent income allowed him to make additions to the house while channeling money to improving his family's rural homestead as well. He never moved to another house or back to the rural homestead, and indeed, seldom left Chitungwiza for more than a few days at a time.

"That's straight," Bennie explained. "Everyone knew he came home at six, and for sure, every day he was there at six." If Sinyoro wasn't at work or at home, he could be found at a nearby shopping center, in the same bar, drinking the same beer, Castle lager. He stopped there every day after work, Bennie said, and spent much of the weekend there as well: "When he was drinking at the bar, I knew exactly which corner he was in if I ever had to go and get him."

AUTHOR: So you don't have your own corner at the bar?
BENNIE: No. If I'm there, it's to do some deal, or maybe I'll be running away from something else. You see? If you go to Rufaro bar at a certain time of day, you'll see so-and-so on this bench, and so-and-so over here, but they're old guys. They know the positions where they meet. They're still living in a way that's straight-forward. But for us to reach that level doesn't happen. No one knows what time I come and go. It could be anytime. There's nothing straight.
MANDOZA: Actually, if you tried to act like them, people would think you're running a con.

Like most young people, Bennie, Mandoza, and their friends considered the rise of the "kukiya-kiya economy" (Jones 2010b) to be an epochal shift, with direct ramifications for the composition of both long-term and everyday forms of temporality. But this exchange demonstrates that it had spatial ramifications, too. Indeed, the trio of places Bennie described—work, home, and bar—was iconic of a whole mode of ethical living, now eclipsed. Those places are not well grasped in isolation from one another. They were nodes of a single geography, and the relations between them were central.

We might conceptualize such relations in different ways. Edward Casey (1996), for instance, speaks of "regions," or "area[s] concatenated by the peregrinations between the places [they] connect" (24). Taking a nod from an analysis of migrants and refugees in neighboring Mozambique, though (Lubkemann 2008), we could also speak of a "lifescape"—a "context of material (including ecological), social, and symbolic resources available to social actors for the realization of the life courses they have been socialized to pursue" (192). Critically, it was the way one *moved* in Zimbabwe rather than staying in place that ensured a straight life, and that movement created not just "regions" but a characteristic rhythm of days, weeks, months, and years. Kukiya-kiya, on the other hand, was synonymous with upset patterns, disorderly movements, and a certain fuzziness of place. Its rise as a general social logic was thus symptomatic of the undoing of the entire lifescape of straightness.

Of course, many features of Sinyoro's lifescape barely predated his generation, and there was ample historical precedent for practices young men like Bennie and Mandoza took to be shocking and new. One cannot discount the immense weight of gender ideology, either: a straight life was a deeply heteronormative life, even if the American notion of "straight" qua sexual identity was absent. Still, the general tenor of their argument was sound: the "regions" of their fathers' generation were crumbling before their eyes, and the lifescape associated with those regions was no longer tenable. The bar, being a metonym for both drinking in general and "straight" masculine sociability, had not physically disappeared, but its "place" in an emergent moral geography was no longer certain. Their tangible experience of such places was being materially "unmade" (Weiss 1996), shifting beneath their feet.

Placing Beer in Twentieth-Century Zimbabwe

How was Sinyoro's lifescape made, though, and how did bars and beer come to play such a central role in it? There is an extensive literature for answering those questions.[7] In fact, it is difficult to talk about Zimbabwe's colonial past *without* addressing alcohol, so I will begin with a short sketch of its key features.[8] Put simply, the work of governing "natives"—as racial others, laborers, consumers, and city dwellers—was inseparable from attempts to govern their drinking habits. Local residents often resisted those efforts; nonetheless, along the way, they were drawn into the discourses and the material logics from which they derived.

By the time British settlers arrived in the 1890s, Zimbabweans had been brewing opaque sorghum and millet beers for millennia. Beer was used to appease ancestral spirits, to gather labor for "beer parties," to facilitate domestic relations, and simply for enjoyment (Colson and Scudder 1988). The situation was already changing, though. The advent of illicit distilling in South Africa in the second half of the nineteenth century was accompanied by massive imports of European spirits to Portuguese East Africa (later Mozambique) and their smuggling to neighboring territories. Labor migration, the growing availability of sugar and yeast, and a commercial market for grain surpluses further affected local practices. Along with other aspects of the market economy, these shifts threatened traditional patriarchal power, as they afforded access to resources that might otherwise be controlled by elders, particularly elder men. Indeed, Willis (2002) has shown that in east Africa, the new patterns of alcohol production and consumption were taken by many Africans as iconic of a crumbling patriarchal order.

The late-nineteenth-century European perspective on native drinking habits, on the other hand, was critical to the colonial venture. As Pan puts it, "the link between alcohol and the origins of European imperialism is by no means tenuous" (1975, 16) Participants in the 1884–85 Berlin Conference, which led to the partition of Africa among European powers, claimed to be intervening in the destructive traffic in slaves and liquor. Both, it was said, led to a "demoralization" of the natives, who were already considered prone to excess and indolence.[9] For a time, European liquor exports to west and central Africa were banned. Although the area that would become Zimbabwe was not subject to those bans (or to the transatlantic trade more generally), the British South Africa Company's colonial charter explicitly enjoined a ban on sales of "spirituous liquor" to natives (Pan 1975, 11). In due course, wine and lager were added to the list; for seven decades, until 1957, they were deemed to be "white" alcohol, and it was illegal for Africans to brew, purchase, or consume them.[10]

Rhodesian colonization was at heart an economic affair, though, and the bottom line was often at odds with crusading rhetoric. First, with respect to productivity, many industrialists (including Rhodes himself) were deeply concerned with alcohol's effects on labor output. Because many Africans resisted incorporation into the colonial money economy, though, employers had to measure the risk of beer-induced indiscipline against the promise that the availability of alcohol would help retain scarce and underpaid Black workers (Ambler and Crush 1992). Following the South African precedent, officials also recognized that native beer was a critical source of calories and vitamins in the otherwise meager diets of native workers (Reader and May 1971; Wolcott 1974). Second, white retailers were often happy to exploit the eager African market for beer and spirits—even when it meant contravening the law—and loath to cede that market to African brewers. Last, policing a colony was expensive, and white settlers were not keen to pay for the necessary infrastructure. The goal was always to extract profits from the Black population, not invest in them.

The solution that emerged appeared to address all of these issues in a single stroke. In 1911, the government passed the Kaffir Beer Ordinance.[11] After reiterating that Blacks were prohibited from purchasing or possessing "white" alcohol, the ordinance gave municipal (and therefore white) governments a monopoly on the commercial production and sale of traditional opaque beer within city limits. Historians call this the "Durban system," after the South African city where it was first tried in 1908 (La Hausse 1992). Independent African brewing was not outlawed, and towns often subcontracted brewing to designated African licensees. But by law, African city dwellers could only *buy* beer at municipal-owned and operated beer halls, and no one else could brew it for *sale*. The benefits were supposedly several. First, the law enabled municipal governments to maintain labor discipline by regulating alcohol content and beer hall hours. Second, it prevented Africans—and white traders of "inferior" stock (i.e., Jewish, Greek, Irish, and Portuguese)—from enjoying all the legal profits of beer production. Third and most decisively, it channeled the profits of the African market into municipal coffers, money that could then be used to govern native locations. As Rogerson and Tucker (1985, 360) put it, in buying municipal brewed beer, the "urban African labour force subsidized the costs of its own reproduction, and . . . minimized the costs of 'native administration' to the settler colonial state."

Still, the appearance of effectiveness was just that. Although some urban authorities were more successful than others (Wolcott 1974), one historian called the monopoly system as a whole a "case study in the limits of colonial power" (Parry 1992, 134). Africans continued to buy and consume "white" alcohol. They smuggled liquor across the border, brewed their own beer, distilled their own spirits, and ran their own drinking spots. In fact, the ways in which policy was undermined, circumvented, and eventually overturned were as critical to colonial life as the policies themselves.

Here we return to the subject of shebeens and skokiaan, because together, they constituted a evolving popular response to the settlers' biopolitical schemes.[12] *Shebeen* is an Irish term, and its use may index the involvement of Irish immigrants in the regional alcohol trade (Van Onselen 1982). *Skokiaan* is Afrikaans, but some trace it to a Zulu term referring to a small hole (*isikokeyana*). If so, its illicit quality is built into the name, because such holes were used to hide tins of beer from police raids. Outside the region, the term is associated with a song of the same name, composed by a Zimbabwean, Albert Musarurwa, and performed by generations of jazz artists since, including, most famously, Louis Armstrong (Chikowero 2015, 187 et passim).

From the earliest days of settler rule, African brewers did a roaring trade in the colony's new towns and mining compounds, and women dominated the business. Some traveled from nearby native "reserves," sold their beer, and returned home (Yoshikuni 2006, 47). Others were urbanites themselves, sometimes staying in municipal locations or squatting on nearby farms. These were the "Shebeen" and "Skokiaan Queens" of local legend (Barnes 1999, 50–54). Not only was their beer held to be superior to that sold in municipal beer halls—and superiority might be measured in taste, high alcohol content, or both—their product was cheaper, could be had at any time of day, and was often shared in more intimate settings (Barnes 1999, 50–54). In a satiric nod to white conventions, Africans in town often held raucous "tea parties" in open fields or just outside city limits, where *tsaba-tsaba* jazz played and "everything but tea" was consumed (Chikowero 2015, 194).

By all accounts, skokiaan culture was very widespread; some contemporary observers suggested that an outright majority of women in town engaged in illicit brewing (Barnes and Win 1992, 96–99). Not all Africans appreciated it, though. Notably, many early representatives of the African bourgeoisie sought to separate themselves (morally and physically) from the native location, shebeens, skokiaan, and the people who drank it (Scarnecchia 1999; West 2002). Their political efforts were "modernizing" in that they sought to establish "civilized" urban lifestyles and promote racial uplift, but they were also conservative, because, as often as not, their model was a highly gendered form of Christian (or outright Victorian) decorum and domesticity. Some became teetotalers, rejecting the beer hall and all it stood for entirely, but others tried to establish more respectable forms of drinking.

In that regard, two issues attracted the most attention. The first was the presence of women in beer halls, so-called joint drinking (West 1997). Their presence carried explicit suggestions of prostitution, and with them both the dissolution of stable family units and the threat of female independence. In the minds of many elites (women as well as men), a respectable woman would have no association with alcohol, much less be seen in a bar. The second issue was the ban on purchasing white alcohol. To start, it was iconic of the refusal to treat "all civilized men" as equal (West 1992). Opaque "native" beer was for the masses—a respectable man would drink lager and spirits—but it also figured in the politics of place. Many elites resented being shoehorned into drinking in the grim municipal beer halls as much as they resented being forced to live in locations.[13]

The ban on white liquor was finally lifted in 1957, and corporate brewing started moving to the fore around the same time. Two corporations were especially important, and eventually they would come under one heading.[14] The first was Rhodesian Breweries, which was first established in 1910 as a subsidiary of the South African Breweries (SAB). In addition to brewing a stable of lagers and ales for white settler consumption, SAB was contracted between 1911 and 1938 by the Salisbury (now Harare) municipal government to produce opaque beer for its beer halls. As in South Africa, its representatives in Rhodesia were eager to begin legal sales of lager to the African market (Mager 2010). The other corporation was Heinrich Chibuku, established in 1955 in the industrialized copper-mining region of Northern Rhodesia. Although the quality of municipal brewing had slowly improved over the first part of the twentieth century, the Chibuku product was widely held to be superior. The company quickly took over municipal production all along the copperbelt, and by the early sixties it owned and operated three large city breweries in Southern Rhodesia as well. In the seventies it assumed ownership and/or production of most of the remaining municipal monopolies, and had established itself in Botswana, Malawi, and Swaziland too. Meanwhile, the Southern

Rhodesian subsidiary of Chibuku had changed hands twice, eventually ending up as part of SAB's local portfolio. This last shift laid the groundwork for the establishment in 1978 of a new holding company: Delta Corporation. From Zimbabwean independence forward, it monopolized the production and supply of both "clear" and "opaque" beer in the country, and much else besides.[15]

Delta's monopoly was vertical as well as horizontal. Its subsidiaries made bottles and containers; produced enzymes, starches, malts, and other beer ingredients; and maintained a massive delivery and bottle return infrastructure. For a time, it owned a major supermarket chain, and it was a local bottler for Coca-Cola products. And although municipal brewing largely disappeared, the beer hall infrastructure stayed in municipal hands, now selling products produced by Delta. Beyond all of that, Delta had all the hallmarks of a modern corporation: rigorous quality control, well-designed sales and promotion tactics, and complex multilevel branding for different market segments. By 2008, it was also the second largest listing on the Zimbabwe stock exchange, with a stock issue at least double that of the next challenger.

Ethical Circulation

With all of this in mind, let us shift to the way the big business of beer intersected with the cultural symbolism of drinking for Sinyoro's postindependence generation. Here it is useful to follow the model provided by Sidney Mintz in his discussion of the transatlantic history of sugar (1986). In it, he differentiates between what he calls the "internal" and "external" meanings of comestibles (1986, 151 et passim). Internal points to the realm of culture and consumption—the way, Mintz maintains, that sugar featured in people's everyday lives, and how it fit into elaborate regimes of symbolic practice. External refers to the (international) order of production—how sugar agriculture was financed, how it affected politics, who did the work, and how it was processed and shipped and integrated into an ever-growing web of industrial food production. The same conceptual distinction works in the case of Zimbabwean beer: much as people had to *have* sugar before it could mean all that it came to mean to them, a great deal had to happen for beer to feature in conceptions of a "straight" life. Space had to be racialized in particular ways; the native location had to be invented and reformed; a legal and biopolitical apparatus had to be developed to govern alcohol production, purchases, and consumption (e.g., zoning, banning, taxation); a beer monopoly had to emerge, and more importantly, saturate the entire market with its products while ensuring their desirability. Moreover, because all of that figured in a larger national economy, beer-related matters were vulnerable to the country's economic collapse. And of course, as with sugar, the influence went the other way as well: African drinking practices and all the ideas surrounding them had to be cultivated for government and business to profit from them.

I have already noted the division of Rhodesian drinking practices along lines of race, as well as the way alcohol was implicated in emergent projects of class, distinction, and gendered propriety. This scratches the surface, though. The same matters were also tied to the rural–urban divide, and with it, a whole chain of subsidiary oppositions, wherein people associated Blackness with rural life, elders, tradition, family, women, and nonmonetary exchange, and whiteness with urban life, modern life, young single men, and the money economy. Throughout the late twentieth century, for instance, a key narrative trope for Zimbabwean fiction was the journey to the city, a tragic shift from Black tradition to white modernity (Chiwome 1996). Bars and uncontrolled drinking were not just features in this tragedy, they were key symptoms. Almost by definition, urban drinking was dangerous drinking, associated with dangerous people: unruly youth, foreign ethnicities, and liberated women.

This model was not what Bennie, Mandoza and company had in mind when they spoke of "straightness," though, at least not exactly. The symbolic oppositions were all familiar enough; every Zimbabwean is exposed to them in heavy doses through school and politics, if not at church or home. But unlike Sinyoro, all of them had been born and raised in town, and a "traditional" rural life—whatever that might mean after a century of colonialism—held no appeal for them. Instead, the symbolism of rural virtues informed an idealized conception of *urban* social space—that "region" I described earlier, comprising "peregrinations" between home, work, and bar. The bridge connecting them was a shared conception of measured movement. And whereas to some, the bar signified the decay of rural–urban migration, to Mandoza and company, it was a positive space, mediating movements between work and home—just as it had been for Sinyoro and his friends.

Movement in this sense involved people, of course, but conceptions of straightness were also caught up with the movement of *money* between work, bar, and home. The masculine ideal was to have a job that provided a large enough regular income to secure men's status as breadwinners at home (i.e., domestic reproduction and expansion) while enabling legitimate excess and release at the bar after work. Even better was a job that provided enough to do all of that while funding the regular consumption of higher-status beer, like the Castle lager Sinyoro favored. Drinking habits that were less than straight were viewed with these ideals in mind. What such drinkers shared was a lack of respect for the boundaries between spheres, or the impropriety of moving between them. A man might spend too much time at the bar, threatening relations at home or at work. He might channel money away from domestic reproduction to beer, or waste funds that might be used for business purposes instead. He might drink or be drunk outside acceptable hours or away from the bar. He might get caught up in cycles of beer debt or agonistic drinking, or neglect home duties for a widely derided class of bar women (*vakadzi vebhawa*). Or, perhaps most threateningly, the drinker in question might *be* a woman—by most accounts, there was no legitimate reason for a "straight" woman to be associated with a bar at all.

After independence, shebeens and homebrew, once associated with insurgent African resistance, slowly became icons of this kind of transgressive, crooked drinking. Shebeens lost much of their original clientele to private bars, nightclubs, and bottle stores, but they continued to operate throughout Chitungwiza and other locations (now renamed "high-density suburbs"), especially in the more cramped neighborhoods. Instead of homebrewed beer, they tended to retail SAB beer at a slight markup, or sell *kachasu*, a kind of moonshine.[16] Kachasu was defined less by taste than the context in which it was brewed (artisanal and illicit), its high alcohol content, and its perceived "heat." Heat referred to the physical sensation of spirits—hence the old term "hot stuff"—but heat was also a symbolic property, capturing a sense of uncontrolled movements and broken boundaries (cf. Weiss 1996, 51 et passim).

A moment's reflection will show that internal meanings of this sort depended on a specific confluence of external meaning, which transcended the lives of individual drinkers in both time and space. Most notably, the practice and symbolism of "straight" drinking was fundamentally shaped by a century of colonial and postcolonial history. In particular, it hinged on a particular form of industrial brewing, and with it the widespread availability, near-uniform pricing, and relatively low cost of beer. Perhaps most decisively for Bennie, Mandoza, and company, straight drinking presupposed an economy where an average man in Chitungwiza could earn a steady living, large enough to cover the costs of both physical and social reproduction, in all its guises. By and large, people of Sinyoro's generation could take such things for granted, as a kind of background on which people's lives, straight or otherwise, played out. The situation in late-2008 Zimbabwe, however, was too chaotic for any of these things to be presumed. As a result, young men were long on ideas of drinking, but short on the substances, relations, and opportunities once associated with those ideas.

Quick to Brew, Fast to Spoil

With this background, we can better understand the import of Mandoza's shebeen. Much like Bennie and his compatriots, Mandoza had come of age amid the country's hyperinflation crisis, and aside from a brief stint as a stock boy in a Harare shop, he had never held a formal job. His father died when he was in high school, and his mother followed soon after. The AIDS epidemic made such losses all too common among Chitungwiza youth; the statistical majority of young men I worked with had lost at least one parent. Mandoza was more fortunate than many orphans in that he was allowed to stay in his parents' house, which they had owned, and could make money by letting out some of the rooms. Still, his prospects were bleak; worse, he had barely limped through local certificate courses in basic carpentry. By comparison, Sinyoro had put Bennie through a well-regarded diesel mechanics course, which afforded Bennie occasional piecework opportunities in the neighborhood.

During the 2000s, Mandoza had worked as a bus tout, made and sold shoddy aluminum pots, hawked cigarettes, sold black-market fuel and sugar, wagered on billiards, brokered deals between friends and associates, smuggled goods across the Botswana and Mozambique borders, and engaged in a variety of petty frauds. Though he himself was a consummate hustler, full of swagger and fast talk, his economic repertoire was not unique in being so wide: again, such was the logic of kukiya-kiya. Nonetheless, carrying on so many schemes at once took some skill, and opportunities had to be both carefully composed and quickly exploited. ·

Mandoza would have considered several factors as he planned his shebeen. First of all, he knew that selling beer could be a moneymaker. In the early 2000s he had watched enviously as Bennie smuggled industrially produced cane spirits across the border from Mozambique, and he was familiar with all the local shebeens. He also had helped others brew. As for demand, he was intimately familiar with local drinking habits and supply, important local players, and the general market for a product like his. Second, he had a highly attuned sense for the game he would have to play to make his venture successful. Years earlier, he had lived with a relative in Plumtree, just across the border from Botswana, and he had made a few forays to Mozambique as well. In both cases he had engaged in a mix of smuggling and legal cross-border trade (for goods other than alcohol). More importantly, he had familiarized himself with processes, people, loopholes, and even the physical terrain.

Several material factors came into play as well. The first and most obvious one was money. Mandoza needed enough to fund his first trip to Francistown, Botswana, and an initial supply of Mnanti (an amount that young men often called "start" in English), but it also needed to be money of the right sort. The ever-plunging value of the Zimdollar made holding onto local currency foolhardy, so he had to convert free funds to foreign currency (especially Botswana pula) and had begun charging his tenants rent pegged to the illegal foreign-exchange rate. A second, less obvious material factor was water and fuel. Piped water supplies were erratic at best by then; often his neighborhood went for a week or more with none. Water could be purchased, but that would cut into his profits, so the solution was for his wife to stand in long lines at nearby wells. Electricity and cooking gas were also limited, which meant boiling the Mnanti using firewood purchased for several dollars a bundle. A third factor, easy to overlook, was a suitable location. Had Mandoza been a lodger, for instance, or under the thumb of his parents, he likely would not have managed to set up a shebeen in the front yard. Such a yard also needed to be suitable for purpose: large, reasonably central, but not overly exposed. Last, he needed traveling documents. Passports were difficult and expensive to acquire in 2008, but skipping border checkpoints both ways would add a good deal of risk to his venture. He opted to leverage some connections in Chitungwiza and get a forged Emergency Travel Document, a stamped paper with his (fake) particulars.

"I won't lie to you," Mandoza crowed to me in mid-2009, "we made loads of money those days [i.e., three months earlier]. I couldn't brew beer fast enough." That was no doubt an exaggeration, but by all accounts, the shebeen was a success, bringing in regular profits while covering costs. Like Chibuku, his Mnanti beer quickly spoiled, which put emphasis on fast turnover of stock. Low capitalization and the added costs and difficulty of smuggling large amounts of mix meant he had to make the trip to Francistown several times a week.

For all its success, though, Mandoza's shebeen only lasted a few months. He subsequently gave me two different stories for its collapse. Both were plausible, and it is possible that both occurred. The first involved a simple miscalculation. Mandoza purchased Mnanti with Botswana pula, and sold the beer for Zimdollars. Though people derided the latter as useless, Zimdollar pricing was actually key to his success: others were selling beer in foreign currency, but his relatively poorer clientele were less likely to have it. He had to source his pula entirely on the black market, though, and because the exchange rate there changed dramatically every day (sometime more than once a day), a misstep in Zimdollar pricing erased his entire margin in the space of hours, leaving him with no capital stock to continue. The second story involved water. Brewing for sale and running a shebeen were both still illegal, but police were hardly being paid at the time, so Mandoza was right to assume he could bribe his way out when they inevitably caught on. However, the water shortage—which was even more severe elsewhere around Harare—had produced a deadly cholera outbreak. That meant his operation was more than simply illegal: it was a designated public health hazard—or so the police claimed.[17] They seized his containers and presumably the remaining money.

One could say many things about this venture, but no one would have called it "straight." In fact, it was constitutively crooked, and a perfect example of kukiya-kiya. It was short lived, situational, and erratic, whereas the ideal job was long lasting, followed a pattern, and carefully planned out. Brewing and consumption could occur Sunday to Sunday, day or night; "anytime is teatime," as Bennie once quipped. There was no paper trail except a fake travel document. The shebeen itself was makeshift, with no special tables, chairs, utensils, or other equipment. Unlike a bar, which would have been physically separated from both domestic space and a workplace, his shebeen blended those spaces with a drinking space. Such again was the spatiotemporal imprint of kukiya-kiya: it respected no spatial or temporal boundaries, nor the conventional pathways that marked out a lifescape. Or rather, it respected them only so far as they could be instrumentalized for profit.

Conclusion

As Mintz suggests in his discussion of sugar, the elaborate symbolic worlds surrounding consumption rest on—and are largely products of—an immense and often invisible material infrastructure. Brewing and beer consumption are no exception. In Zimbabwe, movements between work, home, and the bar were the basis for an entire ethical system—straightness—and with it a specific lifescape, but all of it depended on a welter of historical and material factors that exceeded that lifescape in time and space. By late 2008, that realm of "external meaning" was on the verge of disintegration.

Often this material substrate goes unnoticed. When we talk about brewing and beer in a context like that of United States, for instance, it is easy to take most external meaning for granted. Some US brewing ventures are attuned to elements of it, of course; hence these brewers' drive to source materials locally or engage with local communities. More common, I think, are efforts to create elaborate illusions of place, with all the sheen of nineteenth-century industrialism and none of its dangers. Either way, how many people consider what would happen to the beer industry if clean water were no longer available, or patrons no longer earned enough to buy even the cheapest beer, or the national currency collapsed? But these too are conditions of possibility for brewing and the construction of place in bars and breweries.

In a postcolonial context like Zimbabwe's, external meaning has never been far from the surface of social life. The entire twentieth century has been marked by a crisis of meaning, as local practices shifted in the face of both colonial and postcolonial modes of governance. Still, Zimbabwe's first decade or so of independence was marked by a degree of material stability—enough that in Sinyoro's lifescape, one could attend less to the availability of beer and jobs and houses than to the imaginative dictates of straight living. Though young men like Mandoza were never destined for middle-class lives, the country's economic collapse created such material instability that his cohort came face to face with the structuring facts of external meaning. In the process, the symbolism that attended to places was itself displaced. Everyday patterns and lifeways were materially unmade. Even if Mandoza and his cohort managed to lay claim to their own corners at the bar, the socioeconomic world that made Sinyoro's corner meaningful had disappeared into the shadows. And in any case, the beer was to be found elsewhere.

Notes

1. All names used in this chapter are pseudonyms.
2. Compare the South African brand, King Korn, which also sells nonalcoholic ground sorghum: https://www.facebook.com/KingKornSouthAfrica/.
3. Rhodes's company colonized the territories that are now Zimbabwe, Zambia, and Malawi (then Southern Rhodesia, Northern Rhodesia, and Nyasaland, respectively). The British government soon took over the latter two while ceding control of the first to its white settler population. In 1963, when Zambia and Malawi became independent, the white settlers of Southern Rhodesia (by then just Rhodesia) declared themselves independent as well, only under apartheid-style minority rule. After a long war, majority rule was established in 1980, and the country became Zimbabwe. Unless otherwise specified, my use of *Rhodesia* and *Rhodesian* refers to that territory.
4. The English term was almost always used, but it could also be voiced as *kuswatuka* in Chitungwiza's lingua franca, ChiShona. For more on the material in this paragraph and the next, see my discussion in Jones (2010b).
5. All of the dialogue included here is translated from Shona (intermixed with English terminology).
6. Their language was richly idiomatic. *Hapana yekutamba* refers to draughts (checkers); the suggestion is a state of checkmate. *Haulume* (literally, "you won't bite") is the title of a popular song. Both biting and eating have gendered and sexual connotations in Shona (the word for man, *murume,* could literally be translated as "biter"), but the suggestion here is you will not enjoy success (of the masculine, "breadwinning" sort). *Unopera bhutsu* literally means you'll "wear out your shoes" trying to accomplish something (i.e., a wild goose chase).
7. See the edited collections by Van Wolputte and Fumanti (2010b), Bryceson (2002), and Crush and Ambler (1992), as well as monographs by Akyeampong (1996), Mager (2010), Willis (2002), and Colson and Scudder (1988).
8. Examples include social histories by Chikowero (2015), Barnes (1999), Barnes and Win (1992), Schmidt (1992), Yoshikuni (2007), and Scarnecchia (1994), all of which include discussion of beer and brewing.
9. For example, the Dickensian "Committee for the Prevention of the Demoralization of the Native Races by the Liquor Traffic" was an active participant in debates about colonialism and prohibition.
10. For the US stance on similar prohibition measures for "all uncivilized tribes and races," see Pan (1975), 37–38.
11. *Kaffir* was period settler terminology for an African native. It was and still is a racial slur.
12. For an extended discussion of both phenomena in the Zimbabwean context, see Chikowero (2015), chapters 5–6. See also Chimhete (2018).

13. This dynamic was less pronounced than it was in South Africa, where beer halls were a major target of political organizing; see La Hausse (1992).
14. For more on this history, see Rogerson and Tucker (1985) and Mager (2010).
15. The only real competition for opaque beer came from two remaining independent municipal breweries.
16. The term is derived from the Brazilian term *cachaça*, and its use in the region owes to centuries-old interaction with the Lusophone Indian Ocean circuit. The drink has a long association with Mozambican and Malawian migrants, a uniquely large percentage of whom were either farm laborers or gardeners under white employ.
17. It is not clear whether the brewing process and/or alcohol content in skokiaan is adequate to kill cholera bacteria. In any case, the utensils Mandoza used were cleaned with the same suspect water, and he did not keep a sterile brewing environment.

References

Akyeampong, Emmanuel. 1996. *Drink, Power, and Cultural Change: A Social History of Alcohol in Ghana, c. 1800 to Recent Times.* Portsmouth, NH: Heinemann.

Ambler, Charles H. and J. S. Crush. 1992. "Alcohol in Southern African Labor History." P. 1–55. In *Liquor and Labor in Southern Africa,* edited by J. S. Crush and Charles H. Ambler. Athens: Ohio University Press.

Barnes, Teresa. 1999. *"We Women Worked So Hard": Gender, Urbanization and Social Reproduction in Colonial Harare, Zimbabwe, 1930–1956.* Oxford, UK: James Currey.

Barnes, Teresa and Everjoyce Win. 1992. *To Live a Better Life: An Oral History of Women in the City of Harare, 1930–70.* Harare, Zimbabwe: Baobab Books.

Bryceson, Deborah Fahy. 2002. *Alcohol in Africa: Mixing Business, Pleasure, and Politics.* Portsmouth, NH: Heinemann.

Campbell, Horace. 2003. *Reclaiming Zimbabwe: The Exhaustion of the Patriarchal Model of Liberation.* Claremont, South Africa: David Philip.

Carmody, Pédrag. 1998. "Neoclassical Practice and the Collapse of Industry in Zimbabwe: The Cases of Textiles, Clothing, and Footwear," *Economic Geography* 74(4):319–43.

Casey, Edward S. 1996. "How to Get from Space to Place in a Fairly Short Stretch of Time: Phenomenological Prolegomena." In *Senses of Place,* edited by Steven Feld and Keith H. Basso, 14–51. Santa Fe, NM: School of American Research.

Chagonda, Tapiwa. 2012. "Teachers and Bank Workers' Responses to Zimbabwe's Crisis: Uneven Effects, Different Strategies." *Journal of Contemporary African Studies* 30(1):83–97.

Chikowero, Mhoze. 2015. *African Music, Power, and Being in Colonial Zimbabwe.* Bloomington: Indiana University Press.

Chimhete, Nathaniel. 2018. "African Nationalism, Municipal Beer Outlets and Shebeens in Salisbury, Rhodesia, 1960s–1980." *Journal of Southern African Studies* 44(5):815–31.

Chiumbu, Sarah and Muchaparara Musemwa, eds. 2012. *Crisis! What Crisis! The Multiple Dimensions of the Zimbabwe Crisis.* Cape Town, South Africa: HSRC Press.

Chiwome, Emmanuel. 2002. *A Social History of the Shona Novel*. Rev. ed. Gweru, Zimbabwe: Mambo Press.

Colson, Elizabeth and Thayer Scudder. 1988. *For Prayer and Profit: The Ritual, Economic, and Social Importance of Beer in Gwembe District, Zambia, 1950–1982*. Stanford, CA: Stanford University Press.

Crush, J. S. and C. H. Ambler. 1992. *Liquor and Labor in Southern Africa*. Athens: Ohio University Press.

Duri, Fidelis Peter Thomas. 2012. "Negotiating the Zimbabwe–Mozambique Border: The Pursuit of Survival by Mutare's Poor, 2000–2008." Pp. 122–39. In *Crisis! What Crisis! The Multiple Dimensions of the Zimbabwe Crisis*, edited by Sarah Chiumbu and Muchaparara Musemwa. Cape Town, South Africa: HSRC Press.

Haggblade, Steven. 1992. "The Shebeen Queen and the Evolution of Botswana's Sorghum Beer Industry." Pp. 395–412. In *Liquor and Labor in Southern Africa*, edited by J. S. Crush and Charles H. Ambler. Athens: Ohio University Press.

Hanke, Steve and Alex Kwok. 2009. "On the Measurement of Zimbabwe's Hyperinflation." *Cato Journal* 29(2):353–64.

Jones, Jeremy L. 2010a. "Freeze! Movement, Narrative and the Disciplining of Price in Hyperinflationary Zimbabwe." *Social Dynamics* 36(2):338–51.

———. 2010b. "'Nothing Is Straight in Zimbabwe': The Rise of the Kukiya-Kiya Economy 2000–2008." *Journal of Southern African Studies* 36(2):285–99.

———. 2014. "'No Move to Make': The Zimbabwean Crisis, Displacement-in-Place, and the Erosion of 'Proper Places.'" Pp. 206–29. In *Displacement Economies in Africa: Paradoxes of Crisis and Creativity*, edited by Amanda Hammar. London: Zed Books.

La-Hausse, Paul. 1988. *Brewers Beerhalls and Boycotts: A History of Liquor in South Africa*. History Workshop Topic Series 2. Johannesburg: University of the Witswatersrand.

———. 1992. "Drink and Cultural Innovation in Durban: The Origins of the Beerhall in South Africa, 1902–1916." Pp. 78–114. In *Liquor and Labor in Southern Africa*, edited by J. S. Crush and C. H. Ambler. Athens: Ohio University Press.

Lubkemann, Stephen C. 2008. *Culture in Chaos: An Anthropology of the Social Condition in War*. Chicago: University of Chicago Press.

Mager, Anne Kelk. 2010. *Beer, Sociability, and Masculinity in South Africa*. Bloomington: Indiana University Press.

Mintz, Sidney W. 1986. *Sweetness and Power*. New York: Penguin Books.

Pan, Lynn. 1975. *Alcohol in Colonial Africa*. Helsinki and New Brunswick, NJ: Finnish Foundation for Alcohol Studies; distributed by Rutgers University Center of Alcohol Studies.

Parry, Richard. 1992. "The 'Durban System' and the Limits of Colonial Power in Salisbury, 1890–1935." Pp. 115–38. In *Liquor and Labor in Southern Africa*, edited by J. S. Crush and Charles H. Ambler. Athens: Ohio University Press.

Pilossof, Rory. 2009. "'Dollarisation' in Zimbabwe and the Death of an Industry." *Review of African Political Economy* 36(120):294–99.

Reader, D. H. and Joan May. 1971. *Drinking Patterns in Rhodesia: Highfield African Township, Salisbury*. Occasional Paper 5. Salisbury: Institute for Social Research, University of Rhodesia.

Rogerson, C. M. and B. A. Tucker. 1985. "Commercialization and Corporate Capital in the Sorghum Beer Industry of Central Africa." *Geoforum* 16(4):357–68.

Scarnecchia, Timothy. 1999. "The Mapping of Respectability and the Transformation of African Residential Space." Pp. 151–62. In *Sites of Struggle: Essays in Zimbabwe's Urban History*, edited by Brian Raftopoulos and Tsuneo Yoshikuni. Harare, Zimbabwe: Weaver Press.

———. 1994. "The Politics of Gender and Class in the Creation of African Communities, Salisbury, Rhodesia, 1937–1957." PhD thesis, Department of History, University of Michigan.

Schmidt, Elizabeth. 1992. *Peasants, Traders, and Wives: Shona Women in the History of Zimbabwe, 1870–1939*. Portsmouth, NH: Heinemann.

Van Onselen, Charles. 1982. *Studies in the Social and Economic History of the Witwatersrand, 1886–1914. Volume 1: New Babylon*. New York: Longman.

Van Wolputte, Steven and Mattia Fumanti. 2010. *Beer in Africa: Drinking Spaces, States and Selves*. Münster: LIT Verlag.

Weiss, Brad. 1996. *The Making and Unmaking of the Haya Lived World: Consumption, Commoditization, and Everyday Practice*. Durham, NC: Duke University Press.

West, Michael O. 1992. "'Equal Rights for All Civilized Men.'" *International Review of Social History* 37(3):376–97.

———. 1997. "Liquor and Libido: 'Joint Drinking' and the Politics of Sexual Control in Colonial Zimbabwe, 1920s-1950s." *Journal of Social History* 30(3):645–67.

———. 2002. *The Rise of an African Middle Class: Colonial Zimbabwe 1898–1965*. Bloomington: Indiana University Press.

Willis, Justin. 2002. *Potent Brews: A Social History of Alcohol in East Africa 1850–1999*. Oxford, UK: James Currey.

Wolcott, Harry F. 1974. *The African Beer Gardens in Bulawayo: Integrated Drinking in a Segregated Society*. New Brunswick, NJ: Publications Division, Rutgers Center of Alcohol Studies.

Yoshikuni, Tsuneo. 2007. *African Urban Experiences in Colonial Zimbabwe: A Social History of Harare before 1925*. Harare, Zimbabwe: Weaver Press.

CHAPTER 6

Landscapes of Beer Consumption in Helsinki

KEVIN DRAIN

Introduction

In Helsinki, a cultural shift is visible in the city's spaces of consumption, with some areas witnessing new forms of dining and drinking culture not seen in Finland until the last decade or so. Changing food and beverage consumption patterns overlap with the typical narrative of gentrification—neighborhoods being upgraded, often with an influx of wealthier residents bringing their spending money and distinct tastes—widely observed in Western cities in the early twenty-first century and studied in many fields. Although *taste* is a tricky concept to measure, in Helsinki the growth of the craft beer industry and its accompanying culture is one marker of shifting tastes in the city's changing retail environment.

Through an introduction to retail gentrification as a topic of academic interest, this chapter identifies the experience of food and drink consumption as a driving characteristic of neighborhood change. Following a brief history of the case study neighborhoods and streets, I offer a background of Finland's craft beer scene. I describe a qualitative five-year empirical research study of two Helsinki streets that reveals how the city's retail landscapes have changed and identifies the contribution of bars as social spaces for diverse consumer and social groups. Last, I discuss the results of the study in relation to this retail shift, highlighting the role of beer as a mediator among these groups.

In academic literature, retail gentrification has been addressed as a discrete phenomenon in which the preferences of consumers—often the new, gentrifying class—drive visible changes in retail landscapes (Bridge and Dowling 2001; Zukin 2008; Zukin et al. 2009). Retail gentrification is still often framed either alongside or within studies of other forms of gentrification. Such studies describe the role of small stores—whether they are "local" or "traditional" (i.e., were already there) or are newer "boutiques" that replace local stores—and the emergence of dining and shopping experiences new to an area. They depict the driving force of middle-class consumers seeking authenticity and exercising cultural capital as central and often expressed through their desires for authentic cuisine. Some studies also focus on the negative side effects of changing retail environments, especially for residents still living in an area. Often, the dominant political voices in gentrifying neighborhoods take the view that the only healthy neighborhoods are those that cater to those needs and values of the middle class.[1] This creates further side effects even where regeneration or gentrification has not occurred, as entire areas are labeled as blighted and existing populations marginalized through "symbolically violent" rhetoric along class-based lines of taste and culture (Hubbard 2017, 19).

From the perspectives of gentrification and drinking establishments, then, dive bars tend to have a bad rap among policymakers. In the policy and public discourse of the United Kingdom, for example, "'successful' High Streets are depicted as those that have cast off any taint of working-class consumption while failing ones are depicted as 'toxic,' harboring 'unhealthy' stores potentially off-putting to more affluent consumers and tourists" (Hubbard 2017, 18). However, whereas bars and drinking culture are easy to package in the rhetoric of blight and working-class immorality, craft beers and the bars that sell them easily fit into the habitus of the middle class. Thus, beer lies at a paradoxical intersection of retail gentrification and consumption more generally, one in which culture is expressed through knowledge and affinity for product and provenance rather than the easily moralized excesses of binge drinking and revelry. The case study that follows builds on these themes by comparing the changing bar scenes on two neighborhood streets in Helsinki, Finland.

Helsinki's Kallio and Punavuori Neighborhoods

Constructed in the 1860s during Helsinki's industrialization boom, Kallio has long been regarded as a working-class neighborhood. In

1932, Finnish scholar Heikki Waris published his landmark study, *The Emergence of Working-Class Society North of Helsinki's Long Bridge* (*Työläisyhteiskunnan syntyminen Helsingin Pitkänsillan pohjoispuolelle*; 1932/1973), the first of its kind in Finland. The "Long Bridge," or Pitkäsilta, is actually a short span connecting Helsinki's dense central peninsula with areas to the north. The bridge has a similar symbolic meaning to the American expression "the other side of the tracks," separating bourgeois southern Helsinki from the working-class neighborhoods in the north.

While surveying the case study street of Vaasankatu, north of Pitkäsilta in Kallio, the students who helped me with this project and I encountered many locals and visitors, some of whom shared their experiences of Vaasankatu with us. According to one long-time visitor in his sixties, Vaasankatu used to be called "Knife Boulevard" or "the Meat Counter" in Finnish. Finnish author Arto Melleri affirmed Vaasankatu's moniker of Knife Boulevard by naming his collection of poems after it (in Finnish, *Puukko Bulevardi*). Another man we met, who moved to Kallio from rural Arctic Lapland in the early 1980s, described the horror of seeing a man wandering around with his hand cut off. Even younger locals toast to a memory of Kallio's past. At a bar on Vaasankatu, a man no older than thirty-five lamented, "Before, it was the 'Wild West,' the crazy place where something was always happening." Another man recounted reading a Finnair leaflet warning people not to go to Vaasankatu "because it's full of sex workers, violence, and drunkards," and said he heard rumors that Japanese travel booklets in the 1980s offered the same warning.

These rumors have taken on a life of their own and fit with a narrative of Vaasankatu's past, a liminal zone where those who dared venture could enjoy hedonistic spoils beyond the reach of conservative Finnish laws and customs. The place-myth of Vaasankatu, and Kallio more generally, reaches beyond residents and consumers in Helsinki, as the international press has distributed the frontier narrative of gentrification to a global audience. A March 2013 feature in the *New York Times* Travel section branded Kallio as "a sizzling sector percolating with exotic cafes, sleek restaurants and clubs serving fine cuisine, and inviting walk-in studio-boutiques" (Sander 2013, 1). The article framed the neighborhood in terms of a place that was "once off-limits" to outsiders, where seedy bars still offered the chance for an authentic Kallio experience (Sander 2013, 1). In essence, the street is legendary beyond Helsinki among generations of Finns and, increasingly, an international audience.

The street of Vaasankatu presented an ideal study case in Kallio for practical reasons, especially when compared to our other case study on the mostly pedestrians-only street of Iso Roobertinkatu in the Punavuori neighborhood of Helsinki. Although Vaasankatu is not a major thoroughfare for motor vehicles, it sustains constant foot traffic due to high residential densities and a metro station at one end of the street. Thus, retail spaces are intended to be seen and accessed by pedestrians, and the street is a visibly popular destination both within Kallio and Helsinki as a whole.

· Located on the southern side of Pitkäsilta in central Helsinki, Punavuori is a small district comprising mostly residential blocks with street-level retail along main thoroughfares. Like Kallio, Punavuori was once a working-class neighborhood. Up through the 1950s, the area's "proximity [to] the dockyard and sea made Punavuori the infamous outskirts of Helsinki. There were marine bars, illegal activities and dirty alleyways" (Mustonen and Lindblom 2014, 89). The historical image of Punavuori has all but faded, with little left resembling a working-class or seedy district. Unlike Kallio, where "the legacy of the past decades, when the Long Bridge really separated two worlds from each other, remains," Punavuori is characterized by a "middle-class or even bourgeoisie ethos" (Mustonen and Lindblom 2013, 2). A 2008 article in the *New York Times* Travel section profiled three pricey restaurants in Punavuori, noting the "independently owned, interesting, smaller bistros" had "blossomed" in recent years. The author describes how "attention is paid to the smallest design detail" in the restaurants, and, referring to Helsinki, lauds the authenticity of this "proud paradise" of "inventive and playful" Finnish cuisine (Winer 2008, 10). Punavuori is also promoted by the city as part of the "Design District" area, and many businesses display window stickers branding themselves part of this area.

Iso Roobertinkatu is a shopping street at the heart of the Punavuori neighborhood. The southern portion is open to auto traffic, and there is little retail activity until one moves into the pedestrianized segment (though taxis and delivery vehicles still meander around the central boxed trees). As of this study there were fifty-five retail storefronts along the pedestrianized section of Iso Roobertinkatu, with large windows encouraging gazing and shopping. Traces of the area's former reputation as a red-light district are hardly visible on the street, though the subtle entrance to a gentleman's club, next to a newly opened billiards bar, offers a clue. Given its working-class and sex-work history, as well as the size of its pedestrian-accessible storefronts, the street makes an ideal comparison for Vaasankatu.

Beer in Finland

Both the streets of Vaasankatu and Iso Roobertinkatu have become part of the collective Finnish conscience through artifacts of literature and pop culture, often highlighting both an edgy or marginal sort of nostalgia along with alcohol consumption. For various reasons, including the legacy of twentieth-century Prohibition, strict alcohol-sales laws, high alcohol taxes, advertisement censorship, and a host of cultural explanations, the default way of drinking in Finland seems to revolve around the mass consumption of mass-produced beer. Beer is the drink of choice in Finland, surpassing even soft drinks by a wide sales margin. In 2020, Finns consumed around 380 million liters of beer and cider (Panimoliitto 2022). For a country with four and a half million adults, that translates to around 85 liters per person of drinking age, compared with roughly 120 liters in the United States the same year (NBWA 2021). It has been suggested that 10 percent of the people in Finland consume 50 percent of the alcohol. Most of these drinks are sold under multiple brands by three main Finnish brewers: Sinebrychoff, Hartwall, and Olvi. All three were founded in the 1800s and have remained dominant in the local market since before Finland was an independent country.

The industry is at a crucial moment, however: beer consumption dropped by 2.6 percent in 2018, whereas sales of "long drinks" (mixed gin and fruit soda, most commonly grapefruit) increased by 37 percent. The sale of long drinks still trails that of beer, however, with just over 50 million liters consumed in 2018. Another way in which the beer industry is changing is with a shift toward variety. Although sales of standard lagers and pilsners decreased by 6 percent between 2012 and 2017, other types of beer have grown more popular: over the same period, sales of gluten-free beer, organic beer, and nonalcoholic beer increased by 83 percent, 36 percent, and 41 percent, respectively. The industry is also contracting, with 1,680 people employed in brewing in 2017, compared to 2,930 in 2002 (YLE News 2018).

Amid these changes, a craft-brewing scene has emerged. As recently as 2007, an industry spokesperson lamented that "brewing entrepreneurship is a rare resource in Finland. The combined production of small breweries still represents less than half a percent of total beer sales. In just under ten years [since 1997], every third brewery has stopped" (Nieminen 2007). Hardly ten years later, the opposite is true, and the craft beer market is saturated. Whereas in 2015 there were eighty registered breweries in Finland, the number passed one hundred in 2018. A recent news article reported how currently, "competition in the industry is tough. Small breweries still account for a small share of Finnish beer sales, so brewers are struggling against store shelves and restaurant taps" (YLE News 2018). Those shelves account for most of Finnish alcohol sales, with bars and restaurants composing only 18 percent of total sales. On top of this, although small breweries have grown in number, they only had around 6 percent of the market share for beer sales as of 2020 (Panimoliitto, 2022). Nonetheless, the growing number of small breweries in Finland have influenced both the products available and the country's drinking culture.

Andreas Lundmark has seen a decade of change in Helsinki's beer scene. He began working at the state-owned alcohol retailer ALKO, which controls the sale of all strong beverages (more than 5.5 percent ABV) and has worked as a bartender at four locations. Lundmark now works for a Helsinki craft beer distributor in called Pien. Describing one part of his role, he said, "Most of our business customers know what they are buying from us and are following the world of craft beer. So we try to educate the ones that are coming into this world—the restaurants that haven't really paid attention before and that have customers who maybe don't understand what they are paying for or why it doesn't taste like traditional Finnish beer." According to Lundmark, the number of small breweries is increasing all the time, yet although competition has become very intense, "Finland is a small country and the craft beer scene is still a small bubble. Awareness for the average consumer is still low." Nevertheless, awareness and consumption are growing rapidly. Like the organic beer options pointed out earlier, consumption of varieties is increasing. For example, IPAs are now considered "standard" in the industry, and are widely available from the large breweries. It was small breweries that popularized the variety, and are still doing it better, according to Lundmark: "Mass-market IPAs are still a bit less hoppy and aromatic. The bitterness is there, but not like a proper West Coast IPA. However, craft breweries can offer this."

Helsinki could be considered the epicenter of the beer scene, judged by its number of breweries and festivals, but it does not dominate the country; the city of Tampere is debated as a beer capital as well, with its strong beer culture, and both festivals and breweries can be found all over Finland. What follows, however, is a look at how these changes in Finland's beer scene are reflected on Helsinki's retail landscapes and consumer culture, specifically the bars on Vaasankatu and Iso Roobertinkatu.

Beer Prices

In an empirical qualitative study conducted over five years (2013–2018), with the help of students and friends, I periodically documented the changing prices of beers on draft on two shopping streets in Helsinki: Iso Roobertinkatu in the Punavuori neighborhood and Vaasankatu in the Kallio neighborhood. Beer prices were determined by walking into each bar and reading from the menu or asking staff the price of the *least expensive draft beer*. Data were updated roughly once per year. The data for Vaasankatu were first collected in April 2013 and most recently in August 2018. For Iso Roobertinkatu, data were first collected in February 2014 and most recently in September 2018.

There were ten bars on Vaasankatu in 2013 when the study began. The average price of the cheapest draft beer in 2013 was €3.85, with a very high range—the beer on draft at the most expensive bar was exactly twice the price of the cheapest (€5.80 vs. €2.90). The same ten bars were in the same place as of summer 2018, joined by one new bar. The average price of beer in summer 2018, including the new bar, was €4.30, still with a considerable range of €2.70 between the highest and lowest price. Only two of the existing bars on Vaasankatu changed their presentation significantly. One changed its name and appearance, and although it was formerly the least expensive bar on the street, the price of beer remained below average. Another underwent an extensive remodel and now sells craft beer at significantly above-average price for the street. There were five bars on Iso Roobertinkatu in April 2014, including a nightclub tucked off-strip, with an average price of €5.30 for the cheapest draught beer. There was little variation in price among the bars. In 2018, the average price of beer among all five bars was €6.40, still with little variation (€0.50 range).

Discussion

Whereas Iso Roobertinkatu's retail was in flux throughout the five-year period, including for bars and restaurants, Vaasankatu experienced remarkable stability in its traditional businesses: the bars and sex shops on the street, catering mostly to an existing, working-class population, seemed unfazed by the emergence of additional businesses catering to young or affluent newcomers. In fact, the prices of beer at most bars scarcely increased enough to account for inflation, alcohol tax, and rent increases. The red-light businesses on Vaasankatu, including the traditional bars, represent the kind of establishments disappearing in other cities as the retail landscape is cleansed for middle-class values (Hubbard 2017). With retail gentrification visible throughout the Kallio neighborhood, the fact that these shops did not change significantly in (at least) five years is remarkable under any standard of retail vitality. At the very least, this study demonstrates that these businesses are a solid part of the neighborhood, and are valued enough by their patrons in the community to keep them in business.

While the stability of the bars themselves is noteworthy, their high range in price indicates something else is going on. On Vaasankatu, where a cheap bar is so can be located so close to an expensive bar without their prices converging over five years, the logic of retailing tells us that they are not in competition with each other. This is again in contrast to Iso Roobertinkatu, where pricing suggests that the five bars compete for the same market. There is little variation among beer prices or styles on Iso Roobertinkatu, and the locations are similar, but the businesses compete with differently stylized interiors and themes, as well as product offerings. Indeed, it is here on Iso Roobertinkatu that the influence of craft beer consumption can be seen. When this study began in 2013, the bar Black Door on Iso Roobertinkatu was awarded best craft beer bar in Finland. In 2015, the bar Tommyknocker opened, offering Finnish craft beers in a US-inspired style, with smaller sizes and tastings available from knowledgeable staff. According to their website (tommyknocker.fi), Tommyknocker is a "modern craft beer bar with an American twist. . . . On tap you'll always find real American craft beer complemented by Finnish craft beers as well. We have a bottle selection of over 60 different American craft beers, and various American style Finnish craft brewery products."

The days of cheap beers in Rööperi (local slang for the Punavuori neighborhood) are gone. As the whole neighborhood of Punavuori became more expensive and a wealthier population moved in during the last twenty-five years, the area's retail landscape slowly came to reflect this. By 2013, a cluster of designer furniture and clothing boutiques dominated Iso Roobertinkatu's retail profile, and by 2018 food and drink establishments became the fastest-growing business type. These events coincide with patterns of retail gentrification observed in other cities. Furthermore, the emergence of craft beer coincides with the narrative of consumer culture in which middle classes increasingly concern themselves with the experience of dining and the provenance of their food.

Andreas Lundmark, the craft beer distributor, previously worked at both Black Door and Tommyknocker. He recalled a time when craft beers were emerging on Iso Roobertinkatu, around fifteen years ago, when the street's wild reputation still existed. "Vaasankatu is now like how Rööperi was when I was young. There were people searching for something better [to drink], and there were people interested in straight-up partying, and it was all mixed. Over time, it became more expensive and tuned in for a different sort of people. Now if you look at what's happening in Kallio, it's a mixed bag." Indeed, on Vaasankatu, we can identify two different markets of consumers for two different purchasing decisions. The cheap bars compete at similar price points for the same market: lower-income locals mixed with young people, from the neighborhood and elsewhere, who seem to revel in the crowded, no-frills bar experience as long as the beer is €3 per pint. Meanwhile, the few expensive bars scattered about sell a higher-end product intended for an entirely different consumer market. However, the line between these markets is blurry—the bar Solmu, owned by the brewery of the same name, offers Finnish craft beer for around €4—far cheaper than city-center prices.

The variety of retail types on Vaasankatu—not simply catering to newcomers or the middle class—enables diverse social groups to share the same urban spaces while acting out their own respective consumption practices. People from different social groups—new students and, increasingly, immigrants along with long-time local patrons (perhaps all on a budget)—mix in the bars and on the street between them, as newer, more affluent residents walk among these other groups. Furthermore, the distinctions among bars are not strong beyond what is on the menu, and the prevailing attitude of the neighborhood seems to be that anyone is welcome anywhere.

Thus, while the presence of craft beer bars can be associated with gentrification, it can also be seen as a catalyst for mixing diverse groups of people—at least on a street where traditional bars still exist. For now, at least in Vaasankatu, the emergence of craft beer has not displaced the cluster of pubs, and the more extreme ends of the Finnish drinking culture, at least, remain closer to the street's reputation.

Conclusion

During the five-year study period, the types and prices of beer, as well as the spaces in which it is consumed, have changed in some locations but not so much in others. Although the retail landscape of one study neighborhood has become progressively more gentrified, that of another has retained a cluster of traditional bars. Along Vaasankatu, bars vary in their pricing, product, and atmosphere, thus attracting different consumers from varying socioeconomic backgrounds while remaining side by side—the experience of the street itself is not exclusive to one group or another, but shared. In essence, the diversity of store types, especially bars, enables diverse social groups to share the same urban spaces while acting out their own respective consumption practices.

In the United Kingdom, High Street regeneration policies are guilty of "ignoring the realities of a divided society where different populations consume differently" (Hubbard 2017). The case of Vaasankatu exemplifies a place where different populations consume differently, but often together or side by side.

Thus, beer in Helsinki lies at the nexus of changing neighborhoods, changing cultures of consumption, and a changing drink industry. As small brewers compete against the nineteenth-century mega-breweries and among themselves while bringing new products to the market, bar owners seem keen on the changing tastes of their patrons. Along Vaasankatu such markets coexist with each other, at least for now. Rather than be seen as a blight for new residents to regulate out of existence (or tolerate at best), these businesses could be celebrated as successful local establishments that are savvy enough to endure for years and during turbulent times where others have failed. In the meantime, today's Iso Roobertinkatu resembles a typical gentrified street in Western Europe, or the United States, or Britain—with two identical chain coffee shops on either end of the street, and a cluster of fashion and furniture boutiques and chic restaurants—but has not left its past completely behind. Despite the outward uniformity compared to Vaasankatu, the street is still a place of distinction in Helsinki and even all of Finland. There are even still binge-drinking youngsters lining up at the old nightclub Swengi on weekends. You could say the street still has flavor—and if you ask Andreas Lundmark, the next flavor to hit the scene in Finland just might be sour beers.

Notes

1. *Regeneration* is defined as any attempt to improve urban life. It can be cultural, social, or economic, or can focus on the built environment.

References

Bridge, Gary and Robyn Dowling. 2001. "Microgeographies of Retailing and Gentrification." *Australian Geographer* 32(1):93–107.
Federation of Brewing and Soft Drinks Industry, Finland, 2019.
Hubbard, Phil. 2017. *The Battle for the High Street: Retail Gentrification, Class and Disgust*. London: Palgrave Macmillan.
NBWA—National Beer Wholesalers Association (2021) *Industry Fast Facts*. https://www.nbwa.org/resources/industry-fast-facts
Nieminen, Petri. 2007. "Panimot sakkaavat ahdingossa." *Ilta-Sanomat*, February 13 (https://www.is.fi/taloussanomat/art-2000001496172.html).
Mustonen, Pekka and Lindblom, Taru. 2014. "Creative Districts of Helsinki: Two Distant Relatives. Pp. 87–92. In L. Marques and G. Richards (Eds.), *Creative Districts Around the World*. Breda: NHTV, Breda.
Panula, J. YLE News, June 15, 2018. *Panimoita on Suomessa jo sata, joten massasta täytyy erottua – pieni pohjalaispanimo haluaa oluidensa olevan erikoisempia kuin muilla*. https://yle.fi/uutiset/3-10257233.
Panimoliitto. 2022. *Domestic Sales Statistics*. https://panimoliitto.fi/myyntitilastot/
Sander, Gordon F. 2013. "Sizzling in Helsinki." *New York Times*. March 31, 2013. https://www.nytimes.com/slideshow/2013/03/31/travel/20130331-SURFACING.html.
Waris, Heikki. 1973. *Työläisyhteiskunnan syntyminen Helsingin Pitkänsillan pohjois-puolelle*. Weilin & Göös: Helsinki. (Original work published 1932)
Winer, Laurie. 2008. "The Local Flavor of Helsinki's Food Revival." *New York Times*. December 14, 2008. https://www.nytimes.com/2008/12/14/travel/14Choice.html.
Zukin, Sharon. 2008. "Consuming Authenticity: From Outposts of Difference to Means of Exclusion. *Cultural Studies* 22(5):724–48.
Zukin, Sharon, Valerie Trujillo, Peter Frase, Danielle Jackson, Tim Recuber, and Abraham Walker. 2009. "New Retail Capital and Neighborhood Change: Boutiques and Gentrification in New York City." *City & Community* 8(1):47–64.

Postcard from a Small Town

ROBIN SHEPARD

"Instead of driving through town they are now stopping, and the brewery is the primary reason," says City Administrator Adam Sonntag of Hillsboro, Wisconsin. Hillsboro is a small rural community of about 1,400 residents, and like many such areas throughout the United States, it has experienced significant economic-development challenges in retaining and attracting businesses, residents, and tourists to keep its downtown vibrant and healthy. It is among a growing list of communities that are using craft breweries to leverage interest in their town and to create, re-create—and tap into—a sense of community among residents and visitors.

Local breweries are increasingly seen as an engine of local economic development and community vitality (Barajas et al. 2017). Craft beer has become more intertwined with city development since 2010 as civic leaders and city planners look to the craft beer industry to play a role in their community revitalization efforts (Barajas, Boeing, and Wartell 2017; Hackworth and Smith 2001; Mathews and Patton 2016). Coordinating revitalization efforts and public subsidies with potential breweries can create synergies in the community, especially in proximity to the brewery itself. Renovating buildings, improving streets and sidewalks, and expanding access can maximize the effect on the surrounding economic development.

The Hillsboro Brewing Company is a good example of how beer and a community's sense of place are intertwined. The original Hillsboro Brewery opened in 1870 as the Carl Ludwig and Joseph Landsinger Brewery. It eventually closed (under the name Hillsboro Brewing) in 1943. Since then, local memories of the brewery have faded.

Snapper and Kim Verbsky wanted to bring back that important part of the town's history. Snapper is a Hillsboro native whose family has lived in the area for five generations. His wife, Kim, has lived locally for more than two decades and owns an assisted-care facility in Hillsboro. Snapper, who owns a construction company, had

Hillsboro Brewing Company.

been restoring historic businesses. In 2012, the couple purchased two vacant buildings in downtown Hillsboro and transformed one into the Hillsboro Brewing Company Pub; the other houses a small brewing system.

As Hillsboro Brewing Company gained a reputation as a beer destination, the Verbskys saw expansion as inevitable. In 2018 they completed restoration of another old building, a former Carnation Milk factory, built in the early 1900s, and moved their brewing operation there. This much larger space, at 28,000 square feet, allowed for a new and larger fifteen-barrel brewing system, restaurant, and event space.

The rise of Hillsboro Brewing created greater visibility for other breweries, says Sonntag. "It's a draw to the area and we're now a destination for visitors, many of whom stay overnight because of our rural location."

Hillsboro has seen a handful of younger residents starting new businesses, which Sonntag attributes at least partly to the brewery's success. An all-terrain vehicle dealership, a fitness gym, a hair salon, and a drive-in restaurant are all run by owners under thirty, a highly sought-after age group because they represent long-term investment in the community's economy.

"Some of this may seem pretty small, but when you put it into the context that Hillsboro is only 1,450 people it's pretty remarkable," says Snapper. "I like the fact that my wife and I are providing jobs. It's important to me because the community has given so much to us over the years."

The Hillsboro Brewery employs about twenty people with an annual payroll of $300,000. Across all of their businesses, the Verbskys have forty-seven employees. "We're proud that we support a lot of families in Hillsboro with jobs and health insurance," says Snapper.

In reality, a thriving local economy depends on more than a brewery. But Hillsboro is a vibrant example among several small towns discovering that a brewery—a business that requires a substantial investment, employs area residents, makes a product that is inexpensive yet brings people together, and, perhaps most importantly, can convince other potential small business owners that a town's main street is worth taking a chance on—can be at the center of community revitalization.

Breweries are "a great way to fill empty downtown spaces," says Errin Welty, who focuses on downtown development for the Wisconsin Economic Development Corporation (WEDC). "They're bigger uses than many other businesses, and they come with capital investment and jobs." Welty says that breweries are "in the top things that communities look for most."

"There is a trend," she adds. Having a brewery, a wine bar, and a coffee shop is sometimes seen as the trifecta in the community development game.

Breweries appeal to a wide demographic. "This is not just a millennial thing," says Welty. "Small communities see breweries as a family-friendly business. Lots of people feel comfortable bringing their kids and hanging out. They appeal to all ages."

The American Brewers Association tracks the number of breweries nationwide. In 2018, Wisconsin had 190 craft breweries, a number that has more than doubled since 2012. And, according to the Association those breweries generated over $2.3 billion in total economic impact. (Nationally, the American Brewers Association tracked 7,450 breweries in 2018 that added $79.1 billion to the US economy; American Brewers Association, 2019.)

Those economic impact numbers are a big reason why state economic development authorities like WEDC are working so hard with local communities to design incentive packages that include grants and loans to help attract small breweries. As of early 2019, Wisconsin had directed more than $2 million in state incentives for future brewery development to small communities. To further call attention to local brewing's impact, Wisconsin governor Tony Evers declared September 26, 2019, as Wisconsin Craft Beer Day and embarked on a statewide tour with members of his administration, highlighting seven different breweries that day.

Opening a brewery can cost well over $1 million, and funding is often assembled from multiple sources. Restoring buildings and storefronts in a small rural town increases costs further. At the local level in Wisconsin, both cities and counties may use revolving loan funds to assist breweries. Kurt and Keith Benzine, Randy Sunde, and Tyler Walker renovated a near-century-old building in downtown Columbus to open Cercis Brewing in May 2018. About $160,000 of the $500,000 cost was covered by revolving loan funds from the city and Columbia County. "If we had not received that loan, we would not be open," says Walker.

The brewpub is part of the community's overall plan to revitalize its downtown, along with improvements to its main thoroughfare to ease traffic and be more welcoming to pedestrians. The brewpub's owners were "among the first property owners to make substantial renovations," says Matt Schreiber, Columbus's director of planning and development. "That started a trend with other owner-occupied businesses in making large investments."

In Waunakee, the Lone Girl Brewing Company opened in 2016. The $2 million brewpub proved to be central in a rebirth of activity downtown. "The Lone Girl was a driving force for change," says Gary Herzberg, longtime member of the Waunakee Village Board. "We were like many small towns that had a downtown that was dying off."

Having a brewpub means Waunakee residents don't have to drive into Middleton or Madison for a pint and dinner. And it's much more than just another restaurant, says Herzberg. "Breweries bring new

Cercis Brewing.

excitement. They make a vibrant downtown and bring people to the center of the community."

Kevin Abercrombie, who owns Lone Girl, has noticed increased traffic to neighboring businesses. "People may come here for a beer and then go next door or across the street." Nearby businesses benefiting include gift and home furnishings stores, personal care salons, and other restaurants and taverns too.

"It's definitely a draw; we're complementary to each other. It's the type of business that people remember. The brewery helps us be a place that people will come back to," says Vicky Marsala, who owns the Red Barn Company Store, which sells home décor and furnishings.

Lone Girl contributes to the local economy in direct ways, including employing 75 to 100 persons, ranging from high schoolers to seniors, most of whom live in the Waunakee area. Abercrombie estimates that his brewpub produced more than $3.5 million in economic activity for the downtown in 2018, based on sales and employee payroll, property and excise taxes, the purchase of brewing and restaurant supplies, and services for the brewpub.

Lone Girl's impact doesn't stop there. Like many breweries, it contributes to the community through gifts and donations. Last year the brewpub donated more than $30,000 in charitable contributions to nonprofit organizations, the majority within a thirty-mile radius of Waunakee.

The New Glarus Brewing Company opened in 1993 and has become the quintessential Wisconsin brewery with its iconic flagship beer, a farmhouse ale called Spotted Cow. New Glarus is Wisconsin's largest craft brewery, producing 232,000 barrels in 2018. It also ranks as the sixteenth largest craft brewery in the United States and its twenty-sixth largest brewery overall. Remarkably, New Glarus only sells its beer in Wisconsin, after making a strategic decision to pull its out-of-state distribution in 2002 to focus in-state. "For us, our community is as important as the brewery itself—we exist together and it is a synergistic relationship," says brewmaster Dan Carey.

The brewery sits high on a hilltop overlooking the Little Sugar River Valley and its hometown of New Glarus, Wisconsin, population 2,172, a twenty-five-minute drive from Madison. It employs 120 people and all of them can own stock in the brewery—thus, the brewery is employee owned. "We offer wages that improve the standard of living, pay 100 percent of their health insurance, they live here, own homes, they shop here, go to restaurants. We are definitely intertwined with the Village of New Glarus," says Carey. New Glarus Brewing also creates a ripple effect of direct purchases of $9 million a year from other Wisconsin manufacturers, and contributions to more than three hundred Wisconsin charities. And then there is the tourism multiplier, in which a brewery draws people to itself, even across the state's borders. "A brewery can be an anchor store to a downtown. It creates attention and people seem to follow. Then others may invest in other businesses. It can start a momentum," adds Carey.

The role of a brewery in the community's sense of place is unique and anecdotal to every community in which it is felt. One Wisconsin town with such a unique story is Potosi, population 670, in the far southwestern corner of Wisconsin along the Mississippi River. The original Potosi Brewery operated from 1852 to 1972 (except during Prohibition).

Potosi Brewery.

When the brewery closed, it sat abandoned for nearly thirty years, slowly deteriorating to ruins. In the early 2000s, local residents felt helpless as their town was slowly drying up, much like the taps of the old brewery. That's when they decided to take it upon themselves to bring the Potosi Brewery back to life. "Almost everybody in the community either had family members who worked there or knew someone who did," says Dave Fritz, who serves as president of the Potosi Brewery Foundation.

By 2008 a handful of local residents had raised more than $3 million in their own money that would later be combined with state and federal grants to restore the brewery. That effort returned Main Street's most identifiable landmark. "There would be nothing going on in the south end of Potosi without the brewery," says Fritz. "It's the difference between schools being here and people residing in the community."

A contributing factor to the success of Potosi Brewery came when the restoration efforts led to the creation of the National Brewery Museum within its walls. Potosi had beat out bigger beer towns like Milwaukee and St. Louis to be the museum's home. The brewery also was named a Great River Road Interpretive Center. "We've become a tourism target," says Fritz. Anyone who is traveling through the Midwest who has any interest in brewing history will try to pass through Potosi to go to the Museum." And it's not just beer enthusiasts. Fritz adds that there are a lot of Baby Boomers who stop in Potosi while traveling the country looking for unique things to do. "Potosi makes the Heartland Corridor and Driftless Area something special," says Fritz.

The renovated brewery has continued to grow. In 2015 it opened a new production facility just down the street from the renovated brewery. Today, more than $14 million has been reinvested in the Potosi Brewery, and it's now the town's largest employer. The community passion and energy in restoring the brewery also inspired turning the former brewery farm, across the street from the brewhouse, into the privately run Holiday Gardens and Events Center, which can handle groups up to five hundred. A boutique shop and artisan gallery occupy the brewery's old bottling plant, and even the Potosi Brewery Saloon has a new lease on life, serving locals and visitors. And what's more, hotels and bed and breakfasts in the community have expanded their capacity to handle the increased tourism.

It's a bit of an exaggeration to say every Wisconsin town and village once had its own brewery, but brewing has always been a strong industry tied to a many small communities. Brewing is grounded in Wisconsin's early statehood, through its immigrants, agriculture, and natural resources, and also in the pride residents have in self-proclaiming it "the Beer State." There's a romanticism with beer and the state's image, so it feels natural to bring it back to the center of Wisconsin's small communities.

References

American Brewers Association. 2019. "National Beer Sales & Production Data." Retrieved June 22, 2022 (www.brewersassociation.org/statistics-and-data/national-beer-stats/).

Barajas, Jesus M., Geoff Boeing, and Julie Wartell. 2017. "Neighborhood Change, One Pint at a Time." Pp. 155–76. In *Untapped: Exploring the Cultural Dimensions* of *Craft Beer*, edited by Nathaniel G. Chapman, Slade Lellock, and Cameron D. Lippard. Morgantown: University of West Virginia Press.

Hackworth, Jason and Neil Smith. 2001. "The Changing State of Gentrification." *Tijdschrift Voor Economische en Sociale Geografie* 92(4):464–77.

Mathews, Adam J. and Matthew T. Patton. 2016. "Exploring Place Marketing by American Microbreweries: Neolocal Expressions of Ethnicity and Race." *Journal of Cultural Geography* 33(3):275–309.

Personal Interviews

Abercrombie, Kevin. Owner, the Lone Girl Brewery. March 27, 2019.

Carey, Dan. Brewmaster, New Glarus Brewing Company. November 19, 2019.

Fritz, Dave. President of the Potosi Brewery Foundation. April 4, 2019.

Herzberg, Gary. Board member, Waunakee, Wisconsin Village Board. April 4, 2019.

Marsala, Vicky. Owner, Red Barn Company Store in Waunakee, Wisconsin. April 15, 2019.

Schreiber, Matt. Director of Planning and Development, City of Columbus, Wisconsin. April 2, 2019.

Sonntag, Adam. City Administrator, Hillsboro, Wisconsin. April 2, 2019.

Verbsky, Snapper. Owner, Hillsboro Brewing Company. April 1, 2019.

Walker, Tyler. Co-owner, Cercis Brewing, Columbus, Wisconsin. March 1, 2019.

Welty, Errin. Account Manager for the Wisconsin Economic Development Corporation, State of Wisconsin. April 4, 2019.

CHAPTER 7

"Did You Take the Tour?"

An Analysis of the Spatial Politics of New Jersey's Craft Beer Taprooms

ROBERT A. SAUNDERS AND EMILY A. FOGARTY

The United States is in the midst of a nationwide revival of small-scale brewing, driven by the rise of "craft" beers that are often consumed on brewery premises (Alonso and Sakellarios 2017; Elzinga, Horton Tremblay, and Tremblay 2015; Nilsson, Reid, and Lehnert 2018). The laws governing the space of the taproom, however, vary widely between states. Craft-beer-friendly states like Vermont enjoy a high brewery-to-resident ratio (13.5 per 100,000 adults 21 years and older) compared to more restrictive states like Mississippi (0.7 per 100,000). Although regional cultures clearly contribute to differences in America's craft-brewing revolution (including the predominance of teetotaling religious groups such as the Southern Baptists in the South and Mormons in the noncoastal American West), numerous political and regulatory factors also produce these wide national disparities. In New Jersey (1.6 breweries per 100,000), the country's most densely populated state (2018 estimated population, 8,908,520; total area, 19047.34 km2), these "uniquely restrictive rules on tasting rooms" (Nurin 2018) include zoning restrictions on where a brewery can be established, frequent moratoria on any expansions (including opening outdoor seating), regulations on business hours, prohibitions on food offerings, restrictions on off-premises distribution, and the size and quantity in which beer may be sampled or purchased.

Drawing on both empirical and quantitative data collected at five New Jersey breweries (Beach Haus, Dark City, Kane, Carton, and River

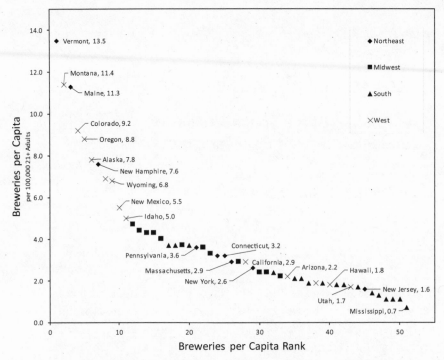

Breweries per capita (per 100,000 21+ adults) versus breweries per capita rank. *Note*: each state is shown by region.

Horse), this chapter examines the policing of brewery spaces, with a special focus on the restrictions the state places on bodies within the taproom. Here we speak of New Jersey's statewide requirement that all visitors to a taproom must first experience a tour of the brewery, purportedly with the aim of making the consumer aware of the artisanal and industrial processes involved in turning hops, barley, yeast, and water into beer. Although we are not averse to the idea of craft beer consumers knowing more about what they are drinking, we argue that such restrictions have been instrumental in situating New Jersey, with its roughly one hundred craft breweries, near the bottom of state rankings on per capita brewery presence—as of this research, forty-fifth in the nation.[1]

Our assertion is especially true when considering the older law prohibiting the onsite consumption at microbreweries that was only abolished in 2012, alongside an increase in the amount of beer that could be sold to a single person for take-home consumption. We main-

IDENTITY, POLITICS, ECONOMICS

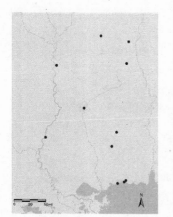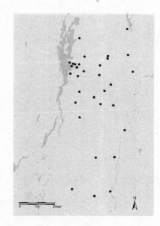

A comparison of the spatial distribution of taprooms in Mississippi, New Jersey, and Vermont.

tain that the poor showing since then effectively situates New Jersey alongside states in the "underdeveloped" Southern tier (Baginski and Bell 2011),[2] despite a host of sociopolitical factors that would otherwise promote a stronger craft beer culture, akin to those of its neighbors Delaware, Pennsylvania, and New York, all of which possess nationally known beer places (e.g., Dogfish Head, Tröegs, and Brooklyn, among others).

Using a mixed-method interdisciplinary framework that draws on culturological, sociological, and geospatial approaches, we interrogate the micro-geographies of these breweries with the goal of providing a case study of spatial dynamics of the New Jersey taproom experience. Contextualized within a comparative framework informed by the authors' frequent visits to New Jersey taprooms as well as those farther afield (especially in Vermont, New York, Florida, Denmark, and the United Kingdom), this chapter is intended to provide an accessible examination of the "placemaking" (Fletchall 2016) that has established the taproom as a unique space in the American drinking experience (see also Elzinga, Horton Tremblay, and Tremblay 2015; Nilsson, Reid, and Lehnert 2018). We also aim to contextualize the New Jersey case against global trends in craft beer production and consumption (cf. Dennett and Page 2017; Hindy 2014; Kirkby 2003; Pritchard 2012; Saunders and Holland 2018; van Wolputte and Fumanti 2010). In terms of methods, analytical approaches, and data collection, this chapter is based on (1) interviews conducted with owners, brewers, and staff at the aforementioned New Jersey taprooms; (2) close readings of the different taproom experiences with a focus on the spatial ordering of touring, drinking, and socializing, including an examination of the micro-geographies of tasting (e.g., curation styles, glassware, flight sizes/varying availability of pints, etc.); and (3) a geographical investigation of New Jersey brewscape clusters and other spatial elements associated with the breweries themselves to reveal the state's micro-geographies of beer, culture, and place.

Using Kerski's (2015) geo-awareness approach, we have selected three breweries within New Jersey's primary brewery cluster, along with two outside this group to demonstrate a contrast. (All were selected based on researchers' preexisting familiarity, thus guaranteeing effectiveness in conveying geospatial information to the wider public.)

The chapter also provides a historical overview and comparative assessment of New Jersey's state and municipal regulations on breweries and taprooms, including commentary on the state's complicated history with Prohibition and its repeal (made famous by the HBO series *Boardwalk Empire*), as well as the powerful sway of restaurant-industry lobbying groups.[3]

The Place and Space of the Taproom

A key element of the microbrewery is the taproom. For start-up brewers and even established craft beer companies, creating a welcoming, cozy environment for beer enthusiasts to sit and sip fresh-produced offerings is a must. Such spaces are visually distinct from other "watering holes" (e.g., lounges, bars, pubs, and social clubs) due to spatial design, sensory engagement, and the lack of other potent potables from which to choose. Most craft beer taprooms share a number of common elements that make them almost instantly recognizable—different from other drinking establishments, but very much like one another. These include the centrality of the beer menu to the space: typically written in chalk, though sometimes displayed using movable-letter boards or digital television screens, the menu needs to allow updates at a minute's notice as a keg goes dry or a new release comes off the line. The taproom is thus an active learning space, a sort of museum of the current, allowing the visitor to partake of not only the consumed product (i.e., tasting the beers) but also the overall processes involved in making it. Drinkers accomplish this via sensory engagement: sight (seeing the equipment and brewers at work), sound (hearing the lecture on artisanal beer manufacturing), smell (sniffing the aroma of spent grains),[4] and even touch (often one is invited to handle ingredients such as hops and barley). As beer writer Pete Brown writes, "If you want to know about [the brewing] process, there's no substitute to seeing it in action" (2017, 18), and that is precisely the idea behind the curated brewery tour.

In the United States, craft beer taprooms are designed as communal spaces that are friendly to families and often dogs, thus providing an American cognate to the German *Biergarten* or the convivial British pub. As John Merklin, the owner of Beach Haus, told Saunders:

> The craft brewery is a fairly unique enterprise to any locality. To any given municipality it represents both a source of industry as well as tourism. Craft breweries are not simply "plants" to produce products. They are also destinations for consumer's to "meet the owners," chat with the brewers, and experience the product. People travel not only across the street but across state lines and increasingly even across the country to visit breweries. Vacation spots are often planned around access to local breweries. (interview, December 1, 2018)

Unlike lounges and other places where the main activity is alcohol consumption, craft beer taprooms are not meant to facilitate new romantic relationships or provide a space that is free from prying eyes of one's neighbors or relations. Instead, the taproom is emerging as a new form of the third space (Soja 1996) that allows for low to moderate levels of beer consumption, an undertaking intended as a taste-based experience rather than a slow descent into spirits-fueled oblivion. This is reflected in the fact that seating at most taprooms is communal: wooden picnic tables, long bars separate from the serving area, beer barrel "tables," etc. Such forced socialization is especially noticeable in the notoriously "rude" state of New Jersey (Kachmar 2015), where the spatial dynamics of the taproom work against self-isolation, generally not "making a place" for a solitary individual to take refuge at the bar (i.e., turned away from others where they can stare at television screen and avoid human contact). This spatial structuring functions

Jersey Girl flight on a paddle in the shape of New Jersey.

as a sort of anti-(b)ordering of space, precluding the sort of territoriality that defines other forms of public drinking (see Anderson 2015; Storey 2012), at least in the United States.[5] Aesthetics are an integral part of the politics of place (see Hawkins and Straughan 2015), geographically determining how people move through an area. In the case of taprooms, most have wood floors, exposed pipes and wiring, and a good deal of room to "breathe," "see," and "do," thus opening the experience up to a number of different uses that are imbued with the locality of the brewery.

By doing so, these open, airy spaces often become dual-use technologies, serving as areas where other (nondrinking) activities can also occur. For example, one of our first case study sites (Beach Haus) hosts live music performances, board game nights, yoga classes, a knitting club, twice-annual animal adoption events (with dogs on the premises) and political fundraisers on both sides of the aisle (though as we discuss later, this way of employing of the taproom as an agora is currently under siege in the state).

The Micro-geographies of Five New Jersey Taprooms

BEACH HAUS BREWERY AND TAPROOM, BELMAR

Housed in the old Friedman's Bakery, the pre-1990s downtown-area anchor of one of New Jersey's most famous beach towns, Beach Haus moved into the space after a period of wandering or "ghost" brewing in New York State. Nestled on Main Street between commercial properties to the west and residential properties to the east, and situated near the train station with ample parking, a balcony, and various food options in the immediate area, the two-story Beach Haus is easily the largest and most popular of our case studies. (For a summary of the percent of each class code in and around the 500-meter buffer around each of the five breweries, see Table 1.) Being walkable from the ample summer beach rentals and with a sizable year-round suburban population, as well as being adjacent to the train station, Beach Haus—unlike Kane and Carton (see following sections)—enjoys a good deal of foot traffic. Owned and operated by John "Merk" Merklin in partnership with Brian Ciriaco and Chris McCallion, Beach Haus's taproom includes a wide variety of elements that pay homage to the former tenant, including repurposed wood from the original space. Indeed, Beach Haus has come to serve as a partial replacement for the shuttered bakery, fueling the downtown's recent wave of redevelopment (unlike most taprooms in the area, it operates seven days per week and opens at noon rather than in the late afternoon).

Table 1. A Comparison of Property Class Summaries within 500 Meters of the Case Studies

NJ Property Classification Code and Description	Beach Haus	Dark City	Kane	River Horse	Carton
Total parcels within 500 meters	330	497	73	36	358
1: Vacant Land	3.94%	5.23%	17.81%	5.56%	5.03%
2: Residential (4 Families or less)	58.79%	61.77%	1.37%	47.22%	60.89%
4A: Commercial	23.64%	21.13%	39.73%	19.44%	18.72%
4B: Industrial	0%	0.20%	0%	2.78%	1.12%
4C: Apartment/cooperative	0.61%	5.84%	0%	2.78%	1.12%
5A: Class I Railroad	0.30%	0.20%	0%	0%	0%
15A: Exempt Public School	0.30%	0.40%	0%	2.78%	0.28%
15C: Exempt Public	7.88%	1.61%	4.11%	16.67%	4.19%
15D: Exempt Charitable	1.52%	2.82%	0%	0%	2.51%
15F: Exempt Miscellaneous		0.80%	0%	0%	0.56%
Unknown classification	3.03%	0%	36.99%	2.78%	5.59%

Note: study used a 500-meter buffer for data collection area around each of the taprooms, as it is 0.31 miles and considered a "walking distance" of roughly six minutes of walking, one way.

The conversion of a bakery into a brewery is somewhat poignant, given that thousands of brewers shifted their production from beer to baked goods under Prohibition (1920–1933) to avoid bankruptcy and maintain their facilities and labor forces until the (anticipated) end of the ban on alcohol production in the United States (see Ogle 2006). The name *Beach Haus* is an amalgam of two influences: the German brewing tradition (Merk is of German descent and spent some years in Europe) and the "Shore"—that is, the Jersey Shore and its attendant culture (Newman 2004). The former manifests in the beer styles, which favor traditional German brews with American flair. In the summer, they offer a variety of Radlers (low-ABV pilsners mixed with lemonade or other fruit juices intended to satisfy the "bike-rider's" thirst, from which the style takes its name); not coincidentally, the site serves as a key stop-off for cyclists who move from brewery to brewery. Beach Haus pours pints in generic Libbey glassware (except for some higher-ABV offerings that are delivered in a smaller, more flavor-friendly vessel) and offers flights for those wishing to sample several of their beers in one sitting. In the winter, Beach Haus produces a powerful seasonal brew called Krampus (Spiced Winter 9.4%), which honors the Austrian/Bavarian traditions of a demonic, goat-like "Christmas monster" that punishes naughty children and has even been known to invades beer halls to ceremonially menace young women.

The Shore influence is signified by local artwork, much of it commemorating the damage to and recovery of the region by Superstorm Sandy in late October 2012. Three beer tanks are exposed behind the bar, but the brewing facilities are mostly out of sight. Indoor seating is at low-slung picnic tables, allowing parties to mingle or groups as large as ten to be seated, which creates an environment vaguely reminiscent of a German beer garden, where making new friends is part of the experience. Tours are available by request (occasionally being made mandatory—e.g., on the day of the St. Patrick's Day parade, when Belmar swells with upwards of 120,000 visitors), thus skirting the letter of the law relating to how New Jersey brewers are supposed to "walk" patrons through the process. Brewing information is instead provided via an obligatory postcard handed to all (new) patrons before arriving in the taproom (as at many of the less formal New Jersey taprooms, regulars are usually exempted from this requirement if staff recognizes them).

DARK CITY BREWING COMPANY, ASBURY PARK

Situated in a renovated building in the fast-developing northern part of the city, Dark City Brewing is a ground-floor taproom on Main Street in Asbury Park, a historical resort area that gained popularity in the late 1800s but entered a period of decay after a 1970 uprising among Black residents caused so-called white flight and businesses closures. As with Belmar, which lies a short drive south, there is an east–west divide in terms of property classes in the area, with light industrial areas west of Main Street and housing to the east, thus allowing for easy access to Dark City on foot or by bike (there is some street parking, but Dark City's location is not as car friendly as other New Jersey breweries). Asbury Park, or "AP" as locals call it, is most famous for its association with Bruce Springsteen, who named his debut album *Greetings from Asbury Park, N.J.* (1973). Betting on further regentrification of an up-and-coming "city of consumption" (Russello Ammon 2015), Kevin Sharpe set up shop in late 2015 in a rather rough-and-tumble part of town (but one that had seen a number of new businesses open as of late), hoping to provide some "liquid creativity," as he called it, for AP's explosive remaking of its identity.

The taproom is a long, rectangular space with highboy wooden tables that seat upwards of eight customers. Flights are available, but so are twelve-ounce pours in elegant tulip-shaped goblets, an amenity that protects flavor and prolongs effervescence. The long bar is staffed by tattooed and knowledgeable "hipster" beer enthusiasts, who religiously require the uninitiated to take a short tour of the back room before their first sip. The names of its beers reflect AP's rich history, from a brew named after the city's foundation year (1871 Winter Beer 11.0%) to geographically named offerings marking out key streets (e.g., Bond Street Brownie 5.1% and Summerfield Session Sour 4.0%) in the ethnically diverse city. Whereas the customer bases of the other breweries we profile in this chapter tend to be painfully white, Dark City is a space where affluent Brooklyn weekenders and Pennsylvania beer tourists rub elbows with African American, Hispanic, and white locals alike. Given the important role that the LGBTQ community has played in the economic resurgence of the city since the late 1980s, Dark City is also popular with some of the city's significant gay population. In addition, on weekends it is rare to enter the taproom and not see one or two canines, thus making human–animal interactions a key part of the micro-geographies of Dark City.

The brewery's offerings mostly tend to be unfiltered, subtly reflecting the gestalt of Asbury Park, a place where all particles of humanity come together without the need to exclude some from the mix. Certain beer names actually reinforce this (i.e., Social Mosaic Weiss 4.3% and Common Area Blond 4.2%). Owner Kevin Sharpe readily affirmed that his brewery is indelibly "bound to the city" via its name and beers, unlike many other microbreweries, which, if necessary, could relocate without damaging the brand (Sharpe, interview with Saunders, August 23, 2018). Reflecting this emplacement, the walls were painted, mostly by local artists, with murals that are unabashedly political in nature, spacing Dark City as a progressive zone (like much of the rest of the city, in contrast to many of the nearby Shore towns, which tend to be quite politically and culturally conservative by statewide standards). Owing to its Main Street location, it is not uncommon for patrons to see police cars screaming by at full speed or unhoused people wandering past the large glass windows, thus making Dark City an outlier among the "average" taproom in terms of socioeconomic placement within (sub)urban space.

KANE BREWING COMPANY, OCEAN TOWNSHIP

Exemplifying the regulation that microbreweries be established in "light industrial zones," Kane is located between two major highways in an area defined by logistics companies, small enterprises, and other businesses that do not require prime real estate to operate (see Table 1). Indeed, upon one's first visit to the brewery (launched in 2011), one usually needs to wander the complex of nondescript buildings to find the entrance—though given its environs, parking is never a problem. (Almost all visitors arrive via car, though an occasional cyclist may risk the dangers of traveling congested New Jersey roads to make their way to Kane.) After entering a space that could easily house *The Office*'s Dunder Mifflin Paper Company, an attendant checks your identification (if you are planning to taste) and stamps your hand before you enter the taproom area.

The first space is a simple bar that also sells T-shirts and other merchandise; deeper into the complex, however, one is confronted with a genuine factory aesthetic. On one's left, the brewing equipment is exposed, with pipes blowing out the frothy by-product of the process.

To the right is a long bar divided into two areas: "pours" and "growler fills." Because most of Kane's beers run to the upper end of the potency spectrum, full pours are limited to twelve ounces and served in shapely glasses that accentuate the refined qualities for which the brewery is known. To the left of the bar is a cordoned-off area stacked high with cans of the product, thus visually affirming the primacy of Kane as the Shore's largest distributor of craft beer for consumption off premises (as well as making the space feel quite industrial).

Patrons, many of whom come nearly every weekend, gather around wine and whiskey barrels that have been used for aging some of the brewery's high-ABV beers (reaching upwards of 14 percent) or at large picnic tables (no drinking is allowed at the bar). No particular stylistic thread draws Kane's offerings together other than a rough balance between American and Belgian styles. There is, however, a surfer/oceanic motif to both the brewery and its nomenclature, including its flagship brew, Head High (IPA 6.6%), as well as Drift Line (Oatmeal Brown Ale 6.2%) and Single Fin (Belgian-Style Blonde 5.0%). This theme is reinforced by the fact that *kane* is the Hawai'ian gloss for "man," though the brewery is named for the founder Michael Kane. Like Dark City and the two subsequent case studies, Kane has limited hours, opening only late in the week and later in the day. The popularity of Head High across the state means that Kane's taproom is often packed, or could swell to capacity when a busload of beer tourists alighted in the large parking lot (organized visits have since been banned). Such popularity precludes a sense of community that pervades comparable establishments, as does the prevalence of nonlocals who have often traveled quite far for the experience. Of all the breweries discussed herein, Kane is the most nonchalant with regard to the tour (or graphically abetted brewing education); however, these are available to interested parties on the hour, thus bringing it in line with many establishments in other states.

CARTON BREWING, ATLANTIC HIGHLANDS

Like many New Jersey microbreweries, Carton was founded by a former New York City executive who decided there was more to life than profits and power suits. However, Carton is unique in having a spatially relevant link to Wall Street, being situated a short walk from the Shore's main ferry connection to the southern tip of Manhattan. The establishment thus serves as a liminal space between the leafy suburbs of New

Jersey and Manhattan's urban canyons. Consequently, the taproom is a favored haunt of commuters, who prefer its laid-back milieu to the dog-eat-dog Financial District. Still, given Carton's location within a wealthy enclave of the upper Jersey Shore, plenty of Atlantic Highlands residents frequent the establishment, gifting it with a bit of a "local" pub vibe.

Founded in 2011 by cousins Chris and Augie, their namesake taproom is situated in a compact two-story facility, with the brewery on the ground floor. New patrons are required to take the tour before ascending the stairs to the tasting room. Rather than buying one's samples outright, customers must purchase tokens or "poker chips" first (available only after proof of the tour is provided) and then trade them in for "small pours." Only a few styles are exempt, such as cask beers, which do not do present well in four-ounce drafts served in concave "taster" glasses. Repeat customers are subtly encouraged to pocket their last token to present upon return and obtain exemption from the obligatory brewing lesson (Augie Carton, interview with Saunders, May 20, 2014). Carton's styles range from the sessionable Boat (Kölsch 4.2%) to high-ABV offerings like 077XX (East Coast DIPA 7.8%).

Themes in naming reinforce place and space, with the adjacent Atlantic Highlands Marina being referenced in the former and the first three digits of the area's postal code in the latter. The tasting room is warm, casually designed, and gemütlich, with many ferry commuters (especially locals) stopping in after a day in Manhattan. Yet because the brewery is near an elementary school and on the very edge of a residential neighborhood, visitors' consumption is well policed, and they are strongly encouraged to depart the premises quietly to avoid complaints to the local municipality. Like Kane, Carton has a large distribution platform; rather than investing in their own infrastructure, however, the brewery relies on third-party mobile canning services via a semi-trailer truck that comes to the brewery (Augie Carton, interview with Saunders, May 20, 2014).

RIVER HORSE BREWING COMPANY, EWING

As one of the older microbreweries[6] in New Jersey (alongside Climax in Roselle Park and Flying Fish in Somerdale), River Horse is interesting as a case study for a number of factors. Regarding its space, the brewery, founded in 1996, was once located in the picturesque New Jersey town of Lambertville on the Delaware River. In its original form, River Horse served as an attractive aside for the many tourists who visit the town, which is partnered with the extremely popular destination of New Hope, Pennsylvania, just across the river (the bridge connecting the two is walkable and many visitors take in both locales). However, the new facility is less inviting, tucked into a nondescript corporate park far from residential neighborhoods or any other attraction (there is always plenty of parking, though). Taking its name from the English translation of "hippopotamus," the brewery is now situated in a free-standing light-industrial facility in a rather unremarkable part of eastern central New Jersey. An ownership change precipitated the move in 2013, increasing the facilities' size from 10,000 to 25,000 square feet (Johnson 2013). As with Kane and Carton, the current iteration of River Horse is the outcome of corporate burnout; as co-owners Chris Walsh and Glenn Bernabeo state on the brewery website, "You don't have to be in a dead end job to feel like you aren't going anywhere. That's the way we felt before River Horse. We were finance geeks living in a world without soul. Grinding it out every day for a fee, wearing suits and kissing butt."

However, as one the authors' first visits to the brewery revealed, there was still a bit of "everyday" pressure on the brewery, because the director of the state's Division of Alcoholic Beverage Control (ABC) lived a few miles from the new facility. With exacting adherence to state regulations, River Horse once required a forty-minute tour of the brewery's innards before letting guests retire to the tasting room (thankfully, small tastes were provided along the way). Today, however, the tour is conducted via View-Master. This 1939 invention was a popular pastime for generations of American children, allowing them to look through toy binoculars to see a story play out in a series of color images and, sometimes, captions. The history of River Horse, as well as the brewing process, is thus conveyed to visitors through a quite original, hipster-chic method; however, they still offer purists a proper tour of the facilities (weekends only, by reservation).

The rather smallish and often lightly attended taproom reflects the facility's aforementioned location, and not the robust distribution of its beer across the state (and beyond). However, if one wishes to imagine how things might have turned out if the brewery had not moved, the original space still stands in Lambertville, romantically adorned with the old logo. Similar to Kane, River Horse tends to brew a number of Belgian-style beers, alongside classic "new" American styles with a few more traditional German offerings thrown in. However, much to the dismay of cerevisaphiles and environmentally inclined customers, beer (including flights) is served in plastic, disposable cups, thus robbing it of some of its quality while generating needless waste. In terms of nomenclature, the brewery's thematic use of its mascot is dominant, with many titles playing on the African mammal's rather unique way of moving through the world. For example, the Imperial Stout (ABV 6.7%) carries the tagline "The third-largest living land mammal requires the best beer," as well as artwork that makes use of the hippo's dimensions, including the rather zaftig example on the Roly Poly Pils (ABV 5.3%) can.

Regulating Spaces, Policing Bodies: The Micro-geopolitics of the New Jersey Taproom

Although dissatisfaction with the corporate world drove some of the founders of our case studies (as well as other owners of New Jersey microbreweries) into a life defined by lautering, mash tuns, and wort cooling, this is not the case for all. The binding thread is a love of beer, which they initially realized through homebrewing. However, as the New Jersey microbrewers interviewed for this chapter affirmed, the journey from giving one's beers away to friends to opening the doors of their taproom was riddled with seemingly endless hurdles, mostly regulatory. As noted earlier, it was only in 2012 that house-brewed beer could be sold on a brewery site; before this, guests had to take a tour before sampling some of the beers in small pours—not full-size glasses. The change also permitted customers to buy up to one keg for offsite consumption (the previous limit was two six-packs). Although licensing is easy on paper and relatively inexpensive ($2,000), a host of restrictions, prohibitions, and injunctions present themselves as a microbrewery seeks to grow, thus forcing brewers to effectively limit themselves to certain "clusters" across the state where the idea of a taproom is somewhat palatable to the local community.[7]

Local concerns about public drunkenness often stymie municipal permissions for establishing new breweries, despite the fact that taprooms tend to sell significantly less alcohol per patron than restaurants or other drinking establishments. In New Jersey, food may be consumed on the premises but must be purchased offsite (in certain breweries, small snacks such as pretzels are sometimes provided gratis); this is largely due to Jersey's powerful restaurant lobby and compounded by the expense of the state's liquor licenses (which can cost

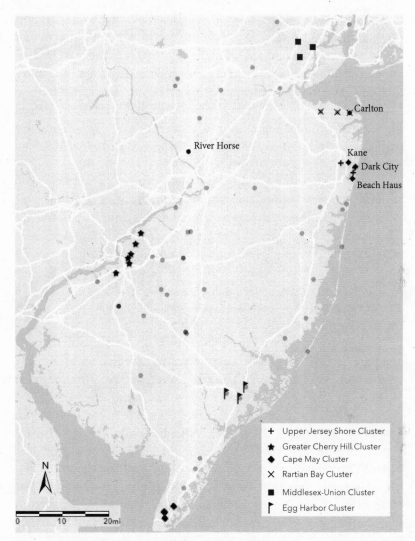

Cluster map of New Jersey taprooms.

over $2 million, averaging about $350,000 statewide).[8] Although this supports the state's burgeoning food-truck industry, it also effectively restricts the amount of time patrons spend in the space (and thus revenues). Reflecting on the common disappointment voiced by some female patrons, Dark City's owner Kevin Sharpe (interview with Saunders, August 23, 2018) suggests that the ban on selling soda, juice, or other drinks at taprooms actually creates a form of gender bias, given that many women are either not fond of beer or do not wish to be *seen* drinking beer in public spaces (see Nichols 2016; Towns, Parker, and Chase 2012). However, there is little to be done as brewery owners do not have any viable options; as one owner lamented, "We have to explain to out-of-state visitors, we are not a bar, we are an educational facility."

Other restrictions (which are not always adhered to or have been phased out in recent years) include a restriction against playing live television, no "guest" taps, limits on the number of gallons a craft brewery can produce, onerous "bartender" certifications for staff, and nonsensical requirements for restaurant-grade equipment when there is no food preparation.[9] Proximity to educational/religious institutions automatically results in restrictions on a taproom's operating hours. As our spatial analysis (see earlier and Table 1) suggests, certain taprooms must tread lightly due to their proximity to schools, churches, and residential housing (with all its attendant "importance" in terms of status in a state with the sixth-highest real estate prices in the country, at the time of this writing), whereas others are free to operate without much concern for their neighbors.

Regardless, the bane of the industry remains the tour requirement, given that the ABC regularly sends in undercover employees to verify compliance. As one brewery owner told me, the ABC's threshold for violating the requirement is rather subjective, fining one brewery for not conducting an in-person tour while not doing so for another that employs a proxy tour. (Examples of "tour substitutes" the authors have encountered include murals, placemats, recorded videos, and River Horse's View-Master). The fine for a violation is $2,000, a nontrivial figure considering that the average customer spends only $20 to $28 per visit (a single flight of beer usually costs about $7 or $8 for a quartet of four-ounce pours). The ABC stipulates that even returning customers must "do the tour"; however, "proper" regulars are typically exempt in practical terms as staff tends to recognize them (thus guaranteeing that they are not undercover agents). In our interview with the vice president of the New Jersey Brewers Association (NJBA), Charles "Chuck" Aaron, he spoke of the "Beach Haus effect,"[10] wherein one brewery becomes known for being lax on observing the laws around taproom visits, and then the ABC sends agents around the state seeking to punish any and all violators. This push for total observance soon dies down and things return to normal (interview with Saunders, April 13, 2019). (For more on Beach Haus as an outlier in key metrics, see Table 2.)

Table 2. A Comparison of Practices among the Five New Jersey Case Study Breweries

	Beach Haus	Dark City	Kane	River Horse	Carton
Pour Size Available	Flights (4 oz.) and full pours (up to 16 oz.) in glass	Flights (4 oz.) and full pours (up to 12 oz.) in glass	Flights (4 oz.) and full pours (up to 12 oz.) in glass	Flights (4 oz.) and full pours (up to 16 oz.) in plastic	Flights (4 oz.) in glass; full pour pints only for cask beers
Hours of Operation per Week	45	26 (fewer in winter)	18	19	23
Tour Type	Postcard/banner-based, except on event days when a full tour is conducted for all patrons	Server-delivered description given at the entrance to the brewing facility at the back of the taproom	Hourly brewer-led tours conducted for interested parties within the taproom	Enhanced-reality "tour" via View-Master; prebooked full tours of the facility	Substantive brewer-led tour of the ground floor brewing facilities required for first-time visitors
Food Options	Take-out menus and good proximity for carry-in food	Food truck on weekends and suggested options for delivery	Not permitted in the taproom	Not permitted in the taproom	Not permitted in the taproom
Dogs Welcome	Yes	Yes	No	Yes	Yes

The microbrewery owners we spoke with estimate that the annual fixed costs of "doing the tour," including staff time lost to the process, printing of supporting material, and the like, run between $4,000 and $7,000 (and this figure does not include fines or variable costs associated with tour infrastructure). Although this is a trivial expenditure in fiscal terms, an additional cost comes with the taping or shrink-wrapping of all growlers filled at the taproom. New Jersey state law stipulates that a growler (even one filled to the top) constitutes an "open container" and can result in a fine of $200 and court surcharges if one is stopped by the police.[11] None of New Jersey's neighboring states have such regulations. Keeping with the theme of Byzantine (bordering on Kafkaesque) regulation, whereas most taprooms that lack exposed brewing equipment allow (well-behaved) canines in the space, and ABC regulations clearly do not prohibit this, as beer is transferred in oxygen-less, closed containers and lines, certain county health departments treat breweries as a restaurants (despite ABC regulation that bars breweries from making food), thus making some owners hesitant to allow dogs into their spaces for fear of fines and closure. Yet rather than lessening the burden on microbreweries, in 2018 New Jersey imposed even more regulations, including a cap on the number of special events (twenty-five per year) and on the ability to show live sporting events like the World Cup (for which Beach Haus brewed and canned a special beer known as Olé). As John Merklin of Beach Haus states:

> The fact that consumer demand across the country and specifically our state has grown exponentially in both areas [new breweries and more local products being served] should be of great excitement. A source of pride for all in the state. Unfortunately, this is not yet the case in New Jersey. In my opinion this is largely due to archaic laws on the books which were designed to address concerns that are very much in the past and now only hurt this growing industry. (Interview with Saunders, December 1, 2018)

David Rible, director of the New Jersey ABC, defended the new restrictions, arguing that such establishments were never meant to have the "same privileges" as restaurants and bars (Pugliese 2018). However, such regulations effectively prevent taprooms from hosting club meetings or board game events—things that would never take place in one of New Jersey's countless Irish pubs or Italian restaurants—thus closing off (beer-abetted) social networking events that cannot exist otherwise in the state's third spaces. Admittedly, most taprooms have just ignored the new regulation, allowing events like weekly trivia nights and Saturday-morning yoga sessions to continue unabated. Two other oft-unobserved regulations are a prohibition on displaying "local restaurant menus that can deliver food to their locations" and a ban on "holding craft shows and pop-up markets," which some legislators have lambasted as ridiculous given legislators' mandate to increase the state's economic output (Miller 2018).

The NJBA previously served as the state's representative for microbreweries and brewpubs with regard to legislative affairs. However, in 2018, a new trade group, the Brewers Guild of New Jersey (BGNJ), coalesced to more effectively lobby Trenton. The BGNJ, which was formed alongside the NJBA by nine of the latter's founding members, now represents the interests of breweries that make 75 percent of craft beer brewed in the state (Nurin 2018). Unlike the NJBA, which is still in existence, the Guild's membership is restricted to those entities that brew at least 2,000 barrels of beer (62,000 gallons) annually (although associate status is now an option for those breweries that do not meet the threshold). In addition to economic issues (as well as questions of fairness), New Jersey's brewers are debating the state over culture, arguing that their spaces are increasingly serving as centers of cultural experience for the communities in which they are located, enabling "opportunities to provide increased awareness for local causes, charities and civic groups" (Merklin, interview with Saunders, December 1, 2018).

This sentiment was echoed by Chuck Aaron, owner of Jersey Girl Brewing Company (Hackettstown) and vice president of the NJBA, who rhetorically posed the question to the authors: "How many restaurants in New Jersey have 10,000 square feet to host an event like a mayoral election campaign?" Speaking with Saunders in 2019, Aaron described his own establishment as a small business "incubator," given that after its establishment, the light industrial area around it blossomed with a host of new enterprises, which in turn promotes goodwill in the local community. He added that the ample space he is able to provide has become instrumental for a variety of nonprofits and school sports teams to conduct fundraising, awards ceremonies, animal adoption events, and the like. Touting New Jersey as one of the fastest-growing craft beer states (alongside partially "dry" Kentucky), Aaron is sanguine about the future under Governor Phil Murphy (D-NJ), a vocal advocate of the microbrewery industry.[12] However, as a lobbyist for the sector, Aaron is aware of the vagaries of New Jersey politics, pointing out that a recent proposal from Trenton was peppered with new ordinances that had never been discussed with stakeholders, effectively stripping breweries of a number of freedoms they had long enjoyed. Echoing the concerns of brewery owners, we find that continuing to restrict access to taproom-based imbibing is antithetical to the spirit of improving the quality of life in the state, something that Trenton should take seriously if it wishes to maintain New Jersey's position among the top ten US states for social cohesion (Wise 2015).

Conclusion

As Bart Watson, chief economist for the Brewers Association, notes: "Tasting rooms are the quintessential location for brand building." Craft breweries generate approximately one-tenth of their revenue in the taproom, and tasting rooms result in faster distribution growth. He goes on to state, "It's in the best interest of distributors to support their brewery partner's ability to directly interact with beer lovers" (qtd. in Nurin 2017). Consequently, New Jersey's regulations are actively throttling the success of its breweries by limiting how people can consume craft beer. As Baginski and Bell (2011) argue, the spatial distribution of microbreweries has less to do with proximity to metropolitan statistical areas, of which New Jersey has many, than with "legal, moral and religious" factors when it comes to being "under-tapped" (2011, 165). Given that New Jersey generally lacks any history of allowing morality or faith to stop the sale of alcohol (beyond a handful of dry townships historically associated with Protestant sects), it is the law that hinders the industry's growth. In the words of Dark City's Kevin Sharpe, New Jersey is definitely *not* a pro–craft beer state, especially when compared to other large states like Illinois, Florida, Colorado, and California or even neighbors New York, Pennsylvania, and Delaware. However, if NJBA vice president Chuck Aaron's reading of the political landscape is accurate, things may be looking up for the Garden State.

Notes

1. According to the Brewers Association, New Jersey fares better in terms of per-capital economic impact of its craft breweries, ranking twenty-eighth.

2. Importantly, New Jersey, a state dominated by Catholic Irish and Italian Americans, and descendants of immigrant Eastern European Jews, lacks the faith-based aversion to consuming potent potables that characterizes states in the American South, where mostly Protestant immigrants embraced abstemious lifestyles in the 1800s and beyond (see Dowell 2015).

3. As Ken Dowell (2015) notes, "This is a state with a long history of resisting any attempts to stem the flow of alcohol, a state which probably produced more beer than anyone during Prohibition, and yet New Jersey ended up with some of the most confusing and restrictive alcohol and beverage laws that you'll find anywhere." Indeed, New Jersey limits the sale of liquor licenses based on township population, thus making it extremely expensive to obtain the right to sell alcohol. Most restaurants in the state are BYOB ("bring your own beer [or wine]"), and those that possess the coveted mandate to serve alcohol are fiercely protective of their revenues to compensate for the massive outlay of cash for the license. With some of the most complex alcohol laws in the country, New Jersey has twenty-nine different types of liquor license, and only permits the sale of alcohol for home consumption at specialty shops—liquor stores, beer distributors, and packaged goods locations (some grocery stores have gained an exemption to sell beer, but most cannot).

4. One of our case studies, Carton Brewing, was forced to invest in an expensive odor-capturing system due to its proximity to a local primary school, to prevent children from being subjected to the smells of the brewing process.

5. Beyond the aforementioned British pub and German beer-hall variants of drinking establishments, Scandinavia, France, Italy, and other countries of Europe all have quite distinct spatial models for drinking in "bars," all of which differ somewhat from the North American model, thus discouraging/ encouraging certain modes of social interaction.

6. Here we differentiate microbreweries from brewpubs, which in New Jersey date back to 1995. Microbreweries initially produced beer for offsite consumption, later opening up taprooms for drinking on site; brewpubs do not allow offsite consumption beyond a single sixty-four-ounce (half-gallon) growler fill, but are permitted to prepare and serve food, as well as sell wine and liquor. Thus, most brewpubs function primarily as restaurants, though ones with house-made beer.

7. These include the Upper Jersey Shore and Raritan Bay clusters, which contain four out of five of our case studies.

8. According to a series of reports by the State of New Jersey Commission of Investigation during the 1990s and early 2000s, organized crime held sway over the issuance of liquor licenses in certain parts of the state, deciding who got to distribute alcohol and where it was and was not available. More recently, entrenched interests in the restaurant community have opposed changing the practice of how licenses are issued to protect their sunk investments.

9. Sharpe (2018) pointed out that some New Jersey brewers have been forced to add grease traps to deal with nonexistent grease, simply because they are regulated like restaurants.

10. Although Beach Haus may have claimed the current mantle for "bending" the rules, other breweries around the state have gained a reputation for violating

ABC regulations, including Cape May Brewing, which—taking advantage of its location as the New Jersey brewery most distant from the state capital, Trenton—has long thumbed its nose at the powers that be.

11. State law requires any previously opened or empty alcohol containers to be placed in the trunk of a vehicle to avoid a fine (including those receptacles taken to recycling centers).

12. Murphy has also promised to sign any bill legalizing recreational cannabis that hits his desk, a factor that may ultimately divert the attention of moral campaigners away from taprooms and toward the "scourge" of dispensaries.

References

Alonso, Abel Duarte and Nikolaos Sakellarios. 2017. "The Potential for Craft Brewing Tourism Development in the United States: A Stakeholder View." *Tourism Recreation Research* 42(1):96–107.

Anderson, Jon. 2015. *Understanding Cultural Geography: Places and Traces* (2nd ed.). New York: Routledge.

Baginski, James and Thomas L. Bell. 2011. "Under-Tapped? An Analysis of Craft Brewing in the Southern United States." *Southeastern Geographer* 51(1):165–85.

Brown, Pete. 2017. *Miracle Brew: Hops, Barley, Water, Yeast and the Nature of Beer*. London: Chelsea Green Publishing.

Dennett, Adam and Sam Page. 2017. "The Geography of London's Recent Beer Brewing Revolution." *The Geographical Journal* 183(4):440–54.

Dowell, Ken. 2015. "Beer in New Jersey: All the Laws We Never Followed." *Off The Leash*, November 1 (https://offtheleash.net/2015/11/01/beer-laws/).

Elzinga, Kenneth G., Carol Horton Tremblay, and Victor J. Tremblay. 2015. "Craft Beer in the United States: History, Numbers, and Geography." *Journal of Wine Economics* 10(3):242–74.

Fletchall, Ann M. 2016. "Place-Making through Beer-Drinking: A Case Study of Montana's Craft Breweries." *Geographical Review* 106(4):539–66.

Hawkins, Harriet and Elizabeth Straughan, eds. 2015. *Geographical Aesthetics: Imagining Space, Staging Encounters*. Farnham, UK: Ashgate Publishing.

Hindy, Steve. 2014. *The Craft Beer Revolution: How a Band of Microbrewers Is Transforming the World's Favorite Drink*. New York: Macmillan.

Johnson, Kelly. 2013. "River Horse Brewing Co. Finds Room to Grow in Ewing." *NJ.com*, August 8 (https://www.nj.com/mercer/index.ssf/2013/08/river_horse _brewing_co_finds_room_to_grow_in_ewing.html).

Kachmar, Kala. 2015. "@ISSUE: Why the $%&@ Are You So Rude, N.J.?" *Asbury Park Press*, July 30 (https://www.app.com/story/opinion/columnists/2015/07/30 /issue-rude-nj/30886957/).

Kerski, Joseph J. 2015. "Geo-awareness, Geo-enablement, Geotechnologies, Citizen Science, and Storytelling: Geography on the World Stage." *Geography Compass* 9(1):14–26.

Kirkby, Diane. 2003. "'Beer, Glorious Beer': Gender Politics and Australian Popular Culture." *Journal of Popular Culture* 37(2):244–56.

Miller, Jennifer Jean. 2018. "Special Ruling Brews Controversy for Craft Beer Industry." *New Jersey Herald*, October 2, (https://www.njherald.com/20181002 /special-ruling-brews-controversy-for-craft-beer-industry).

Newman, Cathy. 2004. "Greetings from the Jersey Shore." *National Geographic Society* 206(2):80–99.

Nichols, Emily. 2016. "'What on Earth Is She Drinking?' Doing Femininity through Drink Choice on the Girls' Night Out.'" *Journal of International Women's Studies* 17(2):77–91.

Nilsson, Isabelle, Neil Reid, and Matthew Lehnert. 2018. "Geographic Patterns of Craft Breweries at the Intraurban Scale." *The Professional Geographer* 70(1):114–25.

Nurin, Tara. 2017. "Pushback against Brewery Tasting Rooms Threatens the Growth of Craft Beer." *Forbes*, June 7 (https://www.forbes.com/sites/taranurin/2017/06/07/pushback-against-brewery-tasting-rooms-threatens-the-growth-of-craft-beer/#4de9bdaf62a8).

Nurin, Tara. 2018. "NJ Brewer's Association Breaks Silence after Founding Members Secretly Form New Group." *Forbes*, March 8 (https://www.forbes.com/sites/taranurin/2018/03/08/nj-brewers-association-breaks-its-silence-ten-days-after-founding-members-secretly-form-a-new-group/).

Ogle, Maureen. 2006. *Ambitious Brew: The Story of American Beer*. New York: Harcourt.

Pritchard, Ian. 2012. "'Beer and Britannia': Public-House Culture and the Construction of Nineteenth-Century British-Welsh Industrial Identity." *Nations and Nationalism* 18(2):326–45.

Pugliese, Nicholas. 2018. "Why Is New Jersey Cracking Down on Microbreweries?" *NorthJersey.com*, September 25 (https://eu.northjersey.com/story/news/new-jersey/2018/09/25/explainer-laws-behind-new-jerseys-crackdown-microbreweries/1420433002/).

Russello Ammon, Francesca. 2015. "Postindustrialization and the City of Consumption: Attempted Revitalization in Asbury Park, New Jersey." *Journal of Urban History* 41(2):158–74.

Saunders, Robert A. and Jack Holland. 2018. "The Ritual of Beer Consumption as Discursive Intervention: Effigy, Sensory Politics, and Resistance in Everyday IR." *Millennium: Journal of International Studies* 46(2):119–41.

Soja, Edward W. 1996. *Thirdspace: Journeys to Los Angeles and Other Real-and-Imagined Places*. New York, NY: Wiley-Blackwell.

State of New Jersey Commission of Investigation. 2004. "The Changing Face of Organized Crime in New Jersey." *Trends in Organized Crime* 8(2):28–117.

Storey, David. 2012. *Territories: The Claiming of Space*. New York: Routledge.

Towns, Alison J., Christy Parker, and Phillip Chase. 2012. "Constructions of Masculinity in Alcohol Advertising: Implications for the Prevention of Domestic Violence." *Addiction Research & Theory* 20(5):389–401.

Van Wolputte, Steven and Mattia Fumanti. 2010. *Beer in Africa: Drinking Spaces, States and Selves*. Münster: LIT Verlag.

Wise, David. 2015. "In Measures of Economic Strength, Social Cohesion, and Fiscal Position, Blue and Purple States Are Generally Outperforming Red States." London School of Economics Phelan US Centre. Retrieved January 3, 2019 (http://blogs.lse.ac.uk/usappblog/2015/03/20/in-measures-of-economic-strength-social-cohesion-and-their-fiscal-position-blue-and-purple-states-are-generally-outperforming-red-states/).

CHAPTER 8

From Consumer to Producer
Pathways to Working in Craft Beer

CHRISTOPHER S. ELLIOTT

Although state laws regarding craft brewing vary tremendously across the country, affecting the balance of power among suppliers, distributors, and retailers, and although the barriers to market entry might be high, with start-up fees and licensing hurdles, one factor in craft beers' growth seems constant: people are inspired by beer. Charlie Papazain was so inspired by it, he started the homebrew movement when it was illegal (Rao 2009). During 2005, in North Carolina, Sean Wilson, the owner and founder of Durham's Fullsteam Brewery, began the "Pop the Cap" movement, petitioning the state legislature to raise its ABV restriction (no beer over 5.9 percent could be sold.) After two years of campaigning and coalition building across the state, the law passed, raising the ABV limit to 15 percent. In the next ten years, the number of breweries in the state would grow from 30 to more than 200 (Elliott 2018.) The more than four thousand brewery foundings between 1990 and 2016 would seem to attest to the personal inspiration driving the growth of craft beer (Brewers Association 2018.) Is this phenomenon—challenging laws to advocate one's hobby—unique to craft beer? Or is the craft beer case a manifestation of some broader moment in Western societies?

This chapter argues that the personal inspiration evident in craft beer's growth represents a broader development in late-capitalist markets. Since the late 1990s, social theorists have suggested that the "Fordist" model of understanding the connection between economy and society has become outdated. The Fordist perspective viewed the workplace, market, and consumer society (i.e., the home) as separate spheres. As capitalism matures, the market logic expands, blurring the lines between these spheres. Hardt and Negri (2000) argue that capitalism has become a global empire, ending the between-nation conflicts over territory and resources, and creating a more abstract terrain of markets and its enemies. Building on this notion, the "social factory" literature argues that all social life is now potentially an opportunity for value creation (Gill and Pratt 2008). Autonomist Marxists suggest value creation is no longer restricted to the hidden abode, but must be understood as circuits, linking consumers to companies in more tightly bound feedback loops (Böhm and Land 2012). Similarly, the critical literature examining "brands" argues that these are specifically created to link consumers, workers, and shareholders in a shared vision, executed by the corporation (Brannan, Parsons, and Priola 2011; Land and Taylor 2010). Misra and Walters (2016) examine the effect of "cool clothes" brands on employment practices. Employers believe they can leverage the cool factor of their brand to offer substandard pay and inconsistent work schedules. Thus, a consumptive identity and a workplace identity are imagined as flowing from the same market-borne message. Across these literatures, a common outcome of this global transformation is a "blurring of the boundaries" between production and consumption. In this view, the market has become a vehicle of empowerment and improvement, whether you are a consumer or a worker. Choosing a career and choosing a wardrobe are both opportunities to improve, upgrade, and construct the (relentlessly rational) self.

A substantial literature examines these changes in the context of job seeking, in which individuals must choose a job in a world saturated by market logic. Literature on the "entrepreneurial self" or "enterprising self" argues that the labor market mandates individuals to actively view themselves as commodities if they wish to become and remain employed (Du Gay 1996; Hong 2014; Vallas and Cummins 2015). This position states that we are all independent, economically rational actors who must accomplish the entrepreneurial self by selecting the right career and organization to "fit" our own personal identity (Vallas and Cummins 2015). Forming this personal identity, a process largely articulated through the language of branding, is the responsibility of the worker. Individuals are expected to know their capacities and then choose the right setting for deploying them. Hong (2014) analyzes career guidance exercises, such as flower mapping or balloon drawing, intended to help job seekers find their true passion as it should manifest in a job, and then go out and find that job. As a labor market commodity, one should strive to understand one's strengths, weaknesses, and passions, and then package them in a way that is easily communicated to potential (i.e., all) employers.

But how do people *know* who they are? How do they form an "authentic" conception of self that would allow them to know their passions? It seems likely that for many people entering the labor market, the answer to these questions lies in the commodities that individuals enjoy consuming and the lifestyles they construct based on those consumptive habits. As consumption increasingly becomes specialized around lifestyle, providing a basis for the conception of self (Arnould and Thompson 2005), an avenue develops by which someone would come to know the passions that should designate their career.

Craft beer certainly provides this platform. Indeed, nonfiction accounts of craft breweries' history suggests these businesses are launched by people who have a passion for making beer and want a lifestyle that enables them to share that passion with others (Hindy 2014). These literatures often celebrate the accounts of homebrew enthusiasts looking to turn their hobby into a real profession, rather than being motivated solely by the chance to earn a lucrative profit in a trendy industry. People who work in craft beer were thus likely motivated by their consumptive-born identities.

This chapter examines the labor market trajectories of persons employed in North Carolina's craft beer industry. In interviewing forty-nine people from various levels of employment in the sector, I found three types of employment trajectories, with "enchanted consumer" being the most predominant. Thirty-five of the interviewees became workers because they identified strongly with the craft beer lifestyle. These pathways illustrate another mechanism by which the boundaries between work and consumption become blurred: consumers who seek to translate into a productive career the fulfillment accomplished through a particular consumptive lifestyle. The spread of craft beer thus illustrates another avenue by which the market logic further penetrates social life in general. However, whereas the social-factory and enterprising-self literatures tend to critically view this market penetration as the expansion of (capitalist) control and hence exploitation, the workers interviewed here seemed empowered by the capacity to bridge their consumptive and professional passions.

The remainder of this chapter is organized as follows. First, I describe the enterprising-self literature in more detail. I then articulate for the purpose of analysis the "ideal pathway" linking an enchanted consumer to craft beer work. I describe the method and sample, then detail three types of labor market trajectories found in the sample: ideal pathways, never macros, and not-fans-prior. Ideal pathways constitute 65 percent of the sample, suggesting workers in craft beer are often drawn from a pool of consumers who have become enchanted by the lifestyle. In the next section I examine the motivations drawing workers into craft beer work in more detail. Last, I discuss conclusions and implications for the enterprising-self literature.

The Enterprising Self

Although the "entrepreneurial spirit" has been a noted feature of capitalistic societies practically since its emergence (von Martin 1963) the "post-Fordist" or late-capitalist society appears to have taken this notion further. Under this system, market logic penetrates into ever more spheres of social life, particularly as consumer markets become awash in cheap goods. Since the late 1970s, neoliberal economic policy, improved mechanization in manufacturing, and outsourcing have reshaped occupational structures (Wyatt and Hecker 2006). The result has been a significant reduction in middle-class, blue-collar jobs in manufacturing (Autor and Dorn 2013). Central to this restructuring is the shift from a "push" to a "pull" economy. The "logistics revolution," or the increased focus on rationalizing the efficiency and capacity of supply chains, is largely responsible for both the proliferation of consumer goods and their falling cost (Bonacich and Wilson 2008; Levinson 2006). The variety and complexity of consumer goods have expanded far beyond what is necessary to reproduce the necessities of social life. Company supply chains increasingly must respond to the "mass customization" of consumer demand (Frenkel et al. 1995). As manufacturing has declined and consumption has increased, the jobs that have grown are in customer service (Wyatt and Hecker 2006). Over the same period, there has been a growth in contingent, or nonstandard, employment practices, where companies increasingly use a collection of part-time employees in place of full-time positions (Kalleberg, Reskin, and Hudson 2000).

As labor market "precarity" (Arnold and Bongiovi 2013; Kalleberg

2009, 2011) has deepened, the workplace discourse increasingly seems to reflect that instability. For example, Jeffrey Sallaz (2014), working six months in a call center, found workers were expected to embody the "permanent pedagogy" of the labor market. Newcomers are constantly having to learn the job, with the expectation that no one will be around long enough to actually develop the requisite skills. Rather than a pedagogy of improvement and stable experience, the workplace reflects, in a fractured way, late capitalism's labor market precarity, providing incomplete skill sets while teaching workers to live with constant turnover.

Researchers began using consumption to understand these new employment relations following Paul du Gay's 1996 book *Consuming Identity*. Cited more than six hundred times in business and organizational journals (Web of Science search, February 13, 2017), du Gay's book has launched intense debate regarding the existence of a so-called enterprising discourse and the extent of the power it may actually have over workers' conception of self. Sparked by an interest in how "new modes of organizational conduct blurred traditional differences between production and consumption identities," du Gay (1996, 5) reasons that, because consumption is becoming more central to the economy, companies must be able to "connect" emotionally with their consumers' needs and respond to their desires—a discourse he labels that of the *sovereign consumer*. The enterprising worker is one who is always thinking about the consumer, no matter their position in the company's hierarchy. Du Gay found that, despite his hope that the sovereign consumer could disrupt traditional power structures in the workplace and give a broader range of workers the ability to determine their own workplace identity, workers nonetheless expressed reserved, almost sullen acceptance of the enterprising discourse.

Researchers have since considered the *enterprising self* a form of workplace control. Spicer (2011) argues that "authenticity" forces workers to monitor their actions in new ways, becoming a new form of self-regulation. One's "true self" is increasingly expected to be reflected in both work and nonwork activity (Fleming and Spicer 2004; Land and Taylor 2010). For example, workers are encouraged to cover their desks with consumer brands, family photos, or whatever makes them feel at home. People arrange their work so they can "be themselves."

Subsequent researchers have been interested in how the discourse of the enterprising self might be evolving—specifically as labor market precarity deepens. Vallas and Cummins (2015) show that job-seeking uncertainty leads people to internalize the belief that, to get a job, they must do "branding work" on themselves. First, the researchers examined the discursive content of advice books offering career guidance. Then, they interviewed people in the labor market, both employed and unemployed. Interviewees without work were likely to invoke the career guidance discourse, describing anxiety over how to use social media platforms, business cards, and résumés to promote a personal brand. Vallas and Cummins found that their participants viewed "personal brand" as shorthand for what kind of work one can do—what kind of labor the employer is going to consume. Workers reported feeling pressure to strategically survey their capacities, then use whatever opportunities were available to create "demand" for that consumption, and thus attain a job.

The degree to which the enterprising discourse functions effectively as a mechanism of control over workers is debated (Bruni, Gherardi, and Poggio 2004; Gabriel 1999; Storey, Salaman, and Platman 2005; Thomas and Davies 2005). Human resources managers have built upon Paul du Gay's notion of the sovereign consumer to detail how consumer–worker interactions may unfold, wherein workers leverage consumers' needs to alter organizational policies (Bolton and Houlihan 2005; Korczynski & Ott 2004; Korczynski et al. 2000). Doolin (2002) examines hospitals in New Zealand, where managerial regimes were restructured based on the enterprising discourse. He found workers' acceptance versus rejection of the new expectations varied according to each department's particular labor needs. Subsequent researchers have examined the extent of the enterprising self in cases such as freelance work in media (Storey, Salaman, and Platman 2005), among doctors and nurses (Halford and Leonard 2006), and among police, social, and educational services in the UK (Thomas and Davies, 2005). In each of these cases, workers mediated the meaning—and the effectiveness—of enterprising discourses. In other words, if there is an enterprising discourse saturating labor markets at the macro level, individuals always contest its effects at the micro level (Cohen and Musson 2000).

Although contested and negotiated by workers, the enterprising self is largely conceptualized as an oppressive form of workplace control. Connecting with the consumers' point of view to provide value is a burdensome activity for workers, yet it is something they must deal with. However, the research just described has investigated the manifestation of the enterprising discourse at two levels of analysis: the macro and micro. Research has either considered the messaging of labor markets or the dynamics of particular workplaces.

Researching the enterprising discourse through the lens of consumption offers a mezzo level of analysis. Craft beer offers a distinct arena of consumption, replete with rituals, institutions, and specialized jargon. Thus, connecting with consumers in this consumptive lifestyle may not be experienced by workers as control, because they may share in the specific values organizing the discourse more generally.

Method

As part of a larger project, I conducted forty-nine semistructured interviews with people from the craft beer industry, mostly in North Carolina's Triangle area. Comprising seven questions, the interview focused on the workers' trajectory from the consumer market (if they had one) into the job they currently possess. The instrument asked them to account for their decision to possess this job, and assessed the degree to which they saw the job as part of their future career trajectory. The sample consisted of seven owners (or people who got their "job" by founding a company), five brewers, six assistant brewers, nine sales/service managers, twelve sales reps, and ten servers or bartenders. Of the owners interviewed, only two were also the head brewer at the time of interview, meaning the breakdown for production versus service jobs was thirteen to thirty-six.

All of the people on the production side, including all of the owners, had some background in homebrewing. A handful of the people holding service jobs had dabbled in homebrewing, having attempted it a few times. Some claimed to have aspirations toward learning to brew and finding work making beer. One male bartender described his desire to get "closer to the source." However, about two-thirds of the sample were not accomplished homebrewers. Men outnumbered women by a ratio of 3:2. Twenty-four respondents were working their first craft beer job at the time of the interview, with the rest on their second or third job in the business. Two were on their fourth job. Average length of tenure in the current job was twenty-three and a half months.

I gathered the sample through a combination of unsolicited emails, approaching random people at bars or festivals, referrals, and (on two occasions) owner encouragement of multiple workers to participate in the interviews. Although some elements were snowballed (a form of chain sampling where subjects refer researchers to other potential interviewees), it was not a difficult population to sample. Therefore, we might expect some degree of heterogeneity with respect to its demographic composition. However, two patterns predominated. First, the respondents were overwhelmingly white (48 of 49). This was not surprising, unfortunately, because the world of craft beer consumption is largely a white one. The demographic composition of consumers observed and workers interviewed appeared closely matched. I did approach people of color and women when possible, and made an effort to include them in the interview sample. Still, I only met three people of color working in craft beer during the period of study, and I was only able to interview one; the other two were willing but the logistics proved prohibitive.

Second, the respondents seemed like very competent people who could have exceled in a variety of working situations. To begin with, forty of the forty-nine participants had at least a bachelor's degree; seven also had a master's, and one had obtained a doctorate in chemistry. Interestingly, twelve of those with a college degree were working entry-level service or sales jobs. Several had plans to attend graduate school that were changed by their desire to pursue careers in beer. Moreover, twenty-one respondents had left a "successful" career (meaning they had earned promotions, or they had gone to school for a particular field and had found work in it) in another industry before coming to work their first craft beer job. The sample thus consists largely of people who had enjoyed some degree of labor market or educational accomplishment before choosing to work in craft beer. Being white, educated, and relatively successful, the sample represents people with the opportunity to "shop" for their preferred career path. They may have had chances to seek their passions, to find jobs that would offer more than just the bare survival of a paycheck. The next section describes how their labor market trajectories were coded for analysis.

Five Steps from Consumer Enchantment to Career

Theoretically, workers may have come to realize their work-related passions are an outcome of their enchantment as consumers. *Enchantment* refers to the hook or pull that consumers experience as market actors

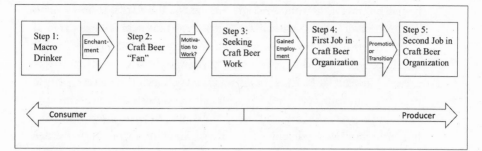

| Step 1: Macro Drinker | Enchant-ment | Step 2: Craft Beer "Fan" | Motiva-tion to Work? | Step 3: Seeking Craft Beer Work | Gained Employ-ment | Step 4: First Job in Craft Beer Organization | Promotion or Transition | Step 5: Second Job in Craft Beer Organization |

Consumer ——————————————————————— Producer

The five pathways into craft beer jobs.

seek to legitimize consumption (Ritzer 2010). For George Ritzer, enchantment begins with the "Cathedrals of Consumption"—massive, capital-intensive spectacles that awe and overwhelm the consumer. He gives Disneyland as the ultimate example. Although Ritzer's conception of enchantment lacks agency for the consumer, it does call our attention to the efforts of market actors to create a positive affinity for the consumptive *experience*. Enchanted people are those that "buy into" the craft beer lifestyle. Figure 9 depicts five potential steps in the pathway of enchantment to a full-time career.

The first step is "macro drinker." This is a designation for people who drink "industrial beer" or "mass-produced beer," which in the United States is one particular style: the American pale lager. Contributing to the $85 billion industrial beer market (by drinking a beer produced by SABMiller, Anheuser-Busch InBev, or Heineken) in the United States, people in this step may have no inkling that beer's color, aroma, mouthfeel, and flavor can diverge vastly from that style. Therefore they represent potential craft beer drinkers. Entering the second stage, individuals develop some passion for craft beer. Perhaps after trying a craft beer at a friend's prompting, or at a party, they find this new world of beer drinking enticing, and seek to learn more. Enchanted by craft beer consumption, they "buy into" the lifestyle. Thus the first two stages are about the potential conversion from American-modal beer drinker to self-identifying as someone who drinks "craft" beers, probably exclusively.

People in the third step, regardless of how they came to appreciate craft beer, have made the conscious decision to find work in craft beer *because they love to consume it*. Seeking to turn that passion into a stable occupation, they seek an avenue for long-term employment. The third step is most critical, since it is here that people have decided to turn their consumer identities into some related occupational identity. Successfully finding work in a particular field requires research, intent, and self-authoring (e.g., résumés, interviews). These people may respond to advertisements, cold-call, send unsolicited résumés, or take longer roads by seeking internships, volunteering, and networking with craft beer industry figures By gaining employment, they enter the fourth stage—their first craft beer job. Now, some people do arrive at this stage for reasons entirely unrelated to craft beer consumption. Maybe they just responded to a "help wanted" sign, and the job happened to be serving craft beer somewhere. Their exposure to craft beer would thus be part of job training versus through the preceding three stages.

In a fifth possible stage, the respondent advances from their entry-level or stepping-stone job, perhaps several times, to eventually arrive at their current job. This transition could be internal via a promotion in the organization, or external with a move to another company or even opening their own brewery. Having invested their time, skill, and experience, people in the fifth stage are now entrenched in their craft beer career trajectory.

This chapter seeks to analyze which people in the sample occupied what steps on this potential trajectory from "macro" beer consumer to bona fide craft beer professional. It addresses three questions relative to those steps. First, how many people traversed stages from one to four or five. On this "ideal pathway," we should observe individuals who became so enchanted by the craft beer lifestyle, they sought to somehow turn that into a job. Second, for workers that did not reach stage four or five, what was the reason? What is the extent of deviation from the "ideal" consumer-to-producer blend? Last, what motivated people to choose craft beer work? Specifically, in the transition from steps two to three, what was it about the consumptive lifestyle that motivated people to seek employment with craft beer companies? My theoretical expectation is that workers draw upon the consumer discourse to legitimize their choices to work in the industry and reasons why they moved from one stage to the next. Thus, the discourses that people draw upon to legitimize their consumption of craft beer may also be used to make sense of why they chose the work.

Types of Pathways

Coding the interviewee's career trajectories according to which of the five steps each respondent occupied yielded nine distinct combinations—or nine unique pathways from consuming beer to working with beer. They may be sorted into three broader categories. First, fourteen of the forty-nine respondents occupied all five steps on the theorized pathway. Eight went from steps one through four, meaning they are essentially on the same trajectory as the "all five" group. They either lucked into a great job immediately or are planning to use their current job as a springboard into craft beer. Taken together, twenty-two people, or nearly half the sample, were macro drinkers enchanted by craft beer who then sought to work in the craft beer field. This group of respondents constitute *the ideal pathway*, as theorized earlier. Ten people occupied a second group of pathways. Described as the *never macros*, they were craft beer fans before ever drinking macro beer. Usually, they had family that drank imported or craft beer, and thus cared about beer quality. Last, the remaining seventeen respondents I have called the *not fans prior*. They chose craft beer work for more "traditional" reasons, such as the need for stable employment in an apparently growing industry, or because they personally knew a manager or owner when a job became available.

Respondents on the *ideal pathway* and the *never macros* have one thing in common: they all specifically sought work in the craft beer field because they were fans of the craft beer lifestyle. Comprising 65 percent of the sample, these are people who at least moved through steps two, three and four. Their interests in craft beer specifically drove them to find work in the field. Consuming craft beer thus appears to be a significant force pushing people to want a related career. The next several sections provide more detail on each of these pathways.

THE IDEAL PATHWAY

People enchanted by craft beer's consumer lifestyle—either by brewing at home or by the desire to taste and try different beers—who then make a protracted effort to turn those passions into a primary income, comprise the *ideal pathway*. These people described drinking "crappy" beer at first because they were in young and underage or in college, or because it was the cheapest option:

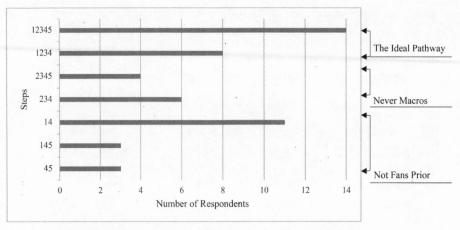

Ideal pathway from consumer to producer.

> You know early college it was case races with Busch Light and Coors Light and things like that. But once I graduated, I started going on vacation and trying different breweries' beers. One of the first ones I remember, I wrote a note on my phone of, I wrote I went to Wilmington and I went to Front Street. I started to notice that I like hoppy beers. I am a hop head. I had never had a beer so flavorful and I loved it. I also liked the fact that it was higher ABV. I could drink three or four and feel just as I could off 12 Busch Light or Bud Light that had no flavor. So at that moment I was totally converted and it was going to the store and getting mixed 12 packs, trying different samplers and trying different styles and stuff like that. —Head Brewer, local brewery, age twenty-nine

Three points in this quote illustrate three predominant trends in the conversion from macro to micro drinker, or how people get enchanted by the craft beer lifestyle. First, the process tends to be viewed as "maturation." College drinking or "case races" is child's play—training wheels for the adult alcohol drinker. The mature drinker is one who tries different styles of beer, explores, and learns to expand their palate. Eleven people in the sample were initially enchanted by the craft beer lifestyle because they were intrigued by the diversity of beer. Exploring and learning beer is thus a major draw for people into craft beer consumptive identities.

Secondly, we see the socioeconomic status in the person's background that enabled them to discover, refine, and control a more

IDENTITY, POLITICS, ECONOMICS

sophisticated level of beer consumption—vacation exploration, and then choosing beers more purposefully, yet still achieving the goal of intoxication. Overwhelmingly, then, people who are motivated to choose craft beer work probably had material means allowing for that initial purchase of a luxury item. A Bud Light at the bar is usually three dollars, whereas a craft beer is five to seven dollars—although, interestingly enough, the respondent did hedge against the notion that craft beer consumption might be viewed solely as a luxury purchase. The same level of intoxication is achieved for the same price. This is consistent with the first point: craft beer is seen as a smarter, more learned way to drink. However the respondent frames it, craft beer consumption is somewhat exclusive. It appears a certain class of people—educated, well off, usually white—become craft beer consumers, and workers of lesser status may be selected out of that pool.

Last, beer tasting is considered to be a process of self-discovery. You do not know which beers are "you" until you taste them. This person found he was a "hop head." Craft beer thus offers a context for making meaningful one's preferences—for discovering and knowing the self. As with this respondent, 45 percent of the sample could remember their first experience of drinking craft beer, *and the name of the beer*. It is described as something like an epiphany: a moment where the person's eyes suddenly opened to a new world. Overall, respondents in the sample thus positively identified their conversion to the craft beer lifestyle as a kind of maturation, a pursuit in self-discovery that is probably costly and limited to wealthier segments of the population.

Despite the ease with which craft beers might be purchased, for many on the ideal pathway, the eventual industry job does not materialize without time, effort and sacrifice. Six of the thirteen people who completed all five steps were doing unpaid work for their first craft beer job—either an internship or a protracted period of volunteering—suggesting a deep commitment to achieve a position in craft beer. A head brewer at a growing regional brewery recounts his time after college. After obtaining a degree in political science, he was unable to secure admission to graduate school, and decided he would try to become a brewer:

> So I told them and I was willing to work for free. I had quit the PetSmart job because I just couldn't do it anymore. I was still working landscaping to pay bills. I told them I can be there for

whatever schedule . . . every other hour that I've got available I want to be here willing to do anything. And I just want to get into the industry. Most were pretty nice about it. They just didn't have an interest in taking me on, but there were at least a couple of the 20 breweries that were kind of rude about it. They pretty much acted like why would you assume? —Head Brewer, regional brewery

The difficulty of breaking into the industry was often recounted in these interviews (especially by people who were trying to work in a brewery but were settling for work as a bartender or server at craft beer specialty bars). Despite offering free labor, this person was turned down multiple times, but his persistence eventually paid off. Owners and brewers also reported how often people would walk into a brewery and ask to volunteer. People want to work in breweries. This respondent eventually visited a small brewery and found the head brewer scrubbing a filter, a task the brewer was happy to hand off. The respondent went on to commute one hour and fifteen minutes, several days per week, to work eight- to ten-hour shifts—without pay—for nearly a year and a half. Finally he was offered a full-time job when the brewery expanded, and he was able to quit landscaping for good. Among respondents, this success story of breaking in was not unusual.

Another five-step respondent, after graduating college and working as a personal trainer, found his initial career plan unsatisfying. He used his life savings to put himself through brewing school. The rigorous and expensive training program—which had him spending six months in Germany—still left him unemployed, however. It took him another two years to find work as a brewer. Again, it was the luck of timing. A head brewer had just quit, and someone working at that brew pub told him now was the time to walk in and ask for the position. He had been there six years at the time of the interview.

As with many people on this pathway, there was no easy or obvious route for working in a brewery. One person, having been laid off from his first job at a library after completing five years of higher education to get a master's in library science, had no other employment prospects. He decided to drive to every brewery in North Carolina. At one stop, pretending he was part of a brewery tour, he lied his way into meeting with a marketing executive, and would not leave until he was offered a position. This level of persistence was surprisingly common in the sample.

Forty-five percent of respondents walked the ideal pathway, either the first four steps or all five. The main difference between the two groups is that those completing all five steps often had an unpaid internship or volunteer period as their first job. The four-step persons were lucky enough to have been hired into a paying position when I interviewed them. The common theme throughout was a deep passion for either brewing or learning about beer, and the desire to make that into a career, even at personal cost.

NEVER MACROS

The second significant group in the sample comprises fans of craft beer who never drank macro beers in their current consumption. These ten people may have drunk macro beers earlier in life, especially when underage, when one drinks what can be had. Aside from this, craft beer never had to enchant them away from the macro side: they had been raised to be fans of craft beers, or at least to see them as normal.

Most never macros had parents or other family who introduced them to craft beer. Sometimes it was because their parents had lived overseas or were homebrewing. In other cases, the person grew up in an area known for craft beer, like Asheville, North Carolina. Often, the never macros were drinking craft beers before anyone else in their peer groups. One described the experience as follows:

> I was the one who in college, you know how everyone has a friend who's a beer snob? Well I was that guy. I mean it was fun, but when I moved back here there was a bottle shop. There wasn't anything like that when I went to high school here. And it would be really cool if I could get a job there, doing that instead of this barista job that I don't like. —Sales Clerk, bottle shop

In other words, the rising popularity of the craft beer scene overall granted these "legacy drinkers" employment opportunities they hadn't imagined before. In the spirit of a rising tide lifting all boats, people raised on craft beer found themselves well positioned to capitalize on the emerging industry. Some of these individuals only chose a craft beer career path after college or other options failed to materialize; however, at some point they did decide to seek craft beer employment.

NOT FANS PRIOR

Seventeen people in the sample were *not fans* of craft beer before trying to find craft beer work. Some were macro drinkers; some were wine drinkers. Some intentionally chose craft beer work, but not because they were fans. For example, one sales representative recounted his pathway as follows:

> I was a history major and I loved that, but I didn't want to be a teacher. So I got a job at a country club. I was a bartender. So I googled recession proof industries. Sounds crazy but that is literally what I googled. The top 5 came up. The first one was accounting. And the last one was the alcohol-beverage industry. The line was "If the economy is good, people drink. If the economy is bad, people drink. —Sales Representative, regional brewery

He used his college degree to land an entry-level job with a distribution company, on the "wine side" of the business. He transitioned to craft beer as he slowly learned more about the coherence of the craft beer lifestyle as part of his job: going to festivals, beverage conferences, and the like. He began meeting people in the craft beer business. Through these connections, he found out a sales-representative position with a successful regional brewery would open up soon, and was able to land the job. Another respondent had a fledgling photography career but had to keep finding new jobs because the companies were closing. She decided to return to community college to retrain. By this time, Asheville (her hometown) had been booming from the craft beer business. Researching the industry, she found ample employment opportunities along with a brewing program at her local college. While completing that program, she worked for a craft beer bottle shop and wrote a column about women brewers. Through these connections, she was able to get a job as assistant brewer with a small local brewery. Others in this group were simply looking for work and happened to have a close personal relationship with an owner or manager.

Regardless, most of these people wanted to stay in craft beer for their careers, and in fact became craft beer fans because they found the work so stimulating. One respondent, working at the time of interview as a waitress at a small brewpub while finishing an undergraduate degree—with the hope of one day becoming a "beer lawyer"— described her first experience:

> Honestly I had just lost my job the week before. One of my friends was like hey there's this new bar; it's really cool. They need hot girls to work there. Go try and work there. I was like well I drink Blue Moon and Yuengling. I guess I know a lot about beer. And I

> couldn't have been more wrong. I knew nothing about craft beer
> . . . when the manager asked me what my favorite beer was and
> I said Blue Moon she just kind of chuckled and said we'll check
> back with you later. —Server, local brewpub

Her work in the craft beer industry thus transformed her into a fan. She recounts the story here with amusement because of her ignorance—Yuengling and Blue Moon are *not* considered craft beers. She described the intensity of "beer school," or the training program her large, franchised corporate employer provided, and the immense satisfaction of learning beer styles. When interviewed, she was on her third position as a craft beer server. During much of the interview, however, she described the experimentation with and exploration of beer styles that she and her family had undertaken. She enjoyed making dessert shakes with beer, and her aunt and father had gotten into homebrewing. This story is common among not fans prior. People who knew nothing of craft beer before their first job were drawn "retroactively" into the craft beer lifestyle.

A subset of this group comprises people who sought craft beer work, surprisingly, because it fit their political beliefs, even though they were *not* craft beer consumers prior. These individuals viewed craft beer's local, hands-on small-business model as consistent with their values. In other words, the chance to work in craft beer offered them the opportunity to work in a place that aligned with their personal political ideology. Only five people in the sample fit this criterion, but their presence provides insight into the kind of economic space that craft beer could represent. For example, this respondent described his motivations:

> So after college I got involved in sustainable agriculture. And I
> worked in that for six years at a nonprofit in Raleigh. On a 6 acre
> farm. It was a teaching farm through that community . . . also
> using ingredients from the farm in beer. I went to Natty Greens
> in Raleigh to pick up their spent grains. . . . So it [craft beer] was
> around my peripherals. But . . . I decided to start looking for new
> employment. And found these guys on craigslist. Applied for the
> job. And they liked me. And gave me the opportunity to work
> here. —Manager, local brewpub

The respondent went on to explain that he only wanted to work for a company that could contribute to his beliefs in sustainability—

something small and local, that would also be involved in community outreach programs, like soup kitchens or fundraisers. People in this group found working with breweries attractive because of their connection to the community, or because they identified with the artisanal nature of the work. We know that people seek work for political reasons: volunteering with nonprofits, nongovernmental organizations, advocacy groups like the ACLU, and so forth. For some, it appears that craft breweries, even though they are capitalistic, for-profit enterprises, fall into this category.

The Motivation to Craft Beer

Regardless of how they became craft beer fans, 65 percent of the sample sought out craft beer work because of their commitment to a craft beer lifestyle, or moved through *at least* steps two, three, and four. What was it about craft beer that drew them to the work? One answer to this probe was generic: "it seemed fun." However, three distinct motivation patterns emerged. First, nine of the respondents were lured by the challenge of brewing—mastering an ancient yet still-evolving craft. One brewery owner said, "Technically I like the science of it. I can probably actually go without ever drinking another beer in my life. Which sounds bad from a person who owns a brewery. But I like the science of it. I like tasting different things." These respondents would often describe beer as "art and science," containing dual aspects that require one to manipulate fermentation processes to achieve a particular subjective experience—a look, aroma, and flavor that matches the brewer's vision. All of these workers were either owners or on the production side. For them, craft beer represented a technical challenge.

The second motivation concerns the service side, or what was driving people who ended up in "auxiliary" jobs. Although all of the brewers were drawn by the intrinsic pleasure of successfully brewing a beverage that others enjoyed, most respondents in consumer-facing roles were drawn because they enjoyed tasting beers and wanted a context where they could teach others how. As consumers who enjoyed learning to explore beers, they were, in many ways, already doing the work. For example, they may have tried "converting" their friends and acquaintances into craft beer drinkers. One sales clerk said, "I figured out that helping people choose beer was my superpower." Craft beer work potentially gave them the chance to keep doing what they were already doing as consumers.

Some of these transitions occurred because their activity as consumers overlapped or filtered into their roles in parallel types of markets. For instance, one person slowly transformed his regular convenience store job into one where he sold craft beer. He was working at a convenience store in 2005, right after Pop the Cap but before craft beer had taken off in North Carolina (only twenty breweries statewide). The store mainly sold American pale lagers, but this person—a craft beer fan since his college days in the late 1990s—convinced the owner to start carrying more craft beers because of the higher markup. As he was able to sell those, talking beer with patrons, the owner began to expand their lineup. This respondent's identity as consumer of craft beer thus directly helped him transform his convenience store clerk role into a craft beer sales position. Several others went from consumer to producer because of familiarity with the establishment:

> All of the bartenders were very friendly . . . it was kind of my own little *Cheers.* Everybody knows my name and everybody's else's name . . . And after going there a little while, I got to know the bartenders and they got to know me, and at the time I wasn't working—I was actually going to school full-time and while I was in grad school I decided I needed some extra cash. And so I asked them if they were hiring. I went on a study abroad trip and when I came back they said they applied for this. —Bottle shop manager

This respondent had been frequenting a craft beer specialty bar for some time, until it became his own *Cheers* (the 1980s–early 1990s American sitcom where an establishment's bartenders and their regular patrons behave like one tight group of friends). Eventually, his familiarity with the atmosphere, where he enjoyed tasting different beers as the draught selection rotated, afforded him the opportunity to switch roles, going from one side of the bar to the other. So, although craft beer consumer culture is driven by the hands-on crafting of beer—the product at the center of this universe—breweries only offer a few such positions at most. What pulls the bulk of craft beer employees into the market are the more numerous peripheral sales and serving jobs. Although these workers are not producing beer—an activity that is presumably directly transferable between homebrewing and commercial brewing—their jobs of selling beer have a parallel skill that *is* transferable. Respondents in consumer-facing craft beer serving roles viewed that work as an extension of their activity as consumers.

Thirdly, craft beer offered a context where labor has an immediate and direct connection with people consuming the product. Some respondents were very explicit about the desire to sell, serve, or make products, while having a direct relationship with people who found the products useful. For example, a bartender at a local brewery said of her motivation, "Because you are showing people where what they're consuming is coming from. . . . Being able to show that to somebody. It is not just a can on a shelf. So it does give you that sense of value and I feel passionate about that. Because they are passionate about it."

This respondent, who was primarily drawn to craft beer because of the desire to be part of local, artisanal organizations, described the tangible process of making beer—being able to show consumers where and how it is made—as being central to her interest in the work. For other respondents, this tangibility was made salient because they had been working the craft beer job as a "side job," alongside a career for which they had trained or been educated. Eventually, the opportunities in craft beer appeared more rewarding, and the respondent decided to pursue them full-time. One brewer got his start by volunteering during three years of college at a local brewpub. After completing an archaeology degree, he continued working his unpaid side job as brew-volunteer until that brewery closed. He then found work as head brewer at a North Carolina brewery, and described the decision by referencing the work for which he had trained in college:

> Archaeology was fun. Not very fulfilling. As far as a life goal. We work. It is a kind of gypsy lifestyle. Living out of hotels. Go where the work is. Work with a team of eight. Or less. And you really don't have interaction with anyone else. So you're in bed about 7:30 because you've been digging holes from dawn to dusk. Go eat some food and then pass out. Because the time sunrise comes you are out in the field digging holes again. . . . Me and many of my brewers spend time talking to the customers at the end of the day. Just having interactions. You know people . . . they'll tell us if they like the beer or not. Whatever it is. It is much more satisfying. Than being a loner out in the woods. —Brewer, regional brewery

This respondent did not consider working closely with a group of people as "interaction," but rather considered himself to have been "a loner out in the woods." It was not the collective process of labor that apparently drew the respondent's interest, but rather the connection of that labor with those who find it useful—the interaction between producer and consumer gives the work significant meaning. Like many people in the sample, this brewer found the work attractive because its connection with consumers was tangible.

One person was working two jobs: one as a sales representative for a new brewery, and another marketing job at a radio station (part of his college program.) He said the enthusiasm of craft beer consumers made his work feel like it was part of a community context, whereas "going to a dance club and seeing a radio guy handing out coasters. . . . That doesn't even make sense at all." By contrast, he felt a genuine interest from the beer consumers, and that made the craft work more interesting to pursue. Likewise, many consumers are drawn to that connection as well—knowing who makes the product and where seems to keep people coming back for craft beer. It also creates a context where people seem drawn to the work.

In other interviews, this sentiment of making products that mattered to consumers manifested in a tirade against products or advertising that potentially took advantage of consumers. One respondent described her experiences of getting a marketing degree, and the feelings she got when designing advertisements for popular national products:

> Enough of these cereal sugary breakfast cereals. I knew of kids who were obese as a result of this product. There's this really cool car. You can buy one but you can't afford to own it . . . tires, repairs, insurance they don't tell you about. Oh, here's a lease that you can barely afford but then in four years you own nothing. And look how cool smoking is. My uncle died of lung cancer. I'm like, I could find something better to do with my talent. —Serving Manager, local brewery

In other words, the respondent felt morally repulsed when designing advertisements for these products. She went on to describe craft beer selling as "authentic" and "true to itself." One did not have to manipulate people to get them to buy beer, just help them find the best beer to suit their tastes. For her, that was the prime reason for choosing the work.

In summation, people in the sample rarely discussed the opportunity to earn money or acquire other designations of material success when deciding to pursue work in craft beer. In fact, people who did discuss money talked about how much *more* their talents or experience would be worth in other industries, working for large companies. Instead, respondents saw work in craft beer as meaningful, either because of the intrinsic tasks of making beer, the chance to continue doing what they had been doing as consumers, or the tangible context it presented where the fruits of their labors would be enjoyed.

Conclusion

Relative to the questions posed at the outset of this chapter, I offer two observations. First, a substantial number of respondents (65 percent) began their craft beer work as enchanted consumers of beer, who then sought to turn that passion into careers. This is consistent with the notion of the enterprising self. These workers believed their calling, their passion, was somehow related to the craft beer industry, and set down that path. Forty-three percent of all respondents left a successful career in another field, sometimes at loss of pay or at least future earnings, to pursue a career in craft beer. Consumer-born passion thus appears to animate labor market choices in this sample.

Second, among those motivated to choose auxiliary or service roles, the ethos of sharing and learning about beer appeared consistently in their narratives. Eleven people were lured to beer because of its variety—there was so much to explore and learn that it stimulated their desire to become a fan of craft beer. The opportunity to share that feeling with others then motivated them to choose the work. Brewers loved the challenge of mastering the craft, in line with research into the intrinsic pleasures of artisanal occupations generally (Hodson 2001; Sennett 2008) and making craft beer specifically (Thurnell-Read 2014). That auxiliary (mostly service) jobs are driven by a parallel facet of the consumer culture—learning and teaching beer—appears in the observations I have recounted. This suggests that the discourses animating the consumer market of craft beer become vehicles for the enterprising self.

The enterprising-self literature argues that workers develop their identity by seeking to know what the consumer desires. Workers wish to understand the market, and portray themselves as positively authentic with respect to those market needs. Moreover, management and organizational scholars see ways to use this logic of embracing the consumer also to give coherence and meaning to organizational culture. As Hardt and Negri (2001) suggest, capitalism becomes ever more entrenched in the lives of workers, and thus a new way of "hooking" the conception of the self for the purpose of monetary valuation emerges. When behavior in consumptive spheres is bent to producing value, as the social-factory literature suggests, organizations and management potentially exploit workers to a greater degree (Land and Taylor 2010).

However, specific consumer cultures such as craft beer may provide meaningful context for how workers engage their tasks. Workers in this study did use the enterprising-self discourse to identify with craft beer work. They described beer as their passion, as their calling. They identified with the intrinsic joys of making beer. They identified with the joys of tasting beer, and with connecting the consumers to their labor. Many of the respondents were consumers of this lifestyle before they began doing the work. Many more came to see themselves as part of this lifestyle after working in craft beer. Rather than seeing that passion for their work as motivated by some abstract need to serve the consumer, they believed that passion to have been animated by a specific collective mission: to spread knowledge and the joy of drinking beer. Moreover, having the skill and knowledge to practice the consumer culture seemed empowering for workers—giving them a sense of ownership over the work. Whereas the social-factory literature seems to view consumer discourses as primarily a new tool for managerial control, and thus part of the terrain of contestation between management and worker, the employees interviewed here had a much different orientation to the consumer discourse. They seemed to view this discourse as enabling them to pursue the larger project of craft beer. The fact that five people chose to work in the industry because they saw craft beer as politically progressive would support this view. More research is needed to understand whether people enjoy fruitful careers, and to determine the characteristics of workplaces or markets that enabled or hindered the fulfillment of those dreams.

Although theorists agree that the boundary between what counts as "work" (i.e., production) and what counts as leisure (i.e., consumption) has become blurred, what that means is still an open question. Previous research finds that the same narratives, beliefs, or discourses that serve to draw consumers into a particular lifestyle also become a logic for employment selection and control. However, those effects on workers and the workplace may depend on how the particular market is constructed. Craft breweries were created by passionate consumers. These small, niche organizations seek to use the market to "live their dreams," but as a particular way of life rather than simply the naked accumulation of profit. The craft beer market may consist of workplaces that are more closely embedded in the spheres of consumption. These connections may allow a collective project to flourish, where the boundary between worker and consumer becomes blurred for a different reason: rather than being a form of organizational control, or maximizing value extraction, workers and consumers engage in a shared project of making and sharing good beer. To continue this research in "blurred boundaries," more theoretical work is needed to develop typologies in how consumer markets are constructed and how workplaces are embedded within those markets.

References

Arnould, Eric J. and Craig J. Thompson. 2005. "Consumer Culture Theory (CCT): Twenty Years of Research." *Journal of Consumer Research* 31(4):868–82.

Autor, David H. and David Dorn. 2013. "The Growth of Low-Skill Service Jobs and the Polarization of the US Labor Market." *American Economic Review* 103(5):1553–97.

Arnold, Dennis and Joseph R. Bongiovi. 2013. "Precarious, Informalizing, and Flexible Work Transforming Concepts and Understandings." *American Behavioral Scientist* 57(3):289–308.

Böhm, Steffen and Chris Land. 2012. "The New 'Hidden Abode': Reflections on Value and Labour in the New Economy. *The Sociological Review* 60(2):217–40.

Bolton, Sharon C. and Maeve Houlihan. 2005. "The (Mis)representation of Customer Service." *Work, Employment & Society* 19(4):685–703.

Bonacich, Edna, and Jake B. Wilson. 2008. *Getting the Goods: Ports, Labor, and the Logistics Revolution*. New York: Cornell University Press.

Brannan, Matthew J., Elizabeth Parsons, and Vincenza Priola. 2011. *Branded Lives: The Production and Consumption of Meaning at Work*. Northampton, MA: Edward Elgar Publishing.

Brewers Association. 2018. "Number of Breweries." Retrieved March 16, 2018 (https://www.brewersassociation.org/statistics/number-of-breweries/).

Bruni, Attila, Silvia Gherardi, and Barbara Poggio. 2004. "Doing Gender, Doing Entrepreneurship: An Ethnographic Account of Intertwined Practices." *Gender Work and Organization* 11(4):406–29.

Cohen, Laurie and Gill Musson. 2000. "Entrepreneurial Identities: Reflections from Two Case Studies." *Organization* 7(1):31–48.

Doolin, Bill. 2002. "Enterprise Discourse, Professional Identity and the Organizational Control of Hospital Clinicians." *Organization Studies* 23(3):369–90.

du Gay, Paul. 1996. *Consumption and Identity at Work*. Los Angeles: SAGE.

Elliott, Christopher S. 2018. "Consuming Craft: The Intersection of Production and Consumption in North Carolina Craft Beer Markets." PhD dissertation, University of North Carolina.

Fleming, Peter and Andre Spicer. 2004. "'You Can Checkout Anytime, but You Can Never Leave': Spatial Boundaries in a High Commitment Organization." *Human Relations* 57(1):75–94.

Frenkel, Steve, Marek Korczyński, Leigh Donoghue, and Karen Shire. 1995. "Re-constituting Work: Trends towards Knowledge Work and Info-Normative Control." *Work, Employment & Society* 9(4):773–96.

Gabriel, Yiannis. 1999. "Beyond Happy Families: A Critical Reevaluation of the Control-Resistance-Identity Triangle. *Human Relations* 52(2):179–203.

Gill, Rosalind and Andy Pratt. 2008. "In the Social Factory? Immaterial Labour, Precariousness and Cultural Work." *Theory, Culture & Society* 25(7–8):1–30.

Halford, Susan and Pauline Leonard. 2006. "Place, Space and Time: Contextualizing Workplace Subjectivities. *Organization Studies* 27(5):657–76.

Hardt, Michael and Antonio Negri. 2000. *Empire*. Cambridge, MA: Harvard University Press.

Hindy, Steve. 2014. *The Craft Beer Revolution: How a Band of Microbrewers Is Transforming the World's Favorite Drink*. New York: Palgrave Macmillan.

Hodson, Randy. 2001. *Dignity at Work*. New York: Cambridge University Press.

Hong, Renyi. 2014. "Finding Passion in Work: Media, Passion and Career Guides." *European Journal of Cultural Studies* 18(2):190–206.

Kalleberg, Arne L. 2009. "Precarious Work, Insecure Workers: Employment Relations in Transition." *American Sociological Review* 74(1):1–22.

Kalleberg, Arne. 2011. *Good Jobs, Bad Jobs: The Rise of Polarized and Precarious Employment Systems in the United States, 1970s to 2000s*. New York: Russell Sage Foundation.

Kalleberg, Arne L., Barbara F. Reskin, and Ken Hudson. 2000. "Bad Jobs in America: Standard and Nonstandard Employment Relations and Job Quality in the United States." *American Sociological Review* 65(2):256–78.

Korczynski, Marek and Ursula Ott. 2004. "When Production and Consumption Meet: Cultural Contradictions and the Enchanting Myth of Customer Sovereignty. *Journal of Management Studies* 41(4):575–99.

Korczynski, Marek, Karen Shire, Stephen Frenkel, and May Tam. 2000. "Service Work in Consumer Capitalism: Customers, Control and Contradictions. *Work Employment and Society* 14(4):669–87.

Land, Chris and Scott Taylor. 2010. "Surf's Up: Work, Life, Balance and Brand in a New Age Capitalist Organization." *Sociology* 44(3):395–413.

Levinson, Marc. 2006. *The Box: How the Shipping Container Made the World Smaller and the World Economy Bigger*. Princeton, NJ: Princeton University Press.

Misra, Joya and Kyla Walters. 2016. "All Fun and Cool Clothes? Youth Workers' Consumer Identity in Clothing Retail." *Work and Occupations* 43(3):294–325.

Rao, Hayagreeva. 2009. *Market Rebels: How Activists Make or Break Radical Innovations*. Princeton, NJ: Princeton University Press.

Ritzer, George. 2010. *Enchanting a Disenchanted World: Continuity and Change in the Cathedrals of Consumption*. Los Angeles: SAGE.

Sallaz, Jeffrey J. 2014. "Permanent Pedagogy: How Post-Fordist Firms Generate Effort but Not Consent." *Work and Occupations* 42(1):3–34.

Sennett, Richard. 2008. *The Craftsman*. New York: Allen Lane.

Storey, John, Graeme Salaman, and Kerry Platman. 2005. "Living with Enterprise in an Enterprise Economy: Freelance and Contract Workers in the Media. *Human Relations* 58(8):1033–54.

Thomas, Robyn and Annette Davies. 2005. "Theorizing the Micro-Politics of Resistance: New Public Management and Managerial Identities in the UK Public Services. *Organization Studies* 26(5):683–706.

Thurnell-Read, Thomas. 2014. "Craft, Tangibility and Affect at Work in the Microbrewery." *Emotion, Space and Society* 13:46–54.

Vallas, Steven P. and Emily R. Cummins. 2015. "Personal Branding and Identity Norms in the Popular Business Press: Enterprise Culture in an Age of Precarity." *Organization Studies* 36(3):293–319.

von Martin, Alfred. 1963. *Sociology of the Renaissance*. New York: Harper & Row.

Wyatt, Ian D. and Daniel E. Hecker. 2006. "Occupational Changes during the 20th Century." *Monthly Labor Review* 129(3):35–57.

PART III

Collectivity and Collaboration

CHAPTER 9

Pop, Pour, Pass
Bottle Shares as Public Rituals

MICHAEL IAN BORER

Introduction

In various craft beer scenes throughout the United States, a common public ritual has emerged as a means for communal tasting and collective aesthetic experience: the "bottle share." Friends and strangers gather with bottles, cans, and recently filled growlers or crowlers at a designated place and time. The vessels are opened and passed around to participants, who take small pours of the soon-to-be consumed elixir. The glasses, or in some cases less-than-ideal plastic cups, are sipped, emptied, and readied for the next beer to taste and discuss.

Though private bottle shares held in people's homes can positively influence a local craft beer scene, I focus here on those that are open to the public, where the cost of entry is often little more than bringing a beer to share with others. Beyond the sharing of often hard-to-find or limited-release beers, public bottle shares have two other characteristics: (1) they take place in open and accessible places like bars, restaurants, or shops, and (2) participants are usually expected to bring products that aren't available in their local market. That is, it's both a part of the ritual etiquette and in some cases a legal necessity to share beers that aren't distributed locally. These two aspects work in tandem as well as in tension because they push and pull on the often taken-for-granted meaning of "local." In academic and popular discourse, "local" is often held up with honor and righteous fortitude, giving romantic credence to a fetishized object as if it held some magical powers that guarantee greater quality and a better sensory experience (Pratt 2007).

On one hand, the simple fact that the places that host bottle shares are physical edifices with unique geographical locations and particular meanings attached to them means that they are "local" in the most obvious sense (Borer 2006; Gieryn 2000). The stages for social interaction are irreducibly local because all cultures, with their shared rules of engagement and collective histories and memories, happen somewhere (Fine 2010).

Yet on the other hand, the craft beers that are consumed during these gatherings are "translocal." That is, they come from elsewhere, and often necessarily so. Counterintuitively, what is considered local doesn't necessarily have to consist of material goods or ideas from a single proximate location. When we think of "beer places," we need to look beyond the place of production—even though the environmental constraints of particular geographies surely affect many aspects of beer—and consider the places of consumption. No local culture in the modern world is a stable and hermetically sealed and bounded entity. The scenes that play out on local stages are not built from scratch (see Irwin 1977). They are neither fully self-referential nor self-contained. Rather, their symbolic boundaries are porous and flexible enough not merely to allow for outside influences but instead to depend upon them. Scenes from elsewhere provide "models of" and "models for" shared and common ritualized expectations and practices that locals adopt and adapt within particular contexts and specific places (Geertz 1973, 90). Scripts are borrowed and reworked in their new context. Props, of which the beers brought to a bottle share are of the utmost significance, are supposed to be—for symbolic and legal reasons—from outside the local vicinity and market.

Many craft beer enthusiasts either travel to other cities to pick up bottles and cans that aren't distributed locally or have brewers ship them. These transported or "muled" beers—the outcome of either physical travel or express-mailed "porch bombs"—often become the targets and progenitors of "oohs" and "ahhs" at bottle shares for their rare status, high quality, or likely both. The "local" of local beer that is transported across state borders takes on a different meaning than "local" as simply something produced at a nearby locale. As such, a beer from *your* city might be symbolically worth more than a beer from *my* city, at least for scene participants who want to expand their aesthetic knowledge of the scene's core significant object.

Here, then, we have an example of a public ritual that is local because the participants are locals, and are embodied and emplaced as such, yet the products they taste together are brewed outside the geographic and symbolic boundaries of what is considered local (even if we take into consideration the Brewers Association's generous definition of local as "within four hundred miles").

In this chapter, I explore the commingling of the local and the translocal in order to show how local craft beer scenes are not beholden to or determined by local breweries, as is often assumed in both academic and popular circles. Yes, local breweries hold economic significance for cities, suburbs, and towns in the way that any small business does. Craft beers from elsewhere, however, may in fact provide greater symbolic value for local craft beer enthusiasts and for the vitality of the local scene itself. As such, the places that host ritualized bottle shares play different and sometimes competing roles vis-à-vis local breweries in a scene's "aesthetic ecology" (DeNora 2011, xi). Moreover, as public rituals, bottle shares work as a social mechanism that provides an integrative function (Durkheim 1965; Etzioni 2000) by bringing "biographical strangers" (Lofland 1973) into contact with one another to experience shared beers and shared desires for said beers along with the collective performance of taste (Hennion 2007).

Doing and Being "Scene"

Across the long oak table, beneath a television that remains off throughout the evening, as it does most days and nights, stand a dozen or so open bottles and cans. These aren't just any containers. They're from some of the most highly regarded craft breweries in the United States. A trendsetting can of Tree House Brewing's Julius, a hazy mango-tasting and mango-looking New England–style IPA, butts up against a golden sour ale aged in oak barrels with apricots from Rare Barrel of Berkeley, California. Another sour beer sits next to it, a Berliner Weisse aged in oak barrels with boysenberries from Tillamook, Oregon's, de Garde Brewing. My lips pucker before I even get to taste them. And I did taste them, at the behest of those who brought these hard-to-find out-of-market treats to share with others that night. And they'll bring different beers next week.

The bottles and cans move around the table, in and out of the hands of those seated at the bar or standing next to one of the empty handful of barrels that serve as tables. Little one- to two-ounce pours enter tiny plastic cups, or small glass snifters for those who arrived early, and are then smelled, sipped, and swallowed. As the first batch empties, new bottles holding sought-after elixirs are opened and passed around.

"Have you tried this one yet?" Rob calls to me from a few tables away.

"No. Is there any left?" I reply.

He shakes the Hill Farmstead bottle gently. "Aw, just dregs. Here, take a sip of mine."

He walks over and gives me his glass. I put my nose in it and breathe in funky red wine aromas. Then I taste it.

"Yum."

I smile, knowing that wasn't the most sophisticated response, while also recognizing that as much as beer geeks like to talk about the intricacies of beer, they also like experiences and expressions of fun. And I smile again when I catch the name of the beer: Civil Disobedience.

Rob gives me a nod and goes back to his table to finish his beer and the conversation he left for a moment. An IT specialist exchanges barbs with a contractor. A Latino sous chef pours a drink for a female social worker. A young Black hotel executive laughs with a female bartender as they clink glasses holding a dark, syrupy imperial stout from a relatively new brewery in San Diego.

Though the beers they're drinking aren't *from* Las Vegas, this is a local crowd, embodied and emplaced *in* Las Vegas. The diversity of the crowd speaks to the desire many have for connecting with others in a city where it's not always easy to do so. Such a desire can lead to connections that span traditional boundaries of social inclusion that are found in urban "ethnic enclaves" and other neighborhoods born from residential segregation.

For the people sharing their beers that night or other nights like it, getting drunk is not the goal (though it can still happen to even the most cautious scenester). They tip their bottles and cans for friends and strangers to sip the vast variety of flavors these crafted libations offer. Taste isn't merely a disembodied and decontextualized marker of difference or social status, as many scholars often deride it (Bourdieu 1984). Instead, taste is performed together, and tast*ing* is the binding activity (Hennion 2007). Craft beer acts as both social lubricant and adhesive. It supplants the exclusivity connected to other craft or artisanal wares available across today's "tastescape," like wines and cheeses, with a greater degree of inclusion, partly because craft beer is more approachable, egalitarian, and (in this case) unifying across supposedly rigid and fixed social attributes and identities.

Bottle shares are commonplace at Khoury's Fine Wine & Spirits, located south-southeast of the Las Vegas Strip and near the Green Valley neighborhood of Henderson, on most Wednesday and Friday nights. It's an open and voluntary practice of giving and receiving that, while less rigidly adhered to, unintentionally mimics the reciprocal exchange of gifts involved in the ancient and cross-culturally ubiquitous potlatch ritual. Marcel Mauss famously wrote that such rituals are morally bounded yet contested means of sharing gifts among "nobles" (Mauss 1990, 7). Bottle shares at Khoury's are symbolic rituals that establish loose hierarchies between and among the upper ranks of local Las Vegas beer geeks depending on what they shared that week. These nobles, however, are more than willing to give away their goods for little more than a smile or nod of recognition. And, as we saw with Rob, they even let people drink out of their own glasses. This type of public intimacy is rare and relatively unprecedented outside of the craft beer scene.

Admittedly, at first I thought it was odd that a store that sells craft beer would allow people to bring in outside goods to be consumed on premise. And this is a store that notably has one of the best selections in the city for sale in bottles and cans *and* on draft (as well as wine and spirits as the name denotes). Between sips of Big Dog's Sled Dog—a locally brewed imperial stout with coffee and cocoa nibs—Issa Khoury, the store's owner and namesake, explains his logic for allowing this practice, summoning a relative degree of affective resistance to the typical and typified Las Vegas bar: "Unlike most places in Las Vegas, we don't have gaming [local parlance for video poker machines] or fifteen TVs blasting all the time. Without as many distractions, people tend to focus on what's in front of them and nine times out of ten they start chatting with the person near them. 'What are you drinking?' 'That looks good.' 'Here, try this.' And that's kind of how the bottle shares started four or five years ago [circa 2010]. . . . I get my shipments in on Wednesdays. A lot of my hardcore craft beer guys knew that and started meeting here to see what I got in. So, one person would buy this bottle, another would buy a different bottle, they'd pop them open and swap them around. And that group of eight or nine has turned into a packed room each week."

"But what about when people bring beers to share that you don't sell?" I push.

A "kill shot" or "graveyard" of empty bottles and cans at the end of a share; a sign of a well-performed ritual.

"The fact that people want to share a cool beer with others they just brought back from Colorado or California or traded for and they want to do it here is cool with me," replies Khoury. "But at the end of the day, we're a business and I have bills to pay. Ninety-nine-point-nine percent of the people get that, and respect it, and are cool about it. As long as you make a purchase in the store, you can open up one bottle. More than that, we'll charge a corkage fee. . . . The first couple of years, we didn't have any rules and then some people started rolling in coolers and not buying anything, so we needed to make some rules explicit to make it fair for everyone. We enjoy the bottle shares; we enjoy the vibe it brings. And the bottle shares get people talking to each other. You've seen it, all kinds of people who've never met before start talking to each other, which is really cool."

By recognizing and purposely cultivating the role his place plays for locals as a gathering spot, Khoury reinforces the notion of a scene's ability "to evoke both the cozy intimacy of community and the fluid cosmopolitanism of urban life" (Straw 2001, 248). Both "a recognition of the inner circles and weighty histories" of his patrons and "a sense of dynamism" (249) allow him to tweak both his own practices and the social norms of his place, thereby changing the taste of the city.

Khoury's is an important node in the Las Vegas craft beer scene. Like other places to which it is connected by affect and aesthetics, it helps foster a scene that offers stability beyond individual selves, which are often separated from one another in this geographically and socially fragmented city. Khoury and his patrons are "doing the scene," as sociologist Pepper Glass puts it, whereby "members, through their everyday interactions, collectively produce these settings" (Glass 2012, 696). "Doing scene" is a creative and practical accomplishment for this group. We should also acknowledge that they are "being scene" by using their bodies to engage in the sensuous activities of performing taste. More specifically, Issa and the folks who buy his wares and drink at the bar or on the patio, sharing beers and laughs with friends and strangers, are *doing and being scene* in ways that elevate local knowledge of taste and tasting.

First, by intentionally choosing not to include gaming, Khoury's watering hole presents itself as unusual. It expresses alternative aesthetic values to the typical ones that saturate the Las Vegas valley. Instead of making grand declarations about craft versus macro- or mass-produced cultural goods, Khoury and his patrons resist the city's dominant aesthetic offerings through the activities they choose and choose *not* to participate in. The acts of sharing, drinking, and talking about craft beers—"fussing" over them, as a 2015 Budweiser commercial, now infamous among craft beer enthusiasts, put it—are embodied rituals of resistance that invert the top-down pressures of corporate popular culture. Only a few craft beer bars have followed Khoury's lead as non-gaming spaces that focus greater attention on the act of tasting.

Second, by regularly putting rare kegs on tap and working with local brewers and distributors to mine their growing lists of craft selections, Khoury is performing taste and implicitly elevating it for those who encounter his shop and those connected to it. When an "outsider" comes in looking for Budweiser or Coors, they are forced to pass full rows and open boxes of local and regional craft selections to reach the last door at the end of the beer cooler. Arranging the selections as such allows the craft beers to communicate something to both the initiated and uninitiated about the nuances of taste and what lurks inside the artfully labeled containers. As Antoine Hennion argues, objects have a "capacity to interrupt, to surprise or to respond. . . . Objects are not already there, inert and available at our service. They deliver themselves, unrobe themselves, impose themselves on us" (2007, 105–6). People like Khoury and places like his use craft beer to help others "unrobe" themselves from preconceived prejudices about drinking that others have reinforced within a particular context, where the bland and boring have ruled the roost. "Offering some of the top brands—Alpine, Almanac, Cascade, we're getting Modern Times soon—brings a lot of attention to this city," says Khoury. "Then other breweries start taking us more seriously and learn that we're more craft-centric than what Las Vegas is generally known for. We have a culture that's growing here; people from out of town are starting to take notice and people here are starting to take pride in local."

The "craft-centric" culture, and the pride that locals have in it, is the product of creative collaborations between people like Khoury and through places like Khoury's. In Michael P. Farrell's analysis of "collaborative circles"—defined as "groups formed by peers who negotiate an innovative vision in their field"—he notes that individuals with "shared values and aspirations" tend to "gravitate toward magnet places" (2001, 12, 19). Farrell focuses his attention on the interpersonal dynamics of small groups and friendship pairs and the ways they work together to create new works of art (like the Impressionist painters in Paris) or new forms of knowledge (like the "Ultras" who started the women's rights movement). In Las Vegas, a more amorphous yet still collaborative scene supersedes Farrell's smaller circles, because the scene is composed of multiple "magnet places" where both producers and consumers, from experts to novices, are drawn for social interaction and craft beer drinking.

Though the scene is not a physically bounded place unto itself, it is made of many places that create, foster, and accomplish it. These places are more than simply inert stages on which the scene plays out (Borer 2006, 181). They are where thoughts and ideas become action.

They are where the scene happens. As Joseph Kotarba contends, scenes exist "in our minds and become visible during interaction" (2013, 95). The most significant interactions for the Las Vegas craft beer scene are those between the people, the people and the places, and the material yet fleeting object (i.e., craft beer) and the people who develop and nurture the local craft beer scene.

Plenty of craft beer drinking certainly happens in homes across the Las Vegas valley during family dinners, parties, and private bottle shares. But scenes require public places that are open and inclusive. Though most of the places are not public in the sense that they are paid for by taxes or owned by municipalities, they are small businesses that function as *shared* places. Owners like Khoury use these places to practice a type of "commercial communalism" that has been an enduring means for sharing experiences and knowledge in American cities since the early nineteenth century (Monti 1999, 105–6). Because each local business relies on a consumer base to keep it afloat, the place itself—as both a stage for interaction and a prop to interact with—is a product of what Herbert Blumer calls "joint action," whereby "participants fit their acts together" (1986, 70–2). The scene is a product of joint actions between multiple actors, including the places and products that are shared and experienced together. The material and symbolic qualities of such places interact with the cognitive and sensuous capacities of people to produce meaning in meaningful and meaning-*filled* places. As a public ritual, the bottle share provides a means for joint actions that affect the ways in which places like Khoury's are deemed meaningful and meaning filled.

Informal Learning of Embodied Knowledge

Though Khoury's was ahead of the curve as a magnet place for local Las Vegas beer geeks to trade beer samples and sarcastic barbs, other shared places across the city have followed suit. Scattered across Vegas's sprawling geography, owners and general managers have opened up their places to bottle shares in order to provide a means of informal learning for both certified beer geeks and craft beer neophytes. Knowledge comes with every pour, or at least that's the idea.

Informal learning of this sort happens during expected encounters or "focused gatherings" where "people effectively agree to sustain for a time a single focus of cognitive and visual attention" (Goffman 1961, 7).

For our discussion, we would add others' senses to Erving Goffman's limited scope because taste is a multisensory engagement that involves more than the nose and the tongue. Regardless, as Goffman notes, the gathering depends on an "official focus of activity" whereby "official" does not mean formal or institutionalized (ibid, 18). Instead, it refers to the defined or understood activity at hand, like a board game (a favored example of Goffman's) or a bottle share (as in our case). That focus often requires a commitment of one's body, whether one is hunched over a multicolored and -patterned board ready to roll a twelve-sided die or doling out pours of the beer they've been hoarding in their cellar for the last three years to mellow the sharp alcohol bite of a particular barleywine.

Tasting and learning about new beers can impel people to attend beer festivals, but attending a bottle share affords more opportunities for deeper engagements. Bottle shares are ritualized "focused gatherings" where the various bottles and cans of craft beers are opened, usually one by one, in a continuous manner that supports participants' "continuous engrossment" à la Goffman in the encounter with the beer and with the others doing likewise. The collectively sustained focus provides newbies and geeks alike a ripe opportunity to learn about craft beer. Though some might not explicitly express that learning is the intended outcome of their involvement, their eyes certainly light up when they get a chance to try beers or styles they've only heard of from others or through websites and social media accounts reporting the latest craft beer trends. As such, we can say that there is a latent informal learning aspect to bottle shares for most attendees.

Moving downtown, on afternoon for one of the Atomic's Second Saturday bottle shares, a few bottles and cans make the rounds among the fifteen or so people gathered. Darren, one of the attendees, asks the bartender to give him the bottle he brought. She takes it out of the ice-filled sink and lets it dry off. "Wow, that's incredible!" says Darren after sipping a dark brown liquid. It smells and tastes like "every breakfast I ever want to have," he exults with a smile as wide as his mouth would stretch. This was his first time trying Funky Buddha's Maple Bacon Coffee Porter. He brought it to the share that day after recently receiving two bottles from a friend in Florida, where Funky Buddha brews its creations. Darren's grin was a permanent fixture as he doled out small pours into the glasses thrust in front of him by eager soon-to-be sippers. This ritual sharing enhances the collective's trove of aesthetic experiences.

A somewhat scattered conversation begins among a few people as each took breaks from talking to swirl the beer in their glasses to bring out all of its aromas, then to gently let the sweet and roasty brew cover their tongues and slide down their throats. Engaged in this moment of sensuous delight together, a small group of four or five, including Darren, begins discussing the differences and merits between porters and stouts.

"They're really the same; porters originally came from England and stouts came from Ireland."

"Isn't it really about ABV, though? Stouts are higher, right?"

"Sometimes. There's a lot of variation within the categories. A Guinness ain't the same stout as a Bomb [brewed by Prairie Artisan Ale]. One's like four percent and the other's like thirteen percent. Both stouts, but totally different."

"Yeah, but Bomb's got like chocolate and vanilla and chilies packed into it. Of course they're different."

"The real difference," another voice chimes in, "is that stouts and porters are made from different types of malts. Stouts use dark roasted malts that give off a slightly bitter coffee taste. That's why there are so many stouts made with coffee—they complement each other—and not that many coffee porters."

"Okay, but this is a coffee porter. And it's fucking amazing!"

"For sure. And it's brewed with bacon and maple syrup. Incredible!"

The conversation went on like this for a while, shifting between topics as different people entered and left the conversation and different beers filled emptied glasses. The informality of the talk was palpable, as was the exchange of knowledge that accompanied the exchange of beers. As many scholars of groups, gatherings, and occasions would note (see Fine 2012; Wynn 2015), this type of interaction helps reinforce scene members' identities *as* scene members.

Craft beer drinkers become *craft* beer drinkers in ways beyond the obvious fact that they're drinking craft beer. Conversations expand participants' knowledge base and are most effective at doing so in focused gatherings, where the sensuous activity of tasting is shared. Discourse *about* and embodied experiences *of* the scene's core object reinforce both aesthetic solidarity and authority through "learning-by-doing."

This type of knowledge exists beyond the sheer pragmatic or mechanical habit; rather, it is "forthcoming only when bodily effort is made" (Merleau-Ponty 1962, 144). Embodied knowledge through visceral contact with an object is foundational knowledge for producers and consumers of other craft wares like cheese (Paxson 2011), blown glass (O'Connor 2005), or cocktails (Ocejo 2012).

What seems to set bottle shares apart, however, is that they are necessarily consumer driven and thus give the impression of being more organic than, say, cheese tastings, where a producer or distributor provides the product. At bottle shares, embodied knowledge is transmitted from consumer to consumer laterally rather than hierarchically. This affords an inclusivity that accompanies the sharing of beer and the knowledge needed to appreciate the beverage at hand—whether one likes it or not. Without "beer places" that allow these open exchanges, craft beer knowledge—and with it, a local scene's growth—likely will be stunted.

Conclusion

Local scenes exist because people interacting with both a place and one another make them happen. All local scenes require places for "participants to commingle, act, and share meanings" (Irwin 1977, 31). As a qualifier, *local* is often applied to the production process of drinkable commodities: local breweries in almost any locale are valorized for their proximity and often tied to marketing strategies that highlight the freshness of their beers, their supposed "authenticity," or their environmentally sustainable practices (see Feeney 2017; Jones and Harvey 2017; Mathews and Picton 2014; Schnell and Reese 2003). This tends to elevate production over consumption, cutting out a large portion of the people who make the scene work (i.e., consumers). I therefore prefer to use *local* as a qualifier that highlights and emphasizes embodiment and emplacement, where sensuous bodies interact in particular locales with each other and with the valorized object (e.g., craft beer) through particular practices (e.g., participating in bottle shares). The scene's very nature as an expressive entity that connects people and places to one another provides nuanced ways for participants to engage implicitly or explicitly in the performance of taste. By being embodied and emplaced, these expressions require bodies and places for any claims about local culture to be made and experiences to be shared.

Focusing on places "where the action is" (Goffman 1967) and the people who take part in rituals like bottle shares opens up new avenues for considering interactions among craft beer, the people who consume it, and where they consume it with others. Without these local places, there is no local scene. These places are the literal and figurative stages where social actors negotiate the ways they act in and on their social world (Borer 2006; Fine 2010; Strauss 1978). Actors negotiate their roles and the scripts they follow or improvise while interacting with others on stages that both liberate and constrain their performances. Craft beer is a core object, a binding object, a significant object that brings significant others together within a local scene comprising places located throughout cities, suburbs, and towns. Participants enact a "symbolic ownership" of the scene in ways similar to neighborhood residents' (Deener 2007, 311–12). The morphing and amorphous collection of actors fosters a cultural logic developed around the sensuous pleasures and fun of taste and tasting craft beer. There are certainly worse things to rally around than pleasure and fun (Fine and Corte 2017). More people in charge of shared places in cities, suburbs, and towns have taken note and are starting to open up their stages for ritualized sharing, tasting, and learning for the sake of the collective symbolic ownership of aesthetic experiences.

References

Blumer, Herbert. 1986. *Symbolic Interactionism: Perspective and Method.* Berkeley: University of California Press.

Borer, Michael Ian. 2006. "The Location of Culture: The Urban Culturalist Perspective." *City & Community* 5:173–19.

Bourdieu, Pierre. 1984. *Distinction: A Social Critique of the Judgement of Taste.* Cambridge, MA: Harvard University Press.

Deener, Andrew. 2007. "Commerce as the Structure and Symbol of Neighborhood Life: Reshaping the Meaning of Community in Venice, California." *City & Community* 6:291–314.

DeNora, Tia. 2011. *Music-in-Action: Selected Essays in Sonic Ecology.* Farnham, UK: Ashgate.

Durkheim, Émile. 1965. *The Elementary Forms of the Religious Life.* New York: Free Press.

Etzioni, Amitai. 2000. "Toward a Theory of Public Ritual." *Sociological Theory* 18:44–59.

Farrell, Michael P. 2001. *Collaborative Circles: Friendship Dynamics and Creative Work.* Chicago: University of Chicago Press.

Feeney, Alison E. 2017. "Cultural Heritage, Sustainable Development, and the Impacts of Craft Breweries in Pennsylvania." *City, Culture and Society* 9:21–30.

Fine, Gary Alan. 2010. "The Sociology of the Local: Action and Its Publics." *Sociological Theory* 28:355–76

———. 2012. "Group Culture and the Interaction Order: Local Sociology on the Meso-level." *Annual Review of Sociology* 38:159–79

Fine, Gary Alan and Ugo Corte. 2017. "Group Pleasures: Collaborative Commitments, Shared Narrative, and the Sociology of Fun," *Sociological Theory* 35:64–86.

Geertz, Clifford. 1973. *The Interpretation of Cultures*. New York: Basic Books.

Gieryn, Thomas F. 2000. "A Space for Place in Sociology." *Annual Review of Sociology* 26: 463–96.

Glass, Pepper G. 2012. "Doing Scene: Identity, Space, and the Interactional Accomplishment of Youth Culture." *Journal of Contemporary Ethnography* 41:695–716.

Goffman, Erving. 1961. *Encounters: Two Studies in the Sociology of Interaction*. Indianapolis: Bobbs-Merrill.

———. 1967. *Interaction Ritual: Essays in Face-to-Face Behavior*. New York: Pantheon Books.

Hennion, Antoine. 2007. "Those Things That Hold Us Together: Taste and Sociology." *Cultural Sociology* 1:97–114.

Irwin, John. *Scenes*. Beverly Hills: SAGE.

Jones, Ellis and Daina Cheyenne Harvey. 2017. "Ethical Brews: New England, Networked Ecologies, and a New Craft Beer Movement." In *Untapped: Exploring the Cultural Dimensions of Craft Beer*, edited by Nathaniel G. Chapman, Slade Lellock, and Cameron D. Lippard. Morgantown: University of West Virginia Press.

Kotarba, Joseph A. 2013. *Baby Boomer Rock'n'roll Fans: The Music Never Ends*. Lanham, MD: Scarecrow Press.

Lofland, Lyn H. 1973. *A World of Strangers: Order and Action in Urban Public Space*. Prospect Hills, IL: Waveland Press.

Monti, Daniel J. 1999. *The American City: A Social and Cultural History*. Malden, MA: Blackwell.

Pratt, Jeff. 2007. "Food Values: The Local and the Authentic." *Critique of Anthropology* 27:285–300.

Mauss, Marcel. 1990. *The Gift: The Form and Reason for Exchange in Archaic Societies*. New York: Routledge.

Mathews, Vanessa and Roger M. Picton. 2014. "Intoxifying Gentrification: Brew Pubs and the Geography of Post-industrial Heritage." *Urban Geography* 35:337–56.

Merleau-Ponty, Maurice. 1962. *Phenomenology of Perception*. London: Routledge.

Paxson, Heather. 2011. "The 'Art' and 'Science' of Handcrafting Cheese in the United States." *Endeavour* 35:116–24.

O'Connor, Erin. 2005. "Embodied Knowledge: The Experience of Meaning and the Struggle Towards Proficiency in Glassblowing." *Ethnography* 6:183–204.

Ocejo, Richard E. 2012. "At Your Service: The Meanings and Practices of Contemporary Bartenders." *European Journal of Cultural Studies* 15:642–58.

Schnell, Steven M. and Joseph F. Reese. 2003. "Microbreweries as Tools of Local Identity." *Journal of Cultural Geography* 21:45–69.

Strauss, Anselm L. 1978. *Negotiations: Varieties, Contexts, Processes, and Social Order*. San Francisco: Jossey-Bass.

Straw, Will. 2001. "Scenes and Sensibilities." *Public* 22/23:245–57.

Wynn, Jonathan R. 2015. *Music/City: American Festivals and Placemaking in Austin, Nashville, and Newport*. Chicago: University of Chicago Press.

Postcard from "The Collective"

ELLIS JONES

Founded in 2005 in Boulder, Colorado, the Brewers Association (BA) is the United States' largest organization of craft brewers and craft breweries. It is focused on protecting and promoting small and independent craft brewers and their related communities. They may be best known for keeping detailed statistics on the growth of the craft beer industry and for their more recent (2017) Independent Craft Brewer's certification label, now found on the cans and bottles of a variety of craft beers. With the rapid adoption of this label, the BA has become a de facto arbiter of authenticity in the craft beer movement. Is a brewer really small enough, independently owned, and truly dedicated to making craft beer? The BA's label is one of the most recognized (if still not perfect) markers for passing those tests. Julia Herz is the Craft Beer Program Director of the Brewers Association, co-author of Beer Pairing: The Essential Guide from the Pairing Pros, *and the creator of the website Craftbeer.com.*

JONES: If you're willing, I'd love to hear a little bit of an overview as somebody from the Brewer's Association at maybe three levels. One, what kind of microgeography of craft beer is everybody working in? Then, if you have a sense yourself of how beer seems different in different parts of the country, you may just have a different perspective on how the micro-geographies show up for you. The last is what it looks like outside of physical geography. How does craft beer look to you in the virtual world?

HERZ: I'll try to go to the first one, the microclimate. It's interesting . . . there is discussion of microclimates because of wine and grape-growing regions, right? And Colorado, the state, has microclimates in temperature. You've got mountains, you've got Front Range, you've got arid, almost desert-like conditions. That is not a variable, though, in brewing. You can brew beer anywhere. You can brew beer anytime of the year. Malt, you know, is dried and converted to barley. It can be transported and shipped anywhere.

So, I think in terms of microclimate, you do have terroir and Mother Nature certainly affecting brewers. You look at the Pacific Northwest, and I think [of] the success of California and breweries like Sierra Nevada, Anchor Steam. And then going up into Washington and Oregon, they are in a mecca for accessible hops.

Colorado, too, has a hop market now. Colorado now has a barley market. So, it's a state that has become one of the meccas. It's been referred to, as former governor Hickenlooper would call Colorado, the Munich of the West. And it's a state known for absolutely advanced beer culture, and often off the charts in terms of number of breweries, you know . . . top of the list behind a few, California of course. And you know Colorado ranked fourth for breweries per capita, ranked sixth for economic impact. It ranks first for impact per capita.

JONES: What is that measuring?

HERZ: Dollar amount. If you go to our statistics section [https://www .brewersassociation.org/resource-hub/statistics-trends], you can compare all the states. And just having been working at the national association that happens to reside in Boulder, as you know—I've been a beer lover, first and foremost, been at my job at BA in different forms for fifteen years. I've watched the culture of Colorado become what others look to follow, look to emulate, look to grow to.

JONES: Was that part of the reason that the Brewer's Association ended up locating here?

HERZ: So, Charlie Papazian, who is our past president and founder . . . he founded it and it had to do with where he was living. Because of where Charlie was living, and because we were founded in Boulder, we had the Great American Beer Festival, which is now more than thirty-five years strong. And this is a sixty-five-thousand-person event. It's the preeminent competition in the United States that we host for commercial beers. And that anchor of this national event, kind of the Super Bowl of beer festivals and competitions, definitely, I think, had a play in advancing Colorado's beer culture as well.

It strikes me at this point that Colorado is awash in beer culture. I am conducting this interview in a space called the Rayback Collective, tucked in between Valmont Road and one of the well-trafficked, multi-use bicycle paths (part of the city's vast network). The Collective began as a Kickstarter campaign and ended up creating a hybrid café-brewpub with solid Wi-Fi, old mismatched furniture to sit on, forty beers on tap day and night, fire pits, and two spaces for rotating food trucks on site so that you don't have to walk more than ten steps to get a bite with your beer. It is a micro-nirvana for craft beer. People around me are working, socializing, holding meetings, bringing dogs in after a long hike, and stopping to grab a quick beer after biking all over town.

JONES: So, do you have a sense of how some of the laws in different places [led to some states being] slower to pick up on craft beer?

HERZ: I haven't thought about it in a while. Let's talk about, for example, self-distribution. So, thirty-plus states have self-distribution. That is absolutely an important variable in looking at sales in the states, and being able to see advanced sales for breweries. You might benefit [from drilling] down on regional and statewide comparisons, and what's working in some states. For example, our economist did an audit of gender and beer purchasing. And in the Pacific Northwest, particularly Oregon, more than 50 percent of those purchasing beer in Oregon are females.

JONES: Wow.

The demographics of both craft beer consumers and, to a much greater extent, brewers skew largely male. This opens up some interesting questions about what breweries in certain states are doing differently to appeal to both men and women. Granted, purchasing and consuming are not the same thing, but it still might lead to some interesting findings.

HERZ: That is incredibly powerful. That's not the case for most states, right?

JONES: Yeah, exactly.

HERZ: Particularly in [certain] regions of the country, we get scan data, for example, from IRI [Information Resources, Inc., a packaged-goods data analytics company]. Whenever an IP code is scanned, they will capture that. Sales data for stores that are over a couple million dollars in sales. So that gives us a trend and a pulse. And we're able to see through IRI certain regions have different successes. They tend to break up the regions in the US into eight groups.

JONES: That's interesting. Well, now that you're hosting more things online, you're having access to more data, I'm wondering more about the digital landscape. Like how in general over the last fifteen years, it has changed not just the way you get this kind of data, but the way you communicate, and the way that the digital sphere has become the avenue for craft brewers and craft beer lovers in a way that it hasn't been before.

HERZ: I'll bring up beer-rating websites. So, beer-rating websites, everything from Untappd to BeerAdvocate and the like, those rating websites are a large driver in two things. One, beer lovers that are not rating, but are looking at that information for cues on what they should purchase. And then, two, brewers look at that for information on how they rated, and then that's feedback in the marketplace [that] could possibly inform their approach to that beer.

JONES: That's interesting.

Ratings are a big deal in the craft beer community, and people tend to have a higher regard for collective ratings from other craft beer drinkers than from the experts. Whereas the wine industry is still largely dominated by expert-driven ratings, craft beer drinkers like to hear from one another on smartphone apps (Beer Buddy, Untappd) and rating sites (BeerAdvocate, RateBeer). From a political perspective, rather than being instructed by sommelier oligarchs, if you will, these citizen-consumers favor a more community-based model of deciding who the winners and losers of craft beer will be. It may seem less sophisticated than drinking wine, but it is significantly more democratic, as the arbiters of taste are the people themselves. Additionally, if someone can't get a well-reviewed beer locally, they can swing by the brewery or liquor store for a visit during their next road trip. Unlike the exclusive nature of most wine regions, solid craft breweries exist in nearly every US state.

HERZ: Untappd and BeerAdvocate are two really good places if you want to get at beer-lover digital data. They have their trends from their networks.

JONES: And do you have a sense of how people are engaging in their house? And I don't know if BA has their own app, but I just get the sense that the beer people I know dive into their phone when they're going to reviews.

HERZ: So, apps are more and more what I see in the beer space a variable. We do have an app called Brew Guru, it's through [the] American Home Brewer's Association. The numbers of users of that do continue to go up, but it's not a rating app. Most beer apps that I tend to hear about and see are tied to tracking and rating your beers. There are a few beer-pairing apps out there, which is also a trend. And craft beer has come of age—my kind-of sound bite is that craft beer has helped beer reclaim its place at the dinner table.

JONES: That's interesting.

HERZ: Craft beer's a full-flavored beverage and it's definitely viewed more as part of the food arts as opposed to just this mass-produced lager.... So, food-rating apps are definitely a piece of it. There are other examples I could bring up in the digital space. Breweries definitely use . . . the model of the internet to even formulate their beers. MobCraft is an open source brewery . . . brewed in Connecticut, is one good example. They literally open-source their recipes. And the ones that get voted on the highest is what they brew.

Some breweries, like Allagash in Maine, allow their employees to submit recipes for test brews. They are brewed in small batches, then other employees vote on them over the course of the year. The most popular recipe is often produced and bottled for the public.

JONES: Wow. You know you mentioned earlier, mass-produced lager. And I'm wondering about your sense of the relationship between craft beer and macro beer? Particularly here in Colorado, you have like Coors—a big macro brewer and always has been a stalwart of macro brewing—but I'm wondering both the sense that you have—like, where is it that you feel the Brewers Association gets along well with macro brewers, where it's maybe neutral, and where it really doesn't get along at all? And where [does] that shows up in the culture of either brewers or beer lovers?

HERZ: Awesome . . . awesome question, very relevant. We're the
national association, but we exist to promote and protect small
and independent craft brewers. So [it's] important to put in the
mix, we also have Big Beer as our members. They just don't happen to be voting members.

This will probably shock most craft beer consumers. In the craft beer con-
sumer community, Big Beer is commonly assumed to be "the enemy" of
craft beer as they have a history of undermining the craft-brewing move-
ment. So the fact that they have seats at the table in the premier organi-
zation for craft brewers in the United States may strike some as "sleeping
with the enemy." Having said that, it makes some sense at a utilitarian level
when craft brewers are seeking legislative changes that may affect breweries
industry-wide. Still, this must make some issues stickier than others.

HERZ: So, it is a new thing, and I love you already come at the question
with where you guys get along, where is it neutral, where do you
not get along. And there's all three of [those] going on. And that's
going to happen within any business category, right, when you get
from the kind of the big to the small, there's just different interests. Um have you noticed, or seen in the marketplace, the independent craft brewers seal?

JONES: Yes, I've seen it everywhere.

The BA's Independent Craft Brewer's seal can be found everywhere at this
point. It is quite popular with brewers and consumers alike. Having said
that, it doesn't always seem to indicate what most craft beer consumers
think (i.e., small, independent, local, artisanal). For example, Sam Adams
beer can be found with the seal despite the fact that the Boston Beer
Company is the fourth-largest brewer of beer in the United States. Here
begin the arguments among craft beer fans of what it means to be "craft
beer" versus "big beer."

HERZ: Great. And yeah, so that's one example to bring up where there is
a need for transparency. That is a two-year-old certification mark.
It was end of June 2017 when it came out. So, the fact that you're
seeing it so prevalent, I think shows unity toward the need for differentiation, and giving the beer lover informed decisions when it
comes to when they're physically purchasing a beer from an independent craft brewer versus a big brewer.

On the other part of it, you know—tax relief, for example. You can find any information on the internet that you want to on this. We've been very public in [seeking] tax relief [with] the recent tax package [Craft Beverage Modernization and Tax Reform Act of 2017], which expires in December [2019]. That was a result of small brewers—us—big brewers, wine, spirits getting together and pushing this through. So, it's an example of collaboration with [alcoholic beverage makers]—big beer and small can work together.

JONES: That's interesting. So it sounds like you have some distinctive interests where you have the label representing small brewers and independent brewers. And then we also have things where you're getting together with them with some of these laws.

HERZ: It's important to think about the fact that the majority of breweries—more than 90 percent of the 7,500+ breweries in the United States—make less than 7,500 barrels a year. And a beer lover doesn't necessarily care how their beer gets to market. But in the case of the Grocery Bill, bringing the enforcement that is now possible with this, the brewers in Colorado—now I'm not speaking on their behalf, I'm only speaking on the history—they fought this. They fought it for years. It kept coming back. This is where Colorado's Brewers Guild could do a great job of articulating their latest and greatest wishes on what they're hoping to see evolve from here.

So, the legislative environment will always affect the potential success, is maybe a theme for craft brewers. And that is one of the reasons why you've got states like Texas—I call it one of the last wild frontiers for craft—sales in Texas are handcuffed. There's great opportunity. They recently did approve a To-Go Bill in Texas—first quarter of 2019—that is giving hope to the Texas brewers to loosen things up. So there were cheers but it's not everything they wanted. And so the legislative environment, the more friendly it is to breweries, the better it's going to be.

I know, talking about legislation can be a snooze fest, but there is some evidence that one reason why some states are experiencing a craft beer explosion while others have only a handful of craft breweries is the morass of laws (many dating back to Prohibition) still on the books today. Most of the country's southern states have a relatively underdeveloped craft beer industry (you can see a visual of this on the Brewers Association website by looking at a map of per capita economic impact). Julia mentioned the recent Texas To-Go Bill, which combats Prohibition-era legislation that bans breweries from selling anything that consumers take home with them (cans, bottles, growlers, etc.). Contrast this with Tree House Brewing in Massachusetts, one of the most highly regarded craft breweries in the United States (and likely one of the most lucrative), which sells their beer exclusively from their brewery—nearly 100 percent of their sales come from to-go sales.

CHAPTER 10

"This Is My Pub, This Is My Brewery"

The Growing Movement of Community-Owned Pubs and Breweries in the United Kingdom

MICHELE BIANCHI

Introduction

As part of British culture, pubs have always been important venues for Britons. Historically, they have also been places for brewing, thus preserving the traditional British ale: a top-fermented cask beer, mostly pale or gold in color, and an alcoholic content usually between 3 percent and 5.5 percent. Over the decades, pubs and breweries have modified their aspect while discarding some of their traditional characteristics in order to respond to market changes. Sport on TV, karaoke nights, Video Lottery (VLT), and offering wine and cocktails are among the improvements that pubs recently have adopted to stave off contemporary competitors. Meanwhile, beer quality has steadily declined, with industrial lager now the benchmark.

Despite this evolution, pubs have not lost their role as social venues and custodians of tradition. In recent years, a new wave of craft beer and community spirit has brought these British institutions back to the public eye. Community-owned pubs and breweries are a new phenomenon in the United Kingdom, and people are promoting collective projects to sustain local businesses through direct participation in ownership and management, rediscovering traditional British ales, and promoting community development (Department for Communities and

Local Government [DCLG] 2015, 2016; Sforzi and Bianchi 2020). Both the need to save historical places and an interest in developing community enterprises are leading many groups to plan collective purchases that will create breweries and pubs strongly rooted in their communities. Local groups selling shares to buy licenses and properties and to support their refurbishment where necessary. This creates a diffuse shareholdership in communities, involving local residents and whoever else is interested in the project. The goal of this research is to contribute to the international debate about breweries' and pubs' role(s) in local communities and beer production itself (Cabras 2018; Cabras and Mount 2017a, 2017b; Cabras et al. 2012; Markham and Bosworth 2016; Sandiford and Divers 2014).

In the 1930s, the Mass Observation organization led first-of-its-kind research in Bolton that studied the anthropological role of pubs in society. In its conclusions, the research team elaborated upon its definition of the pub as "a house where during certain hours everyone is [. . .] participator rather than spectator" (Mass Observation 1943, 17). Through the 2010s, experts with a growing scientific interest in public houses and beer consumption have investigated the sociological and anthropological aspects of these topics (Cabras 2011; Cabras and Bosworth 2014; Cabras and Reggiani 2010; Cabras, Canduela, and Raeside 2012; Dunbar 2016; Markham 2013; Muir 2012; Mount and Cabras 2016; Sforzi and Bianchi 2020; Social Issues Research Centre 2008). Their scientific aim is to demonstrate the deep connections that pubs can create within communities and their capability to strengthen social cohesion. (Note also that local independent breweries play a key role in many communities' social life and economy; they create job opportunities for locals, support charities, and supply local markets; Society of Independent Brewers [SIBA] 2017).

This chapter presents the main features of this new wave in British beer culture by answering two questions: (1) Why are communities collectively buying their pubs and breweries? (2) What do these community-owned pubs and breweries consider to be British ales? I conducted semistructured interviews with two pub and brewery managers to understand how these organizations are preserving British ale and pub culture. This investigation can reveal how community pubs and breweries operate in their territories to foster social cohesion around beer production, consumption, and historical pub preservation.

The Centrality of Public Houses and Ales in British Culture

Historians date brewing in England back many thousands of years. Though its exact start date is not clear, brewing was already well established during the Roman invasion (43–46 CE), when early beers were being made with water, cereals, and natural yeasts. Over the centuries, as in the rest of Europe, monasteries were the custodians of beer recipes, and important breweries and household production were widespread. Since the Anglo-Saxon kingdom began in the fifth century, alehouses have been places for brewing and, most importantly, consumption. Whereas alehouses and taverns have always been social venues for drinks, food, and entertainment, inns offered restoration to travelers (Hailwood 2014; Hornsey 2003). Around the reign of King Henry VII (1457–1509), taverns, alehouses, and inns became known as "public houses," commonly shortened to "pubs." There is evidence of pubs' central role in British culture since the sixteenth century; they were the heart of local communities and, sometimes, the only place where people could gather (Dunbar 2016; Hailwood 2014). Historically, many public houses hosted microbreweries (Hornsey 2003); moreover, brewery companies have owned and managed many pubs in order to sell their own products.

As public houses evolved over the centuries, so have the style and composition of their beers; despite huge variations, they still maintain peculiar characteristics that identify them as British ales. Rooted in Celtic culture and surviving the Roman Empire and Anglo-Saxon conquerors, brewing has always been a key activity in Britain (Cabras 2018; Hailwood 2014; Hornsey 2003). The first British ales were an unhopped alcoholic beverage obtained by brewing malt, water, and yeast in wood barrels. In the fifteenth century, hops were introduced in Britain from the Netherlands; these improved ale's flavor and, most important, preserved the product (Hailwood 2014). Over the centuries, the distinction between *beer* (hopped) and *ale* (unhopped) lost its significance, leaving the term *ale* to indicate the beverage commonly served in brew-houses, taverns, and inns.

British ale is a high-fermented beer with variants such as Mild Ale, Brown Ale, Pale Ale, Old Ale, and India Pale Ale. Also very popular is Bitter, a broad term applied to a well-hopped pale ale between 3.5 percent to 7 percent in strength and pale gold to dark mahogany in color. Bitters also come in various types, such as Best Bitter or Extra Special

Bitter, characterized by the addition of extra hops during the brewing process. Alongside these traditional versions, other kinds of beer have been appearing in the United Kingdom. In London during the eighteenth century, porters in Covent Garden were rewarded for their job with a dark beer brewed from oat grains, which adds to the bitterness and lends flavors of toast, biscuit, or coffee; this special ale was named *porter* for its main drinkers. Porter is the ancestor of stout, which is stronger and fuller bodied, thanks to the use of roasted barley in place of roasted malt. Born in England, it would find major success in Ireland with the brand Guinness (Larson 2014).

As described, UK breweries and public houses have adapted their spaces, entertainment offerings, and beer selection to meet more recent consumer demands. During the twentieth century, introduction of innovative brewing technologies deeply changed beer production. Refrigeration and pasteurization systems enabled breweries to produce and sell considerably greater volumes; these innovations created the "industrial beers" (Cabras and Bamforth 2016) and transformed the brewery sector by letting smaller producers become large firms. Beer became a standard product for massive consumption and lost the distinctiveness it derived from small and craft production (Cabras 2018; Larson 2014). In the 1970s, the rise of large-scale industrialization concentrated the market across six companies—Bass, Allied, Watneys/Grand Metropolitan, Scottish and Newcastle, Courage, and Whitbread—that together produced 80 percent of UK beer. Microbreweries totally disappeared (Cabras 2018).

Historically, many breweries owned pubs to sell their own beer. Alongside many pubs are "free houses" that are owned independently of the breweries that supply them. In 1989, the British government decided to reduce the presence of breweries in the market because they could compromise the competition with free pubs; official statistics counted 65,700 pubs in 1987 (British Beer & Pub Association n.d.), 14,000 of which were owned by beer companies (Pratten 2007). "The Monopoly and Mergers Commission declared that brewers owning tied retail outlets or providing tied loans to retail outlets not owned by them were operating a complex monopoly" (Pratten 2007, 613). The Commission imposed a maximum of two thousand licensed premises per "brewery or group of companies which includes a brewery" (Pratten 2007, 613). The brew companies' strategy was to bypass this obligation creating separate companies for pub management; this decision led to the creation of pub companies, which have many assets around the United Kingdom and have developed franchising systems and economies of scale that allow the reduction of food and beverage prices. During the 1990s, the reorganization of this sector coincided with a period of limited economic growth that affected consumers' spending; to attract new customers; pubs therefore needed a new presentation. This approach to service differed from that of old-fashioned public houses: "They created what was perceived to be a fashionable meeting place providing all day food and a wide range of drinks so as to offer a relaxed atmosphere during the day and a more vibrant mood at night. This is expected to appeal to a wide range of customers, including business people, shoppers and tourists to the younger and fashion conscious who come out later in the day" (Pratten 2007, 615).

Today, the rediscovery of craft beers and brewpubs is leading a renaissance in the UK brewing panorama. Many elements have determined this result, the major one being the constant work of the Campaign for Real Ale (CAMRA). Growing dissatisfaction with commercial lagers and rising consumer awareness regarding beer quality led to the founding in 1971 of a national association that supports breweries and pubs in conservation of traditional British ales (Cabras and Bamforth 2016). Across the United Kingdom, local CAMRA branches have fostered passion and interest in British ales and traditional-pub preservation. In the 2000s, a new wave of microbreweries took the stage; a few years later, they had conquered a considerable share of the British market, thanks to CAMRA's work and innovative legislation on beer production, particularly the Progressive Beer Duty, which reserves a lower taxation level for small breweries (Cabras 2018).

Since the early 2010s, people are reconsidering public houses as social venues—a place to meet friends, create networks, and have a good time. Independent pubs and breweries contribute to their communities' social life in different ways. Historically, they have hosted social activities such as concerts or cultural events; also, local volunteer groups that cannot afford a rental venue commonly take advantage of pubs' free hospitality (Cabras et al., 2012; Sforzi and Bianchi 2020). These establishments also support local initiatives through fundraising events or promoting special weekly dishes to local charities. Moreover, they tend to hire local workers in order to support their local communities and maintain a strong bond with the territory (SIBA 2017).

The aforementioned aspects are crucial in rural contexts where the pub is frequently the only social venue. Because of their great distance from main urban centers, small villages have lost population and, with it, local businesses and retail outlets. In many villages, pubs remain the last public social venue where people can spend leisure time and have a drink. As Smith (2008) points out, small businesses such as pubs are essential in villages across the British countryside: "Their closure induces a sense of angst (as tragedies to be mourned) because they illustrate a passed way of life. The decline in viability of rural and village post offices, corner shops and pubs bring about a sense of communal loss in small communities" (Smith 2008 372). In these cases, the presence of pubs represents a vital element for those communities (Dunbar 2016; Markham 2013; Muir 2012; Social Issues Research Centre 2016).

The Crisis of Traditional Pubs

Despite their rootedness in British culture, the pub crisis has extended for many years. Many factors have contributed to the increasing number of pub closures, including rising beer taxes, lower consumption due to the 2007–9 economic crisis, the cheaper cost of alcohol in off-license shops, and strong competition with pub companies.

Pub companies are the main competitors for traditional public houses. These conglomerates are enlarging the share of pub properties in their portfolio by converting many old pubs into fancy new venues. The Office for National Statistics (2018) shows how small-size pubs are disappearing and big chains are consolidating their position in the market. In the 2000s, pub companies invested in big-size pubs, which could employ many workers from other, closed pubs; this caused a steady pub depopulation in many British regions such as outer-city or rural areas. Many pubs were not able to respond to customers' new demands; others were beaten by the strong pricing competition that big companies presented. The numbers behind this pub crisis are shown in Table 1.

Table 1. Total Number of Pubs in the United Kingdom

1987	1992	1997	2002	2007	2012	2013	2014	2015	2016	2017
65,700	61,600	60,600	60,100	57,500	53,800	52,500	51,900	50,800	50,300	49,000

Source: British Beer & Pub Association, n.d. "Statistics: Pubs," https://beerandpub.com/statistics/pub-numbers/ (retrieved July 2020).

The difference between a commercial pub and a community pub is that the latter predominately serves local residents in a specific neighborhood (Muir 2012). This difference suggests a distinct approach in customer service, because commercial venues are conquering shares of the market with new entertainment elements such as VLT, karaoke nights, weekly special offers, or TVs showing constant sporting matches; instead, traditional pubs thrive more on offering quality beers and a friendly atmosphere. Despite these efforts, free houses are suffering a high rate of closure.

Yet in recent years, these losses of traditional pubs have sparked a new trend: people are mobilizing to save these historical places. Many groups of citizens are starting campaigns to reopen their local pubs, supporting such initiatives by purchasing shares and becoming engaged in the management of these new organizations, called Community-Owned Pubs (COPs).

Community-Owned Pubs and Breweries

A distinction is necessary at this point: the main difference between a community pub and a Community-Owned Pub is the property. In the first case, a publican, with a particular motivation of developing a strong connection with the community, owns or manages the pub. In the second, a group of local residents buys and, in most cases, manages it through a democratic process. The daily administration of the COP is charged to a professional pub manager, but key decisions are made by an elected committee or general members' assembly. The British government supports these initiatives with innovative legislation; the Localism Act (2011) promotes the "community right to bid," an opportunity for communities to structure new local organizations for their own interests.

> The provisions give local groups a right to nominate a building or other land for listing by the local authority as an asset of community value. It can be listed if a principal ("non-ancillary") use of the asset furthers (or has recently furthered) their community's social well-being or social interests (which include cultural, sporting or recreational interests) and is likely to do so in the future. When a listed asset is to be sold, local community groups will in many cases have a fairer chance to make a bid to buy it on the open market. (DCLG 2012, 2)

The Localism Act was part of a wider political agenda, promoted by Prime Minister David Cameron's government, named the Big Society. Its main aim is citizens' empowerment through local self-activation. To achieve this scope, the government promotes legal tools and incentives for groups or networks that aim to take direct control of local services and assets. The policy framework involves a large devolution of power and resources to local authorities and communities, which will have to collaborate for local development. COPs are an outcome of this process because they combine bottom-up independent initiatives with top-down support. From 2012 to 2016, the British government invested more than £5 million in the Pub Loan Fund (DCLG 2015, 2016). The Department for Communities and Local Government planned a reduction of taxation on beers and ciders, supported the leasing of pubs from pub companies to property owners, and gave councils powers to levy discretionary business-rate discounts that could support local community pubs (DCLG 2015).

Various organizations support communities in these projects:

- CAMRA
- Plunkett Foundation (supports community cooperatives)
- Pub Is The Hub (encourages local stakeholders to engage the community in this process of empowerment)
- Locality (the national body of the Community Interest Company)
- Co-operative UK (the national body of cooperation)
- Co-operative Mutual Solution (branch of Co-operative UK)

This initial policy framework has produced significant results, as expressed by Community Pub Minister Marcus Jones, who cites the community-purchased Anglers Rest in Bamford, Derbyshire, as an example:

> Forty communities have already successfully taken ownership of their local pub under community ownership, and a further 1,250 have been listed as "assets of community value" under community rights, highlighting the important role that pubs play in local communities. [. . .] [The Anglers Rest] not only houses the pub itself, but also a cafe and the local Post Office, and offers a much-needed community meeting venue, too. This has helped improve social cohesion and the regeneration of the village, and any profits generated by the Anglers Rest are reinvested back into the local community. (DCLG 2016)

As Dilley, Nakajima, and Natatsuka (2013) report, community-owned pubs can respond to widespread social problems in English rural areas caused by reduction of public services and disinterest of private businesses in low-population villages. Community-owned pubs and breweries can secure local forces and resources for re-creating local businesses that can also manage nontraditional pub services such as post offices, libraries, groceries, internet access points, or meeting halls (Plunkett Foundation n.d.). Many communities decide to host such nonconventional pub services because they are scarce in those areas or delocalized. This practice is beneficial because pubs can enhance their revenues by offering such diverse services while giving communities tangible support. Many public services have been reduced for cost efficiency, but granting them free use of community pub spaces makes them more sustainable. Alongside, many citizens run COPs as volunteers; thus they can ensure the pubs' functioning and support publicans in forging community connections. By generating fresh commitment to communities, COPs are a key element in the strengthening of social bonds among residents, local pubs, and breweries while stimulating mutually reinforcing benefits (Sforzi and Bianchi 2020).

Pumphouse Community Brewery, Ltd., Toppesfield, Essex

Toppesfield is a small but vibrant village in southeast England, assayed in the 2011 Census with a population of 505. Despite being tiny, Toppesfield's small population and isolation have encouraged many residents to become actively involved in their village. They have therefore established several community-owned organizations over the years: a grocery shop, a pub (the Green Man), and the Pumphouse Brewery, one of the few community-owned breweries in the United Kingdom.

The first step was the opening in 2002 of a community shop, promoted by the parish council of the day to provide Toppesfielders with a local store for daily groceries. This belief in local community enterprise was seen again in the purchase of the pub. In 2012, the place's former owners, a large pub company called Admiral Taverns, put the Green Man, the village's only pub, up for sale due to Admiral's precarious financial position, which eventually led to control being taken by its bankers. The village immediately started a campaign to save the pub that ended in the creation of Toppesfield Community Pub Ltd., a Community Benefit Society, with more than 150 shareholders who raised £289,000 for the purchase. The society leases the pub to tenants who are responsible for its day-to-day operation. Under the terms of the pub's tenancy agreement, tenants must organize community-focused activities and events; these include activities for mothers and children after school, and for retired people.

Since the beginning, the pub members had considered the idea of broadening the activities to brewing local beers for local consumption. The opportunity eventually came in 2015 when a small brewery close to Toppesfield stopped production and offered the Toppesfield Community Pub Ltd. committee the chance to purchase a complete brewing production line. Founded that same year, the Pumphouse Community Brewery, Ltd., now produces a range of traditional English ales. Like pub, it is a Community Benefit Society; it employs a head brewer who is in charge of the production and recruits volunteers to support the brewery's community activities. According to Alan Collard, Pumphouse chair, everyone involved has a passion for beer and community enterprises. The mission is simultaneously an occasion for producing something locally, trying to convince people to stop drinking commercial lager and inferior, mass-produced ales, and attracting visitors to Toppesfield.

The head brewer, Pumphouse committee, volunteers, and publicans collectively decide which beer types the brewery should produce, basing their choice on local tastes and people's inclination. The brewer advises what sorts of beer he is happy to brew and publicans indicate which beers are most popular with their customers. By addressing its production toward local tastes, Pumphouse creates a strong bond with the local community, which in turn feels more involved in the project. The result is a range of different ales that tend to be lighter in alcohol; the strongest they make regularly is a golden ale at 4.2 percent ABV, the lightest a basic bitter at 3.6 percent ABV. These ales reflect the preference in rural southeast England for beers that are lower alcohol and light in color:

> We know what kind of beer people drink in this area and they like lighter beers. We do this also to avoid problems with excessive alcohol consumption; people can drink 2 to 3 pints and more and walk home safely. We do not produce beer with exotic flavours or add extra ingredients; it is a good stock of traditional beers, easy

to drink. We are not looking to push the boundaries with our ales.
(Interview with Alan Collard, 2018)

The brewery occasionally makes event-related ales with particular characteristics, such as a 5.3 percent ABV special dark ale for the annual beer festival. For Remembrance Day in 2018, the brewery produced the "19 Elms" ale, a slightly brown, stronger-than-usual beer (4.3 percent ABV) that commemorated the soldiers from the village who died in World War I and the planting of nineteen elms in the parish. Every year, Pumphouse creates a special edition to celebrate Christmas; traditionally almost every brewery in the UK prepares a limited production to celebrate these holidays.[1]

> The feedback from the local community is very positive; they feel [like] owners even if they are not shareholders, because they see their brewery in their village, next door to their pub. On balance, they tend to drink these beers rather than others at the Green Man Pub. In the UK, a hard-core group of people prefers to go for a good ale. People want to know the provenance of what they drink and eat and the more local the better. There is increasing demand for small, local and craft products; of course, assuming the beer is drinkable! Moreover, people like to feel like owners, as it is friendlier, rather than buying beer from a larger, anonymous, and abstract corporation. This strong feeling is growing in the UK.
> (Interview with Alan Collard 2018)

In the future, Pumphouse will explore possibilities for hop and malt cultivation. Traditionally, Essex had hop farms that produced traditional local strains. Nowadays, the varieties have interbred and become distorted, so it is difficult to predict the final beer flavor; for this reason, the brewery is considering a farming project to produce its own hops. Moreover, the planned increase in beer revenues and profitability will allow Pumphouse to invest in community projects and improve quality of life in Toppesfield.

The Duke of Marlborough, Somersham, Suffolk

Since the fifteenth century, the Duke of Marlborough has served its community as a free house. This deep rootedness in Somersham, East England (population 3,810 people per the 2011 Census), was the main reason why residents started the "Save the Duke" campaign to raise money for reopening the pub after years of closure. In December 2014, the previous owner retired, and there were no plans for the future of the venue, which risked being converted into private residences. Moreover, the Duke was the last pub in the village, and its demolition could mean both the loss of an historical building and Somersham's last chance to keep a social venue. The community had already experimented with a collective ownership project in the form of a local shop, so they poured the same spirit into the pub reopening.

Over the course of a year, the Save the Duke campaign raised money and awareness of the community project, which would involve local people and organizations such as the parish and the Mid Suffolk District Council. The campaign committee also received support from the Plunkett Foundation, and became the first project in the United Kingdom to receive a combined grant for the Pub Is a Hub program. The committee has adopted the Community Benefit Society legal form and founded the Somersham Community Pub Limited, which collected £300,000 through the year. Resources came from share selling (eventually tallying more than 250 shareholders), grants, and benefits such as the Social Investment Tax Relief Scheme (which gives tax rebates on loans).

The Duke reopened as a community-owned pub in the summer of 2017 and now serves local craft beers and fresh food every day. Since its first days, the Duke has reclaimed its central role in Somersham social life; people have again a venue where they can meet and socialize. As current pub manager Kevin Long explains, the pub operates in different ways to fulfill its community mission. Except for the manager and the chef, the other employees, nine total, are young residents who work part time during the week; the pub sees this as an opportunity for youths to practice and improve their working skills. Every month, the Duke hosts a pub quiz to raise money for local charities. Elderly people can find here a place to spend time together with other villagers instead of staying home alone. The Duke accepts volunteers who assist staff members in pub management; they work behind the bar or maintain the garden. It now boasts twenty regular volunteers, whom the Duke repays with vouchers that they can spend in the pub for drinks or food. As Kevin explains, they can return with their family and enjoy the pub, which also strengthens bonds with the establishment:

> The good thing in Somersham is that everybody knows everybody pretty much. Everyone is looking out for everyone, if someone is

in need [they] can find support. The pub is a central place in the village where everyone can come and spend time. (Interview with Kevin Long, 2018)

Since the Duke's reopening, the committee has paid particular attention to what the pub serves their customers. Although the participants' main motivation was the safety of this historical venue, the chance to recreate a traditional British pub with good ales was no less important. The pub manager decides the beer menu in collaboration with a separate committee for beer selection. Its members have a particular passion for beers and maintain contacts with seven local breweries; because these breweries also produce seasonal beers, they inform the Duke about their calendars so it can offer an accurate season-focused beer menu. Most of the beers are ales of light color and with an ABV between 3.5 percent and 4.5 percent.

> The [beer committee] is formed by enthusiastic people, they give ideas about what the variety should be and the price should be. Most people come here primarily for the ales; the overwhelming [number of] comments we get from customers are positive, they enjoy the variety we stock and the fact [that] we always change beers and these are not well known; these are beers which you do not find on highstreets pubs. (Interview with Kevin Long, 2018)

Craft beers on tap have replaced industrial lagers at the Duke, which stocks just a few main brands in bottles. The combination of a charming atmosphere, a good choice of local craft beers, and fresh food has been successful; people see in the Duke of Marlborough a place where they can spend time with friends and other people from their village:

> It is different from highstreets pubs because they have [a] younger audience and for them it is more social[ly] expectable to have a bottle rather than a pint and more manageable to not have a pint. Moreover, pub on highstreets are owned by pub companies and can offer cheaper beers and drinks. In general, people come here to enjoy the experience of drinking not to get drunk. (Interview with Kevin Long 2018)

The Duke's renovation has revitalized not just Somersham's social life but also the local economy. The reopening has spread interest in the village, pulling people back to buy residences because now one can find a pub open. This demonstrates how community projects, particularly community-owned pubs, can trigger a renovation in areas around a venue, with positive effects on the neighborhood or village's reputation—a phenomenon one can see in other contexts such as the metropolitan area of London (Sforzi and Bianchi 2020).

Conclusion

The two case studies show how communities are promoting local projects for social cohesion and aggregation. In both cases, the main reason for such promotion is the possibility of having a community venue for social activities and fostering relations. People appreciate the chance to belong to a collective entity that can provide both something practical (e.g., postal services) and more emotional, such as opportunities for social bonding and a sense of community. It is not accidental that citizens are promoting campaigns for pubs; as Muir (2012) shows in his research, people perceive pubs as "the most important social institution for promoting interactions between people from different backgrounds at the local level" (33). The loss of local businesses and venues can trigger negative psychological effects (Smith 2008), whereas their revitalization can improve people's social network and sense of trust and collaboration (Sforzi and Bianchi 2020). Moreover, these elements contribute to enforce general well-being: "Being socially engaged, and taking part in activities like laughing, singing and dancing that are part of that process of engagement, not only make us feel part of the community, but directly and indirectly also enhance our sense of wellbeing and even our health" (Dunbar 2016, 20).

This renovated sense of localism can easily fit into the general movement toward a more local economy that fosters an ethic of "zero-kilometer food" and the rediscovery of local traditions. Both case studies confirm the participants' inclination for British ales rather than other beer styles; furthermore, the studies pay particular attention to local breweries and styles. In both villages, people can share their passion for craft beers with others in a dedicated venue. The necessity for new community projects is as relevant as the renewed attention to pub culture and craft beer; all of these elements forge new bonds between residents and their villages, shaping both a new sense of belonging and local craft products. In this arrangement, people establish direct relationships and involvement with producers and managers, providing their own view on what they drink (e.g., in both villages, a dedicated committee assists professional managers in beer choice). In turn, these groups maintain contact with customers and thus can assess people's taste and preferences. Residents of Toppesfield and Somersham were seeking something new that could also provide an innovative experience of a public house. By establishing these community-owned beer places, they bypassed the pub-company model, preferring a venue where they could share a friendly atmosphere, enjoy company, build a sense of attachment to the whole project, and spurn industrial lagers in favor of local craft ales.

Notes

1. In many countries with a long tradition of brewing (e.g., Belgium, Czechia, and the UK), breweries used to create special editions to celebrate Christmas. They are dedicated to notable clients or available in pubs just for the holiday season.

References

British Beer & Pub Association. n.d. "Statistics." Retrieved July 1, 2022 (https://beerandpub.com/statistics/).

Cabras, Ignazio. 2011. "Industrial and Provident Societies and Village Pubs: Exploring Community Cohesion in Rural Britain." *Environment and Planning A: Economy and Space* 43(10):2419–34.

Cabras, Ignazio. 2018. "Beer On! The Evolution of Micro and Craft Brewery in the UK." Pp. 373–96. In *Economic Perspectives on Craft Beer,* edited by C. Gravaglia and J. Swinnen. Cham, Switzerland: Palgrave Macmillan.

Cabras, Ignazio and Charles Bamforth. 2016. "From Reviving Tradition to Fostering Innovation and Changing Marketing: The Evolution of Micro-Brewing in the UK and US, 1980–2012." *Business History* 58(5):625–46.

Cabras, Ignazio and Gary Bosworth. 2014. "Embedded Models of Rural Entrepreneurship: The Case of Pubs in Cumbria, North West of England." *Local Economy* 29:598–616.

Cabras, Ignazio, Jesus Canduela, and Robert Raeside. 2012. "The Relation of Village and Rural Pubs with Community Life and People's Well-Being in Great Britain." *The Economics of Beer and Brewing: Selected Contributions of the 2nd Beeronomics Conference.* Freising, Germany.

Cabras, Ignazio and Matthew Mount. 2017a. "Assessing the Impact of Pubs on Community Cohesion and Wellbeing in the English Countryside: A Longitudinal Study." *International Journal of Contemporary Hospitality Management* 29(1):489–506.

Cabras, Ignazio and Matthew Mount. 2017b. "How Third Places Foster and Shape Community Cohesion, Economic Development and Social Capital: The Case of Pubs in Rural Ireland." *Journal of Rural Studies* 55:71–82.

Cabras, Ignazio and Carlo Reggiani. 2010. "Village Pubs as a Social Propellant in Rural Areas: An Econometric Study." *Journal of Environmental Planning and Management* 53(7):947–62.

Department for Communities and Local Government (DCLG). (2012). *Community Right to Bid: Non-statutory Advice Note for Local Authorities.* London: DCLG.

———. (2015). *Launch of New Fund to Help Local People Take Control of Pubs at Risk of Closure.* London: DCLG.

———. (2016). *Comprehensive Package of Business Development Support, Advice and Funding to Help Establish Community-Owned Pubs.* London: DCLG.

Dilley, Luke, Masahiro Nakajima, and Masaya Nakatsuka. 2013. "Community Pubs: Factors and Issues." *Journal of the Rural Planning Association* 32(3):374–79.

Dunbar, Robin. 2016. *Friends on Tap. The Role of Pubs at the Heart of the Community, Report for CAMRA.* Department of Experimental Psychology, University of Oxford.

Hailwood, Mark. 2014. *Alehouses and Good Fellowship in Early Modern England.* Suffolk, UK: Boydell & Brewer Ltd.

Hornsey, Ian S. 2003. *A History of Beer and Brewing.* Cambridge, UK: Royal Society of Chemists.

Larson, Michael. 2014. *Beer: What to Drink Next.* New York: Sterling Epicure.

Markham, Claire. 2013. "The Rural Public House: Cultural Icon or Social Hub?" Pp. 267–77. In *Interpreting Rurality: Multidisciplinary Approaches*, edited by G. Bosworth and P. Somerville. London: Routledge.

Markham, Claire and Gary Bosworth. 2016. "The Village Pub in the Twenty-First Century: Embeddedness and the 'Local.'" Pp. 266–81. In *Brewing, Beer and Pubs: A Global Perspective*, edited by I. Cabras, D. Higgins, and D. Preece. New York: Springer.

Mass Observation. 1943. *The Pub and the People: A Worktown Study.* London: Faber & Faber.

Mount, Matthew and Ignazio Cabras. 2016. "Community Cohesion and Village Pubs in Northern England: An Econometric Study." *Regional Studies* 50(7):1203–16.

Muir, Rick. 2012. *Pubs and Places. The Social Value of Community Pubs.* London: Institute for Public Policy Research.

Office for National Statistics. 2018. *Economies of Ale: Small Pubs Close as Chains Focus on Big Bars.* Retrieved November 26 (https://www.ons.gov.uk/businessindustryandtrade/business/activitysizeandlocation/articles/economiesofalesmallpubscloseaschainsfocusonbigbars/2018-11-26).

Plunkett Foundation. n.d. "Case Studies." Retrieved August 8, 2022 (https://plunkett.co.uk/case-studies/).

Pratten, John D. 2007. "The Development of the Modern UK Public House. Part 3: The Emergence of the Modern Public House 1989–2005." *International Journal of Contemporary Hospitality Management* 17(7):612–18.

Sandiford, Peter John and Peter Divers. 2014. "The English Public House as a 21st Century Socially Responsible Community Institution." *International Journal of Hospitality Management* 41: 88–96.

Sforzi, Jacopo and Michele Bianchi. 2020. "Fostering Social Capital: The Case of Community-Owned Pubs." *Social Enterprise Journal* 16(3): 281–97.

Social Issues Research Centre. 2008. *The Enduring Appeal of the Local.* Retrieved July 1, 2022 (http://www.sirc.org/publik/the_local.shtml).

Society of Independent Brewers (SIBA). 2017. *Brewers in the Community.* Retrieved July 1, 2022 (https://issuu.com/societyofindependentbrewers/docs/a5_siba _report_-_brewers_in_the_com?e=28684874/49899335).

Smith, Robert. 2008. "Zzzz. . . . Some Reflections on the Dynamics of Village Entrepreneurship." *International Journal of Entrepreneurship and Small Business* 6:370–89.

CHAPTER 11

Craft Beer Ecosystem or Ecosystems?

Are Craft Beer Cities Functioning Collectively or Individually?

CAROLYN KELLER AND SARAN GHATAK

In this chapter, we use the entrepreneurial ecosystem framework, derived from management studies, to analyze the development and growth of the craft beer ecosystem across the United States, and to determine whether so-called beer towns or cities function as stand-alone ecosystems or are in fact one very diverse, geographically dispersed ecosystem. Empirical studies have explored the emergence of and variation between entrepreneurial ecosystems as geographically bound areas (Cohen 2006; Isenberg 2011; Stam 2006). Because of the embeddedness of ecosystem relationships, geographic distance often generates distinct spaces that do not and cannot transcend boundaries. However, in our analysis of six US cities (Portland, Oregon; Portland, Maine; Cincinnati, Ohio; Kalamazoo, Michigan; Asheville, North Carolina, and Kansas City, Missouri), we found that strong and weak ties within and across beer locales and similarities of the ecosystem components suggest a more unified system.

We conducted qualitative interviews with more than fifty-two craft beer entrepreneurs across six distinct beer cities. Then we combined our analyses of these interviews with extant literature to generate a chronology for the emergence of a craft beer ecosystem. We used a comparative framework to analyze similarities within and between the craft beer cities. Although chronologies of beer locals vary, we show how each of Isenberg's (2011) six domains of an ecosystem emerge and become self-sustaining following largely the same patterns. Furthermore, we were able to demonstrate clear ties from one locale to the next. Our analysis allows us to highlight overarching homogeneity across beer locales.

Our research demonstrates across beer locales that initial policy and market emergence allowed for other ecosystem domains to follow suit. The generation of a geographically diffuse entrepreneurial ecosystem was enabled by a calculated framing of an outside competitor—so-called big beer—thereby creating and reinforcing insider identities through a strong national guild and a shared narrative of craft ideals and local authenticity. Social competence and weak ties across geographic locales generated rich social learning that helped consolidate the system. The establishment of solidarity among craft brewers has produced not only a successful and sustainable entrepreneurial ecosystem with exponential growth but also a model valuing cooperation over competition that spans the United States.

We conclude by arguing that the craft beer industry functions across the United States as a collective ecosystem based on building community and fueled by location-specific resources such as capital, human resources, and supportive policy environment, suggesting that geographically dispersed clusters require ecosystems of support. Although our research explored only one industry, we believe many of the techniques used to sustain the craft beer industry can be adapted by other craft entrepreneurs to increase their levels of innovation and ecosystem sustainability.

Introduction

The rapid development of craft breweries across the United States is striking, especially given overall declines in beer preferences beginning in 2015 as spirits and wine gained popularity (Bhogaraju 2015; Kell 2017). According to industry sources, as of 2016 there were more than 5,200 breweries in the United States, more than half of which appeared between 2012 and 2016 (Brewers Association 2022). This small yet rapidly expanding market segment has emerged as an alternative to the national brands, creating an exclusivity-based niche that attracted a growing consumer base marked by its distinctive taste in beer. Given the segment's extensive and rapid success, it serves as an excellent case study of contemporary industrial entrepreneurship. In this research project, we examined the development and growth of the craft beer industry across the United States to determine the extent of interconnections across entrepreneurial ecosystems. Relying on extant research and on qualitative interviews with over 50 brewers in six cities, we ask if beer towns/cities function as stand-alone ecosystems or if they are in fact one very diverse and geographically dispersed ecosystem. We find that strong and weak ties within and across beer locales and similarities of the ecosystem components suggest a more unified system. The shared narrative of craft breweries positioning themselves as alternatives to "big-beer" with reference to craft ideals and local authenticity generate the basis of ecosystem sustainability.

Entrepreneurial Ecosystems

Extant literature on entrepreneurial ecosystems argues that externalities and contexts play as much a role in entrepreneurial success as do individual characteristics (Feld 2012; Hechavarria and Ingram 2014; Isenberg 2011). Ecosystems provide individual business with the resources (e.g., capital, business-friendly policies, and trained workforces) necessary for their success. These often explain collections of entrepreneurs in specific geographical areas (Cohen 2006; Pitelis 2012; Spiegel 2017; Stam 2015). Importantly, the ecosystems literature has emerged as an alternative to cluster studies of industry-specific analyses, moving analysis instead toward an ecological approach that emphasizes the importance of location and its cultural, political, and economic contexts in promoting entrepreneurial success (Cohen 2006; Isenberg 2010). Although industry-specific analysis can limit the importance of context, we argue that in the case of craft beer, success of craft breweries depends to a large extent on building a conducive business atmosphere in specific locations.

Generally speaking, ecosystem studies focus on small geographic spaces like towns, cities, or regions—places where resources combine to make certain niche businesses flourish. Entrepreneurs measure many variables to determine if certain locations are more suited to their business than others. A good overview of this research can be found in Lee, Florida, and Acs (2004), who analyze the role of creativity, creative classes, and regional diversity as an important entrée into entrepreneurship. Entrepreneur-friendly environments might meet many configurations of the following criteria: plentiful human capital, low tax rates, dense populations, changes in median household incomes and unemployment rates, or readily available financing. Lee, Florida, and Acs (2004) add the interesting dimensions of the Bohemian index—a measure of per-capita creative classes—alongside a diversity measure that they call the Melting Pot Index, or the percentage of foreign-born people in a town. One thought leader in the field, Isenberg, has clearly demonstrated that for an entrepreneurial ecosystem to exist, six different domains must come together to shape and sustain entrepreneurial success: "conducive policy, markets, capital, human skills, culture, and supports" (Isenberg 2011). These domains seem to adequately encapsulate much of the ecosystem discussion. The material resources generated by an ecosystem are undoubtedly important in developing entrepreneurship in an area.

Social Competence and Extending Ecosystem Boundaries

Research has shown that social relationships within the entrepreneurial community also play a very important role. The development of social capital has been identified as intrinsic to entrepreneurial ecosystems (Cohen 2006; De Carolis and Saparito 2006; Ozcan and Eisenhardt 2009). This process is very much evident in the case of craft breweries. Most craft breweries form a relatively close-knit community where business rivalry is less pronounced than in other sectors of the economy. Because these breweries are breaking ground in a new market segment, success in the craft-brewing world requires entrants to build a community ecosystem that will create a reputation for craft brewing in an area, which in turn will likely generate business from both craft beer aficionados and new consumers. These communities exist not only within bounded geographic locations but also across the industry.

Another characteristic that scholars have specifically linked to entrepreneurial success is social competence, which Baron and Markman (2003) define as "entrepreneurs' overall effectiveness of interacting with others" (43). How entrepreneurs interact with others is perhaps as important as their own innate knowledge and substantive skillset, as the latter pair of traits are often shaped by the entrepreneurs themselves. Social competence seems to be linked to financial success because those who are able to connect to a large social network are more likely to connect with consumers, lenders, and important business networks that help build their own businesses. Thus, social capital in this context catalyzes business development and growth. Our research partly confirms how entrepreneurial success isn't just about knowledge but also the networks that create and sustain a business ecosystem. Furthermore, we found clear variation across the various cities where we interviewed brewers. Although the environments and the formulas for success were to some extent place dependent, the importance of ties to ecosystem components were constant and crossed geographic boundaries. We also found that brewers seem to be socially competent. They are very effective at interacting with others and do so locally, nationally, and globally. It is the common feature of brewers' ties to the broader industry that led us to our argument that the craft beer ecosystem is a linked, US-wide phenomenon, not a set of separate places.

Social competence gains additional context when one considers Granovetter's theory of weak ties. As Granovetter (1973) posited (and as empirically supported by the work of many later scholars), for a dyadic relationship to thrive, *weak ties* can be especially impactful in creating coalitions and providing opportunities for mobility. This occurs especially in "professional and technical settings . . . [that are] well-defined and limited in size" (1973, 1373), much like craft beer markets in the United States. In each of the domains of the craft beer ecosystem we studied, we are able to provide examples of weak ties that not only exist within locales but also extend beyond a town or city. Thus, these socially competent brewers are strengthened and buoyed by a diffuse network of weak ties that spans the United States.

Analytic Approach

We conducted semistructured interviews with more than fifty-two brewers and craft brewery entrepreneurs from six cities across the United States in the spring and summer of 2016 to inquire about their start-up processes and any benefits and barriers their day-to-day businesses present. The cities include Asheville, North Carolina; Cincinnati, Ohio; Kalamazoo, Michigan; Kansas City, Missouri; Portland, Maine; and, Portland, Oregon. We also interviewed at a handful of breweries in Vermont and New Hampshire. Our sampling method combined availability and snowballing techniques. We contacted all breweries in each location and met with those staff and owners who had time available in their schedule during our field visit. Upon arrival, we made some additional local connections when craft beer entrepreneurs happened to mention other brewers and owners we could meet.

In each city, we interviewed people at seven to ten separate breweries. We were able to make contact with a wide range of breweries, both established and new, of various sizes. With the exception of Portland, Oregon, which houses more than forty craft breweries, our sample covers at least half of the available craft breweries in each city. We supplemented our interviews with narratives from other brewers who are featured in craft beer ethnographies.

The majority of our sample comprises face-to-face interviews with owners, but occasionally we met with marketing representatives or head brewers. Our brewery contacts were largely determined by the size of the brewery. Individuals at the smaller breweries often performed multiple functions, so in talking to the owner, head brewer, and CFO, we would be interviewing just one person. Larger breweries could handle a more specialized division of labor, so we would talk with either a marketing head, an owner, or a head brewer. In most cases, we met with only one representative per brewery, but occasionally we interviewed two. Some of the breweries where we interviewed had opened in the 1980s; others had been open for fewer than six months. The bulk of the breweries, like most breweries in the country, had opened within the past three years.

All respondents were questioned about their brewery's success, current and previous barriers to growth, their approach to beer, how they as a brewery work to stand out in an increasing crowd, the demographics of their typical consumer, and how local and state policies have influenced their business plans. In essence, we took an ecosystems approach to our data collection—inquiring about individual variation but also cultural, economic, and policy contexts surrounding breweries. Furthermore, we gathered examples that illustrate the types of weak ties that connect the various spaces.

By conducting a brief overview of the growth of the craft beer industry through the lens of Isenberg's six domains, we find at different times and places these domains have varied in import. However, we also find a similar growth trajectory across locales. The story of craft beer in the United States also highlights the importance of recognizing the intersections between these domains, as building an ecosystem requires their mutual interaction. In the early years of craft brewing, the pioneering entrepreneurs built a market niche for a new product by distinguishing themselves from the giant beverage corporations dominating the national beer market. Local policies and ordinances governing the manufacture and sale of beer greatly influenced their initial foray into the market. The success of these pioneers was not limited to the development of a new product, but rather an entire ecosystem with its own organizational ethos. Following these initial successes, new breweries entered the market, embracing and then contributing to it while helping the ecosystem of this new craft business grow and mature.

1800–1920: The Fall of Local Ecosystems of Beer during Prohibition, and Beer in Historical Context

Understanding the craft beer boom first requires a historical understanding of brewing in the United States, which involved an initial wave of diversity, followed by a period in which brewing became homogeneous due to three main factors: technological advances, Prohibition, and conglomerations. As with the current craft beer industry, the United States' original brewing industry was large and diffuse, but for a different reason: each town had a local brewery because the technology available to transport beer long distances did not exist. According to the Brewers Association, the last time there were more than four thousand breweries in the United States was 1873—a number not reached again until 2015. In the mid-1800s, thanks to an influx of German and other European immigrants, towns across the country had many breweries. However, once refrigeration technologies became widespread and affordable, companies like Anheuser-Busch began buying many of the medium-size breweries, and the smallest ones could no longer compete. By 1910, the United States had fewer than fifteen hundred breweries.

Prohibition (1920–1933) further destroyed legal breweries' business, though some of the larger operations were able to weather the period by shifting production to other arenas. Yuengling, for example, refocused their business on ice cream production, using the refrigeration technologies in which they had already invested for brewing until Prohibition ended. This meant some breweries, including Anheuser-Busch and Yuengling, were able to resume brewing beer immediately following Prohibition, whereas most others were unable to make it through the Great Depression and had to sell off their materials and properties. This decline in brewing outlets starkly reduced beer offerings. As one scholar writes, "When beer became popular, it became profitable, opening itself up to large-scale corporate control and consolidation" (Geiling 2015, 1). This marked the end of local craft ecosystems and the beginning of the age of big beer.

1980s–2000: The Pioneers and the Emergence of the Craft Beer Ecosystem—Markets and Policies

The birth of the craft beer movement can be categorized as innovation related to two of Isenberg's domains: markets and policy. Individual entrepreneurs saw an opportunity in the 1980s to revitalize the industry and did so by promoting a buy-local type of brand, drawing connections to America's historical brewing past, or looking to European brewing for inspiration. For example, the D. L. Geary Brewing Company of Portland, Maine, opened the first craft brewery on the East Coast in 1983, beating out Jim Koch and the Boston Brewing Company by a year. Geary himself was trained in Europe. "The first place I ever brewed was a thousand-year-old castle in Scotland [. . .] in a 350-year-old brew house . . . talk about going back to the roots," he said. "Then I traveled around the UK working and brewing for several months." It was in England that Geary hired a brewer before returning home to Maine to open his first brewery. Not only did early craft breweries of the 1980s benefit from European exposure, increased international travel introduced a growing clientele to a greater diversity of flavor.

Jim Koch of Sam Adams began brewing himself in 1981, notably using his great-great-grandfather's recipe to develop today what is known as Boston Lager. That same year in Cincinnati, a city with an extensive brewing past, Christian Moerlein beer—one of Cincinnati's biggest pre-Prohibition breweries—was reintroduced to the local market. Christian Moerlein was a brewery in Cincinnati that was in business for more than sixty years beginning in 1853. Although the company died with Prohibition, the Moerlein family name remained prominent in the region and the Moerlein family money played an important role in endowing local churches and community organizations even into the ensuing decades. The beer's successful reintroduction is notable because "it became the first beer to certifiably pass the strict Reinheitsgebot Bavarian Purity Law of 1516. True to the law since

Christian was the brewmaster, the beer contains only four ingredients: Malted Barley, Hops, Water and Yeast" (Moerlein Brewery 2016). This was the first time an American beer had met a major European standard.

Not one but two major breweries have since leveraged success off of Moerlein's history. Today in Cincinnati, there is a craft brewery with Moerlein's namesake—the Moerlein Lager House— and another incredibly successful brewery, Rhinegeist, began brewing in Moerlein's old brew buildings and selling beer in 2013. So not only did the first cohort of craft brewers play an opening in the market that capitalized on a rich history, they also established ties to Europe and diversified early on. By doing so, brewers quickly grew credible in the market. As David Geary says, successful breweries require something simple: "Good beer, consistently good beer, give people what they expect." Meeting customer expectations and generating a dependable consumer base early on is essential to this ecosystem's success. Koch, Geary, and the Moerlein trajectory all gained legitimacy through weak ties—ties that linked modern beer to traditional brewing in the United States and Europe—in essence creating a value structure related to beer ties to other times and places. Their links to the brewing traditions of yore were complemented by ties with contemporary brewers and beer aficionados, which allowed them to experiment and develop new recipes and brews.

Good beer alone, however, will not build an ecosystem. Early craft-brewery entrepreneurs relied on networks and entrepreneurial innovation from success in other arenas prior to getting started in craft beer. Lessons learned from previous failures in other businesses and shared across entrepreneurial networks proved to be invaluable lessons for the pioneers. On the supply side, as Geary reflected on the market over the past thirty years and lessons learned, he argued that it is important for new brewers to be well capitalized. "If you can't afford to promote your product, if you can't afford to hire the right people, if you can't afford to merchandize, those things can lead to failure . . . living within your means [is important to succeed]." Finding early support from other successful entrepreneurs—either abroad, like Geary, or in town, as in the case of Art Larrance of the Portland Brewing Company in Oregon— helps generate an entrepreneurial network of successful models worth following. As Larrance argued, "The people that got started early on were entrepreneurs. They capitalized themselves early on and they made themselves visible in their companies." The initial success of these pioneering brewers paved the way for other breweries to develop and succeed. Furthermore, on the supply side, as Larrance noted, "the retailers knew they could make more money selling our beer than Budweiser." This way, the successful pioneers paved the way for later entrepreneurs by forging not just the material conditions of business success (capital, technology, knowhow) but also the reputational and cultural conditions. They put their city on the craft-brewing map and attracted a loyal customer base that was instrumental in spreading the word within their own social networks, which then brought new customers and solidified the reputation of the brewery and the area. This, in turn, attracted other brewers and entrepreneurs to the city. There was money to be made and this later wave of brewers found market openings to make it happen. The growth models for craft brewers old and new, big and small, follow similar trajectories because they are talking with one another, looking to history, making connections, and learning socially what works best.

Tapping into an entrepreneurial network and learning from business owners therein was a constant in our data. Interviews were full of craft beer entrepreneurial name-dropping and characterized by informality. Entrepreneurs would occasionally reference other local breweries but more frequently referenced the national scene. At the time of our interviews, Rob Todd, founder of Allagash Brewery in Portland, Maine, was the head of the national Brewers Association. Entrepreneurs in Kansas City and Asheville referenced him as "Rob" as if they were friends. The owner of Migration Brewery, a growing operation in Portland, Oregon, had just visited Rhinegeist Brewery and "met with Bob"—Bob Bonder, the owner of a Cincinnati brewery. Mike Rangel, founder of a pioneer brewery, Asheville Brewing Company in North Carolina, regularly referenced events like the Great American Beer Festival, held annually in Denver, as a space to meet other brewers and share best practices with these entrepreneurs. From the origin of the craft-brewing renaissance and continuing through today, these entrepreneurial ties have existed in all beer locales and extended across the terrain separating the locales, too.

One of the most important moves the pioneer craft brewers made was to attack the three-tier distribution system, a relic from the post-Prohibition era. Following repeal, the federal government left it up to states to implement beer distribution in three tiers—manufacturer, distributor, and retailer. In the fifty years after Prohibition, one was not permitted to brew and sell beer in the same building, largely to avoid tied houses—a model that had created major conglomerates and monopolies in British brewing years earlier. Craft brewers challenged this legislation early on, gradually making way for breweries to sell on premise and thus succeed financially. Our respondents regularly referenced how brewers in Vermont and Oregon were able to achieve great success in tearing down the three-tier system and discussed how their own states had followed similar paths.

The brewers' guilds play an important role in helping new entrepreneurs wade through the remaining red tape to establish a brewery and learn tricks of the trade. This red tape has meant that there are subtle differences between states in how breweries work. For example, in some states, breweries are not allowed to sell beer unless they also sell food. Therefore, brewpubs and larger, distribution-only breweries are the norm. In other states, breweries may only sell beer in small glasses and not larger growlers or kegs out of the door. Most peculiarly, in Missouri, wineries can legally sell wine out of their door but breweries cannot. Therefore, Missouri breweries obtain winery licenses by brewing 100 gallons of fermented fruit beverages to meet the qualifying standard and thus able to sell directly from their production facility. As the brewers informed us, selling direct has the highest profit margins, helps increase beer tourism, and drives growth. State by state, as brewers find workarounds, more and more breweries pop up, because brewers are making these important ties to others across the country within the craft beer industry.

Notably, another important legislative change in the early years was related to the legality of homebrewing. By an accidental oversight, the repeal of Prohibition did not re-allow homebrewing (though it did allow home winemaking). Therefore, it was illegal to brew beer in American homes from the beginning of Prohibition in 1920 until 1979, when homebrewing was once again legalized on a federal level (Homebrewers Association 2017). This legalization played an important role in growing a new American pastime. Homebrewing has grown in popularity and has allowed a forum for potential entrepreneurs to practice and hone their craft. Over half of the entrepreneurs in our sample got their start from homebrewing, which has grown and become increasingly competitive. This means that not only are there more people learning about how to brew, they also play a role in creating a strong and knowledgeable consumer base for craft breweries.

Greg Noonan, head of Vermont's first brewpub, Vermont Pub and Brewery, is an excellent example of how important market openings and legislative changes overlap. In addition to being responsible for changing Vermont's laws related to opening a brewery, Noonan also homebrewed. According to his obituary, it took three years of lobbying (1985–88) to make it possible for a brewer to sell on premise. In addition, Noonan also penned many manuals on homebrewing that are well known in the beer world today. Similarly, in Michigan, Larry Bell began homebrewing and opened Kalamazoo Homebrewing Company; then, two years later, began selling craft beer. Bell's is now one of the largest craft breweries in the country. Stories of Bell regularly visiting the Michigan legislature are known across the state. The brewers we met in Kalamazoo were all happy credit Bell for paving a path for their ecosystem to grow, including legislative distribution precedents set in 2009 that worked to tackle the three-tier system. They also praise Bell for aiding innovation through homebrewing competitions they hold regularly. Eventually, largely due to the legacies established by Noonan and Bell, both Vermont and Michigan would become beer destinations. The states that changed these laws early on continue to be the places where the success of breweries is most established. Areas where we see still a dearth of craft breweries are places (generally in the South) where legacies of blue laws remain; these state-wide relics limit entrepreneurial capacity to capitalize. Policy shifts have been an important factor in setting the stage for the maturation of the ecosystem since 2000. It is a domain in which entrepreneurial learning crosses local boundaries more often than not. Once the markets and policies were in place, this foundation allowed for exponential expansion across the country.

2000–Present: Development and Maturation of the Craft-Brewing Ecosystem—Supports and Finance

The pioneers' success created legitimacy in the market and opened up opportunities to cross-market with other artisanal and food industries, which runs parallel to an increase in opportunities for new breweries to obtain funding. Since 2000, on a local level, policies related to zoning and licensing have been shifted slightly to support the craft beer ecosystem. As the industry expands, these crafters need spaces where they can produce and sell their products at the same time. Alternatively, they need spaces where similar artists, chefs, and local entrepreneurs can highlight and cross-promote each other's products. Direct or near-direct distribution of products yields the highest margins for craft entrepreneurs. Furthermore, cross-promotion helps build up neighborhoods and generates a geographically centered, built-in networking and support opportunity for entrepreneurs in a rising-tide manner. One scholar argues that mixed-use urban development "can create high-wage, low-barrier to entry jobs, diversify urban economies . . . and provide unique retail experiences and a local sense of place" (Cotter 2012, 5). For example, one of the shortcomings until recent years of brewing in Portland, Maine, is that brewers are limited to light-industrial zones. Up to the summer of 2016, restaurants were unable even to be within blocks of the breweries. Furthermore, state law bars breweries from selling food. In the short term, some brewers were able to overcome this shortcoming by relying on food trucks. However, in 2018, restaurants were permitted in one of the city's light-industrial zones, where they quickly proliferated. Nearby breweries like Bunker Brewing Company are hoping these will boost their business. Joint efforts with restaurants such as cross-marketing have been a successful venture for many breweries. Beer dinners are becoming increasingly popular, and being able to sell beer directly to restaurants can play a major role in helping both small businesses get a productive start. Breweries also benefit from being located next to other breweries. As many brewers we interviewed argued, consumers don't ever have just one beer in an evening. Brewers are comfortable sending consumers from one brewery to the next and have little concern of hurting business. Furthermore, the bigger craft breweries share the smaller brewers' attitude of in-group solidarity, which highlights the potential value of social capital in niche industries. Our interviews demonstrated how almost every brewer is aware of the work and offerings of other brewers in the area, and revealed that they spoke about one another in amicable ways. Some of them even pointed out how they were helped both materially (e.g., swapping broken machinery for working gear from another brewery) and through feedback on their products and advice for improvement. Instead of an atmosphere of competition among craft brewers, we saw cooperation and support. They shared the belief that having good experiences at small, local breweries will lead consumers to expand their horizons and try other craft beer. Therefore, it is the quality of craft beer, not the size of the brewery, that reinforces consumer preference for craft beers over big beer.

One new brewer in Asheville pointed out, "Breweries that never had a laboratory to test now have laboratories," because Sierra Nevada in nearby Fletcher had opened their labs to Asheville-area brewers. He went on to discuss the importance of Sierra Nevada and New Belgium's entry to the local market. Although we had expected that the entrance of such big names would create concern and trepidation among small and local craft brewers, we found the opposite: "They've been pretty helpful," noted the new Asheville brewer. Being a member of a guild and working together, he added, helps all the brewers in the association. "Knowing everybody is like playing tennis with a buddy . . . you want to beat 'em but not too badly." Everyone wants everyone to do well. The Asheville brewing community seems to have a congenial culture. This partly derives from the fact that individual breweries do not necessarily eat into the market shares of others in the area. If anything, the assumption is that the entry of new breweries, big or small, will further improve the reputation of the city or neighborhood as a beer destination, in turn attracting more customers to the area. The typical customer of craft breweries is likely to have an adventurous palate and will visit a beer destination to taste new and different brews. This expands the potential universe for innovation and change in brewing while increasing the friendly competition from other area breweries.

Other reasons for the cooperative culture include mentoring and formal legal aid, which state and local brewers' associations have enabled. This implies that once a handful of breweries are established in an area, it will be much easier for an entrepreneur to come in and follow the established model to launch a successful brewery. In other words, the start-up costs in a thriving local brewery ecosystem are lower because of all the existing supports. In addition, cities and towns are increasingly incentivizing brewers to generate new local ecosystems. At some beer festivals we've visited, we've seen local politicians handing out business cards, in an effort to bring breweries to places that don't already have one. For example, Crane Brewery has been a successful startup in the Kansas City area, but they are quick to note they aren't actually within Kansas City limits. Rather, their address is in the adjacent city of Raytown, Missouri. Their choice of location has been a major advantage because town officials have worked to make the start-up process successful. They launched much more quickly than some of their Kansas City–sited peers because of officials' assistance—and they were also the only ones in Raytown doing it.

What stands out most in the entrepreneurial craft-brewing ecosystem are the camaraderie, open sharing process, and networking that characterize the industry. This in-group solidarity existed from the genesis of craft beer in the 1980s and 1990s and clearly remains today. Sharing expertise, skills, recipes, and ideas has been a defining feature of the industry. In the framing of Mike Rangel from the Asheville Brewing Company, from the beginning they created an "amazing atmosphere" among new owners of "gentleman brewers." He went on to tell many stories of working together and collaborating. Nearly all respondents in our sample likewise discussed the willingness of other brewers to help one another out. On the most basic level, this can involve sharing raw material or machine parts. However, it even extends to cobrewing a new beer in some cases. This camaraderie has been institutionalized in the form of brewers' guilds, now present in most beer cities and states. There is also a national brewers' guild (the Brewers Association) that serves an important role of providing support for startups and sharing knowledge freely. When asked if bigger craft breweries are viewed as competition, Chris Gange of Hermit Thrush Brewery succinctly stated, "No. They play an important role in raising the palate. If someone is willing to try a Harpoon or a Sierra Nevada, that makes them much more likely to want to try one of our sour beers." Even as craft breweries have vast differences, they all identify themselves similarly.

These types of network and political supports have meant that there are multiple paths to success in the craft beer ecosystem, with camaraderie and guilds as constants. The rising-tide mentality is so entrenched in the ecosystem, it has even become the name of a brewery in Portland, Maine. Its owner, Heather Sandborn, is the head of the Maine Brewers Association, and she mentioned the phrase many times during our interview in reference to the industry. Local and national ties between breweries has been instrumental for improving the industry's outlook.

Capital, Culture, and Skills

Capital, culture, and skill acquisition via education are essential domains of entrepreneurial ecosystems (Isenberg 2010; Malecki 2018. The case of craft breweries shows how these domains are intrinsically interlinked. Like other manufacturing businesses, breweries require significant initial investment to purchase machinery and for other start-up costs. In most cases, however, the breweries in the sample had little trouble raising capital through loans and owner investment. However, to make sense of a niche sector such as craft breweries, we need to expand the very definition of capital.

Attaining start-up funds for a new brewery is becoming easier because banks are now specializing in loans for craft beer businesses. Banks such as Pinnacle and Live Oak have dedicated units for craft brewery loans. Local brewers' associations are documenting the process of getting Small Business Administration loans (Pierce 2015). This change is recent, because the financial issues of brewers are changing. As many brewers we interviewed noted, the challenge for breweries isn't getting access to start-up money but meeting the increasing demand for the product. Craft beer entrepreneurs are having to write and rewrite business plans and secure funding more swiftly—as Rhinegeist owner Bob Bounder said, he was having to revisit the business plan every four to six months.

Keeping in step with the networks brewers have established around all other domains of the ecosystem, brewers also have generated a way to share, trade, and sell used equipment to meet rapidly shifting demands. Breweries such as Henniker Brewing often begin by using hand-me-down tanks. Portland, Maine, is notable in this case because it has become an incubator for new breweries. All of Portland's breweries are housed within two separate areas zoned light industrial. In these zones, which were designed for breweries, the establishments frequently relocate from one location to the next. Allagash, one of the largest craft breweries by volume, got its start in one of these sites, and the brewers regularly talk about new breweries entering and exiting. In fact, we were unable to connect with a couple of breweries in Maine because they were moving between industrial zones while we were seeking interviews. Rather than bringing in new equipment and starting over, brewers are moving to locations where bigger equipment that meets their needs already exists.

As with any other manufacturer, craft breweries need financial resources to survive, but much of their business is based on other, less tangible forms of capital. In his seminal work on social inequality in advanced industrial nations, Pierre Bourdieu extended traditional understandings of wealth and privilege by distinguishing between multiple forms of capital (Bourdieu 1984). Although money and other financial capital remain some of the most important forms of resources, Bourdieu advocated for including cultural resources such as education, symbolic forms of privilege such as prestige or pedigree, and social relations in order to broaden our understanding of the nuances of social inequality in modern societies. Likewise, in understanding the craft beer ecosystem, we need to expand the traditional understanding of capital's role in business. One of the distinguishing features of the craft beer ecosystem is the distinct culture that surrounds the planning, production, sales, and consumption of the product. Every industry and business sector develops and sustains its own culture, but such development is particularly pronounced in the case of the craft beer industry.

In the case of craft beer, the importance of culture as a factor of business success extends to both the entrepreneurs and the consumers. For the former, it requires knowledge about beer along with technical proficiency in production and other domains of the business. Most craft beer entrepreneurs in our sample had a college degree or higher, but their degrees are not necessarily linked to what has become their profession. Indeed, participants displayed little commonality of educational background, and their degrees ranged from engineering to film studies. What united most of them was some experience in home-brewing or other familiarity and personal connections with the world of craft beer. Some suggested that industrial production of beer using state-of-the-art technology, however small in scale, required a significant amount of on-the-job training, as it was entirely different from their prior experience.

This leads to one of the most revealing findings of the study: these entrepreneurs' education often came from the wider craft-brewing community rather than formal institutions. Many of them suggested that they learned the actual process of running a business from fellow brewers, who in some cases served as mentors and unofficial advisors to their own competitors. Such collaboration partly arises from the fact that social relationships in the craft beer community are generally convivial, because brewers largely are not in direct competition. Indeed, it is in their common interest that a certain critical mass of breweries develops, so the area acquires a reputation that will bring consumers who are likely to sample all their wares. Doug Riley, head brewer of the Asheville Brewing Company, has created a formal apprenticeship program. New brewers are brought in, asked to stay at least two years to learn under his tutelage, and then go out and found their own breweries. As a result, Riley boasted, he has parented many successful breweries across the United States. The representative from Allagash Brewery reminisced about how the head brewer, Rob Todd, got his start, "like many others," at Otter Creek, a Vermont brewery. He also talked about welcoming the new local brewers into town and cosponsoring events that brought in business for everyone.

Our research shows that a sophisticated palate and knowledge about beer characterize the typical craft beer consumer, who also tend to be an educated, white-collar professional. Research shows that knowledge about food and culinary preferences could be seen as attempts to build and maintain distinctions in status (Mellor, Blake, and Crane 2010). Scholars have also described how culinary preferences often move from traditional high-status choices to more exotic or "authentic "cuisine (Bourdieu 1984; Johnston and Baumann 2007). Food certainly has symbolic value with reference to distinction and taste accorded to specific objects of consumption (Cavanaugh 2007). Scholars have also found similar processes at work when it comes to drinking alcoholic beverages and the drinking practices of particular demographic groups (Alasuutari 1985). Craft breweries typically cater to a relatively exclusive market niche that is defined by a certain pattern of taste and consumption generally linked with highly educated, high-status, high-income populations. As craft beer has become more popular, at least a segment of consumers have come to acquire significant knowledge about beer. The breweries themselves often foster this process, as their expansion or survival requires proselytizing consumers into the culture of beer and helping them distinguish craft beer from mass-produced beer.

A co-owner of Hermit Thrush Brewery in Brattleboro, Vermont, highlighted the importance of educating consumers in sustaining and expanding the market. Hermit Thrush specializes in Belgian-style sour beer, which the co-owner said can potentially appeal to the palate of wine drinkers, especially when paired with a meal. However, the problem is lack of overlap between the usual customer bases for beer and wine. Thus, the co-owner asserted that there is a need for "identity-based marketing" to target wine drinkers and emphasize for them the complexity and subtle flavors of their ales, as a wine merchant would do. Such outreach would also involve educating consumers about the exclusivity of craft beer over more mass-market ones they might be accustomed to seeing in grocery stores.

This method of building a brand identity for craft beer would entail imbuing the product with symbolic meanings that in turn would facilitate sustaining the ecosystem. Studies of consumption (e.g., Tian, Bearden, and Hunter 2001) have observed twin faces of consumption cultures: the use of a commodity for need fulfillment or pleasure, but also its symbolic usage—where the need fulfillment or pleasure is derived not only from consumption but also the identity a consumer derives from such practices. In the case of symbolic need fulfillment, scholars point out that consumers' desire for distinction drives their pursuit of authenticity (Tian, Bearden, and Hunter 2001). Carroll (2011) distinguishes between two axes of authenticity when it comes to microbreweries: *craft authenticity* or the commitment to the traditional manufacturing process and product ethos, and idiosyncratic authenticity or the distinctive nature of a specific product or brand that distinguishes it from others in the same commodity category. Craft beer then has become what one respondent referred to as an "affordable luxury."

Very importantly, most of the breweries in the sample make a conscious attempt to distinguish themselves from big beer not just in the product that they are making, but also in their organizational culture. Some of the breweries (e.g., in Asheville) made a case about the need for self-imposed ceilings on growth. The owner of one Asheville brewery asserted that growth beyond a certain level makes a craft brewery lose touch with its "authenticity"—the organizational culture, exclusivity, and commitment to their local customers. With its celebration of relatively small-scale production and craft ideas—that is, privileging quality over quantity and maintaining customer loyalty based on exclusivity—craft beer creates a new model for authenticity (Carroll and Swaminathan 2000). Although this model does not compete on the industrial scale of big beer, it is increasingly seen as successful in building and legitimizing a new way of doing business that is attaining growing acceptance and success. When a certain organizational field comes to occupy a market niche, new organizations emulate its established model, which then becomes the normative form in that industry (Carroll and Swaminathan 1991). Much of craft beer's success was premised on brewers' ability to build a business ecosystem that allowed them to distinguish themselves from mainstream domestic beer or European imports, thus achieving commercial success without surrendering its identity as a niche product.

Conclusion

Although a single craft brewery exists as a business unit with its own compulsion to be profitable or at least sustainable over time, it is also part of a larger network of breweries regionally and nationally. Most craft breweries in the sample have social or business ties with other breweries, and see these ties as an essential part of their survival. Although competition exists between breweries, it is not zero sum, as in most other economic sectors. Personnel attached to older breweries sometimes serve as mentors for newer ones, and many respondents in our sample spoke about personal ties and business cooperation (including sharing or bartering machine parts or raw materials) with other area breweries. This underscores an important point: industries like craft breweries serve as their own ecosystem with endogenous capital, know-how, and personnel, and these interact in manifold ways with other businesses in their localities.

At the same time, we must recognize that even when craft breweries tend to form their own ecosystems, they also tend to be and stay economically and culturally tied to a place. There are certainly exceptions to this norm—indeed, some breweries manufacture beer to transport and sell in other areas. But local authenticity is a hallmark of most small- to medium-scale breweries. One of the main reasons is that these breweries are catering to a market niche that appreciates the whole experience of visiting a brewery and trying products that have a certain story attached to them. This reason also explains why breweries cluster together and the cooperative relations between them. Up to a certain level, development of new breweries adds to the cultural and economic dynamic of the area, and are likely to bring more customers who may also visit multiple breweries. One vital point: there appears to be mutual reinforcement between a city's identity and its craft breweries. Certain places like Asheville, North Carolina, or Portland, Oregon, have an identity of being welcoming for artistic and creative-minded people. Consequently, it has provided a suitable location for craft businesses, including but not limited to breweries. In turn, the development of craft breweries has reinforced the "quirky" identity of these cities.

Symbolic use of actual geographical places has been identified as an important strategy for creating a certain market niche. For example, Seattle's preeminent position in coffee culture has been used to create the brand identity of specialty coffee as against mass-market varieties

(Lyons 2005). Indeed, many city leaders tend to cultivate and foster a distinctive image to differentiate their city from others competing for capital, entrepreneurs, and the so-called creative classes (Markusen and Schrock 2006). However, the widespread acceptance of these images of distinctive identity is the product of interaction and negotiation between geographic locality and market dynamics in which consumption (and facilities for same) plays a key role (Jansson 2003).

This interactive process is very much in evidence when it comes to the interrelation between craft breweries and their location. Given the breweries' increasing popularity, they provide a significant economic boost to a neighborhood. This is particularly evident in places like Cincinnati, Ohio, or Kalamazoo, Michigan, where old industrial districts that had fallen into a long spiral of urban decay are being revitalized by the arrival of breweries and other businesses. In Cincinnati, this rebirth is happening in the old brewing district of the Over the Rhine neighborhood near downtown, the gentrification of which is partly being aided by the revival of local craft breweries. These breweries, along with new restaurants, boutiques, and art galleries that have arrived around the same time, have transformed the neighborhood into one of the more desirable locales for young people living in the city. Meanwhile, Over the Rhine's brewing heritage has in turn enriched the breweries, which sometimes have consciously adopted motifs of the neighborhood's storied past in their marketing operations.

The development of these breweries' local identities is crucially dependent on the ability of these industries to develop surrounding ecosystems of sustenance. Such ecosystems clearly draw from local, regional, and national factors, and there might be sociocultural and locational differences between regions. What might be true for Portland, Oregon, certainly might not be true for Portland, Maine, given their distinct history and respective commercial importance in their regions. Larger and more commercially vibrant cities might draw from multiple existing business ecosystems that might not be available in smaller or economically depressed regions. These ecosystems might have crossover effects; the benefits of one industry might cross into another. Future research might engage with some of the varied factors that influence the creation of commercial and cultural environments in different locales.

The preceding analysis shows the development of an ecosystem in one industry—craft beer. Without an ecosystem approach to our analysis, we would have been unable to fully understand much of the success the industry is currently experiencing. The success of the craft-brewing pioneers paved the way for the next-generation entrepreneurs, whose success depended on developing the ecosystem they inherited. The success of these breweries in turn attracted new interest and investment in these areas. In fact, it is because brewers were able to craft new networks of support, and to leverage particular economic and political opportunities within and across communities, that they continue to grow and succeed. The industry, garnering support from local and national guilds alike, seems able to continue leveraging their success, and brewers are regularly making moves to help stake their claim against big beer. We also have seen much evidence of these entrepreneurs' social competency. By connecting with others, they built an industry with its own organizational culture and a loyal customer base, both of which have sustained their continued development. Last, developing in-group solidarity, generating guilds, and establishing an identity against mass production likely comprises a successful formula for other craft areas to follow. As craft distilling increases and creatives begin setting up shops on Etsy and similar venues, they'd do well to take cues from the strong and transportable model of craft beer. As with brewing, crafting an ecosystem in another creative field might serve to raise tides for other entrants. Indeed, the story of craft breweries shows the potential of renewed industrial entrepreneurship in America at a time of deindustrialization.

References

Alasuutari, Pertti. 1985 "The Male Suburban Pub-goer and the Meaning Structure of Drinking." *Acta Sociologica* 28(2):87–97.

Baron, Robert A. and Gideon D. Markman. 2003. "Beyond Social Capital: The Role of Entrepreneurs' Social Competence in their Financial Success." *Journal of Business Venturing* 18(1):41–60.

Bhogaraju, Sirisha. 2015. "Why Is Beer Losing Ground to Wine and Spirits?" *Market Realist*. Retrieved March 12, 2021 (http://marketrealist.com/2015/03/beer-losing -ground-wine-spirits/).

Bourdieu, Pierre. 1984. *Distinction: A Social Critique of the Judgment of Taste*. Cambridge, MA: Harvard University Press.

Brewers Association. 2022. "Stats and Data: National Beer Sales & Production Data." Retrieved July 29, 2022 (https://www.brewersassociation.org/statistics-and-data /national-beer-stats/).

Carroll, Glenn. 2011. "It's Not About the Beer, Really." Pp. 124–27. In *Market Entry, Competitive Dynamics, and Entrepreneurship*, edited by P. Phan and G. Markman. Cheltenham, UK: Edward Elgar.

Carroll, Glenn and Anand Swaminathan. 1991. "Density Dependent Organizational Revolution in the American Brewing Industry from 1633 to 1988." *Acta Sociologica* 34:155–75.

Carroll, Glenn and Anand Swaminathan. 2000. "Why the Microbrewery Movement? Organizational Dynamics of Resource Partitioning in the US Brewing Industry." *American Journal of Sociology* 106(3):715–62.

Cavanaugh, Jillian R. 2007. "Making Salami, Producing Bergamo: The Transformation of Value." *Ethnos* 72(2):149–72.

Cohen, Boyd. 2006. "Sustainable Valley Entrepreneurial Ecosystems." *Business Strategy and the Environment* 15(1):1–14.

Cotter, Dan. 2012. "Putting Atlanta Back to Work: Integrating Light Industry into Mixed-Use Urban Development." Georgia Tech Enterprise Innovation Institute. Retrieved August 12, 2022 (https://stip.gatech.edu/wp-content/uploads/2012/10/STIP-Dan-Cotter.pdf).

De Carolis, Donna Marie and Patrick Saporito. 2006. "Social Capital, Cognition, and Entrepreneurial Opportunities: A Theoretical Framework." *Entrepreneurship Theory and Practice* 30(1):41–56.

Feld, Brad. 2012. *Startup Communities: Building an Entrepreneurial Ecosystem in Your City.* Hoboken, NJ: John Wiley and Sons.

Geiling, Natasha. 2013. "What Caused the Death of American Brewing?" *Smithsonian Magazine.* Retrieved July 28, 2022 (https://www.smithsonianmag.com/arts-culture/what-caused-the-death-of-american-brewing-21155872/).

Granovetter, Mark S. 1973. "The Strength of Weak Ties." *American Journal of Sociology* 78(6):1360–80.

Hechavarria, Diana and Amy Ingram. 2014. "A Review of the Entrepreneurial Ecosystem and the Entrepreneurial Society in the United States: An Exploration with the Global Entrepreneurship Monitor Dataset." *Journal of Business and Entrepreneurship* 26(1):1–35.

Homebrewers Association. 2017. "Homebrewing Rights Statutes." Retrieved July 28, 2002 (https://www.homebrewersassociation.org/homebrewing-rights/statutes/).

Isenberg, Daniel. 2010. "How to Start an Entrepreneurial Revolution." *Harvard Business Review* 88(6): 40–50.

Isenberg, Daniel. 2011. "The Entrepreneurship Ecosystem Strategy as a New Paradigm for Economic Policy: Principles for Cultivating Entrepreneurship." *Presentation at the Institute of International and European Affairs.*

Jansson, Andre. 2003. "The Negotiated City Image: Symbolic Reproduction and Change through Urban Consumption." *Urban Studies* 40(3):463–79.

Johnston, Josée and Shyon Baumann. 2007. "Democracy versus Distinction: A Study of Omnivorousness in Gourmet Food Writing." *American Journal of Sociology* 113(1):165–204.

Kell, John. 2017. "Incredibly, Americans Drank Less Alcohol in 2016." *Fortune,* June 1, 2017 (http://fortune.com/2017/06/01/americans-drinking-less-alcohol/).

Lee, Sam Youl, Richard Florida, and Zoltan Acs. 2004. "Creativity and Entrepreneurship: A Regional Analysis of New Firm Formation. *Regional Studies* 38(8):879–91.

Lyons, James. 2005. "Think Seattle, Act Globally: Specialty Coffee, Commodity Biographies, and the Promotion of Place." *Cultural Studies* 19(1):14–34.

Malecki, Edward J. 2018. "Entrepreneurship and Entrepreneurial Ecosystems." *Geography Compass* 12(3):1–21.

Markusen, Ann and Greg Schrock. 2006. "The Distinctive City: Divergent Patterns in Growth, Hierarchy and Specialisation." *Urban Studies* 43(8):1301–23.

Mellor, Jody, Megan Blake, and Lucy Crane. 2010. "'When I'm Doing a Dinner Party I Don't Go for the Tesco Cheeses': Gendered Class Distinctions, Friendship and Home Entertaining." *Food, Culture & Society* 13(1):115–34.

Morelein Brewery. 2016. "Christian Moerlein Brewing Honors German Beer Purity Law with New Pilsner." *Brewbound.* Retrieved July 28, 2022 (https://www .brewbound.com/news/christian-moerlein-brewing-honors-german-beer -purity-law-new-pilsner/).

Ozcan, Pinar and Kathleen M. Eisenhardt. 2009. "Origin of Alliance Portfolios: Entrepreneurs, Network Strategies, and Firm Performance." *Academy of Management Journal* 52(2):246–79.

Pierce, Nathan. 2015. "How to Get an SBA Loan for a Microbrewery." *MicroBrewr*, May 26, 2015. (http://microbrewr.com/how-to-get-sba-loan-for-startup -brewery/).

Pitelis, Christos. 2012. "Clusters, Entrepreneurial Ecosystem Co-creation, and Appropriability: A Conceptual Framework." *Industrial and Corporate Change* 21(6):1359–88.

Spigel, Ben. 2017. "The Relational Organization of Entrepreneurial Ecosystems." *Entrepreneurship: Theory and Practice* 41(1):49–72.

Stam, Eric. 2015. "Entrepreneurial Ecosystems and Regional Policy: A Sympathetic Critique." *European Planning Studies* 23(9):1759–69.

Tian, Kelly Tepper, William O. Bearden, and Gary L. Hunter. 2001. "Consumers' Need for Uniqueness: Scale Development and Validation." *Journal of Consumer Research* 28(1):50–66.

Postcard from Helsinki

TEEMU VASS

There is an island just offshore of Helsinki, Finland, that is not only central to the city's history but also has links to the local brewing industry and beer trade. This is the 270-year-old maritime fortress of Suomenlinna, which today is home to Finland's oldest craft brewery. I went there to re-create a strong Baltic porter with a pioneer of the Helsinki craft-brewing scene. The porter was inspired by a style that is part of a long tradition in Finland and all the countries around the Baltic Sea. This is the story of that beer, and also the story of a beer city.

OCTOBER 2018

"This is the biggest amount of malt I've ever put into a beer," Mikko says, emptying bags containing six different types of malts into the kettle.

That is saying something. Mikko Salmi has been a brewer for more than two decades, working over the years with several local breweries. We stand next to the steel kettles in the brewpub of Suomenlinna Brewery, only a fifteen-minute ferry ride from the Market Square of Helsinki, Finland's capital. The front door of the brewpub is only a few steps away from the island's main ferry pier.

In addition to this brewpub, Suomenlinna Brewery also has a bigger brewhouse out of town. The tap beers served on the island are still made on site. This is where Salmi has been brewing all summer, fifteen brews in total, including a pils, a Belgian-style witbier, and a new Hopfenweisse. Now, in October, his last beer of the season is set to be a Baltic porter.

This is a style of beer that draws its inspiration from dark and bitter London beers of the eighteenth and nineteenth centuries. On Baltic shores, however, it evolved in its own distinct ways. Porters were presumably never the number-one favorites of beer drinkers in this country. In fact, even some of the better-known ones such as Sinebrychoff Porter always represented a tiny share of the brewery's output.

The brewpub is located in the nineteenth-century jetty barracks next to the ferry pier. *Photo: Liisa Huima*

But porters have been around the longest. They came when the old top-fermented beers of Finnish cities were already on their way toward extinction, and were there before Munich lagers and other Bavarian and Bohemian styles started to arrive.

This black-beer style is therefore a long, persisting strand in the "beer DNA" of Finland and its capital city. In appearance, it is not unlike the murky waves of the Baltic Sea itself on a cold day. It was first brewed in Helsinki almost 190 years ago, and for a few decades in that distant past it became a must-have in almost every local brewery's beer range.

HELSINKI, A BALTIC BEER CITY

The summer of 2018 has been the hottest in living memory. Even on a bright autumn day, the island of Suomenlinna is still moderately busy. School groups and the last remaining tourist hordes wander among the granite-gray fortifications. Grass now covers most of these, and autumn foliage colors the old trees on the island. Most of the buildings of the once mighty fortress are now museums or private homes, but a naval academy and an old dockyard are still in operation. Many artists have made Suomenlinna their home.

The stone-paved streets surrounding the present-day Suomenlinna Brewery are haunted by the ghosts of two brothers whose name has become almost synonymous with brewing in Helsinki. The "Russian Merchants' Quarter" next to the brewery's backyard within the island fortress was once home to Nikolai and Paul Sinebrychoff and their younger siblings.

While Salmi is filtering mash at the brewery—it's a long process with this amount of malt—I take a stroll around the island. Stepping out of the front door of the modern-day brewpub, I can only imagine the noise and bustle when thousands of marines still occupied the island. They would have walked past here on their way to the canteen where Nikolai Sinebrychoff (1786–1848) sold his food and beverages.

In 1819, the entrepreneurial brothers founded what would become Finland's all-time most successful brewery. Their little Suomenlinna house was its first headquarters. In this tiny brewery, Nikolai produced what he needed to quench his military clients' thirst, before the great Sinebrychoff brewhouse was built on the mainland a few years later.

Although some of the earliest history of Helsinki is lost in the mists of time, one can safely say that this has been a beer-drinking city ever since its beginnings. Founded in 1550, Helsinki is a young city on the European scale. Thus, it has no medieval history going back to the Hanseatic Golden Age. Only with the construction of the Suomenlinna fortress in the mid-eighteenth century did Helsinki's history of commercial beer production start to take recognizable shape.

Even so, imports from German lands may have reached the young harbor town in its early days. Archeologists have unearthed remains of German drinking cups at the site where the Swedish king Gustav Vasa, then the ruler of Finland, had the first foundations of Helsinki built. Apart from the royal estate, several burghers brewed beer for their own houses and were also allowed to sell it to thirsty passersby.

Well into the Sinebrychoffs' glory days, when they had begun brewing on the mainland, Nikolai insisted on living in his wooden house on Suomenlinna. He did so until the end of his life, with his dog Dundas running around his feet and various kinds of cattle and poultry making noise in the backyard. After his death, the house was shipped off the island and still stands next to the Sinebrychoff brewery's nineteenth-century headquarters in downtown Helsinki.

The link between Sinebrychoff and Suomenlinna was finally severed when the brewing dynasty's founding generation passed away. No brewing seems to have taken place on the island for a long time. It most likely lay dormant until the current brewpub opened in 1995, established by two young men who had no connection at all with the Sinebrychoffs.

DESIGNING A PORTER

In the early nineteenth century, discerning drinkers in Helsinki had gotten to know a completely new and fashionable style of beer: *porter*. It was probably first brewed locally by a merchant-brewer called Langeen in 1832, and the style was later adopted by Sinebrychoff and a bunch of other breweries. An inventory from the Sinebrychoff brewhouse shows that porter was brewed only in the winter months. Although strong porters may have been brewed year-round in the Baltic Sea region, there are also more recent examples of Estonian breweries producing special winter porters.

It is appropriate, therefore, that our strong porter in Suomenlinna is also going to be a winter seasonal. Style-wise it is certainly a Baltic porter. But as there has already been talk that the brewpub needs a special winter-warmer beer, we brew our strong porter so that it will have time to ripen in the tanks to be put on tap for the coldest months.

Salmi and I had a chat about our porter some weeks prior to the actual brewing day, to plan what it should be like. Some ideas from Poland had caught on with me after I discussed the topic with Marcin Chmielarz, a Polish expert on Baltic porters, in Warsaw the previous summer. Porter is of course originally a London beer dating back to the early eighteenth century, but by the late nineteenth century it had spread all over northern Europe, including Poland and Finland.

From what Chmielarz told me, I understood that Poles like to make their porters stronger than traditional Baltic porters elsewhere, often 8 percent to 10 percent ABV or even above, and design them so that they keep well in the cellar.

This means using robust German-style malts such as Munich or Caramel and brown malts. The hopping should allow long-term development of the taste, so hop varieties with high levels of alpha acids are not recommended—better to choose one with approximately equal amounts of beta and alpha acids, both preferably low. The original gravity should be considerable, over 20° Plato, and the resulting ABV high enough to exclude excessive sweetness.

Salmi says he tends to mash in at 50°C (122°F) for a porter, but prefers this time to follow the Suomenlinna house style of starting at 45° (113°F) and gradually increasing the temperature. Of the six different malts he throws in, the bulk is Pale Ale malt, but smaller amounts of Caramel 100, Caramel 300, Dark, Chocolate and Black also go in.

Why did we not opt for a specifically Finnish porter recipe? One reason is that virtually no historical recipes seem to have survived. Making a clone of the famous Sinebrychoff Porter did not seem the right choice. For me, this project is at least partly about the mystery of the old black beers that were once so popular and that we now know so little about.

Salmi agreed that we should not stress too much about the particular ingredients but instead try to roughly follow their own initial ideas. We would take malts and hops that the brewery happened to have in store and mix those to end up with a decent recipe. He suggested that I try to get hold of some Polish hops, if for no other reason than to make it a symbolic tribute to the country that is now home to perhaps the most active Baltic porter scene.

I managed to source some Lublin hops, native to eastern Poland, which Salmi now adds to the beer in the whirlpool. The rest of the hop bill was picked more or less randomly from the brewery reserves, and they are all British—East Kent Goldings. I have seen an American homebrewer warn against using UK hops in Baltic porters. But I refuse to be purist about a beer style that, for me, is mainly defined not by a set of orthodox ingredients but its peculiar, multilayered history.

That said, the yeast we use is a lager yeast. Thus the beer will be (at least in terms of yeast genetics) a relative of the porters made by major brewers in Poland, Estonia, Latvia, Lithuania, Russia, and Denmark—but not of Sinebrychoff Porter, which, like some new craft-brewed versions of the style, is made with ale yeast.

Baltic porter as a stylistic term is in fact hard to define on any grounds other than geographical origin. It seems to have been coined by British beer writer Michael Jackson, writing in the early nineties about East European porters that were brewed with bottom-fermenting

yeast and probably tasted markedly different from any English porter or stout. But Baltic porter cannot be defined simply as a "porter
brewed with lager yeast"; Jackson himself praised Sinebrychoff's top-
fermenting porter as one of the best specimens of the Baltic porter
tradition.

Later, in early November, Mikko would send me a text saying he'd
had a little try of the beer: he considered it technically flawless and
added that the taste was very promising. Starting from an original gravity of 20.4° Plato in October, the ABV has settled at somewhere under
8 percent, which is suitable for the style.

A SENSE OF OPTIMISM IN THE AIR

Until the 1980s, Sinebrychoff's porter—then the only Finnish remnant of the style—had long been considered an oddity in an otherwise
extremely uniform beer scene dominated by pale lager. Audiences did
not immediately warm to it when Sinebrychoff reintroduced it in 1957,
and even much later it was regularly blended with mild lager to soften
its "extreme" taste and strength. As in many other countries, it took
a British beer scribe to inject confidence into the Finns and make us
realize that interesting beer was brewed here.

Something began to stir at the turn of the 1990s, albeit slowly. I
asked Olli Majanen, a pub manager and beer sommelier with more
than thirty years' experience in the trade, to share with me some of his
reminiscences about those days. In the early nineties, Majanen worked
at Pub Angleterre and William K, both Helsinki frontrunners in the
country's newfound interest in special beers.

As we chat, we sit in front of the brewing kettles at Bryggeri
Helsinki, a brewpub where Majanen is now manager. This place is right
in the center of the oldest part of the city, fifty meters from the Market
Square. I'm drinking their strong porter, put on tap a couple of weeks
earlier as a seasonal special.

"In the late eighties, you could see something new was going on as
it became easier to import beers," Majanen says. In a country where the
state monopoly controlled all aspects of alcohol policy, imported beers
had been nearly nonexistent after Prohibition (which Finland repealed
in 1932). At the turn of the nineties, Guinness came to be on tap at
Angleterre and a couple of other pubs and was well received. In the following years, draught foreign specialty beers arrived in Helsinki one by

Pouring a porter at the Suomenlinna brewpub. *Photo: Liisa Huima*

one. Hoegaarden wheat beer from Belgium was a revelation for many, as was the Yorkshire classic Old Peculier.

Beer culture was a new term the local media was increasingly using. Finnish beer had an image of being folksy and underappreciated, and many felt that this perception could—and should—be changed. Where once a discerning customer had walked up to a bar to order a gin and tonic, it was believed, they should now be offered a selection of world-class beers.

In the early nineties, however, virtually no one in Finland brewed specialty beers. Sahti existed, of course, but it was a beer made at home—mostly in the countryside—or available from a handful of tiny commercial producers in the inland provinces. Apart from this, the sole Finnish beer that deviated significantly from the lager norm was Sinebrychoff Porter, an export stout-style beer at around 7.5 percent ABV.

Despite its local fame, this remnant of the Finnish porter tradition was only available in bottles, never on tap. It took Olli Majanen's tenacity to persuade the brewery to keg some of the black stuff for his pub. He finally achieved this in 1995 when the beer appeared as a draught specialty at William K. In collaboration with Marston's Brewery, Sinebrychoff's master brewer has once, in 2009, brewed it for cask distribution in the United Kingdom. Apart from such rare occasions, Sinebrychoff Porter was and still is virtually always a bottled beer.

Majanen recalls an occasion when Sinebrychoff used its famous pub tram to boost the renown of the porter. The tram, named SpåraKoff, is still very popular and circulates every summer in Helsinki, the ride lasting just long enough to enjoy a leisurely pint or two. But in 1996, a special experience was offered to Michael Jackson, who was in Helsinki for one of his many visits. Writing for a Finnish beer publication, Jackson had listed Sinebrychoff's porter among his top ten beers worldwide. To make his tram ride perfect, the brewery hosts arranged for porters to be served on board. Sadly, for regular punters of the pub tram, nothing but pale lager is on offer.

In the mid-1990s, Helsinki already prided itself on its wide array of pubs and bars offering a large assortment of the world's best beers. By the time I reached the legal drinking age, Vanha, a pub at the Old Student House, had a choice of more than two hundred beers. Another pioneer was the "fish pubs" chain, which emerged in 1992 with pub names such as Janoinen Lohi (Thirsty Trout) or Hilpeä Hauki (Perky Pike).

These pubs, with their strange newfangled beers, made an impression on many people who had a budding interest in beer. One of them was Jussi Heikkilä, a young engineer with not much prior experience of specialty beers. In the course of a discussion with a friend in a pub, the idea came about to make his own brews. Heikkilä's friend suggested he start a brewery on the island where he was living, Suomenlinna. In early 1995, that wild idea came to reality when Heikkilä and his business partner, Jari Tapaninen, received a license to start brewing.

Theirs was one of the first operating licenses granted for new breweries in Finland since the establishment of the state alcohol monopoly in 1932. For decades, the official line had been that Finland "needed" no more breweries than the handful of lager giants already extant. Suomenlinna Brewery became the first new independent commercial brewery in Helsinki, only narrowly preceded by the training brewery of the Perho hospitality school. By 1995, Finland had slightly over thirty microbreweries, most of them brewpubs like Suomenlinna.

The center of Helsinki is a fifteen-minute ferry ride from Suomenlinna. *Photo: Liisa Huima*

Helsinki, which generally had been dismissed as "gray and over-controlled," turned livelier and more permissive in a relatively short time. Its burgeoning pub and restaurant scene was a key element in the transformation of urban culture that occurred in the last two decades of the twentieth century. Here lay the foundations for the next phase in the evolution of urban life in Helsinki, characterised by citizen activism and autonomous groups that often organize themselves through social media.

DECEMBER 2018

In mid-December, I walk through heavy sleet to a small, wooden house in the former working-class neighborhood of Kumpula. I've come here to see how Helsinki beer culture looks in the age of social media. This is where HOMBRE Helsinki—the Facebook community of Helsinki-area homebrewers—is holding one of their meet-ups. I am greeted at the door by Pate Pesonius, the founder of the group, who offers me a glass of imperial stout from a plastic canister.

Pesonius set up HOMBRE in 2014. It grew quickly and has now more than 1,800 members. Not that homebrewing in Helsinki is something new as such. Home beer competitions have been organized at least since the early 1990s, and a handful of activists have been brewing their own beer for more than thirty years. But the HOMBREs are a generation of serious beer geeks, who take it for granted that their favorite beer styles—however obscure these might be—can be easily found in Helsinki or any other major city.

About twenty people attend tonight. Everyone has brought with them a liter of a homebrewed beer. We try one brew after another and discuss the beers we have just tasted. They represent a plethora of styles, from low-alcohol mild ale through strong Belgian dubbel and hibiscus-raspberry saison to vanilla ice-cream rye porter.

In a survey one member posted in the community, the most popular style brewed by HOMBRE members turned out to be IPA, followed by American pale ales and wheat beers. But Helsinki homebrews are not, of course, all pale or wheaty: porter and stout were also among the styles receiving several mentions in the survey.

The imperial stouts we drink as a welcome toast at the homebrew evening (one with *Brettanomyces* yeast and one without) are imitations of Yeti Imperial Stout by the Colorado-based Great Divide Brewing Company. Despite its American influences, it is, of course, part of the same family tree as the strong porters brewed in this city for the past two centuries. Checking the Facebook group a few days later, I also notice that three members are currently trying their hand at Baltic porters.

I am impressed by all this enthusiasm, both from complete novices and more experienced homebrewers. Undoubtedly, the hobby has recently become popular on a scale never witnessed before. Some of the most devoted homebrewers end up working in one of the professional craft breweries or even setting up their own at some point. Along with Pesonius, our host for the evening, two other HOMBRE members around the table have worked for Suomenlinna Brewery.

The rise to prominence of homebrewing activists is a global phenomenon. So is the unprecedented rate at which the number of breweries has grown worldwide since the early 2010s. Finland has now more

Tasting the Baltic porter at Suomenlinna: Harry Berg (left), Mikko Salmi (middle), and Jussi Heikkilä (right). *Photo: Liisa Huima*

breweries than ever before, with the total hovering around a hundred, ten of which are in Helsinki. The number had stagnated after the first surge in the late 1990s, but a new generation has now managed to tap into the recent international trend and make it work for everyone's benefit.

TASTING THE BALTIC PORTER

Winter dusk has turned to darkness in Helsinki's South Harbor early in the evening when I head back to Suomenlinna to taste the porter Mikko Salmi and I brewed two months earlier. It is only a few days until Christmas. As the ferry edges away from the dock, the strings of lights above the Esplanadi Park and the City Hall quarter come into full view.

Gone are the Asian tourists who lined the railings of the ferry deck with their cameras on my October visit. The streets of Suomenlinna are almost deserted now, but there are lights in some windows. The brewpub, an old building with arched windows and wooden floorboards, is dimly lit for a cozy Friday evening. It offers refuge from the wind that slowly covers the island with snow. Except for their Christmas holiday, the brewpub will stay open on Wednesday to Saturday throughout the winter months.

The house beers of Suomenlinna are mostly named after personalities involved in the construction and running of the naval fortress in the eighteenth and nineteenth centuries. Currently on tap are their pils—Höpken—and a witbier called Piper. The third beer now on tap, simply called Helsinki Porter (5.4%), has long been one of the staple beers of Suomenlinna Brewery and considered a fine tipple by many connoisseurs, including Olli Majanen. For this winter, the top-fermenting porter will receive a stronger sibling.

Indeed, our strong Baltic porter is not ready yet; it is still in the lagering tanks in the brewery behind the barroom. Salmi meets me at the bar and we slip to the back corridor. In the tank room, the cold-loving lager yeast has worked its wonders for six weeks now. The plan is to mature the beer for at least another month, to let it come into its own.

We pour ourselves two glasses of the strong porter. It is dark brown, nearly black but with reddish hues visible when held against light. There is a good head of beige foam. The aroma is slightly earthy, almost reminiscent of a dark Belgian abbey beer. Tastewise, it is straightforward and well balanced, not too sweet, with licorice, lightly roasty tones and moderate hopping (33 IBU).

With this beer, the Bryggeri porter, and a couple of others, there are perhaps more old-style Baltic porters available in Helsinki this winter than at any point since the late nineteenth century. But never before has it been as likely for three or even thirteen new beers to go by unnoticed in a flurry of novelties as it is now.

Perhaps we should make more noise about our faithful old porters and stouts in this part of the world. As happy as I am about all the new, enthusiastic breweries, craft beer bars, and homebrewers reinventing Helsinki as a beer city, I want to see styles and brands that proudly acknowledge their heritage. We need renewal, but perhaps we also need beers that will still be there after fifty years, or even a hundred.

Bibliography

BeerFinland.com. 2018. "Paikkakunnat: Helsinki." Retrieved April 2, 2021 (http:// beerfinland.com/suomen_panimot/helsinki.htm).

Bonsdorff, Seppo. 1997. *Suomen Panimot. Matrikkeli Portteri-, Olut- Ja Sahti Panimoista 1756–1996.* Helsinki: Panimoliitto.

Cornell, Martyn. 2003. *Beer: The Story of the Pint. The History of Britain's Most Popular Drink.* London: Headline.

———. 2007. "The Forgotten Story of London's Porters." *Zythophile,* November 2 (http://zythophile.co.uk/2007/11/02/the-forgotten-story-of-londons-porters).

European Beer Guide. 2010. "European Beer Statistics: Number of Breweries Per Country." Retrieved February 22, 2021 (https://www.europeanbeerguide.net /eustats.htm).

Helminen, M. 1997. "Helsinki olut kaupunkina." Kvartetti. City of Helsinki Urban Facts.

Kähkönen, Heikki. 2017. "Kantapöydässä: Kaverini halki vuosikymmenten—Koffin portteri." *Viisi Tähteä,* November 2 (https://viisitahtea.com/juoma/olut /kantapoydassa-kaverini-halki-vuosikymmenten-koffin-portteri/).

Lehtinen, Anikó. 2017. "Itsenäisen Suomen oluthistoria osa 1—Kieltolaista keskio- luen vapautumiseen." Retrieved January 24, 2021 (https://olutposti.fi/itsenaisen -suomen-oluthistoria/).

Lindström, Ida and Marjo Tiirikka. 2016. *Kohtalona Suomenlinna: Suomenlinnan Salatut Elämät.* Helsinki: Into Kustannus.

Mårtenson, Gunnar. 1969. *Sinebrychoffin panimo 1819–1969.* Helsinki: Sinebrychoff.

Mäkelä-Alitalo, Anneli, Sakari Heikkinen, and Minerva Keltanen. 2009. *Sinebrychoffit.* Helsinki: Sinebrychoff Art Museum.

Nelimarkka, M. 2017. "Koffin Porter—60-vuotias klassikko." *Olutposti,* November 3 (https://olutposti.fi/10755-2/).

Niemi, Jalmari. 1952. *Suomen Panimoteollisuuden Vaiheita.* Helsinki: Panimoteollisuus Yhdistys.

Pattinson, Ronald. 2014. *Porter. Mega Book Series Volume I.* Amsterdam: Kilderkin.

Rokka, Jussi. 2011. "Finland" In *The Oxford Companion to Beer,* edited by Garrett Oliver. New York: Oxford University Press.

Ruoppila, Sampo and Timo Cantell. 2000. "Helsingin ravintolat ja kaupunkikult- tuurin elävöityminen." Pp. 35–53. In *Urbs: Kirja Helsingin kaupunkikulttuurista,* edited by Eeva Maaria Linko. Helsinki: Edita. Retrieved January 24, 2021 (http:// www.kaupunkikettu.fi/kaupunkikulttuuri.html).

Thunaeus, Harald. 1968. *Ölets historia i Sverige 1–2.* Stockholm: Almqvist & Wiksell.

Turunen, Matti. 2002. *Jos täytätte mun lasini. Suomalaisen panimo- ja virvoitusjuo- mateollisuuden vuosisata.* Helsinki: Panimo- ja virvoitusjuomateollisuusliitto.

Personal Interviews

Chmielarz, Marcon. Personal interview. July 15, 2018.

Majanen, Olli. Personal interview. November 20, 2018.

Salmi, Mikko. Personal interview. October 2, 2018.

Zwierzyna, G. Personal communication. 2018.

CHAPTER 12

The Collaborative/Competitive Dynamics behind Local Craft Beer Scenes

PAUL-BRIAN McINERNEY, TIMOTHY ADKINS, TONY PEÑA, AND SETH BEHRENDS

Introduction

As noted in this volume and elsewhere, craft breweries derive meaning from and give meaning to the specific localities in which they are situated (Barajas, Boeing, and Wartell 2017; Cserpes and McInerney 2017; Paulsen and Tuller 2017). The literature on craft brewing and cities brings the new-urbanism perspective to bear on the dynamics of a growing industry (Cabras 2017; Zukin 1997). Instead of focusing exclusively on place, in this chapter we address the phenomenon of *scene*, which we define as a geographically limited strategic action field constituted by a group of individual and collective actors who share a common identity as it relates to place. Scenes give meaning to groups of actors in a given place. They provide a communal identity (a sense of "we-ness") around which collective and individual actors organize. In the modern era, scenes are spaces of identity-based production and consumption. For example, music scenes provide literal and figurative venues for the expression of identity through specific rituals of production and consumption.

Beer scenes operate according to similar principles as other spaces of identity-based production and consumption. Craft beer drinkers present themselves as savvy consumers with discerning tastes and appreciation for both traditional and esoteric brews and brewing processes.

In this chapter, we focus on the production side—the craft brewers. Craft brewers formulate an organizational identity primarily predicated on their opposition to large actors in the field (Mathias et al. 2017). We focus on the emergence of a collective organizational identity, one predicated, beyond opposition to macro brewing, on collaboration tempered by competitive realities. We begin to explain the collaborative/competitive dynamics that operate in local craft beer scenes. We argue that scenes are co-constituted by cultural and relational facets: collective organizational identity creates the culture that unites members of a scene, and collaborative/competitive dynamics form the relational "glue" that binds organizations together as members of a scene.

We start by reviewing the literature on scenes. We then turn to the literature on organizational identity to uncover its theoretical underpinnings for a notion of collective organizational identity. Uniting these notions, we identify the theoretical pieces that bring together the cultural and relational aspects of scenes. Following a brief discussion of our data collection and analysis methods, we present our findings, which combine formal network analysis with qualitative interviews to show how fields are co-constituted by culture and relations. We end with a discussion of the implications of these findings. First, we found that the notion of scenes contributes to the literature on both organizations and culture by showing how collective organizational identities are formed and put to work in the collaborative/competitive dynamics among craft brewers. Second, we recommend that future studies employ this multifaceted approach to further develop a notion of scenes, among craft brewers as well as other industries constituted by cultural organizations, including the obvious ones like music and art, but also the less obvious, such as restaurants, bike shops, tattoo parlors, and the connections among them. Scenes give meaning to place. By studying the organizations that generate and maintain scenes, scholars can understand a key mechanism by which place is constructed.

Scenes

We continue to live in an "age of scenes" (Irwin 1977). In this chapter, we articulate how the interplay of culture and structure inform the formation of local craft beer scenes. We understand a local scene as a historically and geographically limited strategic action field constituted by a group of individual and collective actors who share a common identity as it relates to place. Existing literature on scenes reveals three key features: (1) scenes are sites of expression, consumption, and/or cultural production; (2) scenes are historically specific phenomena; and (3) scenes involve networks of actors. We explore these characteristics of scenes further next.

First, scenes are sites of expression, consumption, and/or cultural production. In his classic volume on scenes, John Irwin writes, "The label indicates that these worlds are expressive—that is, people participate in them for direct rather than future gratification—that they are voluntary, and that they are available to the public" (1977, 23). This expressiveness of scenes for people's direct gratification means that scenes are important to identities. Beer scenes allow brewers and consumers to directly participate in expressions of taste. Craft brewers advertise the freshness of their product, often announcing keg tappings or the release of some limited-edition beer. This feature of craft brewing creates an immediacy, which plays on consumers' fear of missing out, but also helps maintain relationships between brewers and drinkers. Pfadenhauer (2005) writes that scenes involve "material and/or mental forms of collective self-stylization [*sic*]." Craft brewers create elaborate branding strategies, telling consistent stories through various sites of consumer interaction (e.g., product labels, websites, tap handles, and taprooms). Relatedly, drinkers of craft beer present themselves as informed, savvy consumers with exclusive tastes. Websites of craft-brewing companies usually have biographies of brewers and staff that align with their organizational identity.

Second, scenes have histories and are themselves historically specific phenomena. They are born; they often get co-opted; and they eventually die (Irwin 1977). For instance, the Chicago beer scene was ostensibly born with the founding of Goose Island Beer Company in 1988. It was co-opted with the sale of Goose Island to Anheuser-Busch in 2011. However, the Chicago beer scene shows no sign of dying anytime soon. Rather, like other beer scenes throughout the country, Chicago's continues to grow. As historically specific phenomena, contemporary scenes emerge out of the social fragmentation of the postindustrial era, which exhibits "no overarching symbol system . . . capable of imparting unequivocal meaning to everyday life" (Nash 1979, 435). Silver, Clark, and Yanez (2010, 2293) explain that "scenes grow more important in less industrial, more expressively-oriented and contingent societies where traditional constraints fall and self-motivated action around consumption, leisure, and amenities is a more important feature of social cohesiveness and interaction." The United States certainly fits this description, which may explain the proliferation of various scenes, from the punk and disco scenes that took root in the 1970s to the beer scenes of today. Pfadenhauer (2005) calls scenes a form of "post-traditional community building." Craft brewers employ myriad strategies to build communities around their brands, but also among themselves. Examples of the former include hosting events at their breweries and organizing festivals. Examples of the latter include sharing recipes, techniques, and ingredients among themselves.

Third, scenes involve networks. Pfadenhauer (2005) observes that they are a "thematically-focused cultural network of people." This facet of scenes expresses their meso-level structural and cultural components. Scenes emerge from the co-production of personal, organizational, and locational identities. In this chapter, we limit our analyses to relationships among producers. However, there is strong evidence of ties among consumers as well. For example, the beer rating app Untappd has several built-in community-building features, such as being able to connect with other users and read their reviews. Maher (2009) calls for more use of network theory in scene studies. Network theories encompass both formalist and relational frameworks, meaning that while some apply formal social-network analytical methods to uncover structural features of social worlds, others focus on the intersubjective nature of relationships as well as the meaning and content of ties (Erikson 2013). In this chapter, we bring together formalist and relational approaches by modeling the networks of collaborations among craft brewers in the Chicago scene and presenting interview data about the content of the relationships that define the scene. Silver, Clark, and Yanez (2010) see scenes as characterized by a "cluster of amenities" that serves the scene's needs of consumption, interaction, and cohesion. In beer scenes, such amenities include beer festivals and guest taps, not to mention release parties for new products.

In sum, the literature on scenes identifies three key aspects that we have reviewed here and that apply to beer scenes. However, this literature has primarily studied the consumer side of scenes, and lacks an awareness of the importance of organizations in the (re)production of scenes. Organizations are implied in these definitions, dubbed "amenities," "contents," or "establishments," but are not articulated.

By contrast, our analysis of scenes focuses on the producer side.

We believe organizations structure a scene and act upon it—this being one of the meso-level mechanisms through which individuals define, participate in, or claim membership to scenes. Whereas consumers may voluntarily participate in scenes out of an expression of distinctive tastes, we contend that both cultural taste expression and the pursuit of profit may motivate organizational behavior in the scene. This duplexity is what is implied in the notion of collaborative/competitive dynamics that we explore in this chapter.

With an eye toward bringing organizations into focus within scenes, we limit our analysis here to the behavior and network structure of organizations in craft beer scenes, rather than the full interplay of the individuals and organizations that constitute them. We use a mixed-methods approach that combines quantitative analyses of organizational behavior and structure with in-depth interviews where individuals-as-organizational-actors expound this behavior. To facilitate an organizational analysis of scenes, however, it is useful to introduce the concept of *fields*.

The focus of this chapter, scenes, is deeply connected to the concept of field. The literature on fields offers insights that complement theories of scenes, especially in their organizational composition. Fligstein and McAdams (2012, 9) define a strategic action field as "a constructed meso-level social order in which actors (who can be individual or collective) are attuned to and interact with one another on the basis of shared (which is not to say consensual) understandings about the purposes of the field (including who has power and why), and the rules governing legitimate action in the field." Thus, although the literature on organizational fields is vast, one of the connective tissues of field studies is actors' development of shared meanings and the emergence of formal and informal rules that govern legitimate behavior and organizational forms within them (Bourdieu 1996).

Through our focus on scenes, we are able to draw an analytical connection to fields. We can draw two key conceptual differences between scenes and fields to make the letter a useful designation in the literature on organizations and markets. The notion of scenes highlights different mechanisms at work in the emergence and maintenance of a group of organizations, which may also limit the use of the concept to specific arrangements among certain types of organizations.

First, scenes are geographically delimited—that is, they are highly localized in space. Members of scenes tend to operate within the same city, town, or region. In the empirical case that follows, we use data from the craft-brewing scene in Chicago, which includes key members from the suburbs and even a neighboring state (Three Floyds in Munster and 18th Street Brewery in Hammond, both in Indiana). In certain instances, scenes may be virtual, such as a group of music fans who communicate over the internet to discuss goings-on in their chosen genre (Bennett and Peterson 2004). Similarly, actors in fields need not be geographically proximate (Martin 2003; Scott 1994). For example, ranking agents, such as *U.S. News and World Report*, have come to play an important role in the legal education field, which itself spans the country (Sauder 2008). In the beer scene, such actors include Untappd and RateBeer, which provide virtual venues for consumers to interact through ratings and friend networks. Similarly, beer groups abound on Facebook and other online sites. Some are discussion based, whereas others coordinate bottle exchanges, which allow for translocal involvement in beer scenes.

Second, scenes consist of individual and collective actors who share a collective identity that ties members to a local scene. Collective identity is a key component of how members recognize others in the scene. Localized collective identities unite members of a scene. For example, San Diego has a particularly strong craft-brewing scene. Its members identify themselves based on their connection to the locality, which is reflected in both their branding and the styles of beer they tend to offer.

Thus, we define scenes as historically and geographically limited strategic action fields constituted by individual and organizational actors who share a common identity as it relates to place and who act toward scenes' cultural and organizational reproduction.

Collective Organizational Identity among Craft Brewers

According to our definition, scenes are predicated on collective identity— a certain sense of "we-ness" shared by their participants. Our argument following this is that scenes are co-constituted by consumers and producers. Much of the literature on scenes focuses on the production and maintenance of collective identities among consumers of culture, such as the straight edge movement in hardcore music (Haenfler 2004). Complementarily, we focus on the organizational component of scenes, which necessitates a discussion of collective *organizational* identity. The formation of collective organizational identity takes place in scenes as organizations relate to one another, often defining themselves in opposition to some kind of perceived threat. For craft brewers, this threat takes the form of incumbent macro-brewers (Mathias et al, 2017).

Organizational identity provides the framework for answering the existential dilemma many collectives face as to "who we are as an organization." Early considerations in developing a response to this dilemma drew upon the perspectives of the internal actors within an organization to identify characteristics that were distinctive and enduring core features (Albert and Whetten 1985). These features, in turn, emerge as a set of commitments, actions, and official claims (Gioia and Hamilton 2016) that establish the organization as a social actor. The internal constituents of the organization are then enmeshed in a recursive process of sense making and sense giving—the latter being conducted through top management—via a continual negotiation "with each other and their environment to arrive to some understanding of who they are" (Gioia et al. 2010, 6) and comprising a set of individual-level processes of discourse, cognition, and behavior that fosters the identity (Kreiner and Murphy 2016). In this regard, organizational identity becomes linked to organizational identification, where the individual actor's membership in the collective is affected by the organizational environment through various levels of interaction, and primacy is placed on interactions and cognitive processes.

This perspective provides insight into how internal membership plays a role in framing the identity of an organization and, more specifically, how this interaction generates a relational identity between individual actors and the collective organization. Organizations—particularly those that have shared characteristics, values, and goals—tend to occupy a similar social space (Clegg, Rhodes, and Kornberger 2007) or population (Carroll 1985; Hannan and Freeman 1984; Negro, Visentin, and Swaminathan 2014) that also shapes organizational identity. Identification occurs among microbreweries to provide legitimacy and affirm identity, whereas the large-scale microbreweries (or those operating with a microbrewery label) provide a disidentification referent.[1]

Within the realm of organizational identity, specifically among specialist organizations that have limited focus and resources (Carroll 1985), two additional factors come into play that relate to production processes, presentation, and final product (which returns to the external audience as a status signal). The first factor, authenticity, is an essential component of organizational identity within the small-scale food and service industry. Authenticity describes the ways in which an organization stays "true to craft," or in line with its categorization, while holding onto central values that make it distinctive through moral or idiosyncratic means (Carroll and Wheaton 2009). The second factor is collaboration. When breweries collaborate, a complex identity unfolds in which the product not only establishes the market identity of the breweries involved but also acts as a link between the organizational identity of one brewery to another, potentially increasing the lesser-known brewery's perceived authenticity and legitimacy within the industry. The aggregation of collaborations and identities produces the structural and cultural dynamics of a scene. Among craft brewers, collaborative dynamics are tempered by competition, to which we now turn.

Collaborative/Competitive Dynamics in Scenes

Despite a collective identity that is tied to a locale, craft-brewing scenes are marked by collaborative/competitive dynamics among producers. Such dynamics, often called *coopetition* in the management literature, are a feature of many industries (Walley 2007). Among craft brewers, collaboration takes place informally as firms share ingredients, recipes, techniques, and equipment, and formally as firms create periodic, limited-run, cobranded products. Collaboration among craft brewers takes place against the backdrop of competition. In the industry, material competition takes place for consumers, shelf space in stores, and tap handles at bars and restaurants. Symbolic competition also happens as craft brewers compete over authenticity—the degree to which organizational identity aligns with audience expectations of being "true to form." To examine these collaborative/competitive dynamics, we collected quantitative and qualitative data about the structure and culture of the craft-brewing scene in Chicago.

Methods

The data for this chapter come from a National Science Foundation–funded multimethod study of the craft-brewing industry (Award #1734503). In it, we combined formal social network analysis and qualitative interviews. Formal social network analysis entailed collecting data from online sources to model collaboration networks for all the craft breweries in our sample. The larger project includes craft brewers in California, Colorado, and Illinois. For this chapter, we limit our analysis to the Illinois dataset. We conducted qualitative interviews with a sample of craft brewers in Illinois, based on our network analysis. Formal social network methods captured the structural aspects of scenes, including collaborative dynamics. Qualitative interviews captured the cultural aspects of scenes, including competitive dynamics. Illinois provides an excellent field site in which to explore the cultural and structural aspects of scenes. The state boasts a robust sample of craft brewers (n = 269). From this sample, we generated 231 collaborations between 2009 and 2016. Illinois craft brewers tend to be concentrated in Chicago (n = 75) and its nearby suburbs (n = 119). Chicago has also recently become the US city with the largest number of breweries in its metropolitan area (Watson 2018). As the chief economist at the Brewers Association notes, "I don't think Chicago is thought of with places like Seattle or Portland. . . . But certainly these numbers underscore a huge development in Chicago's brewing scene in the last few years" (Noel 2018b).

Network Data Collection and Analysis

We created a dataset of collaborations between two or more brewers in which at least one of them had been located in Illinois for the years 2009 through 2016.[2] Collaboration data were collected from several websites that track individual beer releases and provide user ratings, including RateBeer and Untappd. The collection processes started with a list of brewers who were members of the Brewers Association and located in Illinois, then grew as other smaller and newer brewers were added (and are continually being added as new breweries are founded in the state).

To capture the ephemeral collaborations among brewers, we generated a list of collaborative beers from the beer-rating site RateBeer. RateBeer is a user-driven website on which beer enthusiasts post tasting notes, reviews, and ratings of various beers. Despite being user driven rather than industry driven, RateBeer provides a comprehensive list of brewers and the beers they produce. Using the site's search features, we identified all collaboratively produced beers with at least one review or rating. Since we collected these data, RateBeer has been fully purchased Anheuser-Busch InBev, leading some craft brewers to pull their ratings from the site. We verified collaboratively produced beers and expanded our list with data from the beer rating app Untappd. Using these sources provided a robust list of collaborations. The advantage of this technique is that it captures all beers that reach the market, even products that did not make it into stores but rather were sold exclusively in taprooms or bars.

To further verify the collaborations in our dataset, we alphabetized the list, then individually researched each brewer to find instances of their collaboration products not captured through RateBeer and Untappd.

From this search, we generated a list of 231 collaboration beers. We entered data in an Excel spreadsheet to track and record variables of each collaborative beer. Variables included the collaborating brewers (up to three), their respective locations, the facility in which the beer was brewed, the initiator of the collaboration process, the number of user reviews for the specific beer, the date of the first review (used to approximate release of beer), the actual ratings in both a mean and adjusted average (which takes into account smaller numbers of ratings and permits comparisons across beer styles to other ratings), the beer name, the beer style, and the website link to find the collaboration (on RateBeer, BeerAdvocate, Untappd, the brewer's website, or in other articles). Both the number of ratings and the rating values were recorded from the specific website of the link given. Importantly, we excluded contract brewers from our sample, as we are interested in collaborative rather than subcontracting relations. We also excluded collaborations between breweries and individual brewmasters or homebrewers as well as those involving restaurants or other non-brewery entities (e.g., PseudoSue Pale Ale, Toppling Goliath's collaboration with Chicago's Field Museum).

We analyzed and plotted network data in R using the statnet and ggplot2 packages. Among the analyses we conducted was to determine the centrality of brewers' network relationships. Rather than reporting centrality scores for all the breweries in our sample, we report betweenness-centrality (BC) scores—a measure of network position in which an actor sits on more or fewer shortest paths between other brewers—for respondents in the citations for their quotes. This gives some indication for the reader of how the respondent's brewery is situated vis-à-vis other breweries in the network. In the next section, we describe our interview strategy.

Interviews

Because ours was a mixed-method study, we also conducted interviews with a sample of Chicago craft brewers. Respondents were selected based on their position in the formal collaboration networks described in the previous section. Rather than focusing on the core actors in the network we worked to obtain a sample that represented a wide swath of positions. As a result, we identified 62 respondents (out of approximately 220 craft brewers in the state) to target for interviews. This research draws from our analysis of twenty-four interviews. Seven craft breweries in our sample closed before we could interview a representative from their organization, and one declined to participate. We continue to solicit interview respondents at the time of this writing.

Interviews generally lasted between forty-five and ninety minutes. Substantively, interviews focused on the history and structure of the organization, aspects of their relationships to other brewers (including formal and informal relationships), and respondents' sense of the scene and their position in it. Most of our interviews were conducted with the owners or head brewers in their respective firms. At times they were the same person. Most craft breweries in our study were relatively small firms (fewer than ten people), which ensured that the respondent with whom we spoke was knowledgeable about the workings of the firm.

Interviews were digitally recorded and later transcribed by a professional transcription service. We checked transcripts for accuracy, then conducted iterative thematic coding (Emerson, Fretz, and Shaw 1995). First-pass coding identified general themes. Iterative coding refined these themes. We were then able to connect respondents' coded data with their positions in the collaborative network to show differences in responses between core and peripheral actors in the scene. Core and periphery followed geographic lines, as craft breweries located within the city of Chicago tended to collaborate with local brewers, whereas suburban craft breweries tended to collaborate with other craft breweries located there.

Findings

Chicago's beer scene exhibits the features in the preceding "Scenes" section. We begin the presentation of our findings with evidence of the collective identity among craft brewers and how that helps connect members of the scene. From there, we explain the structural and cultural aspects of scenes and how the two interplay to undergird competitive/collaborative dynamics among craft brewers. We outline four features of scenes that temper scene members' responses to the competitive realities they face: (1) geographic subdivisions, (2) size and market footprint, (3) style and product portfolio, and (4) collaboration.

COLLECTIVE ORGANIZATIONAL IDENTITY IN CHICAGO

As mentioned earlier, research has shown that the organizational identity of craft brewers is predicated on their competition with macrobrewers (Mathias et al. 2017). However, craft brewers in our sample are aware of the limits of this practice. As one craft brewer told us, "We're taking fewer and fewer people away from Bud, Miller, Coors at this point. We're slowly reaching our critical mass. Once people are in the craft pool, they're in the craft pool" (Personal interview 8-29-2018, BC = 0). Here, this brewer is explaining his perception that the consumer part of the scene is growing, but that growth is slowing. As a result, basing organizational identity on competition with macro-brewers is becoming less viable as a strategy. Similarly, as another told us, "Honestly, Budweiser's not our biggest competitor by any stretch. The people who come to buy beer are not, 'I don't know. Am I gonna get this Bud Lite, or this $25 750 [ml bottle] of wild beer, aged?' [Budweiser is] not our competition in any way, shape, or form" (Personal interview 6-28-2018, BC = 932).

Instead, craft brewers in the Chicago scene developed an alternative basis for a collective organizational identity, one that connected them to one another and the city. As these craft brewers explained:

> Regardless of how you think about big beer in America, there's a heap of brewers there that love their jobs as much as I love my job here in this small brewery. I really respect those guys, not only for caring as much as I do, even though they're still working in a very large. . . . it's essentially a factory that just has a brewery inside of it, maybe, is a good way to think about it. They still love their job as much as I do. They still care about the final product, as well as they're a part of Chicago beer history. Part of the reason Chicago beer is on the map is because of these people are there. They're, as a group, important people. (Personal interview 9-7-2018, BC = 0)

I think part of it is the breweries that are kind of the signature breweries in Chicago, [which] are all run by very technologically sound brewers. So, some of the very flawed beer that I've tasted in other states is a little bit more rare here. . . . So, that's really nice about Chicago. The bar is set a little higher and you can pretty much get anything here. This is the birthplace of barrel-aging, right? As far as we know, Goose Island back in 1991 or whatever. We also have some of the best IPA producers here like Half Acre and Hopewell. I'll throw Three Floyds in there even though they're in Indiana, but they're in the metro area. (Personal interview 10-25-2018, BC = 128).

These two brewers identified the salience of Chicago as a geographic delimitation of a particular beer scene with its own actors and history. The end of the first quote suggests that such a place-based identity transcends the boundary of craft and macro-brewing, particularly when the actors are important to the scene's collective history. The second quote reinforces this emphasis on actors' important contributions to the scene and draws on Chicago brewers' high standard for technical mastery to construct the scene's collective organizational identity.

THE STRUCTURE OF SCENES

Seeing scenes as strategic action fields gives import to both the typical cultural elements found in scene studies as well as the structural phenomena more commonly approached by organizational scholars. By plotting the scene's network ties and using some descriptive statistics, we can attend to the structural element of craft beer scenes.

The following graph presents a network diagram reflecting collaborations on cobranded beers brought to market among craft brewers in Illinois between 2009 and 2016. As the diagram indicates, there are several clusters, indicating denser collaboration relationships between brewers, similar to social cliques. On the periphery, there are small, isolated networks where an Illinois brewer is the center of several connections with brewers outside the scene.

In general, we find that craft brewers operating within Chicago city limits collaborated on a cobranded beer at twice the rate of brewers located in the suburbs. Specifically, 52 percent of craft brewers in the city collaborated with at least one other brewery between 2009 and 2016, whereas only 24 percent of Illinois craft brewers outside Chicago

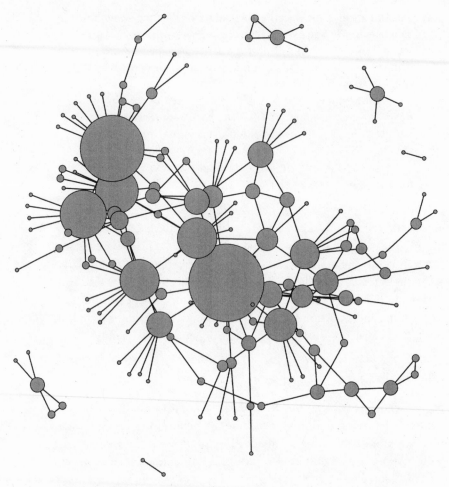

Network of Illinois craft beer collaborations, 2009–16, with most active five collaborators (and Dryhop as center node). *Note*: this graph uses a traditional Fruchterman–Reingold layout.

city limits collaborated with other breweries during that span. Of those Illinois craft brewers who did collaborate on a cobranded beer between 2009 and 2016, 59 percent were brewers located in Chicago, compared to 41 percent from elsewhere in the state. As an illustration of the geographic boundedness of scenes, networks of craft brewers in the Chicagoland suburbs appear to be clustered around specific suburban regions (e.g., southwestern suburbs vs. western suburbs). However, networks among suburban brewers tend to be less dense than networks of breweries in Chicago. Beyond these specifics, our results show how the greater Chicago area is made up of multiple interconnected scenes.

CULTURAL ASPECTS OF COLLABORATION/COMPETITION

Craft brewing is marked by collaborative/competitive dynamics, what management scholars often call *coopetition*. One of the most obvious forms of coopetition in Chicago's craft beer scene we mention throughout this chapter is collaborating on a cobranded, cross-promoted beer. Additionally, through interviews, we heard about a host of less visible tactics, such as sharing recipes and equipment or making collective bulk ingredient orders to reduce each brewer's costs. In a 2018 *Chicago Tribune* article, Hagen Dost, cofounder of Chicago's Dovetail Brewery, explained his brewery's participation in a Sierra Nevada–led fundraising event for California wildfire victims: "It's emblematic of what's great about craft beer. . . . Technically Sierra Nevada and every other brewery is our competitor—at least [they would be] in any other industry. It's just not the way craft beer works. It's a cooperative environment, and when somebody's down, you help them out" (Noel, 2018c).

Although many brewers participate formally or informally in various forms of collaboration, all are aware that they operate in an increasingly competitive market. A representative from a brewpub told us, "We're all competitors, technically, first. I mean, we're less of a competitor to folks whose main gig is distributing" (Personal interview 11-19-2014, BC = 3937). Another brewer explained the new competitive dynamics his brewery faces: "We sell to craft beer bars. We don't sell to Chili's. That's [where] the people that we actually compete against are. . . . We are all competing in Chicago for the same tap handles. There's not enough room for everybody anymore" (Personal interview 6-28-2018, BC = 932). The competitive realities are simultaneously offset by the collective organizational identity that unites members of the scene. Another brewer noted, "Obviously there's competition among other craft breweries but it doesn't feel that way. None of us behave in a way that is adversarial for the most part" (Personal interview 8-16-2018, BC = 1891).

In interviews, features of the scene tempered competitive dynamics. Specifically, craft brewers discussed four features: (1) geographic subdivisions, (2) size and market footprint, (3) style and product portfolio, and (4) collaboration. Such features temper competition within scenes of all kinds. For example, scholars have found that art scenes feature the same factors operating among galleries and museums (Velthuis 2005). The art scene in 1980s New York City featured cutting-edge galleries in the East Village and SoHo neighborhoods, with up-and-coming artists showing on the Upper East Side and well-established artists having runs at Midtown and Uptown museums. Galleries were also differentiated from one another and from museums by size. Last, galleries and museums were known for showing certain kinds of art. Respondents in our sample often expressed these factors as coexisting. We elaborate next on these features in the case of Chicago craft beer.

Geographic Subdivisions: The Hyperlocality of Scenes

Most craft breweries operate at the neighborhood level. Some brewers think about the scene as constituted by competitive neighborhood-level niches. As one brewer told us,

> we consider ourselves [this neighborhood's] craft brewery. We're the only one over here, we want to be this neighborhood's brewery that they come to and get their beer in their neighborhood. For us, it's about being connected to the community and you know those five blocks around us, north, west, east, south, and connecting with the people that live near us. I think that's what every other brewer does in the neighborhood that they're in as well. (Personal interview 11-19-2014, BC = 3937)

Explaining his choice to locate in a certain neighborhood in Chicago, another craft brewer told us, "The setting is fresh. We can see that it's gonna happen any moment. We want to be the cornerstone for a new place to hang out in the city. We believe that everybody in this neighborhood feels the same way" (Personal interview 8-3-2018, BC = 0).

Many craft breweries take advantage of Illinois's self-distribution laws to brew and sell for a specific neighborhood, such as DryHop and Haymarket, which are both brewpubs. Others, like Two Brothers, Revolution, and Half Acre, have become regional players. Goose Island Beer Company has a national market through their acquisition by Anheuser-Busch. However, they still operate their barrel-aging program while still brewing for the local market in Chicago (Noel 2018a).

Like any scene, Chicago's beer scene is constituted by actors of different sizes. We do not have systematic access to sales, production volume,
and personnel data for many of the breweries in our sample, though
we do have self-reported data from our interviews. Respondents in
our sample reported annual brewing capacity as small as 188 barrels to
as large as 15,000 barrels and employing as few as two and as many as
eighty-three people.

Size is a competitive advantage in many markets. In craft brewing, size provides economies of scale and increased negotiating power,
which allows firms to distribute their products more broadly. As
one craft brewer explained, "It starts to feel a little bit like Revolution
[Brewing] might be a competitor because of their sheer size and how
they are everywhere." He went on to explain how craft brewers that
gain the support of macro-brewers also gain competitive advantages:
"Because of their distribution network and their economies and scale,
it halts growth of craft beer. Just by the nature of that curve, there
were going to be a lot of breweries that are going to be now shut out
of airports, you know. So, it stops that level of growth and really makes
it hard for those types of breweries" (Personal interview 8-16-2018,
BC = 1891). Such recognition is remarkable given the respondent represents a fairly well-established brewery, which is also very central to
the collaboration network and, by extension, the scene.

Size differentiation among firms creates conditions for market partitioning (Carroll and Swaminathan 2000). Large firms in our sample
tended to have greater capital investments that allowed them not only
to produce greater volumes but also to can or bottle on demand, which
gave them access to distribution channels that smaller firms did not
have. Smaller firms often shared or rented equipment, such as canning
lines. They were also more likely to engage in self-distribution, either by
offering taprooms or delivering to bars and restaurants themselves. In
such instances, craft brewers did not see themselves competing across
scale. As one mid-size (8,000 barrel-per-year) craft brewer said, "You
have 15 breweries all making the exact same beer, all trying to sell it in
the exact same way. That's not helping anybody. They find a segment of
the market that really likes that. It seems to be working for them now.
I just don't see that as a long-term success strategy. . . . But again, we're
kind of an outlier anyways too, by trying to be. . . . We've always tried

to be very niche-y. Fortunately our niche, so far, carried us" (Personal interview 6-28-2018, BC = 868).

Style and Product Portfolio

Others discussed niches as defined by brewing certain styles of beer. As one craft brewer told us, "People are like, 'Oh, are they a competitor of yours?' And you're like, 'No. We make this kind of beer, and they make that kind of beer. That's why we're okay with each other.' And generally it is" (Personal interview 8-3-2018, BC = 0). As another craft brewer in the city explained,

> I don't necessarily think that a lot of people are competitors. I like to think of my local breweries [more] as peers than competitors. Let's take that brewery down the street, for example. I'm probably not going to make a lot of Belgian Pale Ale. The brewery over this way, that is what they do a lot of. A lot of Belgian IPA's, and a lot of Belgian beer in general. The other brewery that's north of us makes some really cool, classic, British styles of beer. As a Mexican influenced brewery, it's very hard for me to write a narrative where a British beer fits into that. Again, I'm probably not going to be making a lot of British Mild." (Personal interview, 8-16-2018, BC = 1891)

Another craft brewer located in the suburbs explained, "We walk a tightrope. We're small. We do creative stuff, but we like to style things. We want to be in your fridge. I really like just a great pale ale, just something straightforward, that you can pop anytime. We make a rye Kölsch. Those aren't bold brash beers, so we have to think about both those things because we're a little country, we're a little rock and roll. We have to be very careful we don't fall so in the middle that we're just left behind" (Personal interview 8-29-2018, BC = 0).

Collaboration

Collaboration reflected an important mechanism for tempering the competitive forces in the growing market. As one craft brewer explained, "[Collaboration] is a great marketing tool to talk about how you are working with your. . . . fellow industry [members]. . . . I mean it's obviously for all, in a competitive market, in terms of selling our beer to folks. But at the end of the day like I said everyone's goals are the same: to be exposed to craft beer. And collaboration certainly helps with that" (Personal interview 11-19-2014, BC = 3937). This brewer's comments highlight the tempering effect of collaboration on competition, especially in how it signals working with similar organizations in the scene. It also suggests that part of craft brewers' mutual interest in collaboration rather than strict competition is prioritizing scene development over competing for existing craft consumers. Nonetheless, there is a thread of collaboration as a conscious business strategy running through this quote. Seeing collaboration as a "marketing strategy" and aiming for people to be "exposed to craft beer" evince the competition in this field. Informally, craft brewers found that the spirit of shared organizational identity tempered the sense of competition among them. One craft brewer described it as follows:

> I guess we are all competitors in some sense, but I really still feel a sense of kinship. . . . There's basically nobody who I would wish ill on. Like in any large group of people, there are a couple jerks who I like less than other people, but for the most part, I wish well for all of the other brewers that I associate with, and we have a good time when we go to events and stuff like that. (Personal interview 8-16-2018, BC = 0).

Another explained in detail:

> Because of the nature of craft beer, it's all about hospitality, and community, and camaraderie. That melts into everything that we do as a company and as an industry. Everybody works well together. Everybody communicates with each other, everybody gets together on a regular basis. People do collaborations. We have hung out with so many different breweries and talked about all sorts of cool ideas that we'd all love to be doing. We field questions with each other, it is not uncommon for me to get weekly Emails or texts from brewers around the area. (Personal interview 8-22-2018, BC = 0)

Discussion: Toward a Structural/Cultural Theory of Scenes

Scenes are venues for cultural production and consumption. In this chapter, we focused on the production side of scenes, showing how the dynamics of competition and collaboration among groups of firms with a collective organizational identity create the "glue" that connect members of a scene. Organizational identity answers the question "Who are we as an organization?" whereas *collective* organizational identity provides a sense of "we-ness" across firms in a scene. In the case of craft brewing, much has been made of opposition to macro-breweries as the basis for organizational identity. We have explained here the limits of such opposition for forming a collective organizational identity. Rather, in the Chicago craft brewing scene, collective organizational identity was predicated on a sense that local craft brewers had a shared stake in developing and maintaining the scene. This sense operated structurally through collaborative networks. Formal ties often resulted in cobranded products. Less formal ties created networks of organizations that shared techniques, recipes, ingredients, and equipment.

With more than 150 craft breweries concentrated in and around Chicago, these firms were constantly aware of the competitive environment they faced. Craft brewers in our sample reported competing most frequently over shelf space in retail outlets and tap handles in bars. However, the "scene-ness" of the local industry means that competition was tempered by geographic subdivisions, size and market footprint, style and product portfolio, and collaboration. These scene features helped craft brewers maintain a collective organizational identity while allowing them to differentiate themselves by forming unique organizational identities, as reflected in their branding.

The features we outline in this chapter are applicable to a broad range of craft-brewing scenes. However, future research should test our claims against craft-brewing scenes in different cities and in varying levels of competitiveness. Although Chicago may host the greatest number of craft breweries in the United States, it is not the country's densest market for craft beer, nor is it the largest per capita. Competitive pressures vary across cities. We suspect that increased competitive pressure would hamper the development of collective organizational identities in different scenes. As we expand our project, we will be testing this hypothesis in additional US cities.

Last, by focusing on producers in the Chicago beer scene, we hope to shed light on the benefits of looking at scenes with an organizational lens. Whereas most scene studies focus on consumers and consumption-based identities, we highlight the producers' behavior and recursive influence on the scene. Specifically, we believe that an examination of organizations in scenes not only highlights this often-missing segment of actors but also melds scholarship on scenes with that on fields. Through interviews with brewers and structural analysis, we argue that scenes constitute strategic action fields that are historically and geographically delimited and held together by a shared, place-based identity. This redefinition allows us to simultaneously view the cultural and structural phenomena comprising scene activities. We hope that future scholarship builds on this fuller approach to industries and their subcultural communities.

Notes

1. The audience plays another central role in maintaining organizational identity. *Audience* in this context can refer to any number of actors that provide evaluation of that identity. Thus, audiences may include internal members such as employees and managers, or external members such as consumers, vendors, and other producers (Bishop Smith 2011; Carroll and Wheaton 2009; Gioia, Schultz, and Corley 2000; Kim and Jensen 2011).
2. Though technically located in Munster, Indiana, we include Three Floyds Brewery in our sample because it is considered by our respondents, among others in the Chicago craft beer industry, to be a major player in the local scene.

References

Albert, Stuart and David Whetten. 1985. "Organizational Identity." Pp. 263–95. In *Research in Organizational Behaviour, Vol. 7*, edited by L. L. Cummings and B. M. Shaw. Greenwich, CT: JAI Press.

Barajas, Jesus M., Geoff Boeing, and Julie Wartell. 2017. "Neighborhood Change, One Pint at a Time: The Impact of Local Characteristics on Craft Breweries." Pp. 155–76. In *Untapped: Exploring the Cultural Dimensions of Craft Beer*, edited by Nathaniel G. Chapman, Slade Lellock, and Cameron D. Lippard. Morgantown: West Virginia University Press.

Bennett, Andy and Peterson, Richard A. (Eds.) 2004. *Music Scenes: Local, Translocal, and Virtual*. Nashville, TN: Vanderbilt University Press.

Bishop Smith, Edward. 2011. "Identities as Lenses: How Organizational Identity Affects Audiences' Evaluation of Organizational Performance." *Administrative Science Quarterly* 56(1):61–94.

Bourdieu, Pierre. 1996. *The Rules of Art: Genesis and Structure of the Literary Field*. Stanford, CA: Stanford University Press.

Cabras, Ignazio. 2017. "A Pint of Success: How Beer Is Revitalizing Cities and Local Economies in the United Kingdom." Pp. 39–58. In *Untapped: Exploring the Cultural Dimensions of Craft Beer*, edited by Nathaniel G. Chapman, Slade Lellock, and Cameron D. Lippard. Morgantown: West Virginia University Press.

Carroll, Glenn R. 1985. "Concentration and Specialization: Dynamics of Niche Width in Populations of Organizations." *American Journal of Sociology* 90(6):1262–83.

Carroll, Glenn R. and Anand Swaminatham. 2000. "Why the Microbrewery Movement? Organizational Dynamics of Resource Partitioning in the U.S. Brewing Industry." *American Journal of Sociology* 106(3):715–62.

Carroll, Glenn R. and Dennis Ray Wheaton. 2009. "The Organizational Construction of Authenticity: An Examination of Contemporary Food and Dining in the U.S." *Research in Organizational Behavior* 29:255–82.

Clegg, Stewart R., Carl Rhodes, and Martin Kornberger. 2007. "Desperately Seeking Legitimacy: Organizational Identity and Emerging Industries." *Organization Studies* 28(4):495–513.

Cserpes, Tunde and Paul-Brian McInerney. 2017. "The Spatial Dynamics of Organizational Identity among Craft Brewers." Pp. 177–99. In *Untapped: Exploring the Cultural Dimensions of Craft Beer*, edited by Nathaniel G. Chapman, Slade Lellock, and Cameron D. Lippard. Morgantown: University of West Virginia Press.

Emerson, Robert M., Rachel I. Fretz, and Linda L. Shaw. 1995. *Writing Ethnographic Fieldnotes*. Chicago: University of Chicago Press.

Erikson, Emily. 2013. "Formalist and Relationist Theory in Social Network Analysis." *Sociological Theory* 31(3):219–42.

Fligstein, Neil and Doug McAdam. 2012. *A Theory of Fields*. New York, NY: Oxford University Press.

Gioia, Dennis A. and Aimee L. Hamilton. 2016. "Great Debates in Organizational Identity Study." Pp. 22–38. In Michael G. Pratt, Majken Schultz, Blake E. Ashford, and Davide Ravasi (Eds.), *The Oxford Handbook of Organizational Identity*. New York: Oxford University Press.

Gioia, Dennis A., Kristin N. Price, Aimee Hamilton, and James B. Thomas. 2010. "Forging an Identity: An Insider-Outsider Study of Processes Involved in the Formation of Organizational Identity." *Administrative Science Quarterly* 55(1):1–46.

Gioia, Dennis A., Majken Schultz, and Kevin G. Corley. 2000. "Organizational Identity, Image, and Adaptive Instability." *Academy of Management Review* 25(1):63–81.

Haenfler, Ross. 2004. "Collective Identity in the Straight Edge Movement: How Diffuse Movements Foster Commitment, Encourage Individualized Participation, and Promote Cultural Change." *The Sociological Quarterly* 45(4):785–805.

Hannan, Michael T. and John Freeman. 1984. "Structural Inertia and Organizational Change." *American Sociological Review* 49:149–64.

Irwin, John. 1977. *Scenes: City & Society*. New York: SAGE.

Kim, Bo Kyung and Michael Jensen. 2011. "How Product Order Affects Market Identity: Repertoire Ordering in the U.S. Opera Market." *Administrative Science Quarterly* 56(2):238–56.

Kreiner, Glen E. and Chad Murphy. "Organizational Identity Work." Pp. 276–93. In Michael G. Pratt, Majken Schultz, Blake E. Ashford, and Davide Ravasi (Eds.), *The Oxford Handbook of Organizational Identity*. New York: Oxford University Press.

Maher, Dana Nell. 2009. *The Sociology of Scenes: The Sacramento Poetry Scene*. UNLV Dissertations and Theses (https://digitalscholarship.unlv.edu/cgi /viewcontent.cgi?article=2125&context=thesesdissertations).

Postcard from Alameda

DEAN BRIGHTMAN

According to Ron Silberstein, cofounder of Admiral Maltings in Alameda, California, geography was the primary driving force in the development of the earliest beer styles, which evolved due to local "sources of energy, sources of water, sources of hops, sources of barley. The water—is it soft water, is it hard water, is it going through limestone, is it going through sandstone? *all* of that contributed to and created the original styles of beer. [Local brewers asked,] 'What can we make well here? Oh, this [ingredient] is available, that [ingredient] is available.'"

For example, "Pilsner, from the Pilsen Republic, with their soft water, noble hops, and the way they kilned or heated the malt to dry it out, versus the porters done in England with the way they coal-fired their plants."

The advent of the industrial revolution and the development of transportation systems that enabled shipping over great distances resulted in the homogenization of beer. Uniqueness of localized styles gave way to consistency. Industrial brewers grew ever larger, opening factories hundreds of miles apart that had to produce identical beers. Ingredients needed to be uniform, abundant, and cheap.

For efficiency and economy, malted grain was augmented with rice and corn, which were added not for flavor but simply to provide additional fermentable sugars for yeast to convert into alcohol.

It was in this landscape that the earliest "microbrews" (such as Anchor Liberty Ale and Sierra Nevada Pale Ale) began to appear in the late 1970s and early 1980s. These beers featured a return to all-grain brewing with no adjuncts and an emphasis on hops for flavor and aroma.

As craft brewing has evolved since the 1980s, hops have taken center stage. The runaway popularity of today's India Pale Ales, in all their variations, has turned beer labels and tap lists into virtual hop-varietal marquees, sporting names like Mosaic Promise, Galaxy Supernova, Centennial IPA, Citra Ninja, Sorachi Ace, and so on.

Admiral Maltings and its pub, the Rake, in the former Naval Air Station in Alameda, California. Admiral is one of the new wave of malt houses across the country offering customized malts to local craft brewers.

Only very recently has malt, the essential building block of beer (aside from maybe water), gotten anything close to the same attention. Although brewers by and large have been able to play and experiment with ever more exotic hop varieties from ever more local sources, they've mostly been stuck with malt from the same large, centralized malt houses that have been around for decades.

As Silberstein notes, Coors particularly took malting consistency to its highest efficiency. "They had the same variety of barley, grown in different regions of Colorado, malted the same, and made the same beer. The only difference was where it was grown. They maintained those references and called them a, b, c, d, e, f, g. A's the best, b's second, etc.

"They repeated the tests over a number of years, ranked them con-

Grain germinating at Admiral Maltings. The malt-house floor features a radiant cooling system to keep the grain at the optimal temperature for germination, especially during the summer months.

sistently each time with only minor fluctuations, and used those benchmarks to determine which areas of Colorado produced the barley most suited to their style of beer, and malted them in their own facility."

Finally, during the 2010s, the situation has shifted. The rise of the "farm-to-fork" movement has highlighted locally sourced ingredients and reconnected the relationship among farmers, crops, and consumers.

It wasn't until 2013 that the Craft Maltsters Guild formed in North Carolina—with *eight* malt houses. As demand for local ingredients has increased, that number has risen from eight to sixty-four in six years. Along with breweries, distilleries, growers, researchers, equipment manufacturers, and more, total membership has grown to more than three hundred, from all parts of the country.

A craft maltster is defined by the Guild by the following traits (Cioletti 2017; Kuehl n.d.):

- Relatively small scale. Craft Maltster produces between 5 metric tons (5.5 US tons) to 10,000 metric tons (11,000 US tons) per year.
- Source ingredients locally. Over 50 percent of grains are grown within a 500-mile radius of the Craft Malthouse.
- Independently owned. The Malthouse must be independently owned by a 76 percent majority of ownership.

According to Executive Director Jen Blair, the rise in craft maltsters has led to more parts of the country having access to local malt. "Most of the growth has been in areas considered to be non-traditional malting barley growing areas, such as New York, Michigan, and North Carolina. However, we now have craft malthouses in every region of the US."

Especially in California.

California has the fifth-largest economy on the planet (Segarra 2018). According to the California Department of Food and Agriculture, the state produced more than $50 billion in agricultural cash receipts in 2017. California grows a third of the country's vegetables and two-thirds of its fruits and nuts, and accounts for 13 percent of its total agricultural value (California Department of Food and Agriculture n.d.).

And the state seems ripe for diversification of crops. From the University of California Agriculture and Natural Resources (Mathesius 2017):

> When wheat prices drop low enough, farmers begin looking for other options. Recently, the combination of wheat prices at a 15-year low and the rise of craft brewing culture in the American west has generated inquiries into the possibility of growing malting barley.
>
> The virtual non-existence of local malting facilities is somewhat puzzling when one considers the volume and enthusiasm for craft breweries springing up in the state, not to mention the existence of the Chico-based power house, Sierra Nevada Brewing.
>
> This required step in the journey from seed to beverage has historically created a bottleneck between California's would-be barley growers and the brewing locales that specialize in creating a certain widely-enjoyed beverage.
>
> Despite the vast amount of farmland in the surrounding region

Malt sacks at Admiral Maltings, awaiting shipment to local breweries to be made into fresh, local beer.

and Sacramento's much-touted title as the Farm-to-Fork Capital, California's malting barley has largely been Washingtonian, Idahoan, and Canadian barley processed by maltsters throughout the American northwest and then shipped to California by rail. Recently however, that has begun to change.

Nile Zacherle, owner/brewer of Mad Fritz in St. Helena, California (one of the few breweries with its own malting floor), illustrates how relatively easy it could be to find local parcels to grow barley.

"Let's say you have a property in Napa Valley you're not doing anything with, that's right down the street from us. But it's just sitting there fallow, and it was left to you by your great-grandmother, and you say 'Hey, I can grow something.'

"I'll say, 'Okay, let's put in three acres of this, and two acres of that,' we can put anything in. And once you start growing grains you realize it's not really that hard."

More local growers not only equals more variety but also less reliance on industrial growing techniques. Silberstein is an evangelist for sustainably grown grain:

> All of our barley is sustainably grown. That's critical to us. I read this book called *The Soil Will Save Us*. It talks about how more carbon is sequestered in the soil than anywhere else on land. More than in the trees, more than in the Amazon, etc. Every time we plow and till the soil, you get massive releases of CO_2.
>
> So every time you plow and till until you completely disturb this synergistic world of the microbiome in the soil, a certain amount of moisture also evaporates into the atmosphere. So you need to add more moisture to the soil. Especially in areas where drought is an issue, no-till agriculture can allow you to grow something dry farmed with only rain.
>
> Lastly, especially in the Midwest where they learned this during the Dust Bowl era, when you use no-till agriculture, you don't get wind erosion or rain erosion. Often more topsoil is lost in those two forms of erosion than can be reproduced, so we rely more and more on single inputs—i.e., petroleum-based fertilizers to be put into the soil.

Indeed, Silberstein's biggest challenge has been finding and educating enough growers to fill the demand. After peaking at around 2 million acres in the 1950s, acreage for grains today is roughly only 60,000. As Silberstein details about planters' choices:

> It just shifted to tomatoes, grapes, almonds, walnuts, and we went away from cereal grains. But cereal grains are ideal because they are drought-tolerant. We can dry-farm our barley. Most of what we use, very little of it, if any, is irrigated. Some is grown on land that can be irrigated, and they might, because a key amount of water at a key time takes stress off the plant and lowers the protein level.
>
> The big thing with growing barley is that you want lower protein. If you're a traditional farmer you want high yields, because you want to grow three tons on your one acre, as opposed to two tons. But we, in contrast, want lower protein, which will lower the yield. We have to teach our farmers not to use too much fertilizer.

Admiral Maltings uses the time-honored, labor-intensive practice of floor malting. As opposed to industrial malting, which uses automated machinery in silos to turn and aerate the grain, Admiral spreads it out by hand over a large concrete floor (Hieronymus 2014; Williams and Shapiro 2018).

Once the grain has been steeped and dried multiple times to begin germination, it is then spread over the floor and hand-turned with a large rake over several days (Craft Beer and Brewing n.d.-b). This specially designed rake keeps the grain at an even depth, to manage oxygenation, keep a uniform temperature, and prevent the grain's rootlets from tangling. (Indeed, Admiral Malting's onsite pub, where all taps feature beer made with their malt, is named "the Rake"; Mobley 2018, Pershan 2017).

Traditionally, floor malting could not be done during the summer months, as the ambient temperature would keep the grain too warm to germinate properly. Admiral, however, has added a modern twist to be able to malt year-round—radiant floor cooling.

Silberstein likens the superiority of locally grown, hand-turned, freshly kilned malt to comparing fresh-baked, straight-from-the-oven bread to the loaves kept in cellophane at your local grocery store. "We think it's better. The aromatic qualities are better. But you still have to make a good beer. Having a good malt doesn't excuse a brewer. You still have to know how to combine the ingredients."

Silberstein should know. He's also the owner of ThirstyBear Brewing in San Francisco, the city's only certified organic brewery. He noted the benefits of using local malt in his beers—primarily, less reliance on specialty malts.

Base malts are essentially the workhorses of malt, whose primary function is to provide enough enzymatic power to convert its starches into fermentable sugars for the yeast to then convert to alcohol and CO_2 during fermentation (Craft Beer and Brewing. n.d.-a). These types include Pilsner and pale malts.

Specialty malts are often darker in color and more thoroughly roasted. These malts are used more for color, flavor, and mouthfeel, and include Caramel, Chocolate, and Black Patent.

Silberstein credits Admiral Malting's traditional, hand-raked floor-malting process with giving their malts additional complexity and expressiveness that can be found using more modern methods. "We use less

Mad Fritz localizes ingredients down to the water source. Waters from three different sources—which are often used in identical beer recipes just to demonstrate the effects different sources can have on the same beer—are pictured here. *Photo: Author*

specialty malt because our base malts are more aromatic and have more substance, more backbone, more soul. We don't use as much Caramel, or as much Munich, or some of the lighter Caramels and Munichs.

"You can dispense with those, because you don't need to add mouthfeel and texture, and bready and slightly kilned notes."

Admiral Maltings' top purchaser is Almanac Brewing Company. Perhaps not coincidentally, the two are neighbors in the same building. The malt is delivered by forklift.

"They use two tons, plus, of our malt a week," says Silberstein. "They, almost more than anyone, represent the idea of geographically based beer."

Almanac's tagline? "Farm to Barrel."

Indeed.

References

California Department of Food and Agriculture. n.d. "California Agricultural Production Statistics." Retrieved April 23, 2021 (https://www.cdfa.ca.gov /Statistics/).

Cioletti, Jeff. 2017. "Grain Trust: Craft Malt, Craft Beer and What It Means to Be Local." *Craft Beer.com*, May 16 (https://www.craftbeer.com/craft-beer-muses /grain-trust-craft-malt-craft-beer-what-it-means-to-be-local).

Craft Beer and Brewing. n.d. "The Oxford Companion to Beer Definition of Base Malt." Retrieved April 23, 2021 (https://beerandbrewing.com/dictionary /Kq8N9DxS2y/).

Craft Beer and Brewing. n.d. "The Oxford Companion to Beer Definition of Floor Malting." Retrieved April 23, 2021 (https://beerandbrewing.com/dictionary /yq2r7ePj7z/).

Hieronymus, Stan. 2014. "The Malting Process." *Pro Brewer*, April 24, 2014 (https:// www.probrewer.com/library/malt/the-maltingprocess/).

Kuehl, Kelly J. n.d. "Malt and the Malting Process." *The Country Malt Group*. Retrieved April 23, 2021 (http://www.ahaconference.org/wpcontent/uploads /presentations/2010/Malt___The_Malting_Process-Kelly_Kuehl.pdf).

Mathesius, Konrad. 2017. "Alternative Crops: Malting Barley." *Sacramento Valley Field Crops*, March 23 (https://ucanr.edu/blogs/blogcore/postdetail.cfm ?postnum=23616).

Mobley, Esther. 2018. "The Rake Is a Temple to Beer's Most Important Ingredient: Malt." *San Francisco Chronicle*, May 1 (https://www.sfchronicle.com/food/article /The-Rake-is-a-temple-to-beer-s-most-important-12878922.php?psid=kV2yy).

Pershan, Caleb. 2017. "California's First Craft Malt House Wants to Make Malt the New Hops." *Eater: San Francisco*, September 29 (https://sf.eater.com/2017/9/29 /16375644/admiral-maltings-craft-beer-malt-san-francisco).

Segarra, Lisa Marie. 2018. "California's Economy Is Now Bigger Than All of the U.K." *Fortune*, May 5 (https://fortune.com/2018/05/05/california-fifth-biggest -economy-passes-united-kingdom/).

Williams, Gail Ann and Steve Shapiro. 2018. "Admiral Maltings—Kilning It in California." *Celebrator*, March 4 (https://www.celebrator.com/2018-02-exclusive -admiral-maltings-kilning-it-in-california/).

CHAPTER 13

A Social Geography of Craft Breweries

Digital Representations of Brewery Collaboration Networks in Asheville, North Carolina

RACHEL SKAGGS AND ETHAN GIBBONS

A post of a pairing menu comes up while scrolling through Instagram. First pairing: avocado-glazed mini doughnut with chocolate crumble, paired with The Fire Within Chili Pepper IPA, 7.2% ABV. Second pairing: creamy brie–glazed mini doughnut, topped with spiced walnuts, paired with Madness of Crowds Wine Barrel-Aged Tripel with Apricot & Black Currant, 10.5% ABV. Third pairing: blueberry-rosemary and ginger-glazed mini doughnut, paired with Dark Matter Oatmeal Stout, 10.5% ABV. This is Twin Leaf Brewery's most recent collaboration with local donut shop DoughP Doughnuts, both of Asheville, North Carolina. Beer and donuts are an unexpected pairing in comparison to more typical pub grub, but there has been a recent boom in the number of Asheville craft-beer-and-donut pairing events. If the Twin Leaf and DoughP Doughnuts pairing is not what you are looking for, walk the 0.1 miles to Burial Beer Company where you can sip their brews along with pairings from Vortex Donuts. If you walk another 350 feet from Burial, you can partake in hop-free pairings of DoughP Doughnuts with a hard cider flight from Urban Orchard Cider Co. Nationally recognized Hole Doughnuts (Delany 2016) has yet to partner with a brewery for beer pairings, but their special weekly donut flavors have included donut glazes featuring ingredients procured from other local businesses, like hibiscus and wild blueberry (Rayburn Farms), Heart

Path Tea (Mother Mountain Herbals), Chocolate Sorghum Bourbon (French Broad Chocolates), donuts made with local Carolina Rye flour (Carolina Ground Flour), and herbal glaze blends of tulsi, lemon balm, and rose from the doughnut shop's own garden.

Beyond pairing finished food items with beers, Asheville's craft breweries take on additional ingredients and focus on brewing with hyperlocal yeast strains to produce microbrews that could not be from anywhere else. In another take on the local focus of Asheville's brewing community, the sours-specific Funkatorium taproom takes hyperlocalism seriously, following the city's commitment to "Unchain AVL" by rejecting chain stores and restaurants and relying on local supply chains. Their current beer selection includes Aicha, a barrel-aged American Sour Ale fermented with tea from the neighboring Dobra Tea. A local tea shop that incorporates a flair for consuming tea in a more naturalistic setting by offering customers cushions on the ground for seating, Dobra has locations in downtown Asheville and in the bohemian neighborhood of West Asheville. Complete with a menu of hundreds of tea varieties, a selection of Asian-fusion dishes, and several beverages and treats infused with hemp oil and CBD, Dobra Tea embodies the countercultural vibes of the city. As collaborators, Dobra Tea and Funkatorium exemplify this hyperlocal collaborative community nestled in the mountains of western North Carolina.

Each of these pairings represents a local collaboration that builds the Asheville community. Often, these collaborations are made more visible through the digital platform of Instagram. Because of this social media outlet's visibility, and users' norm of tagging other accounts, interested customers are able to see and interact with the breweries, get excited about new releases, and easily find information about them. In this chapter, we use Instagram posts in a different way: to reconstruct and analyze the complex collaborative webs that connect Asheville's breweries to individuals, local businesses (including fellow breweries), and other organizations. Along with interspersed vignettes based on participant observation in Asheville, this chapter relies on social network analysis to create a map of the social geography of the connections between Asheville's breweries and their collaborators in the city and elsewhere. This chapter's key takeaway is in conceptualizing the structural patterning of relationships between local breweries and other community members as a site of collaboration, community building, and mutual economic benefit contained in one locale. In light of this book's focus on landscapes and geographical regions, this chapter contributes to thinking around digital representations of geographically colocated space. It also extends thinking about space and place that also considers social connectedness—a social geography of craft brewing in one community. Our analysis does the kind of mapping that at first seems invisible but ultimately uncovers the interwoven roads and pathways of collaborations.

Asheville as a Case

Asheville, North Carolina, has become the premier regional beer destination in the southeast. Expanding from their first craft brewery, Highland Brewing, built in 1994, the city now boasts well over fifty, including three locations of large national craft breweries. Among southern metropolitan statistical areas, Asheville is anomalous in its number of breweries (Baginski and Bell 2011). As the city's brewing community has grown and expanded, brewers in Asheville have done what Anne Fitten Glen (2017) calls a game of musical chairs by moving from brewery to brewery. Through this process, their networked relationships have built a strong sense of connectedness among brewers, breweries, and the brewing community. The community also has formed an industry association, the Asheville Brewers Alliance (ABA), which includes sixty-one breweries and exists to promote the regional industry. The ABA has even collectively built a Habitat for Humanity home, which they dubbed "the house that beer built" (Fitten Glen 2012). The overarching sentiment about the brewing community in Asheville that Fitten Glen portrays in her book is that it was a space that encouraged collaboration over competition. She describes one particularly compelling case of collaboration over competition. When Asheville Pizza and Brewing Company (now called Asheville Brewing Company) had an issue with their HVAC system, their colleagues from Catawba Brewing, Highland, and Green Man brought glycol over to cool the three tanks of beer that otherwise would have been ruined by the outage.

Although Asheville is a mecca for beer tourism, locals still make up the majority of brewery patrons in the city's many taprooms. In one study, 62 percent of North Carolina brewery patrons were residents of the county in which the brewery was located (Kraftchick et al. 2014). Beyond simply visiting brewery taprooms and purchasing beer, local beer hobbyists in Asheville compete in the annual "Just Brew It" home-brew festival, in which winners have their recipe brewed by a local craft brewery (Fitten Glen 2012). Further broadening the audience for Asheville's reputation among beer cities, it was a multiyear winner of the now defunct Beer City USA Poll, and others in the brewing community have commented that Asheville punches above its weight in terms of beer, brewing, and beer culture (Fitten Glen 2012).

The city's brewing culture and industry, among other factors, was enough to attract three national beer brands to put their second location in Asheville. Sierra Nevada Brewing Company, New Belgium Brewing, and Oskar Blues Brewery all built East Coast headquarters in Asheville, further raising the city's profile and contributing to its unique combination of local and national presence on the brewery scene. Though one might expect blowback from the local brewing community with three big craft breweries coming to town, this was not the case, as new entrants to the brewing community made intentional efforts to be good and welcome community members. A tour guide at Sierra Nevada Brewing Company told us that Ken Grossman, the owner and cofounder of the brewery, called Oscar Wong, the founder of pioneer brewery Highland Brewing, to ask if Sierra Nevada would be welcome in the community. Wong said that he thought so, and, together with the ABA, held a town hall meeting to discuss the issue. Ultimately, the ABA welcomed Sierra Nevada, saying that they expected it to increase the profile of Asheville as a beer destination. In an effort to integrate themselves into their new brewing community, Sierra Nevada invited local craft brewers to their annual beer camp and brewed different beers together. When New Belgium announced that it too was coming to Asheville, they gave out bottles of their Fat Tire Amber Ale with an attached flyer listing the reasons they chose Asheville (Fitten Glen 2012). The list said that they chose Asheville because of its integration of work and life, strong community, respect for the environment, being full of culture, love of beer; and love of bikes.

Collaboration in Asheville's Brewing Community

One aspect of craft brewing that interests us is the collaboration, coordination, and organization that characterizes the supply chain from which brewers obtain the materials and means of production in order to create and distribute craft beer so that customers can ultimately purchase and enjoy it. Specifically, we are interested in relationships between breweries and local artists, marketing and PR services, and distributors that facilitate the marketing and distribution of craft beer. When it comes to acquiring the ingredients and antecedents of brewing, many craft brewers consider locally sourced ingredients to be closely aligned to their brewing philosophy and conception of themselves as members of both their local community and the craft brewing community (Jones and Harvey 2017). An additional area of interest in this study is the relationships that connect breweries to their communities, including collaborations with local charitable organizations as well direct connections with their customers and employees.

Our initial sampling frame included each of the fifty-seven breweries profiled in the Summer 2018 Field Guide to Asheville Breweries. This guide is ubiquitous in its distribution through Asheville breweries and is generally located in a wire basket next to the door. Each brewery profile therein describes the brewery's amenities, such as whether it is dog friendly, has a full kitchen or food trucks, has live music, or is kid friendly. Of these fifty-seven breweries, twenty-five are located within Asheville, with the other thirty-two in the surrounding areas of western North Carolina. For this chapter, we chose to focus only on breweries that the Field Guide designated as located within Asheville.

Theoretically, our concern was in understanding the ecosystem of collaboration among craft breweries, and we did this by examining breweries' Instagram presence. Instagram is a popular platform for businesses to promote themselves, and we theorize that tags are a useful measure to indicate that the account is highlighting particular collaborations with another entity. A tag is a direct mention of another user account in Instagram that is structured as @UserName. This kind of tag alerts the tagged user that they are mentioned in the text post that accompanies a photo posted on Instagram. We collected data from Instagram during July 2018 with the intention of capturing digital representations of affiliation between local breweries and other businesses, organizations, and individuals. That is to say, we measured collaboration in terms of what breweries chose to highlight on their public Instagram accounts by counting each time a brewery tagged another account in their posts as a digital affiliation. Breweries are highly collaborative and require a complex supply chain to make and distribute beer, so our operationalization allows us to track the relationships they have highlighted and publicly displayed, but it is not inclusive of every instance of collaboration or aspect of the supply chain among Asheville breweries.

By selecting one month of focus for this initial inquiry into using affiliation data from an online social network, we chose to focus the empirical approach on a meaningful and discrete period. We selected July as the focal month to align with our sampling frame, the Summer 2018 Field Guide to Asheville Breweries. Rather than picking another summer month, we chose July because it contains a major national holiday (Independence Day). We thought that a month with a major holiday might be one in which we would see a variety of different kinds of posts about special themed beer releases and public events at breweries. Because July is also in the summer, we expected that breweries would post about outdoor activities like festivals, river cleanups, and vacationing.[1]

Within the initial sampling frame, we found the official Instagram accounts of these breweries and collected information about each post from each brewery during July 2018. For each post, we collected the number of likes, number of comments, information about who is tagged (either in the photo or in the text of the photo description; we refer to these as "tagees"), and which type of account(s) are tagged. The four tag types are

1. individuals whose Instagram accounts do not identify them in a primarily professional role (e.g., a brewer's personal Instagram would count as an individual, but a tattoo artist's business page would not);
2. individuals or businesses selling goods or services, but not other breweries;
3. organizations that are charitable or mission-driven, rather than profit driven; and
4. another brewery, local or not.

Collaborations of Craft Breweries in Asheville

The twenty-five Asheville-based craft breweries posted 541 times to Instagram in July 2018 and tagged an average of 0.56 other accounts per post (302 total tags; median = 0, mode = 0). The average number of likes per post was 278.65 (median = 89, mode = 43), and the average number of comments per post was 7.55 (median = 2, mode = 0).

Individuals were tagged by breweries fifty-five times (18.2 percent of total tags) during the study period. Posts tagging individuals included breweries introducing a new staff member, crediting photos in customers' Instagram posts that they reposted, tagging the brewer of a new beer that the brewery was promoting for release, and tagging the winner of a contest or giveaway. In one Instagram post by UpCountry Brewing, for example, a photo of an employee hugging a large piece of particleboard was captioned:

> #flashback friday to one year ago when we got our canning line from @wildgoosecanning! @trulyblackzac was particularly excited. Come grab some cans to go for the weekend!

This caption and post is typical of the kind of post in which an individual was tagged (although UpCountry Brewing also tagged a business in this post, the manufacturer of canning lines that breweries use to package cans of beer). Generally, posts tagging individuals were humorous and more personal to the individuals who run the brewery (e.g., tagging patrons or employees), as compared to a more aloof, staged, branded, or professional image evoked in posts that did not tag individuals.

Breweries tagged businesses 173 times in July 2018 (57.3 percent of tags). This was perhaps the most diverse category of digital affiliation and one that represents collaborations with, for example, business services affiliated with making, packaging, and marketing beer; artists whose work they feature digitally and physically (e.g., on their cans and walls); restaurants whose baked goods the brewery offers for sale; DJs whose music is featured regularly in brewery events; and a collaborative pork taco dish with a local meat purveyor. Many such tags represented repeated collaborations between breweries and local restaurants. Typifying such crossovers in social and spatial geography, Hillman Beer tagged Rise Above Deli in seven of their twenty-three July posts as a result of the deli being located within the brewery itself. An example of a collaboration between a brewery and a local artist is the following post from Hi-Wire Brewing promoting an anniversary event with live music:

> JUST ANNOUNCED: @empirestrikesbrass to headline our 5th Anniversary Party! General Admission is FREE Saturday, July 28 at Big Top from 3–10PM. The Digs & @porch40 are also performing live on the @henconorth Main Stage. See all the details and grab a VIP Pass which includes unlimited access to the

Sour & Wild Ale tent, including free food and 5 ride tickets at hiwirebrewing.com.

Literature on breweries suggest that collaborations with local businesses are part of a larger philosophy of brewing (Jones and Harvey 2017). Respondents in a study of craft brewers in the northeastern United States compared themselves to the slow food movement. The authors emphasize how the brewers "described their commitment to sourcing local ingredients, their role in the community, and keeping their products in the region," viewing the resulting beer as a version of the popular "farm to table" ethos in food (Jones and Harvey 2017, 124).

Extending their collaboration in the local community beyond other businesses, the breweries tagged organizations twenty-nine times (9.6 percent of total July tags). These organizations and the reasons why a brewery tagged them were quite varied. Several such posts type tagged the Southern Appalachian Highlands Conservancy. For example, a post by Wicked Weed, recently purchased by Anheuser-Busch InBev, advertised that part of the profits from a new session IPA would go to the conservancy:

> Appalachia Session IPA is in distribution now! This beer is being served all throughout Western North Carolina with a portion of every beer that's poured going to support @appalachian_org. The Southern Appalachian Highlands Conservancy strives to protect plant & animal habitat, clean water, farmland, scenic beauty and outdoor recreation in the mountains of North Carolina and Tennessee. Enjoy a pint today and join us in supporting this amazing organization. #WickedWeed #Appalachia #SessionIPA #SouthernAppalachianHighlandsConservancy.

As part of an Asheville community that values the natural beauty of the surrounding mountains, these breweries sought to highlight their charitable donations to conservation-minded organizations. We found, for instance, a variety of initiatives to collaborate with @fbriverkeeper, a local nonprofit that works to clean up the French Broad River and help others enjoy it through paddle sports and recreation. French Broad River Brewery posted on July 19 that they were releasing a beer collaboratively brewed with a local river rafting company, with 10 percent of profits going to @fbriverkeeper.

Though we did not visit French Broad River Brewery, we did spend some time sipping locally brewed craft beer while overlooking the

French Broad River. New Belgium Brewing's Liquid Center taproom and brewery are located on the French Broad Biver in West Asheville. A key narrative through-line of the brewing facilities' official tour, as told by the tour guide, is New Belgium's commitment to rehabilitating the formerly polluted brownfield on which their campus now sits, as well as continuing their efforts to clean up the river, plant native species, and maintain LEED certification in their buildings. The brewery is employee owned, workers make a living wage, and each quarter they decide which organization will receive donations given in the Liquid Center. From our Instagram data, we know that in July 2018, they raised money for Mountain Pet Rescue Asheville; supported Light a Path, a yoga nonprofit that provides services to incarcerated and at-risk community members; and held a music event to benefit the local River Link environmental conservation organization.

In the final tag category, breweries tagged other breweries forty-five times in their Instagram posts (14.9 percent of July tags). Posts in which breweries tagged other breweries included shout-outs to nearby breweries in Asheville and Western North Carolina; collaborative beer releases with local breweries and those across the United States and abroad; and advertisements for events that brought together more than one local brewery or highlighted another local brewery's event. Notably, Burial Beer Company tagged a variety of other breweries located both near and far from Asheville as they collaborated with Zillicoah Beer (Woodfin, North Carolina), Other Half Brewing (Brooklyn, New York), Creature Comforts Beer (Athens, Georgia), J. Wakefield Beer (Miami), TRVE Brewing (Denver), Anchorage Brewing Company (Anchorage, Alaska), and 18th Street Brewery (Hammond, Indiana). Burial's digital representations of its affiliations with these seven other breweries indicated that they have a broad network of collaborators, including high-status and well-known breweries like Other Half, which is a trendsetter among US craft breweries (Pomranz 2018). Burial's caption on a July 30 Instagram post featuring a photo of an amber-colored draft beer in a glass bearing their logo with a thick head of foam next to a corked bottle of Jeppson's Malört Liqueur reads:

> The triumph of creativity knows no bounds, and we celebrate those things that pique our intrigue. The Closed Mind Withers Malort Saison is a test of boundaries. When our friends @18thstreetbrewery came last October, we made 1 easy beer and 1 hard beer. Among the windy billows and tireless bar scene

in Chicago, Malort reigns supreme as the trier of palates. Our blended mixed culture saison utilizes a heavy dose of necessary, yet extremely bitter, wormwood, balanced with a delightful bouquet of honey and tea-like crystal hops. Get it in the taproom today. #burialbeer #18thstreetbrewery #avlbeer #malort #facesofmalort

Although not included in the dataset, an example of collaboration between breweries that caught our attention while in the field was a collaborative beer made by Archetype Brewing and New Belgium. Wittily called the "Neighborly Lager," in reference to the short spatial distance between the two West Asheville breweries, the Archetype menu proudly described this Kellerbier as a "New Belgium Collab." After discussing the possible reasons for this sort of collaboration between ourselves, we asked the bartender at Archetype Brewing why they had decided to collaborate with the much larger brewery down the street. "It's just kind of the culture around here," she said. "We learn a lot from the bigger guys about how to make good beer and they love to spread the knowledge around." This echoes the statement given by New Belgium's CEO, who "emphasized the company's commitment to working with the local brewers in a 'spirit of collaboration' and 'sharing our groovy toys'" when they opened their new brewery in Asheville (Fitten Glen 2012, 144).

The bartender added that, in addition to collaborating in creating the beer itself, the two breweries (both of which offer the beer on tap) donate $1 from the purchase of every pint of Neighborly Lager to the organization PeopleForBikes, which promotes safety for cyclists around the country. According to her, "A lot of us here ride our bikes to work and, of course, New Belgium is really into bikes. It just seemed like a cool thing for us to do." By collaborating with New Belgium, Archetype's brewers were able to gain information about brewing from established experts in the field. In addition, New Belgium's brewers benefit from the arrangement by building a more connected local brewing network, establishing roots in the community, and associating their brand with both collaboration and charitable giving. As our conversation with the bartender showed, folks in Asheville's brewing scene don't see other breweries, even the large ones, as competitors, but rather as part of the local brewing community, sharing resources and knowledge as well as giving back by donating to meaningful charitable organizations.

Archetype Brewing's taps with "Neighborly Lager" visible at the bottom left side of the sign. *Photo: Rachel Skaggs*

These examples of brewery collaboration is a notable trend in the literature on brewing. Brewers in the United Kingdom engage in swapping beers, exchange information about experimentation and industry opportunities, and "tend to create collaborative relationships with other breweries mostly located close by" (Cabras 2017, 46). Cabras identifies this kind of approach in brewing as a "collaborative-competitive" environment that "stimulate[s] creativity and innovation" (2017, 47). Likewise, Jones and Harvey (2017) discuss collaboration in brewing, saying that it is a key part of "beer culture." Two examples of collaboration they cite are collaborative brewing recipes among local New England breweries that then would be featured at another local brewery for a release night, and a more mundane collaboration in the form of equipment sharing between breweries. So, although Asheville is not unique for having highly collaborative breweries and brewers, it exemplifies the collaborative nature of the national craft brewing community.

Mapping Social Connections in Asheville's Craft Beer Scene

Using a concept that is more frequently employed to examine the contributions of artists and the arts to communities, Paulsen and Tuller (2017) studied the role of breweries in "creative placemaking," saying that microbreweries are responding to a demand for local flair by supporting other businesses. *Creative placemaking* is the theory and public policy practice of shaping the physical and social space of a community through various artistic, economic, building, and social efforts (see e.g., Frenette 2017; Markusen and Gadwa 2010; Paulsen and Tuller 2017). In the current era of globalization and homogenization, placemaking efforts must be "active, conscious, and ongoing" in order to be distinct and differentiated (Paulsen and Tuller 2017, 106), even as patterns of breweries emerge and cluster according to external factors like geographic locale, market concentration, and organizational dynamics (Carroll and Swaminathan 2000; Cserpes and McInerney 2017).We furthered these lines of thought around creative placemaking, the ongoing work of creating community spaces, and of how breweries cluster by measuring and mapping the relational social clustering of one geographic cluster of breweries.

In addition to listing the quantity and type of digital affiliations presented on Asheville breweries' Instagram accounts in July 2018, we constructed a two-mode network visualization to better understand the patterns of affiliation between breweries and other entities represented in these Instagram posts. Two-mode networks link two different types of social actors—in this case, breweries and the entities that they tag (vs. one-mode networks, which would link breweries to one another, for example). In the network visualization hereafter, the four large squares are "nodes" that represent each tag category (labeled according to type: individual, business, organization, and other breweries) and the twenty-five small circles are nodes that represent each brewery. The lines of various thickness are "edges" that represent a brewery's affiliation with each entity type. The size of the weighted edge lines connecting breweries to the tagee categories represents the relative frequency with which each brewery tagged that type of entity. The spatial arrangement of the various nodes reflects the social-network analysis program

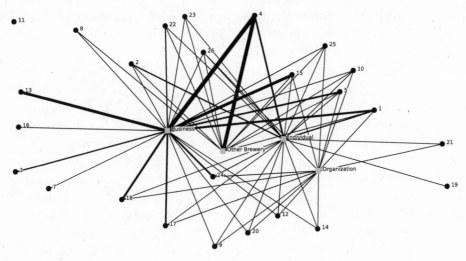

Asheville Networks.

that we used (UCINET) and its visualization algorithm (NetDraw), which prioritizes nonoverlapping edges and general readability of the diagram, rather than indicating any specific relationships between the nodes beyond the affiliations that we describe in this chapter.

In other words, the figure shows the otherwise invisible points of connection and affiliation that Asheville breweries share. Rather than serving as a cartographic map of structured geographical closeness, the thickness of the edge lines maps the social affinity and structured connectedness between breweries according to the kinds of affiliation they display on their Instagram accounts. In the case of Asheville breweries, this visualization provides a more granular look at the larger social geography within which the breweries operate, reflecting Jones and Harvey's argument that, when brewers and breweries see and present themselves as a "networked ecology," they become "part of a larger movement" (2017, 125).

As noted, the thickness of the lines in the network diagram represents the strength of the tie between the brewery and the type of collaborator. One striking part of this network diagram is the bold lines extending from the number 4 brewery, Burial Beer Company, to businesses, other breweries, and individuals. We might think of Burial as a quintessential example of the collaborative brewing community in Asheville. Burial combines a quirky and macabre aesthetic with an intimate atmosphere partly defined by the presence of the brewing equipment in the bar itself. According to the "Our Story" video on their website, the founders chose to locate in Asheville for the sense of community they perceived in the city. Highlighting the positive impact of the brewery on the community, the video says that when Burial moved into the South Slope neighborhood, the area had yet to gain its now well-known moniker. Part of Burial's success has been in contributing to the new neighborhood as a place to be for locals and tourists alike. The founders also consider their approach to brewing to be slightly abnormal, choosing to "resurrect" older styles of European beers rather than following popular trends. Burial often collaborates with local artists to design unique labels for each can, inspired by the creation story of the beer itself.

The relative boldness of the lines branching from the Burial node reflects the collaborative spirit of the brewery. In particular, Burial's Instagram page indicated a high number of collaborations with businesses ($n = 28$, mean = 6.92) and other breweries ($n = 24$, mean = 1.80). Furthermore, the network diagram reflects a high number of collaborations with individuals ($n = 11$, mean = 2.20) relative to the rest of the breweries in the dataset. Interestingly, in the period sampled, Burial Beer did not collaborate with any charitable organizations ($n = 0$, mean = 1.16). Of course, it is unclear whether this reflects a lack of collaboration between Burial and nonprofit organizations or simply a limitation in the data. Either way, our data show that Burial is now solidly socially embedded in the Asheville brewing community that initially drew them to the South Slope.

It is also informative to compare Burial Beer to Green Man Brewing, number 10 on the network diagram. This brewery is the only "isolate" in our dataset, which in network terms describes an entity with no social ties. Because Green Man Brewing did not tag any other accounts in their posts during July, using this criterion it appears to be an isolate. Although the lack of tags between Green Man Brewing's Instagram page and individuals, businesses, other breweries, and organizations does not necessarily indicate that Green Man is not involved in the collaborative culture of the Asheville beer scene, it does indicate that, at least in July 2018, the brewery chose not to highlight any collaborations they may have been involved in. Located less than a five-minute walk from Burial Beer, the seeming difference in community involvement is striking. Interestingly, their website describes them as one of the oldest breweries in Asheville (founded in 1996), and also specifically asks local citizens to think of them when organizing fund-raising events. Again, it may be the case that Green Man simply chose not to use their Instagram account to highlight their collaborations. Alternatively, Green Man Brewing may now be focusing on building a larger national brand as they seek to grow their distribution. The newly built three-story, 22,000-square-foot packaging hall and specialty brew-house that includes a "brewtique" and an indoor/outdoor taproom certainly asserts Green Man's place as a more-developed organization relative to the quainter premises of Burial Beer.

Another informative comparison can be made between two national breweries that the Field Guide designated as within the city limits, New Belgium (number 16) and Sierra Nevada (number 19). In visits and walking tours at both of these breweries, tour guides told stories of a small group of individuals starting the breweries in Fort Collins, Colorado, and Chico, California, respectively. As described earlier, both chose Asheville as a strategic expansion location as they continued to grow. Reasons included a central location along the Eastern Seaboard for convenient distribution, a burgeoning local beer scene, and the natural beauty of the surrounding mountains. However, the network diagram reveals slight differences between the two brewer-ies. In the period of study, both breweries collaborated with businesses, individuals, and nonprofit organizations. As shown by the varied thick-ness of the edge lines, New Belgium more frequently collaborated with businesses ($n = 9$, mean = 6.92) and organizations ($n = 3$, mean = 1.16) than Sierra Nevada ($n = 1$ collaboration for both businesses and orga-nizations). This difference reveals the intersection of social and spa-tial geography in Asheville. As mentioned, New Belgium's campus sits directly adjacent to the French Broad River, within biking distance of downtown and walking distance of the River Arts District as well as local favorite Hole Doughnuts. In addition to describing their com-mitment to environmental improvement and equitable employment practices, the tour guide at New Belgium frequently mentioned the work the brewery did to ensure it would have a positive impact on the community, including choosing a location where employees could bike to work and communicating with nearby residents in order to coordi-nate the most convenient trucking route. Both Sierra Nevada and New

Belgium top the list when it comes to sustainability in brewing, and it is notable that environmental concerns often trump social and political justice concerns in the craft brewing industry (Jones 2018). That New Belgium's tour focused so heavily on community impact along with their ecological footprint may indicate a growing attention to incorporating a variety of concerns within sustainability initiatives.

Conversely, Sierra Nevada's compound is situated about a thirty-minute drive away from downtown. To arrive at the brewery, one must drive on I-26 to an exit that is otherwise sparsely populated and drive down a road named "Sierra Nevada Way." The site itself is both beautiful and environmentally considerate, as is readily visible in the porous pavement in the parking lot, which allows rainwater to flow into the soil, and the solar panels interspersed between the rows of parked cars that generate some of the brewery's power. Inside the complex itself, a massive hunting-cabin-style restaurant and tasting room was teeming during our visit with beer enthusiasts gleefully tasting their favorite varieties at this Disneyesque monument to brewing. The tasting rooms, gift shop, and various lounging areas encompass multiple floors and tens of thousands of square feet of immaculate but rugged Sierra Nevada–themed décor. Behind the brewery itself is a large open-air concert venue with a garden full of a variety of fruits, vegetables, herbs, and flowers.

Despite the impressive nature of Sierra Nevada's brewery, its distance from Asheville proper means that it feels somewhat disconnected from the collaborative local scene. In comparison, though the New Belgium Brewery campus is a beautiful location in its own right and is close enough to downtown to conceivably be a stop on a local brewery tour, Sierra Nevada's Brewery is a destination of its own. Although Sierra Nevada, as noted, was initially sensitive to the local brewing community, its ensuing social media approach (at least in July 2018) did not highlight collaborations with fellow breweries or other local businesses. In contrast to New Belgium's Asheville location, Sierra Nevada's appears to have followed the pattern noted by Jones (2018) in which craft brewers seeking to be sustainable focus on environmental efficiencies at the cost of neglecting social integration and community outreach. New Belgium, Sierra Nevada, Burial, and Green Man all represent variations in how breweries can demonstrate their commitment to Asheville's collaborative culture. However, each also contributes the overall sense that Asheville is committed to brewing.

Conclusion

Taking a relational approach to understanding the structure of craft brewing in the Asheville community allowed us to conceptualize new measures of social geography, meaning, and collaboration. The categories we developed based on breweries' Instagram posts contain a wide variety and number of individuals (e.g., brewery patrons or employees); businesses (e.g., those who sell brewing equipment, artists whose work is featured on cans or in breweries, marketing companies, local ingredient providers); and other breweries from around Asheville, the United States, and even some outside the country, as well as organizations with different foci (e.g., environmentalism, food security, poverty alleviation). When thinking about how well our measures held up to our participant observation in Asheville, we believe that the measure of digital affiliation accurately represents many of the instances of collaboration that are happening in the Asheville brewing community. Although digital affiliation does not capture all collaborative activity, it represents the relationships and events that breweries elect to highlight as part of their digital identity.

The comparisons we offer, along with the network diagram, demonstrate that through our use of Instagram tags as a proxy for collaboration, we were able to observe a vibrant culture of collaborative engagement in Asheville's brewing scene. Within the city's spatial geography and its surrounding area, a social geography has been created in which brewers collaborate with individuals, businesses, other breweries, and organizations to create a distinctive brewing culture. Variations in this culture demonstrated in these comparisons reflect the different needs and cultures of the breweries themselves. Despite these differences, all of the breweries in Asheville contribute to its growing reputation as a regional and national beer destination.

In an example of fortuitous timing and external validity, we learned that one of the breweries in our study, Lexington Avenue Brewery (LAB), would be closing and would shortly be replaced in its physical location in downtown Asheville by a new brewery tenant. Though LAB is one of the first craft breweries established in Asheville, it was not well linked in the affiliation network we present here. Their numbers of posts, followers, and accounts that they follow were relatively low, and they only tagged individuals, rather than companies, nonprofits, or other breweries in their Instagram posts through July 2018. We also discovered in our participant observation at LAB that, in our initial Instagram data collection, we had identified the wrong account as LAB's official Instagram account; the account listed on their advertisements and chalkboard (@lexingtonavebrew) was different from the one we had previously identified as the official account. This appeared to be because the brewery had started one account (@lexingtonavenuebrewery) but did not use it after posting once in 2013 and later starting the second account. For this case in particular, being participant observers in the physical space greatly informed and changed our conception of LAB's social location in the network of Asheville breweries before it closed.

In LAB's place on Lexington Avenue will be CANarchy, which describes itself as a "disruptive collective of like-minded brewers dedicated to bringing high-quality, innovative flavors to drinkers in the name of independent craft beer." This craft brewing collaborative is made up of Oskar Blues Brewery (Longmont, Colorado; Brevard, North Carolina; Austin, Texas), Perrin Brewing Company (Comstock Park, Michigan), Cigar City Brewing (Tampa, Florida), Squatters Craft Beers and Wasatch Brewery (Salt Lake City, Utah), Deep Ellum Brewing Company (Dallas, Texas), and Three Weavers Brewing Company (Inglewood, CA). Their new space in Asheville will be the "front door" of the collaborative, bringing them to a single location after more than two years of collaboration, resource sharing, collectively ordering materials in bulk, and generally working together to unite in the face of an increasingly competitive craft brewing industry. This example of collaboration between independent craft breweries in Asheville and independent craft breweries based mostly in other states shows the value of social connectedness and emphasizes the potential power that social geography may ultimately have to shape spatial geography.

Notes

1. To ensure that our results in July were not an aberration, we analyzed posts from June and August 2018 for the four breweries we compare in-depth below (Sierra Nevada, New Belgium, Burial, and Green Man). All four breweries had tagging patterns for August and June very similar to those in July, further supporting our one-month time frame. Scholars interested in these data and analyses directly may contact the authors.

References

Baginski, James and Thomas L. Bell. 2011. "Under-tapped? An Analysis of Craft Brewing in the Southern United States." *Southeastern Geographer* 51(1):165–85.

Cabras, Ignazio. 2017. "A Pint of Success: How Beer Is Revitalizing Cities and Local Economies in the United Kingdom." Pp. 39–58. In *Untapped: Exploring the Cultural Dimensions of Craft Beer*, edited by Nathaniel G. Chapman, Slade Lellock, and Cameron D. Lippard. Morgantown: West Virginia University Press.

Carroll, Glenn R. and Anand Swaminathan. 2000. "Why the Microbrewery Movement: Organizational Dynamics of Resource Partitioning in the American Brewing Industry after Prohibition." *American Journal of Sociology* 106:715–62.

Cserpes, Tünde and Paul-Brian McInerney. 2017. "The Spatial Dynamics of Organizational Identity among Craft Brewers." Pp. 177–99. In *Untapped: Exploring the Cultural Dimensions of Craft Beer*, edited by Nathaniel G. Chapman, Slade Lellock, and Cameron D. Lippard. Morgantown: West Virginia University Press.

Delany, Alex. 2016. "How Our Favorite Doughnut of the Year Is Made." *Bon Appétit*, August 31 (https://www.bonappetit.com/story/favorite-doughnut-of-the-year).

Fitten Glen, Anne. 2012. *Asheville Beer: An Intoxicating History of Mountain Brewing.* Charleston, SC: American Palate.

Frenette, Alexandre. 2017. "The Rise of Creative Placemaking: Cross-Sector Collaboration as Cultural Policy in the United States." *Journal of Arts Management, Law, and Society* 47(5):333–45.

Jones, Ellis and Daina Cheyenne Harvey. 2017. "Ethical Brews: New England, Networked Ecologies, and a New Craft Beer Movement." Pp. 124–36. In *Untapped: Exploring the Cultural Dimensions of Craft Beer*, edited by Nathaniel G. Chapman, Slade Lellock, and Cameron D. Lippard. Morgantown: West Virginia University Press.

Jones, Ellis. 2018. "Brewing Green: Sustainability in the Craft Beer Movement." Pp. 9–26. In *Craft Beverages and Tourism, Volume 2*, edited by S. L. Slocum, C. Kline, and C. T. Cavaliere. Cham, Switzerland: Palgrave Macmillan.

Kraftchick, Jennifer Francioni, Erick T. Byrd, Bonnie Canziani, and Nancy J. Gladwell. 2014. "Understanding Beer Tourist Motivation." *Tourism Management Perspectives* 12:41–47.

Markusen, Ann and Anne Gadwa. 2010. *Creative Placemaking.* Washington, DC: National Endowment for the Arts.

Paulsen, Krista E. and Hayley E. Tuller. 2017. "Crafting Place: Craft Beer and Authenticity in Jacksonville, Florida." Pp. 105–23. In *Untapped: Exploring the Cultural Dimensions of Craft Beer*, edited by Nathaniel G. Chapman, Slade Lellock, and Cameron D. Lippard. Morgantown: West Virginia University Press.

Pomranz, Mike. 2018. "NYC's Other Half Brewing Announces Second Location outside of Rochester." *Food and Wine*, retrieved January 11, 2019 (https://www.foodandwine.com/other-half-brewing).

Postcard from East Bristol

SCOTT TAYLOR, NEIL SUTHERLAND, AND CHRIS LAND

From the beginning of human agriculture, brewing has been part of what happens with crops, inevitably differentiated by place. Alcohol has also formed the backbone of countless cultures, providing social lubricant, spiritual aid, and gateway to community (Baron 1962; Flack 1997), connecting place through agriculture and culture. The association of place with beer changed during the late twentieth century through the advance of "lagerization," as relatively homogeneous, industrially produced beers, differentiated only by branding, eroded the market share of more locally specific brews. More recently, particularly in the United Kingdom, pub closures have disconnected beer drinking from the kinds of sociality described in *The Pub and the People* (Mass Observation 1943), as alcohol purchasing shifted to supermarkets and consumption increased in homes. The recent craft beer revolution can be understood as a reaction to these trends, resocializing alcohol and emphasizing an anti-industrial social imaginary rooted in a distinctive mix of tradition, innovation, DIY work ethic, and new consumption communities.

What is less clear in the craft revolution so far is how it interests space and place. On one hand, a craft brewery can be defined as "a small place using traditional methods and ingredients to produce a handcrafted, uncompromised beer that is marketed locally" (Cottone 1986, 9; quoted in Rice 2015). This emphasizes tradition, personalized production, and localism. Paradoxically, contemporary craft beers are known for their intense use of hops, mostly grown in the United States, mainland Europe, New Zealand, and Australia, so in the United Kingdom at least the ingredients are anything but locally sourced. Similarly, although craft bars and micropubs might be represented as a challenge to the decline of social beer consumption, they are not a simple replacement for the local community pub. Rather, brewery taprooms as drinking destinations often move the place where alcohol is consumed to out-of-town locales or edgeland industrial estates more reminiscent of scenes in a dystopian late-modernist novel by J. G. Ballard than the Moon under Water, Orwell's idealized local 1940s pub. These developments can be interpreted more as aspects of gentrification rather than a revival of traditionally emplaced communities (Barajas, Boeing, and Wartell 2018), with relatively affluent consumers performing distinction through expert knowledge of hops, yeast, and must-have, edgy collaboration brews.

We explore these tensions and challenges to craft brewing as production and consumption through conversation with the founders of Good Chemistry Brewing, based in Bristol in the southwestern United Kingdom. We present a much more complex and nuanced account of the emplacement of small breweries as they navigate localized responsibilities, creating new ecosystems and walking a line between building a sustainable, local, community economy and avoiding the risks of gentrification and the associated dissolution of local distinctiveness. For Good Chemistry Brewing, at least, the rootedness of craft brewing holds potential for local regeneration based on attitudinal change: establishing communities of like-minded people; engaging alienated individuals; diversifying drinking communities; and working with other local organizations, not simply for instrumental gain but to reclaim an ethos of collaboration, collective responsibility, and mutual aid.

THE CITY OF BRISTOL

Bristol grew from the eleventh-century settlement of a strategically important river crossing in the southwest of England. It became one of the country's most populous towns over the following three to four centuries, then experienced very considerable economic and population growth in the eighteenth and nineteenth centuries. For a brief period in the early nineteenth century it was the largest city in the country. Growth was mostly mercantile rather than in manufacturing, as a result of the city's location on the west coast of England, making it an ideal geographical point in the colonial slave and commodity trading triangle formed of West Africa, the Caribbean, and Europe.

Alongside this, nineteenth-century Bristol was also built on a more morally respectable group of small-scale artisanal producers, contrasting with the more industrial, factory-based economies of Manchester and Birmingham. What large scale industry Bristol did develop—docks, shipbuilding, tobacco, and aerospace—largely disappeared between 1970 and 1990. Following this decline, Bristol rapidly developed a service-based economy, with higher than average employment growth. The last half century is usually divided into four overlapping time periods: 1971–82, characterized by slow growth and a weak recession; 1983–94, a period of boom and bust; 1995–2010, featuring sustained growth; and then recession and slow recovery, bringing the city and its inhabitants to the present day (Sunley 2017; Tallon 2007).

Contemporary Bristol has a reputation as a hub for countercultural activities, particularly in its intertwined music and art scenes, which have gained notoriety and significance since the 1970s. With a considerably more diverse population than the surrounding region, Bristol has birthed various high-profile artists, including the legendary graffiti artist Banksy and bands like Massive Attack and Portishead. Each year, UpFest—Europe's largest "urban painting" festival—is held in the city, as buildings and businesses are decorated with murals, tags, spray paintings, and designs. Politically speaking, Bristol has also attracted attention through large-scale Occupy and Extinction Rebellion camps; antiwar, anti-Brexit, and anti-austerity demonstrations; large-scale opposition to the influx of supermarkets and large businesses; and riots and protests that have sought to highlight civil injustices. In short, Bristol is a city that is proud of its "alternative" heritage.

Bristol is also recognized as a hub for craft beer brewing in southwest England. The city hosts a wide variety of independently owned craft breweries, taprooms, micropubs and "popups." Organized tours of these venues, as well as regular beer festivals, have grown from and contributed to the popularity of craft beer in the city. Bristolian craft brewing is often explicitly articulated and paired alongside other countercultural activities—including DIY music events, tattoo culture, and local festivals—further cementing the city's reputation as a driver of cultural innovation and taste making.

Good Chemistry (GC) Brewing grew from and into this milieu, founded in 2015 by co-owners Bob Cary and Kelly Sidgwick with a ten-barrel kit in East Bristol. The business has grown steadily since then, and employs a number of people in the brewery, back office, taproom, and most recently in a micropub nearby. The account that follows attempts to prioritize Kelly and Bob's interpretations on how the brewery has simultaneously grown from and shaped its place in the city, and in East Bristol particularly.

CHOOSING A LOCATION: BUSINESS OR COMMUNITY?

We began by directly addressing the importance of place and space. Setting down the roots of a brewery is more than just an instrumental business decision; like other decisions, this one was informed by a variety of social and cultural factors:

> We looked at places like Bedminster [a suburban district on the southern edge of the city]. All of the advice we got was to go to areas . . . on the outskirts of Bristol, [with] big industrial estates, more modern buildings, better value and all the rest . . . they [estate agents and business advisors] looked at this place [where the brewery is located] and said "I wouldn't take that place because it is old, it's not insulated, it doesn't have a yard." But we looked at this and thought, well, there's a brewery right next door to us . . . so, there's lots of opportunities if you can get people to come here . . . this is a major thoroughfare for people coming from St George and Redfield into work . . . so, why can't that area start to be a hub?
>
> And it's starting to happen: there's a theatre that's opened, there's a bakery, florists, upholsterers and coffee shops. Artisan businesses . . . it seems to be really good in that it's . . . all small . . . independent people who are setting up their businesses. We know a lot of the business owners and they're just other . . . youngish, independent people kind of setting up their own businesses doing what they love doing . . . it's quite important for us also to know and to use where we can our local businesses. We've used the upholsterers on Old Market to do some work for us for the pub; the florist lady did get in touch with us and said I'm having an opening party could we have some beer, and I said, "Yes, do you want to swap some beer for some flowers?" The coffee shops we have supplied. . . . The bakery we would swap beer for bread for here last year for the Brewery Tap . . . [which is] a way of having them [customers] come to your place and see the space and see, you know, what it actually looks like and talk to you directly . . . there is no price to put on that.

A commercial logic of decision making is contrasted here with less calculative, value-rational decision making, focused on collaboration, community, and collective regeneration, rather than cost-effectiveness or competition. By emphasizing "one of a kind settings and products" (Daniels, Sterling, and Ross 2009), this kind of so-called neolocalism "resurrects a feeling of community tied to a specific land-scape" (Schnell and Reese 2003, 66). The rejection of an instrumental logic established a form of oppositional authenticity while connecting to Bristol's wider countercultural sensibility (Taylor 1991). This authenticity is further anchored in the visibility of the process and the direct connection that the brewery's location, and its taproom, permit between consumer and producer. Such visibility defetishizes production by enabling consumers to feel that their beer has been made not by a machine, but by a skilled laborer—"creating a sense of self-esteem and self-efficacy" (Lewicka 2008, 211). Drinkers are able to connect directly to the brewers through visiting the brewery, which also enables them to experience the "magic" of the production process firsthand, turning consumption into an experience (Thurnell-Read 2019). To continue Bob and Kelly's account:

> People like to come here because it's something different . . . sitting in a warehouse is different to going to the pub. But it's also [because] people like to think they've gone to the best place as well. They can say to people, "Oh, we go to the brewery and drink the beer." And it's just interesting to be able to come down and see where something's made. I don't know why people go for that, why that's a thing. But it's the same as going to Hart's Bakery [a successful and renowned independent in the city center] and seeing everyone making the stuff in the background. They could have a cafe in Clifton [a middle-class area] but it wouldn't be the same as going to the bakery to buy something.

OCCUPYING THE SPACE: REACHING OUT TO OTHERS?

The brewery space is, as GC's cofounders cheerfully recognize, an unprepossessing building. It's a classic British modern light-industrial unit in a short cul-de-sac. It has, however, the ability to be shaped internally, as Bob and Kelly note:

> We have a bar here in the brewery which is open Fridays and Saturdays through the summer months. . . . It is a bit of an odd one because when you stack it all up it's a warehouse which isn't particularly warm, in a weird industrial estate . . . not far from the tip [the town dump]. There's a scrap yard on the other side; there's all sorts of weird businesses around here that you wouldn't necessarily visit on a day to day basis. Or ever, really.

Nonetheless, they decided to use the building as best they could:

> The first event that we ever opened for was May bank holiday 2016. We'd been selling beer for two months by that stage. We opened up and ran the East Bristol Brewery Trail; this coming May bank holiday will be the seventh . . . there's five breweries [involved] all together . . . it's just got bigger and bigger and bigger . . . and that's something, you know, that's helped to anchor us to here and draw people into the area . . . three years down the line you can do the East Bristol Brewery Trail any weekend you like through the summer because all of the breweries now have a tap-room that's open. It's had a really big impact on how people look at coming to drink beer at breweries in Bristol [here and in other areas].
>
> [The brewery location near] Old Market is an area . . . well, it used to be the main street that ran from this side of Bristol . . . but it's since been cut off . . . and the businesses have declined . . . it wasn't sort of a place that a wide variety of people would come to. But since we've been here—I'm not saying that that's a causation— but there have been other businesses that have moved into Old Market and seen it as a place that can develop because it is really close to the city centre.

Beyond acting as a community hub for consumers, therefore, craft breweries are also at the forefront of a more cooperative business model, where neighboring breweries are seen not as competition that must be destroyed or dominated, but as potential allies, partners, and friends. Rather, the competition is the large, industrial breweries, which represent a completely distinct logic. "Collaboration" brews, for example, where two or more breweries join forces and pool expertise or resources to produce a unique limited-edition beer, are common, as is "cuckoo-brewing," when inexperienced brewers without machinery use a more established company's equipment to produce their beer. From here, it is possible to see the logical jump toward some breweries becoming more involved in broader community development initiatives—either internally or externally hosted—solidifying themselves as linchpins of the local area (Daniels, Sterling, and Ross 2009). Rather than thinking about themselves in an insular fashion, GC follows many other craft breweries in considering other sorts of establishments in their local area.

CONSTRUCTING AN OPEN COMMUNITY SPACE: THE PUB

While working to make the brewery itself open, and to embed it into a chain of similar spaces within a few minutes' walk of each other, Bob and Kelly began to think about opening up space in the commercial and residential areas around the industrial sector. The obvious, but unlikely, decision was to open a pub. Obvious, because they brew beer; unlikely, because pub closure rates in the UK are high. Nonetheless:

> We've taken on a really small pub—I think you can probably get about 40 people in it then it's really busy . . . it's sort of a way of creating a good customer for us for the brewery, a good shop window for our beers, [and] a good . . . way of interacting with other breweries, building relationships with other breweries by buying their beer putting on events with them. And also a good way of interacting with the local community of course. It allows us that, kind of, direct interaction with customers all the way through the year . . . exposing our beers to new customers as well and new people.

This is a particular kind of pub, one that challenges the modernist convention of small-brewer separation from retail via "tied houses," which mainly sell beer produced by one brewer, with a few options from other smaller brewers that must be supplied through the pub-owning company (or "PubCo"):

> We don't deal with any PubCos; in order to get into those [tied houses] you need to get onto a list which normally has a ceiling price. . . . We know that if we sell them [the pub-owning company] a cask of beer for . . . £60, £65, the actual tenant or landlord will end up paying probably £90 to £100 and they're not allowed to buy directly from us. And that isn't a very nice way of working. We'd basically be giving money to a "PubCo" . . . they're just glorified property companies. Because you do things differently [running your own independent pub] and you do things better and you do things locally and independently and you have a focus and a . . . not a theme but, yes, a way of doing things I think.

This point about PubCos being "glorified property companies" is an important one. For a PubCo, the viability of a specific pub is a simple question of return on investment. If the pub can be sold, and the money invested more profitably elsewhere, they will close up and sell. In contrast, for a small brewery like GC, a pub doesn't need to make any money itself, as long as the brewery has a stable outlet for beer and can make money that way. This can create a sustainable business for a locally embedded, brewery-owned pub in a way that a tied pub cannot.

This is about more than a niche business position, however. Working with tied pubs is not only bad business but also flies in the face of the spirit of independence that animates the craft beer scene. Worse yet, the economic logic of tied pubs drives down the quality of beer:

> I think when you look at what pubs are closing mostly they're crap pubs. And the reason they're crap is because they're tied. They have to buy beer from their PubCo which is more expensive than if they went to the cash and carry and bought it. So, they end up buying the cheapest they can possibly buy because it's the only way they can make any margin. All of their customers know that they can go to the supermarket and buy exactly the same beer, the big industrial brands . . . at a much cheaper price. So, they can't compete on price, they can't compete on the actual beers they have to offer; it just becomes like a race to the bottom. And then if you can't serve food and make your money on food then you just go out of business. So, I think a lot of it [the decline of pubs in the United Kingdom] is down to the PubCos and the way that they run their properties as pubs . . . they're not interested in running good pubs, they're interested in getting as much money out of their tenants as possible before they move on and the next one comes in. Even their [tenants'] rent is based on how much money they make, so the more money they make the more rent they have to pay. We're not bound by any of that; we can buy whatever we want from whoever we want . . . I think that's also the reason why you see the [recent] rise of micro-pubs. They are all independent, run by, you know, individuals.

This kind of rejection of large-scale PubCos has a clear place in craft brewing history. Indeed, some have argued that the upsurge of interest in craft beer more generally (both producing and consuming) is as an active reaction to the lagerization of culture that took root in 1960s and 1970s tied houses (Banks 2010). Criticism centers on the notion of beer being literally and figuratively diluted and bureaucratized, leaving no space for organic human interactions or autonomy.

This David and Goliath theme has most notably been popularized and marketed by craft brewing giant BrewDog (although others have criticized *them* for performing exactly the same kind of homogenization) and generally features heavily in craft breweries' advertising, writings, and rhetorical devices (Rice 2015).

PLACE AS A LIMITING FACTOR?

Alongside space and location being considered as a benefit for the identity of a local craft brewery, Kelly and Bob also argued that although having ties to a particular place might create a sense of community and empowerment for those "in the loop," it can also be responsible for a more exclusionary atmosphere for certain people and organizations:

> I think you do get caught up in . . . this feeling of involvement . . . especially if you feel like you belong to a place—we are both from Bristol. That is something that we talk about an awful lot is being from Bristol and kind of belonging here—and we want you to feel like you belong here as well, whether you've moved to Bristol last year or you've lived here all your life like we have. Bristol is very supportive of Bristol businesses and things made in Bristol. And people like things that are from Bristol in Bristol. So, we know that breweries outside of Bristol have difficulty selling into Bristol. So, there's a lot of national brands, well-regarded craft beer brands, a lot of London breweries, that you don't see on taps in Bristol because they can't get onto the taps, even though pubs all around the country are trying to get hold of these beers. You will go into pubs in Bristol that will have almost exclusively Bristol brewery lineups.
>
> There isn't this big movement of "drink local" or "buy Bristol" or anything like that. It's just what people do. I've spoken to a few people who don't really know much about the wider brewing or beer kind of industry or community or what's going on . . . but they are fiercely local and will always drink Bristol breweries and will visit Bristol breweries and know a lot about what's going on.

These new cultural "revolutions," linked so closely with Bristol as an area, can have detrimental effects on those living outside of particular social groups. Critiques of craft brewing being a middle-class pursuit that signals the transformation and gentrification of traditionally working-class areas are not new (Barajas, Boeing, and Wartell 2018), and are something that Bob and Kelly are very aware of:

There's been . . . these discussions of gentrification over the last few years . . . then there's been this contrasting campaign of "make Bristol shit again," which, you know, having lived here for a long time . . . I can understand it and I do sort of see where it's coming from I think.

Although there are a variety of perspectives on the place of craft brewing in contemporary gentrification processes—from those that suggest that the organizations *cause* change in neighborhoods (Matthews and Picton 2014), to others who argue that craft industries *follow* the change (Bartlett et al. 2013)—it is significant to note that the inception and ongoing proliferation of new cultural industries does bear a potential human and material cost. This dynamic is not directly driven by the breweries, however, who are seeking to establish localized, solidarity economies, but rather by the wider economic processes of the neoliberal city.

CONCLUDING THOUGHTS: BREWING IN PLACES WITH PEOPLE

Alongside novelty beer flavors and catchy marketing, Bob and Kelly's account of their part in the British craft-brewing revolution speaks to a wider cultural desire for reconstructing place through community-based organizations, rejecting large-scale organization and economic instrumentality in favor of re-traditionalized practices and locally emplaced organizing principles. According to Kelly and Bob, this movement is founded on moving beyond distinctions between producers and consumers. Doing so allows for strong collective identities to emerge, as craft breweries play an important role in "establishing an industry ethos closely aligned with local food movements, indie attitudes or artisan production" (Rice 2015, 258) alongside the emergence of new communities of taste.

Through "tapping into the local historic and environmental landscape of the region" (Feeney 2017, 28), craft breweries are able to reinforce a local Bristolian revolutionary spirit that underscores the importance of countercultural behavior, and a business logic that is quite distinct from the rootless, homogenizing logic of global organizing. Although breweries are shaped by logics of effectiveness, efficiency, and economic sustainability, they are also shaped by heterogeneous logics of social sustainability and the specificities of place. Bristol has long had a reputation for thinking differently about cultural and social problems, and with the craft-brewing revolution developing there in a very particular way, it appears that this influence will continue.

References

Banks, Mark. 2010. "Craft Labour and Creative Industries." *International Journal of Cultural Policy* 16(3):305–21.

Barajas, Jesus M., Geoff Boeing, and Julie Wartell. 2017. "Neighborhood Change, One Pint at a Time: The Impact of Local Characteristics on Craft Breweries." Pp. 155–76. In *Untapped: Exploring the Cultural Dimensions of Craft Beer*, edited by Nathaniel G. Chapman, Slade Lellock, and Cameron D. Lippard. Morgantown: West Virginia University Press.

Baron, Stanley. 1962. "Brewed in America: A History and Beer and Ale in the United States." Boston: Little Brown.

Bartlett, Dan, Steve Allen, Jack Harris, and Larry Cary. 2013. "Revitalization One Pint at a Time: How Breweries and Distilleries Contribute to Main Street." Presented at the Oregon Main Street Conference, Astoria, OR, October 2–4.

Cottone, Vince. 1986. *Good Beer Guide: Breweries and Pubs of the Pacific Northwest.* Seattle: Homestead Book Company.

Daniels, Evan, Chandler Sterling, and Eli Ross. 2009. "Microbreweries and Culture in the Greater Madison Area." *Geography* 565(12):1–19.

Feeney, Alison E. 2017. "Cultural Heritage, Sustainable Development, and the Impacts of Craft Breweries in Pennsylvania." *City, Culture and Society* 9:21–30.

Flack, Wes. 1997. "American Microbreweries and Neolocalism: 'Ale-ing' for a Sense of Place." *Journal of Cultural Geography* 16(2):37–53.

Lewicka, Maria. 2008. "Place Attachment, Place Identity and Place Memory: Restoring the Forgotten City Past." *Journal of Environmental Psychology* 28(3):209–31.

Mass Observation. 1943. *The Pub and the People: A Worktown Study.* London: Faber and Faber.

Mathews, Vanessa and Roger M. Picton. 2014. "Intoxifying Gentrification: Brew Pubs and the Geography of Post-industrial Heritage." *Urban Geography* 35(3):337–56.

Rice, Jeff. 2015. "Professional Purity: Revolutionary Writing in the Craft Beer Industry." *Journal of Business and Technical Communication* 30(2):236–61.

Schnell, Steven M. and Joe Reese. 2003. "Microbreweries as Tools of Local Identity." *Journal of Cultural Geography* 21(1):45–69.

Sunley, Peter. 2017. "Case Study Report: Bristol. ESRC Urban Transformations Initiative, Working Paper 7." Structural Transformation, Adaptability and City Economic Evolutions Project.

Tallon, Andrew. 2007. "City Profile: Bristol." *Cities* 74(1):74–88.

Taylor, Charles. 1991. *The Ethics of Authenticity.* Cambridge, MA: Harvard University Press.

Thurnell-Read, Thomas. 2019. "A Thirst for the Authentic: Craft Drinks Producers and the Narration of Authenticity." *British Journal of Sociology* 70(4):1448–1468.

CONTRIBUTORS

Timothy Adkins earned his PhD from the Department of Sociology at the University of Illinois at Chicago in 2020. He is interested in research that uses multiple methodologies to study the recursive effects of culture on work, workers, and organizations. He recently defended his dissertation examining the emotional and economic demands of "dream" jobs with an empirical focus on fishing guides in the Florida Keys.

Julian Bakker is a geographer currently completing his PhD at the University of Victoria. His professional interests include the aesthetics of public space, craft brewing, and the phenomenology of place.

Seth Behrends received a BA in sociology from the University of Northern Iowa in 2016 and an MA in sociology from the University of Illinois at Chicago in 2019. Behrends's research interests lie at the intersection of race and gender, workplace dynamics, and organizational culture. His current works focus on the US craft-brewing industry and the US military.

Michele Bianchi is currently a postdoctoral researcher at the University of Parma and works on the socioeconomics of the third sector. He was formerly employed by the Yunus Centre for Social Business and Health at Glasgow Caledonian University, where he carried out a project on community-based initiatives and implementation of the Sustainable Development Goals set by the United Nations.

Michael Ian Borer teaches and researches urban and community sociology, popular culture, religion, and qualitative methods. He is primarily interested in the creative ways that people make sense of their social and physical environments through their interactions and experiences with people, places, and things. He is the author of *Vegas Brews: Craft Beer and the Birth of a Local Scene* (NYU Press, 2019), *Sociology in Everyday Life* (Waveland Press, 2016), *Urban People and Places: The Sociology of Cities, Suburbs, and Towns* (SAGE, 2014), and *Faithful to Fenway: Believing in Boston, Baseball, and America's Most Beloved Ballpark* (NYU Press, 2008).

Dean Brightman is a craft beer enthusiast and blogger based in the San Francisco Bay Area. His blog, the Beerverse (thebeerverse.com), features the latest news about the Bay Area craft beer industry. He holds a Craft Beer Appreciation certificate from Sonoma State University.

Michaela DeSoucey is associate professor of sociology at the University of North Carolina State University and the author of *Contested Tastes: Foie Gras and the Politics of Food* (Princeton University Press). Her research interests include culture, consumption, markets, risk/trust, and authenticity.

Kevin Drain is a PhD candidate at the University of Helsinki and holds degrees from the geography departments of the London School of Economics and the University of California, Los Angeles. Drain splits his time between Finland and Southern California.

Christopher S. Elliott is an assistant professor with the Department of Sociology and Criminology at the University of North Carolina Wilmington, where he teaches courses on work, organizations, and the economy. His research largely centers on how workers make their jobs meaningful and develop a conception of self in relation to the tasks they perform. Most recently, he has focused on consumer cultures as possible contexts for making work meaningful. After an examination of craft beer work in the North Carolina Triangle area, he found that the passion of craft beer enthusiasts energizes the work of brewers, servers, and even sales staff. He has published ethnographic research on competitive work cultures that emerged in a warehouse where labor was digitally controlled.

Emily A. Fogarty is an assistant professor in the Department of History, Politics, and Geography at Farmingdale State College. She obtained her PhD in geography from Florida State University in 2009. Her previous research involved spatial and temporal variation in tropical cyclone activity related to large-scale climate variability. Fogarty's current areas of interest focus on the geography of the tattoo industry, understanding the virtual geography of social media landscapes, and geospatial education for K-12 teachers/students. Fogarty serves on the New York State (NYS) GIS Association board, the NYS Geospatial Advisory Committee, and the Long Island GIS User Group

Steering Committee. In 2017, Fogarty was recognized as GIS Champion by the NYS GIS Association.

Saran Ghatak is an associate professor of sociology and anthropology for the Sociology, Anthropology, and Criminology Department at Keene State College. He received his PhD in sociology from New York University. Ghatak's professional interests include law, knowledge/science, medical sociology, politics, culture, and crime. He is a member of the American Sociological Association, the Eastern Sociological Sociology, and the American Society of Criminology.

Ethan Gibbons is a PhD student at Vanderbilt University, where his main areas of study are environmental sociology, sociology of food and agriculture, and science and technology studies. His work focuses on the ways in which the producers of food (and other consumer products, like beer) use scientific knowledge and environmental values to both inform their own production practices and add value to consumer products. He is particularly interested in the ways that producers and consumers influence and are influenced by contested narratives in social, popular, and news media.

Jeremy L. Jones is an associate professor at the College of the Holy Cross. His academic research is broadly concerned with the interweaving of economic action and everyday life. In his current project, Jones focuses on young, formally unemployed men living in an urban township near the Zimbabwean capital Harare. He pays special attention to these youths' experience of Zimbabwe's record-breaking bout of hyperinflation and their strategies for making money in seemingly impossible circumstances.

Carolyn Keller is an associate professor in the Social Sciences Department at the University of Wisconsin–Platteville, where she is also the director of academic assessment. She received her PhD in sociology from The Ohio State University. She is a comparative sociologist interested in economic changes and stratification.

Amanda Koontz is an associate professor of sociology at the University of Central Florida. Her primary areas of interest include the sociology of culture and consumption, social inequalities, and identities. Her current work focuses on connections among constructions of authenticity, identity work, racialized authentication, art world boundaries, and definitions of success. Her articles on related topics of authentication claims and types of identity work appear in such journals as the *Journal of Consumer Culture*, the *Journal of Popular Culture*, the *Sociological Quarterly*, and *Social Currents*.

Chris Land is Professor of Work and Organization at Anglia Ruskin University, where his research examines the changing nature of work and value in the burgeoning craft beer scene. This has included a study of gender in the brewing industry and an ongoing ethnographic study of consumer behavior and staff–customer interactions in craft beer pubs. This work is part of a broader project examining the relationship between economic value and substantive values, and the implications of that relationship for work.

Paul-Brian McInerney is associate professor in sociology at the University of Illinois at Chicago. Broadly, his research focuses on economic and organizational sociology, social studies of technology, social movements and collective behavior, and sociological theory. McInerney explores how groups of people try to overcome the contention that arises from diverse ways of understanding problems and accomplishing goals. Most recently, McInerney has been studying the network dynamics of innovation in the craft-brewing industry. McInerney received his PhD and MPhil in sociology from Columbia University in 2006. He holds an MA and BA in sociology from St. John's University.

Isabelle Nilsson is an assistant professor of geography at the University of North Carolina at Charlotte. Her research interests include transportation, housing, and local economic development. Her most recent work has focused on rail transit investments' effect on residential mobility and income segregation and the craft-brewing industry's impact on urban neighborhoods.

Tony Peña received a master's in higher education leadership from Northeastern Illinois University and a master's in arts in sociology from the University of Illinois at Chicago, where he is working on completing his PhD in sociology. His research and professional interests center around critical approaches to race, organizations, higher education, and organization identity. As a publicly engaged researcher, Peña is currently researching professionalization as a means to neutralize or obscure racialized relations in colleges and universities.

Neil Reid is Professor of Geography and Planning at the University of Toledo. His research interests include the urban geography of craft breweries, cluster-based development strategies, and local economic development. His most recent work has focused on the craft-brewing industry's impact on urban neighborhoods.

Jeff Rice is the chair of the Department of Writing, Rhetoric, and Digital Studies at the University of Kentucky. He is the author of *Craft Obsession: The Social Rhetorics of Beer* (Southern Illinois University Press).

Nathan Roberts is a graduate student at North Carolina State University. His research interests include the relationship between culture and markets, consumption, social theory, economic sociology, and environmental sociology.

Robert A. Saunders is a professor in the Department of History, Politics, and Geography at the State University of New York. His scholarship explores various intersections of popular culture, geopolitics, and national identity. His scholarship has appeared in *Social & Cultural Geography*, *Progress in Human Geography*, *Political Geography*, *Politics*, and *Geopolitics*, among other journals. He is the author of five books, including *Popular Geopolitics and Nation Branding in the Post-Soviet Realm* (2017) and *Geopolitics, Northern Europe, and Nordic Noir* (2021). He is an honorary fellow of the Russian Center at University of Leeds and an affiliate partner of the Center for Transnational Media Research at Aarhus University.

Robin Shepard is the author of a series of guidebooks titled *Searching for the Perfect Pint*. He writes at https://isthmus.com/ and tweets at @BeerHereWriter.

Rachel Skaggs is the Lawrence and Isabel Barnett Assistant Professor of Arts Management at The Ohio State University. Dr. Skaggs completed her PhD in sociology at Vanderbilt University, where she was a fellow at the Curb Center for Art, Enterprise, and Public Policy. Her research focuses on how workers in postbureaucratic employment situations (freelance, project based, self-employment, and other forms of free agency) are able to craft careers out of a series of self-directed projects and jobs, particularly in creative industries. She is especially interested in how workers in these situations collaborate and cooperate along the way. Her research has focused on topics such as the importance of social networks in music industry careers, arts entrepreneurship, how artists learn to deal with rejection and failure, and the public perceptions of artists in local communities.

Neil Sutherland is a senior lecturer in organization studies at the University of the West of England. He writes and teaches about the theory and practice of organizations. His interests focus on the rise of craft brewing and artisanal work in the United Kingdom and the performance of leadership in "alternative" organizations, including radically democratic social movements.

Scott Taylor is the Business School director of admissions and Reader in Leadership and Organization Studies at the University of Birmingham. He previously worked at Essex, Exeter, and Loughborough Universities. He has visited and taught at the Universities of Auckland, Delhi, FGV-EAESP São Paolo, Jeddah, Melbourne, and Lapland. He is currently a section editor for the *Journal of Business Ethics*.

Teemu Vass is a Helsinki-based beer writer and blogger. His main interests include beer history, Belgian beer, Baltic porter, and various aspects of the current craft beer culture. He blogs at https://olutkoira .wordpress.com/.

INDEX

community-owned pubs (COPs) / breweries, 22, 269–70, 275–83
competitive dynamics, 22–24, 336, 361; craft beer culture, 339–43
conglomerate culture, 138
connectors, 128
consumer culture, 138
consumer reviews, 32, 33, 40, 134. *See also* ratings websites
consumptive identities, 218–19, 221, 226, 238–40
Conway, Pat and Dan, 73
cool authenticity, 33–34, 37
coopetition, 23, 124, 332, 339
Coors, 124, 128, 265, 350–51
Copenhagen, Denmark, 135, 143–46
Courtyard brewery (New Orleans), 95, 98
craft authenticity, 305
craft beer culture: authenticity, 11–12, 14–18, 32–33, 105, 125–40, 305; basic recipe, 4; brewing traditions, 110–13; business challenges, 85; capitalist markets, 21; career trajectories, 21, 217, 219, 223–38; charitable giving, 44, 188, 211, 270, 273, 280, 363–68, 372; clustering, 11, 16, 20, 23, 72, 73, 370; Colorado, 117–24, 261–67; community-owned pubs/breweries, 22, 269–70, 275–83; competitive dynamics, 22–24, 336, 339–43; consumer knowledge, 304; consumer reviews, 15–16, 32–33, 40–49, 54–57, 134, 264–65, 333–34; contemporary studies, 6–7; definition, 24, 86; demographics, 263; digital relationships, 23–24, 360–61, 363–76; diversity and inclusivity, 7; economic challenges, 117–21; economic impacts, 72–74, 78, 82, 86, 183–90, 212, 262–64; entrepreneurial ecosystems, 22–24, 287–308; Finland, 66, 171, 175–81, 311–22; food pairings, 359–60; gentrification, 19–20, 72, 77–78, 171, 178–80, 307, 379–83, 387–88; growth measures, 31, 71; historical perspective, 74–78, 101–2, 106–9, 271–72, 293–301; independent retailers, 121–22; local scenes, 23; Louisiana, 93–99; market focus, 84–85; marketing practices, 294–96, 298–99, 304–7, 342–43; motivational factors, 234–39; neighborhood revital-

ization, 11, 16, 71–74, 77–81, 137, 183–90; neolocalism, 11–12, 105, 109, 113, 382–84; New England, 3–4; New Jersey, 193–210; North Carolina, 16–17, 101–3, 217, 219; place-based identity, 35–37, 101; policy shifts, 298; popular-culture representations, 126; price variations, 177, 178–80; ratings websites, 15, 32, 40–41, 134, 264–65, 328; regulatory factors, 43, 79, 81, 83–84, 193–96, 205, 206–8, 210–14, 266–67, 298; research methodology and analyses, 40–57, 105–6, 223–24, 291–93, 329–30, 332–36, 363–64; retrojection, 103–4; ritualized bottle shares, 245–57; self-distribution, 263; sense of community and place, 249–51; social geography, 23–24, 359–76; social media, 23–24; sociocultural aspects, 5–6, 8–9, 382, 388–89; sociopolitical and economic implications, 18–19; spatial considerations, 9, 11, 15–18, 32, 37, 39–47, 49–57, 193–206; three-tier distribution system, 296–97; United Kingdom, 22, 269, 273, 278–83, 379–89; upper-class versus working-class consumers, 19, 172–75, 178–81; Wisconsin, 183–90. *See also* Asheville, North Carolina; Charlotte, North Carolina; collaborative dynamics; cultural quarters/scenes; sense of community and place; taprooms; Triangle region (North Carolina)
Craft Beverage Modernization and Tax Reform Act (2017), 267
Craft Brew Alliance (CBA), 119–20
Craft Brewers Guild, 66, 101
craft culture, 131, 132, 137, 138, 306
Craft Maltsters Guild, 351–52
Crane Brewery (Raytown), 300
crawfish season, 95
creative cities, 16
creative class, 16
creative placemaking, 24, 370
Creature Comforts Beer (Athens), 367
crossover beers, 123
cuckoo-brewing, 384
cultural homogenization, 35, 36–37
cultural quarters/scenes: branding strategies, 327–28; characteristics, 256–57,

Hickenlooper, John, 73, 262
Highland Brewing (Asheville), 361, 362
Highland Park Mill (Charlotte), 74, 75, 77, 80
Hill Farmstead (Massachusetts), 61–64, 67, 130, 248
Hillman Beer (Asheville), 365
Hillsboro Brewing Company (Wisconsin), 183–85
Hillsboro, Wisconsin, 183–85
Hill, Shaun, 63, 64
Hilltop, Pennsylvania, 7
Hilpeä Hauki (Helsinki), 318
Himmeriget (Copenhagen), 146
historically and geographically limited strategic action fields. *See* cultural quarters/scenes
Hi-Wire Brewing (Asheville), 365–66
Hogan, Kurt, 80
Hole Doughnuts (Asheville), 359
HOMBRE Helsinki, 319–20
homebrewing ventures: entrepreneurial spirit, 217, 223, 231, 233, 235, 303; Finland, 319–21; New Jersey, 206; regulatory factors, 297–98; Zimbabwe, 150, 162–65
Hopewell (Chicago), 337
Hopewell, New Jersey, 20
hops: agricultural cultivation, 262, 279, 379; beer tastings, 229; brewery tours, 194, 197; brewing process, 314–15, 322; British ales, 262, 271–72; contemporary craft beers, 379; Danish beer, 144; flavor components, 9, 63; local sources, 4; regulatory factors, 110–12; terroir, 262; United Kingdom, 279; varieties, 279, 315, 349–51
hot authenticity, 33–34
hyperlocalism, 15–16, 84, 341, 360

I
iconic authenticity, 37, 38
ideal pathways, 21, 220, 226, 227–31
identity, 14; collective organizational identities, 23, 326–27, 330–32, 336–37, 339, 343–45; consumptive identities, 218–19, 221, 226, 238–40; cultural quarters/scenes, 36, 325–45; self-identities, 37. *See also* place-based identity

idiosyncratic authenticity, 305
Illinois: craft beer culture, 49, 103, 336–45; cultural quarters/scenes, 333
imperial stouts, 130, 248, 249, 320
InBev, 103, 135, 225, 333, 366
Independent Craft Brewer's seal, 266
independent retailers, 121–22
indexical authenticity, 37–38
Indiana, 130, 330, 337
individual perception, 34–35
industrial beers, 108, 225, 272, 281. *See also* macro-brewers
industrial malting, 355
industrial neighborhoods, 18, 50–51, 71, 77, 79–82, 307
industrial spaces, 105, 136–37, 183–90, 198–99, 383–84
inebriation, 127
informal learning opportunities, 253–56
in-group solidarity, 288, 299, 301, 308
inns, 271
Instagram. *See* social media
Intuition Brewing (Jacksonville), 132
investment capital, 301–3. *See also* venture capital investments
IPAs: Belgian-style, 342; Finland, 320; local production, 337; New England-style, 61, 66, 130, 247; place-based identity, 105; popularity, 176, 320; taprooms, 139
Irish Channel neighborhood (New Orleans), 96, 99
Iso Roobertinkatu street (Helsinki), 19–20, 174–75, 177–79, 181

J
Jackson-Becham, J. Nikol, 7
Jackson, Michael, 315–16, 318
Janoinen Lohi (Helsinki), 318
Japanese beer, 14
Jarnit-Bjergsø, Jeppe, 144, 146
Jersey Girl Brewing Company (Hackettstown), 211
job opportunities, 218–23
Johnston Mill (Charlotte), 74, 75
joint actions, 253
joint drinking, 159
Jones, Ellis, 3–4
Jones, Marcus, 276
J. Wakefield Beer (Miami), 367

Kingdom, 379–83, 387–88; Helsinki, Finland, 172–74, 178–81

neolocalism, 11–12, 105, 109, 113, 382–84

network dynamics: collaboration, 328, 333–35, 337–39, 341, 344, 360, 363–76; cultural networks, 137–38; cultural quarters/scenes, 328, 337–39; distribution, 31, 341–42; entrepreneurial ecosystems, 290–91, 295–96, 299, 301, 302, 306, 308; research methodology and analyses, 332–36; social networks, 10, 128, 211, 273, 282, 332–33, 360–61, 363–76; visualization techniques, 370–74

Nevada, 248, 249–54

never macros, 220, 227, 231

New Albion Brewing (Sonoma), 86, 129

New Belgium Brewing (Fort Collins/Asheville), 101, 120, 122, 123, 300, 362, 367, 368, 373–74

New England, 3–4, 7, 61–70, 131, 247, 369. See also Massachusetts; Vermont

New Glarus Brewing Company (New Glarus), 188

New Glarus, Wisconsin, 188

New Hampshire, 291

New Hope, Pennsylvania, 205

New Jersey, 20, 129, 193–214

New Jersey Brewers Association (NJBA), 208, 211

New Orleans, Louisiana: craft beer culture, 93–99; localized authentication, 37; locavorism, 4–5; neighborhoods, 98–99

New York Times Travel section, 173, 174

NoDa Brewing Company (Charlotte), 78–79, 81

NoDa district (Charlotte): craft beer culture, 6, 77–80; historical perspective, 74–78; neighborhood revitalization, 72, 76–81; population trends, 77–78

NOLA Brewing (New Orleans), 94, 96

nonalcoholic beers, 14, 175

non-places, 134, 136

Noonan, Greg, 298

Nørrebro Brewery (Copenhagen), 145

Nørrebro, Denmark, 143

North Carolina: brewing historiographies, 106–8; craft beer culture, 16–17, 101–3, 217, 219; historical perspective, 109–10; Prohibition, 102; taprooms, 135, 136; textile industry, 74–75, 77. See also Asheville, North Carolina; Charlotte, North Carolina; Triangle region (North Carolina)

North Carolina Craft Brewers Guild, 101

North Charlotte, North Carolina. See NoDa district (Charlotte)

not-fans-prior, 220, 227, 231–34

no-till agriculture, 354

O

Ocean Township, New Jersey, 202–3

O'Dell brewing (Colorado), 120, 122

Ohio: craft beer culture, 72, 73–74, 130, 287, 291, 294–95, 302; neighborhood revitalization, 307

Ohio City neighborhood (Cleveland), 72, 73–74

Olde Mecklenburg Brewery (Charlotte), 78

Olvi brewery (Finland), 175

opaque beers, 150–51, 157, 159

Oregon: craft beer culture, 247, 262, 263, 297. See also Portland, Oregon

organic beers, 145–46, 175, 176, 355

organizational identities, 23, 326–27, 330–32, 336–37, 339, 343–45

original objects, 37–38

Orwell, George, 135

Osborne, Joe, 117–18

Oskar Blues Holding Company, 118, 120, 122, 362, 376

Other Half Brewing (Brooklyn), 367

Otter Creek Brewery (Vermont), 304

Over the Rhine neighborhood (Cincinnati), 307

P

Pabst Blue Ribbon, 126, 140

pale ales, 63, 145, 271–72, 320, 342, 349. See also IPAs

pale malts, 355

Papazain, Charlie, 217, 262

Parleaux brewery (New Orleans), 95, 98

Pearl District (Portland, Oregon), 72

People's Pint (Massachusetts), 4

Pepper Distillery district (Lexington), 136–37

Perrin Brewing Company (Michigan), 376

personal branding, 221–22
Pesonius, Pate, 320
pet-friendly taprooms, 197, 198, 209*t*, 210, 363
pilsners, 64, 175, 200, 349, 355
Pine Hill Orchards (Massachusetts), 4
place-based identity: alcohol production, 107, 382–83; branding strategies, 110, 202, 305, 330; cultural quarters/scenes, 325–45; entrepreneurial ecosystems, 288–89, 306–7; experience economy, 35–37; retrojection, 101, 105–6, 108–13
placemaking theory, 10–18, 20; beer drinking culture, 151, 160–62; consumer reviews, 33; creative placemaking, 24, 370; entrepreneurial ecosystems, 287–89; lifescape modes, 154–55, 166–67; localized authentication, 33, 36–37; spatial dynamics, 195–206, 382; spatio-temporal considerations, 152–55, 165–66
Plunkett Foundation, 276, 280
Poland, 314
"Pop the Cap" law, 102, 108–9, 217
Popular Culture Association, 6
porters, 255, 272, 311–18, 320–22, 349
Portland Brewing Company, 295
Portland, Maine: collaborative dynamics, 117, 123; craft beer culture, 287, 291, 294; ecological sustainability, 8; employee involvement, 265; entrepreneurial networks, 296, 301, 302; regulatory factors, 299
Portland, Oregon: craft beer culture, 78, 130–31, 287, 291, 295; craft culture, 306; neighborhood revitalization, 72, 74
Port Orleans brewery (New Orleans), 98
postmodern hotels, 134
Potosi Brewery (Potosi), 188–90
Potosi, Wisconsin, 188–90
pours: bottle shares, 245, 247–48, 253–54; comparison studies, 209*t*; localism, 47; regulatory factors, 206, 208; taprooms, 130, 200, 201, 203, 204
preservation considerations, 13
Progressive Beer Duty, 22, 273
Prohibition, 102, 200, 267–68, 293–94, 297, 316
Protagonist Clubhouse brewpub (Charlotte), 85
Protestant abstinence, 212, 213

Pub Angleterre (Helsinki), 316
Pub Is a Hub program, 280
public houses/pubs: collaborative dynamics, 385–87; as communal spaces, 271, 273–74, 275, 276–83; community-owned pubs/breweries, 22, 269–70, 275–77; community support organizations, 276–78; competition and economic crises, 274–75, 274*t*, 385–86; food service, 273, 280–82, 386, 388; historical perspective, 271–72; management practices, 272–73
public rituals, 37, 245–57
Pub Loan Fund, 22, 276
pub-owning companies (PubCos), 385–86
Pumphouse Community Brewery, Ltd., 278–79
Punavuori neighborhood (Helsinki), 19–20, 174–75, 177, 179
Purity Law (1516), 111, 294–95

Q

quality considerations, 42–47, 54–55
Quartersawn Woodworks (Charlotte), 81

R

Raleigh, North Carolina. *See* Triangle region (North Carolina)
Rangel, Mike, 296, 301
Rare Barrel brewery (Berkeley), 247
RateBeer, 134, 264, 330, 333–34
ratings websites, 15–16, 32–33, 40–41, 134, 264–65, 328, 330, 333–34
Rayback Collective (Boulder), 263
Rayburn Farms (Asheville), 359
Raytown, Missouri, 300
real objects, 37–38
Red Barn Company Store (Waunakee), 187
Red Oak Brewery (Whitsett), 111
reflexive consumerism, 7
refrigeration technologies, 293
regional breweries, 31, 229–30, 232, 236, 306, 340, 361, 375
Regulator Brewing Company (Hillsborough), 109
Regulator Movement (1766), 109–10
regulatory factors: craft beer culture, 205, 206–8, 210–14, 296–99; homebrewing ventures, 298; mixed-use districts,